P9-CWE-670

ACCLAIM FOR

Diane Ackerman's

A NATURAL HISTORY OF LOVE

"By turns playful, serious, poetic and scientific, Ackerman has drawn upon a vast variety of sources to create a compelling compendium of that great intangible, love." —*Los Angeles Daily News*

"In a glorious tumult, Ackerman looks at the siren call of mermaids, the Indy 500, and the ecstasies of a levitating seventeenth-century saint. And her exploration of young girls' love for horses takes her to Lascaux, where she wonderfully and wonderingly describes the 'floodtide of horses' crashing down through our dreams." —*The New Yorker*

"An atlas through the mysterious ways of the human heart. . . . Ackerman tackles her subjects with a Sherlock Holmes-ian zeal, employing equal parts philosophy, mythology, history, science, even erotica, to shed light on this most noble of human emotions." —*USA Today*

"Studded with accurate, witty versions of all the facts that made biology class interesting. . . . *A Natural History* is a wide-angle vision of love—informing, reminding, entertaining." —*Harper's Bazaar*

"Ackerman is an alchemist who transmutes leaden data into literary gold. Her book is a voluptuous valentine to a most exalted emotion, a lusty ballad to erotic pleasures, and an ode to romantic attachment." —*Hartford Courant*

"Ackerman's language is so rich as to be practically carnal. . . . What throbbing stuff she has gleaned from history's sheets." —*Columbus Dispatch*

BOOKS BY Diane Ackerman

A Natural History of Love

The Moon by Whalelight

Jaguar of Sweet Laughter: New and Selected Poems

A Natural History of the Senses

Reverse Thunder

On Extended Wings

Lady Faustus

Twilight of the Tenderfoot

Wife of Light

The Planets: A Cosmic Pastoral

Diane Ackerman

A NATURAL HISTORY OF LOVE

Diane Ackerman was born in Waukegan, Illinois. She received her B.A. from Pennsylvania State University and an M.F.A. and Ph.D. from Cornell University. Her poetry has been published in many leading literary journals, and in the books *The Planets: A Cosmic Pastoral* (1976), *Wife of Light* (1978), *Lady Faustus* (1983), *Reverse Thunder: A Dramatic Poem* (1988), and *Jaguar of Sweet Laughter: New and Selected Poems* (1991).

Her works of nonfiction include, most recently, *A Natural History of Love* (1994); *The Moon by Whalelight and Other Adventures Among Bats, Crocodilians, Penguins, and Whales* (1991); *A Natural History of the Senses* (1990); and *On Extended Wings* (1985), a memoir of flying. She is at work on a second book of nature writings, *The Rarest of the Rare*.

Ms. Ackerman has received the Academy of American Poets' Lavan Award, and grants from the National Endowment for the Arts and the Rockefeller Foundation, among other recognitions. She has taught at several universities, including Columbia and Cornell, and she is currently a staff writer for *The New Yorker*.

A NATURAL HISTORY OF LOVE

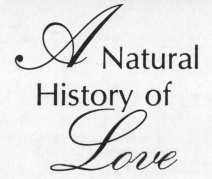

A Natural History of *Love*

DIANE ACKERMAN

VINTAGE BOOKS
A DIVISION OF RANDOM HOUSE, INC.
NEW YORK

FIRST VINTAGE BOOKS EDITION,
MARCH 1995.

Copyright © 1994 by Diane Ackerman

All rights reserved under International and Pan-American
Copyright Conventions. Published in the United States by
Vintage Books, a division of Random House, Inc., New York,
and simultaneously in Canada by Random House of Canada
Limited, Toronto. Originally published in hardcover by
Random House, Inc., New York, in 1994.

A portion of this work was originally published in different
form in the August 1992 issue of *Allure*.

The section entitled "Kissing" was originally published in
slightly different form in *A Natural History of the Senses* by
Diane Ackerman (Random House, Inc., New York, 1990).

Permission acknowledgments for previously published material
can be found on pages ix-x.

Library of Congress Cataloging-in-Publication Data
Ackerman, Diane.
A natural history of love / Diane Ackerman. — 1st Vintage
Books ed.
p. cm.
Originally published : New York : Random House, c1994.
Includes bibliographical references and index.
ISBN: 0-679-76183-7
1. Love—History. 2. Man-woman relationships—History. I.
Title.
[HQ801.A513 1995]
306.7—dc20   95-1910
CIP

Book design by Oksana Kushnir

Manufactured in the United States of America
10 9 8 7 6 5 4 3 2 1

For George,
whose heart is bright as summer

PERMISSIONS

Grateful acknowledgment is made to the following for permission to reprint previously published material:

Branden Publishing Co.: Excerpts from *The Symposium* by Plato, translated by B. Jowett. Reprinted by permission of Branden Publishing, Boston.

Doubleday, a division of Bantam, Doubleday, Dell Publishing Group, Inc.: Excerpt from entry about Ludwig van Beethoven from *Encyclopedia of Great Composers* by Milton Cross. Reprinted by permission of Doubleday.

Harcourt Brace and Company and Peter Owen Ltd., Publishers: Excerpt from *The Diary of Anaïs Nin 1931–1934* by Anaïs Nin. Copyright © 1966 by Anaïs Nin. Rights throughout the world excluding the United States, Canada, and Israel are controlled by Peter Owen Ltd., Publishers, London. Reprinted by permission of Harcourt Brace and Company and Peter Owen Ltd., Publishers.

Indiana University Press: Excerpt from *The Art of Love* by Ovid, translated by R. Humphries. Reprinted by permission of Indiana University Press.

Alfred A. Knopf, Inc. and Faber and Faber Ltd.: Three lines from "Connoisseur of Chaos" from *Collected Poems* by Wallace Stevens. Copyright © 1942 by Wallace Stevens. Copyright renewed 1970 by Holly Stevens. Rights throughout the British Commonwealth are controlled by Faber and Faber Ltd. Reprinted by permission of Alfred A. Knopf, Inc., and Faber and Faber Ltd.

Jon Landau Management: Four lines from "Fire" by Bruce Springsteen. Copyright © Bruce Springsteen: ASCAP. Reprinted by permission.

William Morrow & Company, Inc. and Lescher & Lescher, Ltd.: Excerpts from *French Lovers: From Heloise and Abelard to Beauvoir and Sartre* by Joseph Barry. Copyright © 1987 by Joseph Barry. Rights throughout the British Commonwealth are controlled by Lescher & Lescher, Ltd. Reprinted by permission.

New Directions Publishing Corporation: Excerpt from poem on pages 14–15 of *Love Poems of Ancient Egypt* by Ezra Pound and Noel Stock. Copyright © 1962 by Noel Stock. Reprinted by permission of New Directions Publishing Corporation.

New Directions Publishing Corporation and David Higham Associates: Two lines from "When All My Fine and Country Senses See" and eleven lines from "If I Were Tickled by the Rub of Love" from *Poems of Dylan Thomas* by Dylan Thomas. Copyright © 1939 by New Directions Publishing Corporation. First published in *Poetry*. Rights throughout the world excluding the United States are controlled by David Higham Associates. Reprinted by permission of New Directions Publishing Corporation and David Higham Associates.

Penguin Books Ltd: Excerpt from the Introduction to *Romeo and Juliet* by William Shakespeare, edited by T.J.B. Spencer (Penguin Books, 1967). Introduction copyright © 1967 by T.J.B. Spencer. Reprinted by permission.

Random House, Inc.: Excerpts from *Remembrance of Things Past, Volume Two* by Marcel Proust, translated by C. K. Scott Moncrieff and Terence Kilmartin. Translation © 1981 by Random House, Inc. and Chatto and Windus. Published in the United States Kingdom by Chatto and Windus. Reprinted by permission of Random House, Inc.

Routledge: Excerpts from *Women in Athenian Law & Life* by Roger Just, published by Routledge. Reprinted by permission.

Scarborough House and MBA Literary Agents Limited: Excerpts from *Sex in History* by Reay Tannahill. Copyright © 1980 by Reay Tannahill. Originally published by Stein & Day. Rights in the British Commonwealth are controlled by MBA Literary Agents Limited, London. Reprinted by permission of Scarborough House Publishers and MBA Literary Agents Limited.

Sterling Lord Literistic and The Hogarth Press: Excerpt from *The Aeneid* by Virgil, translated by Cecil Day-Lewis. Copyright © 1932 by Cecil Day-Lewis. Published in the United States by Oxford University Press. Rights throughout the world excluding the United States are controlled by The Hogarth Press, London. Reprinted by permission of Sterling Lord Literistic and The Hogarth Press.

ACKNOWLEDGMENTS

Some sections of this book (in different versions) first appeared in *Parade, The Condé Nast Traveler, Travel-Holiday, The New York Times Magazine, Allure, The New York Times Book Review,* and *American Photo.* I'm grateful to the editors of those periodicals for their hospitality and encouragement.

Special thanks to the following friends and colleagues who have been generous with their time, expertise, and encouragement: Ann Druyan, Chris Furst, Lindy Hazan, Jane Marie Law, Linda Mack, Jeanne Mackin, Nancy Skipper, Meredith Small, Deva Sobel, and Paul West.

CONTENTS

THE HEART IS A LONELY HUNTER: IDEAS ABOUT LOVE

ALL FIRES THE FIRE: THE NATURE OF LOVE

A NECESSARY PASSION: THE EROTICS OF LOVE

PASSING STRANGE AND WONDERFUL: LOVE'S CUSTOMS

POINTS FOR A COMPASS ROSE: VARIETIES OF LOVE

INTRODUCTION:
LOVE'S VOCABULARY

Love is the great intangible. In our nightmares, we can create beasts out of pure emotion. Hate stalks the streets with dripping fangs, fear flies down narrow alleyways on leather wings, and jealousy spins sticky webs across the sky. In daydreams, we can maneuver with poise, foiling an opponent, scoring high on fields of glory while crowds cheer, cutting fast to the heart of an adventure. But what dream state is love? Frantic and serene, vigilant and calm, wrung-out and fortified, explosive and sedate—love commands a vast army of moods. Hoping for victory, limping from the latest skirmish, lovers enter the arena once again. Sitting still, we are as daring as gladiators.

When I set a glass prism on a windowsill and allow the sun to flood through it, a spectrum of colors dances on the floor. What we call "white" is a rainbow of colored rays packed into a small space. The prism sets them free. Love is the white light of emotion. It includes many feelings which, out of laziness and confusion, we crowd into one simple word. Art is the prism that sets them free, then follows the gyrations of one or a few. When art separates this thick tangle of feelings, love bares its bones. But it cannot be measured or mapped. Everyone admits that love is wonderful and necessary, yet no one can agree on what it is. I once heard a sportscaster say of a basketball player, "He does all the intangibles. Just watch him do his dance."

As lofty as the idea of love can be, no image is too profane to help explain it. Years ago, I fell in love with someone who was both a sport and a pastime. At the end, he made fade-away jump shots in my life. But, for a while, love did all the intangibles. It lets us do our finest dance.

Love. What a small word we use for an idea so immense and powerful it has altered the flow of history, calmed monsters, kindled works of art, cheered the forlorn, turned tough guys to mush, consoled the enslaved, driven strong women mad, glorified the humble, fueled national scandals, bankrupted robber barons, and made mincemeat of kings. How can love's spaciousness be conveyed in the narrow confines of one syllable? If we search for the source of the word, we find a history vague and confusing, stretching back to the Sanskrit *lubhyati* ("he desires"). I'm sure the etymology rambles back much farther than that, to a one-syllable word heavy as a heartbeat. Love is an ancient delirium, a desire older than civilization, with taproots stretching deep into dark and mysterious days.

We use the word *love* in such a sloppy way that it can mean almost nothing or absolutely everything. It is the first conjugation students of Latin learn. It is a universally understood motive for crime. "Ah, he was in love," we sigh, "well, that explains it." In fact, in some European and South American countries, even murder is forgivable if it was "a crime of passion." Love, like truth, is the unassailable defense. Whoever first said "love makes the world go round" (it was an anonymous Frenchman) probably was not thinking about celestial mechanics, but the way love seeps into the machinery of life to keep generation after generation in motion. We think of love as a positive force that somehow ennobles the one feeling it. When a friend confesses that he's in love, we congratulate him.

In folk stories, unsuspecting lads and lasses ingest a love potion and quickly lose their hearts. As with all intoxicants, love comes in many guises and strengths. It has a mixed bouquet, and may include some piquant ingredients. One's taste in love will have a lot to do with one's culture, upbringing, generation, religion, era, gender, and so on. Ironically, although we sometimes think of it as the ultimate Oneness, love isn't monotone or uniform. Like a batik created from many emotional colors, it is a fabric whose pattern and brightness may vary. What is my goddaughter to think when she hears her mother say: "I love Ben & Jerry's Cherry Garcia ice cream"; "I really loved my high school boyfriend"; "Don't you just love this sweater?" "I'd love to go to the lake for a week this summer"; "Mommy loves you." Since all we have is one word, we talk about love in increments or unwieldy ratios. "How much do you love me?" a child asks. Because the parent can't answer *I* (verb that means unconditional parental love) *you*, she may fling her arms wide, as if welcoming the sun and sky, stretching her body to its limit, spreading her fingers to encompass all of Creation, and say: "This much!" Or: "Think of the biggest thing you can imagine. Now double it. I love you a hundred times that much!"

When Elizabeth Barrett Browning wrote her famous sonnet "How do I love thee?" she didn't "count the ways" because she had an arithmetical turn of mind, but because English poets have always had to search hard for personal signals of their love. As a society, we are embarrassed by love. We treat it as if it were an obscenity. We reluctantly admit to it. Even saying the word makes us stumble and blush. Why should we be ashamed of an emotion so beautiful and natural? In teaching writing students, I've sometimes given them the assignment of writing a love poem. "Be precise, be individual, and be descriptive. But don't use any clichés," I caution them, "or any curse words." Part of the reason for this assignment is that it helps them understand how inhibited we are about love. Love is the most important thing in our lives, a passion for which we would fight or die, and yet we're reluctant to linger over its name. Without a supple vocabulary, we can't even talk or think about it directly. On the other hand, we have many sharp verbs for the ways in which human beings can hurt one another, dozens of verbs for the subtle gradations of hate. But there are pitifully few synonyms for love. Our vocabulary of love and lovemaking is so paltry that a poet has to choose among clichés, profanities, or euphemisms. Fortunately, this has led to some richly imagined works of art. It has inspired poets to create their own private vocabularies. Mrs. Browning sent her husband a poetic abacus of love, which in a roundabout way expressed the sum of her feelings. Other lovers have tried to calibrate their love in equally ingenious ways. In "The Flea," John Donne watches a flea suck blood from his arm and his beloved's, and rejoices that their blood marries in the flea's stomach.

Yes, lovers are most often reduced to comparatives and quantities. "Do you love me more than her?" we ask. "Will you love me less if I don't do what you say?" We are afraid to face love head-on. We think of it as a sort of traffic accident of the heart. It is an emotion that scares us more than cruelty, more than violence, more than hatred. We allow ourselves to be foiled by the vagueness of the word. After all, love requires the utmost vulnerability. We equip someone with freshly sharpened knives; strip naked; then invite him to stand close. What could be scarier?

If you took a woman from ancient Egypt and put her in an automobile factory in Detroit, she would be understandably disoriented. Everything would be new, especially her ability to stroke the wall and make light flood the room, touch the wall elsewhere and fill the room with summer's warm breezes or winter's blast. She'd be astonished by telephones, computers, fashions, language, and customs. But if she saw a man and woman stealing a kiss in a quiet corner, she would smile. People everywhere and everywhen understand the phenomenon of love, just as they understand the appeal of music, finding it deeply meaningful even if they cannot explain exactly what that meaning is, or why they respond viscerally to one composer and not another. Our Egyptian woman, who prefers the birdlike twittering of a sistrum, and a twentieth-century man, who prefers the clashing jaws of heavy metal, share a passion for music that both would understand. So it is with love. Values, customs, and protocols may vary from ancient days to the present, but not the majesty of love. People are unique in the way they walk, dress, and gesture, yet we're able to look at two people—one wearing a business suit, the other a sarong—and recognize that both of them are clothed. Love also has many fashions, some bizarre and (to our taste) shocking, others more familiar, but all are part of a phantasmagoria we know. In the Serengeti of the heart, time and nation are irrelevant. On that plain, all fires are the same fire.

Remember the feeling of an elevator falling in your chest when you said good-bye to a loved one? Parting is more than sweet sorrow, it pulls you apart when you are glued together. It feels like hunger pains, and we use the same word, *pang*. Perhaps this is why Cupid is depicted with a quiver of arrows, because at times love feels like being pierced in the chest. It is a wholesome violence. Common as childbirth, love seems rare nonetheless, always catches one by surprise, and cannot be taught. Each child rediscovers it, each couple redefines it, each parent reinvents it. People search for love as if it were a city lost beneath the desert dunes, where pleasure is the law, the streets are lined with brocade cushions, and the sun never sets.

If it's so obvious and popular, then what *is* love? I began researching this book because I had many questions, not because I knew at the outset what answers I might find. Like most people, I believed what I had been told: that the idea of love was invented by the Greeks, and romantic love began in the Middle Ages. I know now how misguided such hearsay is. We can find romantic love in the earliest writings of our kind. Much of the vocabulary of love, and the imagery lovers use, has not changed for thousands of years. Why do the same images come to mind when people describe their romantic feelings? Custom, culture, and tastes vary, but not love itself, not the essence of the emotion.

"Animal attraction," we sometimes call it. After a passionate encounter, a woman might describe her bedmate as "a real animal" and mean it as a sexy compliment. If she says it to his face, she might toss in a mock growl for good measure, and that's usually enough to start festivities all over again. In fact, animals have much to teach us about our own romantic habits. There are many parallels. Male animals often give the equivalent of engagement rings, females often check a male's bank balance, and "modesty" or "playing coy" is as much a trump card for female birds or insects or reptiles as for humans. In this book, I sometimes refer to the mating habits of other animals, although not at great length because I've written on that subject in detail in other books. I think it would be a mistake to repeat—out of context and in different language—what I have struggled so hard to say elsewhere (with one exception: my thoughts about kissing. See page 249).

For the history section of this book, I consider a mideastern culture (Egypt), where we find the earliest writings about love, and then I explore love's changing nature in the ancient and modern western world, so that I can follow a single thread as far as possible.

However, when it comes to the history of love, one must keep in mind that we know more about the love lives of the fairly well-to-do than about the love lives of common people, who had little leisure, and lived in caves or small rooms, sharing their beds with many people; their romantic lives would have been distinctly different from those blessed with spare time and privacy. The most remarkable time for the poor might have been that newlywed period, perhaps only nine months long, when they were alone. Happily, love is a peasant emotion and thrives as well in stables as in palaces.

It's tempting to think of love as a progression, from ignorance toward the refined light of reason, but that would be a mistake. The history of love is not a ladder we climb rung by rung leaving previous rungs below. Human history is not a journey across a landscape, in the course of which we leave one town behind as we approach another. Nomads constantly on the move, we carry everything with us, all we possess. We carry the seeds and nails and remembered hardships of everywhere we have lived, the beliefs and hurts and bones of every ancestor. Our baggage is heavy. We can't bear to part with anything that ever made us human. The way we love in the twentieth century is as much an accumulation of past sentiments as a response to modern life.

When I began researching this book, I scouted libraries for reputable studies of love and discovered how little serious research had been done. For example, the microfiche Human Relations Area File, an anthropological database representing over 300 cultures around the world, includes entries on everything from divorce to nose ornaments. It has no separate main category or code for love. Why has there been so little research into love? Surely it's not just that love seems a subjective field with unprovable assumptions, too emotional for social scientists to take seriously (and receive funding for). After all, there are countless studies on war, hate, crime, prejudice, and so on. Social scientists prefer to study negative behaviors and emotions. Perhaps, they don't feel as comfortable studying love per se. I add that "per se" because they *are* studying love—often they're studying what happens when love is deficient, thwarted, warped, or absent.

Why did love evolve? How does it make sense in evolutionary terms? What is the psychology of love? Are erotic and nonerotic love essentially the same? Who is naturally more loving, a man or a woman? What is mother love? How does love affect our health? Do men and women have different sexual agendas? What is the relationship between lack of love and crime? What is the chemistry of love?

Are we monogamous by nature, or were we born to cheat? How has the idea of love changed through the ages? Do aphrodisiacs really exist? Do animals feel love? What are some of love's customs and extravagances?

We have the great fortune to live on a planet abounding with humans, plants, and animals; and I often marvel at the strange tasks evolution sets them. Of all the errands life seems to be running, of all the mysteries that enchant us, love is my favorite.

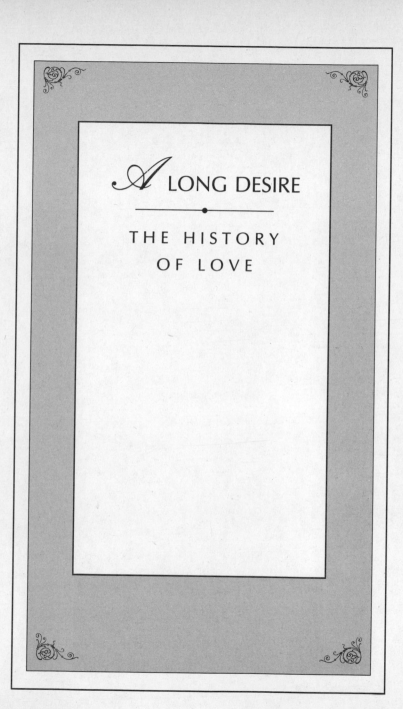

$\mathscr{A}$ LONG DESIRE

THE HISTORY OF LOVE

EGYPT

HISTORY'S PARAMOUR, THE SERPENT QUEEN

Cleopatra. Her name conjures up an Orient of mystery and romance. Thousands of years after her death, she still rules men's fantasies and sparks women's envy. We may sigh over Helen of Troy as the incarnation of feminine beauty, but we envy Cleopatra for an allure so elemental that she could sail into any man's life and steal his heart. We picture her as a human aphrodisiac, a woman redolent with sensuality. That part of us still a child, which secretly trusts in magic, wants to believe that her wand-like power could bewitch one Caesar after another. Her legend tells us more about our own fantasies and yearnings than about the woman herself.

Cleopatra was born in Egypt in 69 B.C., the daughter of King Ptolemy XII, who was descended from a Macedonian general. Although her mother isn't known, royal marriages between brother and sister were usual, and that would make Cleopatra mainly Greek. However, a purely incestuous line of descent would have produced frail and feebleminded offspring, whereas freshening the gene pool by only one indiscretion would be enough to ensure some genetic variety and healthy offspring. In all likelihood, royal women occasionally became pregnant by outsiders. So it's safest to say that Cleopatra was mainly Greek, but she may have been a mélange of other ancestries as well.

Although writers and artists of her time described her in much detail, those accounts have vanished. What survives is Plutarch's biography, written two hundred years later, based on the memoirs of people who saw or met her. They reported that she was not pretty but very charming, with a strong personality and a musical voice. Her portrait on Egyptian coins minted during her reign was bound to have been flattering; no artist would have wanted to insult the queen, and she wouldn't have wished her subjects to carry around unflattering likenesses of her. The woman whose profile we find in relief on those coins has a large hooked nose, bony face, sharply pointed chin, big eyes, and a rather narrow forehead. Second-guessing beauty in ancient days in distant lands is not a game for the faint of heart.

What she had was style. Glamorous and dramatic, Cleopatra was a one-woman pageant. Silks and perfumes, veils and precious stones, exotic makeup and ornate coiffures, fawning slaves and sinewy dancers—all were part of her repertoire and retinue. When she wanted to impress her own people or visiting Romans, she produced elaborate ceremonies on land and sea, wore opulent clothes, knew just what tableau to stage. She might have written stirring speeches instead, and indeed some books have been credited to her, but most of her people were illiterate, and she needed to express herself in a way that would transcend the written word, and also not require much translation. She chose a dramatic, full-body hieroglyphics, in which nothing was spoken but much was understood. Plutarch reports that, when she sailed to Tarsus to meet Antony, she arrived on a scented barge of purple and gold, dressed as Aphrodite (the Greek goddess of sexual love), with boys as cupids fanning her.

> Her rowers caressed the water with oars of silver which dipped in time to the music of the flute, accompanied by pipes and lutes. . . . Instead of a crew the barge was lined with the most beautiful of her waiting women attired as Nereids and Graces, some at the rudders, others at the tackles of the sails, and all the while an indescribably rich perfume, exhaled from innumerable censers, was wafted from the vessel to the river banks.

Sometimes merged with Isis, Egypt's patron goddess, Aphrodite was an important goddess to the city of Tarsus, whose religious history told of her union with an eastern god. Imagine the wildness of the scene, when the people of Tarsus beheld their goddess arriving in clouds of perfume. They flocked to the harbor to welcome and adore her. Not a bad entrance. Antony would have been impressed by the opulence and grandeur at Cleopatra's command, and he would have gotten the message that their union was written in the stars.

We don't remember her in Egyptian terms, as a powerful and able monarch, whose people valued and even worshiped her. Instead, we accept the Roman propaganda of her as a depraved seductress, the ruin of great men. This should not surprise us. Rome was her enemy, and it was in Rome's best interest to vilify her during wartime. If she wasn't depicted as a beautiful, debauched, hot-blooded enchantress, how could one explain Roman generals joining forces with her?

Was she depraved? Apparently she did contrive to kill her siblings in order to be queen. Did she have many lovers? She is reported to have taxed some men dearly for spending a single night with her. After lovemaking, she sometimes had a man killed. Because she was a goddess, any lover became a demigod in her arms. Perhaps she felt well rid of certain dangerous and attractive men, and no guilt, knowing that they would be destined for eternal life. As the ruler of a large and tumultuous kingdom, she might not have had endless time for dalliance; but I doubt that she was abstinent for years on end, as some scholars argue. Cleopatra appears to have been flamboyant and nervy, earthy and spiritual.

If she seems unreal to us now, we must remember that even in her own lifetime she was something of an invention. Her Roman enemies mythologized her as an evil enchantress; she mythologized herself as a beneficent goddess. Did she believe her own divine version of herself? Only the goddess figure appeared in public, and we have no record of what she was like in private. We know very little about her, except that she was clever, learned, cultured, and fascinating to be around. She spoke several languages, including demotic Egyptian, the language of the common people. That, along with the fact that she worshiped Egyptian deities rather than Greek, endeared her to them. She is said by many to have written treatises on cosmetics, gynecology, weights and measures, and alchemy. Al-Masudi, a tenth-century historian, wrote that she was "well versed in the sciences, disposed to the study of philosophy and counted scholars among her intimate friends. She was the author of works on medicine, charms, and other divisions of the natural sciences. These books bear her name and are well known among men conversant with art and medicine."

Was she really a siren, who lured and beguiled? Cleopatra's greatest charm was Egypt itself, the wealthiest kingdom in the Mediterranean, and any Roman who yearned for mastery of the world needed her power, her navy, and her treasury. An alliance with Egypt made superb military sense. Caesar and Antony were questing for power, not love, even if she was supremely lovable, as she may well have been. Antony and Cleopatra did live together off and on for six years—he was frequently away on military campaigns—during which she bore him two sons and a daughter. When Octavius defeated them at Actium, they committed suicide because everything was lost—empire, power, wealth, esteem. The romantic version of their double suicide argues that they were unable to live without each other. That may be true, but they also knew the Roman habit of parading vanquished enemies through the streets in an orgy of humiliation, torture, and display. And Cleopatra thought herself immortal, after all, an embodiment of Isis who could look forward to a rich reception in the afterlife. Despite her fright or any last-minute lapses of faith she might have suffered, she staged her death carefully, dressing herself in the rich robes of Isis, and making sure she would be discovered on a bed of pure gold.

My intuition is that Cleopatra and Mark Antony shared an exuberant love and respect, along with a sense of divine mission. Was she irresistible? She was ingenious, brilliantly manipulative, and wise about male psychology. She may well have had a deep, lagoonlike sensuality, hypnotic as quartz. *Quartz.* From Middle High German *quarz,* from West Slavic *kwardy.* From Indo-European, *twer-. Twery-en,* "she who grasps, binds, enthralls; in Greek, *seiren,* siren." Quartz was a frozen siren that held you in her grasp forever, hard and pure, a woman with a hundred faces. She could be opal, she could be flint. She could contain fire, or she could cause fire. Quartz had nothing to do with will or desire. This was a mineral love, it enchanted from the bones outward.

Each culture invents Cleopatra anew, depending on the social climate and morals of the time. Our version is the one bequeathed to us by her illustrious enemy, Rome. Octavius was so proud of crushing her and claiming Egypt for the Roman empire that, in 27 B.C., when he declared himself "Augustus Caesar," he chose to give his name to the month of August because that was the time of year when he had conquered his toughest enemy, Cleopatra—history's paramour, the serpent queen. In an ironic twist of the love-your-enemy libretto, it was her downfall that made his heart and future bright.

ART IN ANCIENT EGYPT

History is an agreed-upon fiction. Even during Cleopatra's reign, scholars did not see her without makeup and regalia, nor were they privy to the key events affecting her life. They may have misread some of her actions, or been dangerously biased. People close to her—family, lovers, priestesses—may not have been totally in her confidence. If they were, they may not have had a penchant for writing things down. And, if they did, such documents may not have survived. Of those that did, some may be exaggerated or hide political motives. The best we can do is *surmise,* that sunstruck word that sounds like an ancient kingdom.

Nothing reveals more about the inner life of a people than their arts, and the arts thrived in ancient Egypt. Visitors often commented on the abundance of music, dance, storytelling, and song. They were dazzled by the size and sophistication of the statues, the pageantry of the paintings, the variety of the dancers, and the agility of the wordsmiths. Nineteenth-century European composers would create "tone poems," in which they tried to capture in music such natural wonders as a pasture, a skylark, or the afternoon of a faun. In ancient Egypt, dancers *became* the movement of the wind, the openness of the sky, the heat of the sun. Lyric poetry (a song accompanied by the lyre) blossomed, and writers spun imaginative tales, moral fables, and even a narrative about a sailor's adventures that most likely was the inspiration for Homer's *Odyssey.* Performing regularly at feasts, religious ceremonies, and casual parties, musical groups played the harp, lyre, tambourine, sistrum, drums, lute, cymbals, and flute. When a Greek potentate attended a royal banquet at Memphis, he was entertained by a band of musicians, and then

two dancers, a man and a woman, went among the crowd and beat out the rhythm. Then each danced a solo veiled dance. Then they danced together, meeting and separating, then converging in successive harmonious movements. The young man's face and movements expressed his desire for the girl, while the girl continually attempted to escape him, rejecting his amorous advances. The whole performance was harmoniously coordinated, animated yet graceful, and in every way pleasing.

Through art, the Egyptians celebrated their gods and pharaohs, but they also praised the Nile, rejoiced in the wonders of the garden, and recorded the ways of city and rural folk. They celebrated beauty wherever they found it, among people or in nature. But there was another aspect to Egyptian art that made it quintessentially relevant and, at times, a matter of life and death.

The Egyptians believed that to imagine something was to make it real. If one carved a statue of a donkey and placed it in a tomb, it would come to life to serve the deceased in the other world. Art was powerful. It could transform matter, bend time, escape death. It had a magical purpose. Most of the art we associate with Egypt was, in effect, a kind of fetishism. Beautiful art was practical art. But, by practical, they meant clay becoming flesh, paint becoming sheaves of wheat, a gemstone eye awakening the protection of a deity.

In paintings, men are shown bare chested, straight and strong, with wide shoulders tapering to a narrow waist—the shape of the hunter in the constellation Orion. Women are tall and bosomy, and often glamorously dressed, with stylized eye makeup, and long black hair carefully plaited and perfumed with unguents. Egyptian women did not take part in government (except for the occasional female pharaoh), but they traveled freely, enjoyed many of the same pastimes and activities that men did, and commanded more respect than women in other lands.

The hieroglyphic word for love (as a noun or a verb) consists of a hoe, a mouth, and a man with a hand in his mouth. No doubt Egyptians spoke of love without dwelling too long on the etymology of the word, just as we refer to our muscles without thinking about mice running under our skin.* The sign literally meant "to want, choose, or desire," but it could also include the idea of duration, to

*Muscle comes from the Latin musculus or "little mouse."

want over a period of time, or, as we say, to love. Most Egyptologists don't regard the mouth and hoe symbolically, but rather as sounds, just as we would the letters *l* and *v*. I would like to think the letters sounded like the wind blowing through the sand, and that you had to purse your lips into a waiting kiss just to utter them. But we have no idea what ancient Egyptian sounded like, any more than we do the Greek of that era. The man with a hand to his mouth is a sign that frequently occurs at the end of words having to do with eating, drinking, speaking, thinking—anything that involves functions of the mouth or of the heart. (Feelings were thought to reside in the brain.)

It is interesting to look at what their word for love implies. To a Freudian, it might be a sexual euphemism, with the long, stiff hoe representing a penis, the mouth a vagina, and the man with a hand in his mouth lovemaking. Interpreted this way, the word would emphasize how fixated we are on the oral. Or perhaps the word is entirely agricultural—lovers till the earth of a relationship, raising the food of love, with which they nourish each other. Perhaps it is economic. Marriage is chiefly an economic institution, joining clans, forging alliances between families, uniting properties. There is no woman in this picture, unless she is symbolized by her mouth, a disembodied kiss. So perhaps it depicts love from a man's point of view, filling his days with labor and his nights with kisses.

The garden was a favorite setting for romance in Egypt, and poems often draw on such sights and smells. In ancient times, in desert worlds, few things were more soul-drenching than the idea of an oasis. A hidden garden in the aridity of life soon became a metaphor for love. In the biblical Song of Solomon—which was preceded by similar songs in ancient Egypt and Sumeria—King Solomon sings to his intended that her virginity is like a luscious garden he will soon enter. Then he mentions one by one all the fruits he will pick, all the scents he will inhale. We tend to forget that King Solomon's frequent marriages were part of a pagan fertility ritual. He had 700 wives and 300 concubines. If he courted even a few with the same degree of devotion and poetry, then one can only lament the volumes of his writings that have been lost. And where are Cleopatra's love poems? Given her youth and disposition, and her long separations from Antony, she must have committed her heart to paper.

THE HIEROGLYPHIC LOVE POEMS

Egyptologists have found fifty-five anonymous love poems, on papyri* and vases, dating back to around 1300 B.C. Certainly there were poems written earlier; but papyri and vases are extremely perishable. Although we don't know the authors of the poems, they were most likely written by both men and women. Some of them are alternating duets between lovers. Told first from one point of view, then the next, they show psyches torn by uncertainty, hearts on fire. Here is part of a typical hieroglyphic love poem, "Conversations in Courtship," in which a man describes his darling as

> More lovely than all other womanhood,
> luminous, perfect,
> A star coming over the sky-line at new year,
> a good year,
> Splendid in colours,
> with allure in the eye's turn.
> Her lips are enchantment,
> her neck the right length
>   and her breasts a marvel;
>
> Her hair lapis lazuli in its glitter,
> her arms more splendid than gold.
> Her fingers make me see petals,
> the lotus' are like that.
> Her flanks are modeled as should be,
> her legs beyond all other beauty.
> Noble her walking
> (vera incessu)
> My heart would be a slave should she enfold me.

In another poem, "Pleasant Songs of the Sweetheart Who Meets You in the Fields," we find a woman hunting birds:

*We get our word *paper* from the Greek *papyros,* the word given to a material used by the Egyptians for writing and wrapping. To make papyrus, the Egyptians flattened and crisscrossed strips of pith from the long stalks of a sedge, *Cyperus papyrus,* which grew tall in the Nile Delta. This wasn't true paper, which requires a grinding and mashing process that turns fibers into a soupy mixture that is then spread across a screen to drain and dry. The latter process is said to have been invented by a Chinese eunuch in A.D. 105 and spread slowly to Europe, entering Spain around A.D. 1200.

My darling—my beloved—whose love empowers me,
Listen to what I tell you:
I went to the field where birds gather.
I held in one hand a trap, and in the other a net and
  spear.
I saw many birds flying from the land of Punt
Laden with sweet fragrance to alight on Egypt's soil.
The first snatched the bait from my hand.
He had a beautiful odor and his claws held incense.
But, for your sake, dear beloved, I will set him free,
Because I would like you, when far away,
To listen to the song of the bird
Scented with myrrh.
How wonderful to go to the fields when one's heart
  is consumed by love!
The goose cries out, the goose that snatched the bait
  and was trapped.
Your love distracted me and I could not keep it.
I will fold the nets, but what can I tell mother
When I return each day without birds?
I will say I failed to set my nets,
Because the nets of your love have trapped me.

Although these poems were written over three thousand years ago,
they weave together many of the same themes, worries, and rejoicings
we find in love poems today. They tell us what mattered to Egyptian
lovers (and still vexes us). A few of their key themes:

1. *Love's alchemy, or the power to transform.* Sad as it seems,
human beings have always been unhappy with who they are. Even the
most comely of us feel like eternally ugly ducklings who yearn to be
transformed into swans. One of the bad jokes of evolution is that we
have evolved brains which can imagine a state of perfection we
cannot achieve. When Plato wrote that everything on earth has its
ideal version in heaven, many took what he said literally. But for me
the importance of Plato's ideal forms lies not in their truth but in our
desire for the flawless. No one can live up to perfection, and most of
us do not often expect it of others; but we are more demanding with
ourselves. Egyptian lovers, feeling transformed by love, based their
belief on a subconscious faith in magic. In a world menacing and
implausible, only faith could explain it, only magic control it.

Another feature of love's alchemy is the idea of improvement. Why are we so obsessed with *improving* everything around us: our lawn, our aluminum siding, our chances, ourselves? Regardless of talent, looks, or good fortune, we feel ourselves to be inadequate and in need of some extra genius or flair or energy or serenity. Perhaps this is because so much of our experience of life happens as thought, interior monologue, and dream. Language helps to define our feelings, but many of our moods and tempers cannot be articulated. And memory provides us with a circus of shortcomings. It doesn't matter that those events happened when we were younger, in dire straits, frightened, or less wise. We sense that we are impostors. Keeping our failings a secret, we assume no one on earth is as neurotic, no one as uniquely flawed. The rampantly beautiful person we are attracted to couldn't possibly be as frail. He is a contagion of virtues. Loving him, we sing his praises, highlighting all his good points. We redefine him to himself. Through love one learns to feel lovable.

2. *Idealizing the beloved in images drawn from nature*. Why should it flatter a person to be compared to stars, gemstones, flowers, or perfumes? Why not compare one another to skyscrapers, Persian rugs, filigree ironwork, covered bridges, or steaming macadam? Sometimes we do, especially in modern poetry, but lovers mainly rhapsodize about each other's body and its parts in terms of sun and moon, plants and hillocks. The lover rationalizes his carnal worship by saying to himself, in effect, "Her brown eyes are as absolute as nightfall, her mouth as dew-struck as morning." Or as the author of the Egyptian courtship poem puts it: her black hair glitters like lapis lazuli, and her arms are the pure gold of an idol. Love speaks in absolutes, but the only absolutes we know are the workings of nature or the mastery of gods.

3. *Love as enslavement*. Sometimes I think all of life can be seen as a struggle to keep one's own freedom or to steal someone else's. We are so alike you would think one voice could speak for all of us. But let a dictator arise—of a country or of a family—and rebellion eventually ensues. Freedom is an idea worth killing for. Throughout our lives, we feel trapped by family, society, age, gender, job. Also by many intangibles: tradition, religious teachings, and our own and others' expectations of ourselves. How we shudder at the thought of being enslaved to an illness or an injury. Being an automaton isn't

human, and we prize the curious hallmarks of our humanity. To take orders is to be low man on the totem pole, and we upright apes are forever clambering toward the top.

Yet in love we become willing prisoners. If you remove the idea of the beloved and replace it with the tyrant, but keep the same degree of obsession, servility, sacrifice, uncertainty, and loss of freedom, what do you have? A police state. In the banana republic of the heart, petty tyrants can drag one away by nightfall for some gentle terror. Love makes mania respectable. Not only does it enslave, it issues proclamations and directives. Love speaks, gives its own orders.* In poems, lovers frequently report: "Love bid me go, and I followed." Love is often depicted as a state of mnemonic possession, in which the spirit of love speaks through someone, urging them to act in uninhibited ways. We allow only our rulers and gods to possess us body and soul, as if we were nothing more than ventriloquists' dummies, to dictate our actions and determine our fate. We build love temples and shrines, where we enter as supplicants, practice love as a form of religion, complete with personal savior, acolytes, and rituals. How can we explain the recklessness, the sheer abandon of love, if we don't see it as the work of a despot or a force of nature, a divine tornado that has swept us up?

4. *Being disabled.* So it follows, paradoxically, that love is both a fortifying and a disabling emotion. Lovers moon about, sigh, fantasize about each other. They can't keep their minds on their work, they abandon their normal pursuits. The beloved becomes a mantra that focuses the lover's thoughts in a cleansing way. All else is distraction. The lover lives in a waking faint. We describe such lovers with words of drunkenness or witchery. Their condition is so familiar to us we don't find it particularly odd that, every now and then, people go haywire, lose their ability to think clearly, have stomachaches, can't sleep properly, and spend hours daydreaming. Such a state has all the earmarks of disease and, as the Egyptian love poems remind us, people have always described love as a sickness.

5. *A secret kept from one's parents.* No one wants to tell his parents that he has fallen in love. Why be furtive about it? One's

---

*At that level of high-voltage emotion, there's a thin line between sweet fanaticism and acute psychosis. Twist the love just a little, keeping the same intensity, and you are in a dangerous fixation that leads to violence.

parents have flirted, fallen in love, felt sexy. Yet lovers feel embarrassed by the extravagance of their obsession, try to disguise their feelings, and worry that their kin will know. There is a sense of wickedness or shame attached to it. I suspect that this is because it feels like a betrayal, an act of treason, that will carry them away from the family. Love for parents will be superseded by love for spouse and children. They will sneak away into another tribe and pledge devotion to outsiders.

6. *Redoubling of the senses.* "Her fingers make me see petals," the hieroglyph poet writes. Love produces synesthesia. All the usual categories blur and one experiences the world freshly, as a waterfall of sensations. We often indulge in platitudes about how love makes us "young again," or "brings out the child in us." But you can look at it from the opposite perspective, too. Watching young animals at play, one sees them unwittingly practicing all the essential behaviors of courtship. Love returns us to a time when there were fewer people to worry about, when we were powerfully dependent on parents who gave us everything—food, warmth, attention, affection, tenderness.

MY SISTER, MY BRIDE

One custom of the ancient Egyptians that shocks most of us is incest. Lovers in the poems frequently address one another tenderly as brother or sister. Yet to us, and to peoples throughout the world, throughout the ages, incest is a taboo, a practice horrible to imagine, unnatural and damning. Parent-child incest is regarded as the most heinous, because it thrives on exploitation, power, and domination. The older family member is seen to be preying on the younger, who is innocent and helpless. In Greek tragedy, Oedipus was doomed to blindness and wandering because he had slept with his mother, though unknowingly. There is something particularly offensive about the idea that he reinserted part of himself into the place from which he was born. Centuries later, Freud would be jeered in psychiatric circles for suggesting that male children felt Oedipal desires—jealousy toward Father, a yearning for union with Mother. His colleagues were not simply disbelieving of his theory; they were appalled.

Another reason for the powerful incest taboos, which exist among other animals as well, is that incest is the ultimate form of inbreeding. If individuals marry only within a small family group, the same genes will be passed to all the offspring. But the environment changes, new diseases evolve, the harvest sometimes fails, herds vanish, new predators arrive. In an unstable world, only the ingenious survive. Evolution works by mixing bloodlines, so that there will always be someone around who can adapt to change. Variety is not just the spice of life, it's evolution's crucial ingredient. We need genetic variety to deal with the changing landscape and the caravan of frights we encounter in a lifetime. Inbreeding for only twenty generations will produce homogeneity.

An example of what happens if incest goes unchecked can be seen in the animal world today—the predicament of the cheetah. Because cheetahs are highly endangered, and there are precious few of them in the wild, they have inbred for some time. A microscopic look at their DNA is disturbing. They are essentially clones of one another. They all look the same, all heal the same; no new traits or strengths are being passed along to the young. A virus that can kill one cheetah can kill every cheetah. Throughout the animal kingdom, hybrids are stronger, produce larger litters, and live longer. There's no doubt that the incest taboo has a biological basis, but there are also many sociological, psychoanalytical, and anthropological theories. The strongest argument is a combination of genetic and social.

One thing we know for sure is that in our distant past there were fewer people. A million years ago, the entire worldwide human population was about 500,000, smaller than the cities of Oslo or Nairobi. Incest was essential then for the species to survive. Infant mortality was high. But as tribes grew in number, so did the possibilities for genetic mixing. And for romance. Desirable women were swapped to form political alliances. As Reay Tannahill reminds us in *Sex in History,* " 'love at first sight' is possible only between strangers." The Bible often refers to (and condones) incestuous marriages; in the days of the Old Testament, relatives were encouraged to marry. By the time of the Egyptians, marrying out of the family was normal, but it was also common for brother and sister to marry if it seemed convenient. This doesn't mean that they consummated the union, or were faithful to each other, bearing each other's children. Among the

Egyptians, incest was a practical way to keep real estate in the family, since women could inherit property. It was a custom based on economics, not familiarity. Even so, one hears of brother and sister marrying, not parent and child. A family is like a city-state in which everyone has an important role to play, depending on their relationship with one another. Here is the tangle of role reversals that would be produced by a father-daughter marriage:

> A resulting son would be a half-brother of his mother, his grandmother's stepson, his mother's brother's half-brother, and not only his father's child but his grandson as well! Note the problems of identity and exercise of authority: should he act toward his mother as a son or as a half-brother; should the uncle be treated as an uncle or as a half-brother? . . . if a brother and sister were to marry and then divorce, could they readily revert to their original relationship?

Not only would the integrity of the family be impossible to maintain, daily life would be plain confusing. In any case, marriage was useful for forging kinship bonds and establishing individuals' roles in society. Incest kept love on a tight leash, but the family in control.

A LONG DESIRE

At first glance, the ancient Egyptians seem exotic, glaringly different from us, and in some ways they were. But not when it comes to loving. Our attitudes about love are as old as the pyramids. The Egyptians were sentimental and romantic about love. Their word for love meant something like "a long desire." Relying on a rich array of metaphors, their love poems are, even if sometimes sappy, free of guilt, self-abasement, or that curious combination of love/hate we see so often today. We don't have Egyptian writings about homosexual love per se, but *The Egyptian Book of the Dead* includes a passage in which the deceased swears that he hasn't had sex with a boy. Homosexuality must have been commonplace, the seduction of boys a frequent temptation, or it wouldn't have been forbidden. We do find fetishism, masochism, and other fringe elements, plus a practical concern with contraception, for which women used a pessary of elephant and crocodile dung. Love is sometimes thought of as a sweet trap, sometimes as a sickness one craves. But no god or goddess steers the course of lovers, foiling their efforts, tempting their faith. Though they feel swept away by love's power, they blame no one. Poetry records the heartbeat of a people, and thanks to the Egyptian poets we know that love thrived in ancient days, a familiar, modern sort of love, which had little to do with the hard currency of marriage. They felt the same sweet calamities that lovers do today.

GREECE

THE WORLD OF THE CITIZEN KING

Thinking about the late sixties, I remember the anxious thrill of trying to reinvent society. A generation defined by love-ins, hallucinogenic drugs, and the Vietnam War, we lived in a state of daily commotion. Cynicism and idealism went hand in hand in us. Inherited truths no longer fit; we felt it was both our privilege and our duty to reshape them. The roller coaster we rode sometimes took wild curves and left the tracks. Fun meant outlandish public pranks. Rock and roll besotted us with high-decibel slogans. "The War" loomed over everything and everyone. We championed integration. We protested. We were arrested. We enlisted. We were drafted. We evaded or fled. We staged sit-ins. We practiced free love. We sampled drugs and learned about extremes of consciousness. Like every generation, we lived with moral dilemmas. On campus, we discussed politics before, after, and even during classes, whose curricula we rewrote.

That atmosphere of upheaval, social change, and hope comes to mind when I picture the city of Athens in the fifth century B.C. War and politics led to the radical idea of a bustling democracy, in which citizens could air their views, however novel, and vote their minds in the state assembly. Any citizen over thirty was eligible for public office. The daily intrigues of this vigorous new self-government must have filled the law courts and fueled the gossip mills. Athens was a world of only about 30,000 people, not much larger than my hometown in upstate New York. And yet it produced a band of luminous thinkers and creators whose ideas were the source of western civilization. Most of them would have been friends, crossed paths regularly, or at least known one another on sight. It was a tight, competitive city—the Greeks adored staging contests of body and mind. To be a citizen of Athens meant status, prestige, economic opportunity (only citizens could own real estate), and a sense of nobility (you had to be the child of two Athenian parents—indeed, in the fourth century, it was illegal for Athenians even to marry non-Athenians). Athens revolved around its citizenry, and sanctified their rights. As Pericles proudly explained, in sentiments that would later be adopted almost word for word by colonial America:

> Our constitution is called a democracy because power is in the hands of the people, not a minority. When it is a question of settling private disputes, everybody is equal before the law: when it is a question of putting one person before another in positions of public responsibility, what counts is not membership of a particular class, but the actual ability which the man possesses. No one, so long as he has it in him to be of service to the state, is kept in political obscurity because of poverty. . . . This is a peculiarity of ours: we do not say that a man who takes no interest in politics is a man who minds his own business; we say that he has no business here at all.

Among such ideals, in an intellectual free-for-all, politics must have fed Athens like a tonic. However, it was a stimulant enjoyed only by men. Women were not allowed to be citizens. Politics might be too invigorating for them; it was common knowledge that women were by nature irrational, hysterical, gluttonous, given to drunkenness, and sex-obsessed. They were not thought to be rational or strong-willed enough for so vital a responsibility as self-government. Or for spirited conversation. A wife didn't dine with her husband, and if he brought home a male visitor, all the womenfolk were expected to retreat to the women's quarters. Any woman seen at a male gathering—even if she engaged only in talk—was assumed to be a prostitute. It's not that the men didn't cherish their women. One often finds women referred to tenderly in Greek literature, and domestic scenes lovingly depicted on vases. Courtroom speeches frequently include a sentimental appeal on behalf of the litigant's mother, sister, wife, or daughter. Men wouldn't resort to such ploys if they didn't think they would work. But a family could only be sure of its bloodline by keeping a strict watch over the wife, whose place was in the dim vault of the home with the other forms of wealth. A purebred Athenian girl had to marry young, be a virgin, and not even have mingled socially with men. Men married late (usually in their thirties), and weren't required to be chaste. This meant that neither men nor women had equals of the opposite sex to fall in love with. In a typical scenario, a cultured, educated, sexually experienced, politically active middle-aged husband would return home to his sheltered, illiterate sixteen-year-old wife. Teenage girls were not visible on the streets for men to idealize or fantasize about. Beautiful teenage boys were, though, and they alone provided the erotic siren of youth. Friends often met at gymnasia, where they could watch the young men of Athens exercise naked (with the foreskin tied over the tip of the penis to protect it). Since Athenian women were off-limits, it was common for men to have young male lovers or female courtesans, to whom they turned for companionship, as well as sex, since respectable women were social exiles.

Married couples sometimes fell in love; but love had nothing to do with marriage, which was intended to produce children. According to Menander, the marriage formula went like this: "I give you this woman (my daughter) for the ploughing of legitimate children." Women were associated with agriculture, fields to be sown and reaped. Men stood for reason and culture; women for the wild forces of nature men were to tame.

THE WOMAN'S WORLD

Above the fireplace in my living room hangs a large etching entitled "Diana's Chase." Leaping and dodging, with all body parts swinging, the voluptuous goddess and her female followers race nearly naked through the forest, hunting a buck as if it were zest incarnate. Also known as Artemis, this "huntress chaste and fair" exuded sensuality and energy. She rejoiced in nature at its most savage and free. As "Mistress of the Beasts," she was the official protectress of wild animals, and she moved among them with the delicate brawn of the wind and the ethereal dynamism of the sun. A high point of the Greek wedding ceremony came when the girl renounced her patron goddess, Artemis, and swore fealty to Demeter, goddess of agriculture and married women. Demeter (literally "earth mother") somehow managed to be both nonerotic and fecund. The perfect wife was wilderness tamed. She was the fugitive land cleared and turned to production. All of a man's social, intellectual, cultural, and romantic needs were to be filled elsewhere.

Women in ancient Greece celebrated two special holidays. Athenian matrons held a yearly Thesmophoria, whose exultations excluded both women of lower class and any men, and required a period of sexual abstinence. As a counterculture holy day, courtesans, prostitutes, and their lovers celebrated the openly licentious festival of Adonia, honoring Aphrodite's lover Adonis. This was more of a flesh-and-blood carnival, which included the symbolic planting of grains in pots on the rooftops. Under the blinding Mediterranean sun, the plants would sprout fast, spurting color, and just as quickly wither. The seeding of this small thatch of earth was quick and exciting, but it was not expected to be fruitful. Perhaps they quoted these lines from Mimnermus' poetry:

> What is life, what is joy without golden Aphrodite?
> May I die when these things no longer move me—
> hidden love affairs, sweet nothings and bed.'

If high-spirited women in Athens who were intellectual, cultured, fun-loving, and proud of it wished to speak in mixed company about things that mattered, they became courtesans. Although their lives were uncertain, and at times degrading, at least these women could enjoy the riches of Athenian culture. They were stylish and witty, versed in art and politics, and, in calling, somewhere between a geisha and a prostitute. Men admired precisely those talents in the courtesans they forbade in their wives. But Athens was full of paradoxes. While debating and championing democracy, citizens frequently owned slaves, with whom they sometimes found pleasure. At a cheaper rate, with less emotional ballyhoo, were streetwalkers, one of whose sandals has survived the millennia. On its sole, studded so that it would brand the dust with each step, is the invitation: *Follow me.*

MEN LOVING MEN

Loving relationships, not merely sexual liaisons, also evolved between older men and teenage boys, a combination of romance and tutelage that was blessed by society and praised in philosophy and art. "The aristocratic ideal," as historian Charles Beye points out, "was a combination of athletic exercise to create a beautiful body and music and poetry to create a beautiful personality." There is a section of Aristophanes' *Clouds* that instructs a boy

> how to be modest, sitting so as not to expose his crotch, smoothing out the sand when he arose so that the impress of his buttocks would not be visible, and how to be strong. . . . The emphasis was on beauty. . . . A beautiful boy is a good boy. Education is bound up with male love, an idea that is part of the pro-Spartan ideology of Athens. . . . A youth who is inspired by his love of an older male will attempt to emulate him, the heart of the educational experience. The older male in his desire for the beauty of the youth will do whatever he can to improve it.

Anyway, that was the theory—pederasty as a refined stage in a boy's education. But the system didn't always proceed so chastely. Greek literature sizzles with scenes of love brazen or tawdry, tormented or betrayed, drunken or homicidal. In Aristophanes' *The Birds,* one older man says to another: "Well, this is a fine state of affairs, you damned desperado! You meet my son just as he comes out of the gymnasium, all fresh from the bath, and you don't kiss him, you don't say a word to him, you don't hug him, you don't feel his balls! And you're supposed to be a friend of ours!" Plato has Socrates and his friends discussing randy matters casually as they dine. His *Symposium* (from the Greek word for drinking companion) offered a banquet of the senses as well as ideas. To this day, we find the dinner party, or the brown-bag lunch, a good place to hone ideas and swap tales of entanglement.*

My first teaching job, at the University of Pittsburgh, introduced me to the voracious minds of blue-collar students. A graduate poetry seminar ran late one evening. We all retired to the nearby Pitt Tavern, where my students liked to drink boilermakers of Jameson's Irish Whiskey followed by Iron City Light beer. Hard-boiled eggs doused with Tabasco sauce passed as dinner, and there amid the ruckus of gritty dialect and workingman's music they held their own impromptu symposium. No one described it as such, but when pensive young minds get together they're often drawn to similar topics. Among those they discussed easily were nature versus nurture, aesthetic ideals, the purpose of love—without realizing it, they were talking Plato. "Which do you think is more important," a young woman asked me that evening, "truth or beauty?" "No difference," I answered glibly, offering her the ideal established in Greece millennia ago, and later used by John Keats in his "Ode on a Grecian Urn." " 'Beauty is truth,' " Keats said, " 'truth beauty,'—that is all/ Ye know on earth, and all ye need to know." In Athens, handsome people were assumed to be morally good. How could it be otherwise in a world of symmetry, balance, and harmony? We still subconsciously believe that faulty equation today, crediting attractive people with high motives, rare intelligence, good character. Study after study shows that pretty schoolchildren get better grades; attractive criminals get lighter sentences. But in Greece a handsome man was also morally sublime—innate goodness had to express itself as beauty. So it followed that homosexual love affairs could take on a religious zeal and cosmic rightness. It's easy to imagine this leading to soul-drenching devotion, and the religion of two we call romantic love. When women expressed love, they were thought wanton and irrational. When men loved men, they adored flesh and virtue simultaneously, all wrapped up in the form of the beloved. Anything less was heresy.

Men must also have enjoyed sex with their wives, or a play such as Aristophanes' Lysistrata—in which the women stage a sex strike to force the men to stop the Peloponnesian War—wouldn't have

*See Plato, "The Perfect Union," for a discussion of Plato's theory of love.

made sense. But the idea of the self-sufficient married couple, who met most of each other's needs, was not in the air, nor was that of the private man, who kept amiably to himself. Our word *idiot*, for example, comes from the Greek disapproval of any man who wasn't politically active.

THE FAMILY

Growing up in the women's quarters, as if in a harem, children rarely saw their fathers; thus their exiled mothers must have been exceptionally strong forces in their lives. In all probability there was a lot of pent-up anger, rejection, envy, and frustration on display. What example of love did this set? For a little girl, it would be a particularly heart-torn existence. If she aspired to a life of the mind, or any brand of adventure, it would mean embracing immorality and repudiating the sanctity of motherhood. In agricultural Greece, a land obsessed with the harvest, the mother loomed as an earth goddess, a figure of honor and magic. A pregnant goddess contained the forces of nature, her breasts poured forth the stars. A pregnant woman going about her daily chores symbolized all that mysterious fertility.

In this highly charged world, fed on vivid myth, which most people took literally, the gods and goddesses were all related. In the pantheon, the family was everything. But the family was not one household in Athens; it was the city itself, whose affairs all men knew and played a role in. Once legitimate heirs were born to a man, things loosened up slightly for the wives, who could then divorce to get out of a particularly nasty marriage. It's not that Athenian women didn't sometimes have premarital or extramarital affairs, but those who did were thought shocking and immoral. And what chance had they to meet men? Plutarch reports in his *Life of Solon* that if a woman left the house in daylight she had to be chaperoned, and could take nothing with her but the equivalent of a shawl and a light snack. After sunset, she had to travel in a lighted carriage. Some women turned to lesbianism, or "tribadism,"* as it was known, following the example set by Sappho, one of the most adroit and sensual of lyric poets.

---

*From the Greek verb "to rub."

Others no doubt found homelier solutions, such as the one described by historian Reay Tannahill:

> Masturbation, to the Greeks, was not a vice but a safety valve, and there are numerous literary references to it. . . .
> Miletus, a wealthy commercial city on the coast of Asia Minor, was the manufacturing and exporting center of what the Greeks called the *olisbos,* and later generations, less euphoniously, the dildo. . . . This imitation penis appears in Greek times to have been made either of wood or padded leather and had to be liberally anointed with olive oil before use. Among the literary relics of the third century B.C., there is a short play consisting of a dialogue between two young women, Metro and Coritto, which begins with Metro trying to borrow Coritto's dildo. Coritto, unfortunately, has lent it to someone else, who has in turn lent it to another friend.

I think it's safe to assume that married life was less than bliss, and rarely became a focus of love for either party. Men were able to find romance openly, whereas women had to search in makeshifts and in shadows.

And yet, unlike other ancient cultures, the Greeks worshiped two love gods—Aphrodite and Eros. The idea of love played an important role in their lives, and troubled them enough that they needed two full-time gods to beseech or blame. According to Homer, it was Aphrodite's toying with Helen that led to the Trojan War. Love was a feeling so automatic and powerful that it had to have some other-worldly origin. In *The Origin of Consciousness and the Breakdown of the Bicameral Mind,* Julian Jaynes suggests that what we now call "conscience" or "reflection" prehistoric people heard as a sort of ventriloquial command, which they perceived as the word of god telling them what to do. Love makes such mischief that the idea of mortals causing it by themselves seemed impossible. Homer doesn't explore the psychology of love, as Greek lyric poets would later. Told from the outside, with the keen eye of an observer, Homer's love stories conquer hardship and distance and end happily. We know that King Menelaus had a young wife named Helen, and that when she was kidnapped the king fought a war to get her back. But we don't know much about the couple's feelings for each other. It was Christopher Marlowe, in seventeenth-century England, who claimed that beautiful Helen had a "face that launched a thousand ships." Was the Trojan War fought for the love of a woman, or because a king's private property had been stolen?

ORPHEUS AND EURYDICE

The Greek myth of Orpheus and Eurydice better illustrates the depths of a man's love for a woman. Orpheus was the son of Apollo and the muse Calliope ("she of the fair voice," the muse of epic song), who gave birth to him alongside the river Hebrus in the land of Thrace. His father was mortal, a Thracian prince. The Thracians were known throughout Greece as masterful musicians, and Orpheus was regarded as the most gifted of the Thracians. When he played the lyre and sang, he became psychokinetic, and nothing could resist him, not people, not animals or plants, not inanimate objects. His music entered all forms of matter at the level of atom and cell, which he could rearrange, changing the course of rivers, moving rocks and trees, taming wild animals. His song could make the sun leap up as it vanished, and coat the hilltops with a mist of pearls. An Argonaut in his youth, he set the measure for the oars, and saved his comrades from the fatal music of the Sirens. When they sang their eerie, mesmerizing song, the oarsmen rowed to them and a rock-festooned coast. But Orpheus played an antidote to the narcotic call, a song of such piercing clarity that it shook the men alert, giving them a chance to regain their wits and row to safety.

We do not know how he came to meet Eurydice, or any of the details of their courtship, though he is bound to have wooed her with song. She was a "nymph," one of the young maidens who lived in the forests and caves, free spirits in wildest nature, children of the earth. The nymphs hunted with Diana, feasted with Dionysus, and spent time with mortals, whom they sometimes wed. But Orpheus and Eurydice had little chance to enjoy their marriage. Soon after the wedding, Eurydice was walking across a meadow when she encountered the lecherous Aristaios (one of Apollo's sons), who pounced on her. She managed to pull free and run away, but she was so addled by his attack that she didn't see a snake sleeping in the sun in her path.

Before she could stop herself, she stepped on the snake's tail, and it spun around and bit her on the ankle, killing her. Hours later, Orpheus found her lying dead in the field. Bludgeoned by grief, he resolved to go down into the subterranean realm of death to find his bride and bring her back. He'd heard a rumor that a cave at Tainaron led down to the Underworld, and so he went there, carrying his lyre. This was a fearsome journey he planned, but he couldn't bear the thought of losing his beloved, and he knew his music was a pacifying weapon of great power, which nothing on earth could resist. He reasoned

> With my song
> I will charm Demeter's daughter,
> I will charm the Lord of the Dead,
> Moving their hearts with my melody.
> I will bear her away from Hades.

As he journeyed deeper and deeper into the cave, he played the sweetest, saddest song, music forged on the anvil of his heart. The cave spirits took pity on him and left him unharmed. A tearful Charon ferried him readily across the River Styx. Cerberus, the ferocious three-headed dog with hair of snakes that guarded the gates of the Underworld, lay down and let him pass. With his song of grief, Orpheus charmed his way into the kingdom of Hades. There he sang until earth was saturated with his voice, sang so beautifully that the dead rejoiced, and those vexed by punishments were granted a day of freedom so they could listen to his serenade. The king and queen of the Underworld, stirred by his pitiful lament, grew infatuated by the music. His song reasoned with them in a new, unexpected way that bypassed thought and turned their hard hearts to quicksand. So the king granted Orpheus a favor never before allowed a mortal—he could take his bride back to the world of light. But there was a stipulation.

"One thing," King Hades warned. "You must not look behind you. She may follow you into the upper air. If, however, you but once look back to see her ere you both have stepped fully into the light, she will be lost to you forever." Orpheus agreed, Eurydice was summoned, and he led her back along the way he had come, singing songs of hope and deliverance as he once more gained safe passage past

Cerberus, across the River Styx, and into the cave. There he began a steep ascent, clambering over the skiddy rocks, worrying that Eurydice might slip, trying to find the easiest path for her. As he climbed toward the entrance of the cave, just above, his song became wilder and more ecstatic. At last he reached the top and leapt into the blaze of daylight. Joyously turning to Eurydice, he saw to his horror that he had turned too soon; she was at the mouth of the cave, getting ready to step out. He lurched after her, but that fast she fell backward, into darkness, into death, crying "Farewell" as she disappeared down the throat of the cave. Wild with despair, Orpheus dived after her, found Charon again and begged to be taken once more across River Styx. There would be no need for a return passage, he explained; he would join his bride in death. But the boatman would not ferry him. Nothing would persuade Charon. For a week, Orpheus sat sobbing on the shore, starving away to nothing, covered in mud and slime. Finally, he brokenheartedly returned to Thrace, where he spent the next three years wandering alone, trying to erase even the thought of women. In time, he became a priest, performing simple duties in a small temple in the country. Celibate, solitary, he played his lyre for the plants and animals. As ever, his songs enchanted the woodlands and moved nature itself. That is, all but the maenads, wild-eyed, scruffy-haired, frenzied followers of Dionysus who hated him for every reason and no reason, but especially because he resisted their orgies and the favors of all womankind. They were punks with quick tempers and savage tastes, and easily annoyed. His music hit them like rock salt. It soured their mood, and it gave them the willies. So one morning this pack of bare-breasted assassins lay in wait for him outside the temple, and when they saw him they went murderous wild, attacking him with spears and rocks, then clawing him apart with their bare hands. They ripped off his arms and hurled them into the grass, yanked his legs loose, and when the ground was drenched with his blood, they ripped his head off and threw it into the river along with his lyre. That should have been the end of him. But, drifting downriver, his lyre began playing music all by itself. It played a low, mournful dirge, and then, miraculously, the tongue began to move in Orpheus' severed head. Singing his own funeral song, he floated out to sea and sank beneath the waves, above which the sad song lingered.

Few myths have been retold and reimagined as often as this one.

Why did Orpheus look back? I've often wondered. Because he didn't trust the gods? As an all-too-human reflex when he didn't hear Eurydice's movements—that is, because not even his magical gifts could protect him from his human traits? Out of a self-destructive, Freudian desire to fail in his life? In arrogance, because he thought his music made him more powerful than the gods? Was it a natural oversight linked to his gift (he was a transcendental musician, someone for whom time was fluid)? Because the author of the myth had a strong sense of drama, or—as it's so tempting to say while reading a whodunit—otherwise there wouldn't be much of a story? Because the gods, who understand human nature better than human beings do, knew all along that Orpheus would look back, so they weren't risking anything in letting Eurydice go with him? In this scenario, it is Orpheus' destiny to turn back, and their sadistic pleasure to let him go as far as possible, to the ultimate edge, to let him think he had won, so that their Schadenfreude would be the sweeter. Because no gift can be enjoyed without paying the price? Perhaps its lesson is about knowing one's place, in essence: *This is what happens if you try to best the gods.* Or is it a social lesson having to do with gender definition—as a musician, Orpheus was a person with a sensitive, intuitive nature, and that wasn't considered manly. In Greece, a woman was a man's property, so he would naturally assume that when he stepped into the light his possessions went with him. Perhaps his tragedy was that he didn't think of Eurydice as having a separate destiny.

In Balanchine's ballet, set to music by Stravinsky, it's all Eurydice's fault. During the entire trip back, she clings to him, tugging, yanking, desperate that he turn to look; and she finally wins, turning him around and pulling the mask from his eyes. This sounds a lot like blaming Eve for the world's sins. However interpreted, the story captured the hearts and minds of the Greeks, and every generation after them, as an example of loving devotion, self-sacrifice, and the power of love to survive everything, even dismemberment and death. In this myth, although the lovers are dead, the melody of their love continues to play without them. It has a fate of its own. It reminds us that love is the most resurrecting emotion in the world, which can carry one into the depths of hell and out again, provided one believes. Perhaps the simple moral is that, in love, there's no turning back.

ROME

THE NIGHTMARE OF GIRLS

Cornelia, the little girl next door, does not yet know she shares her name with Cornelia Gracchus, mother to a family of Roman statesmen in the first century A.D. As I write this, I'm watching her play on a fallen tree trunk which bridges our two yards. Neighbors always know where their property begins and ends. The line is the same for both, but we call the nearest edge "the beginning," as we do birth; and the farthest edge "the ending," as we do death. I suppose this is because we have a processive notion of time and life—the first of which our kind invented long ago,* the second of which each person invents anew. But so much of one's personality and actions are inherited. There must be a shyness gene. My friend's son, Isaac, was a flirt from the day he was born. Last year, as a seven-year-old, he met me at the door to their Long Island house, flung his arms around me, squeezed tight, climbed all over me, then said: "Who are you?" Affection pours from him, spontaneous as a mountain stream.

At five years old, Cornelia is sociable and forthcoming, but not huggy. I've known her all her life, and she's always had a bold, self-sustaining curiosity. She loves snakes and worms and caterpillars and slugs. This is not the perverse fascination with things gross or scary that one often finds among little boys who have discovered how to appall grown-ups and spellbind girls by wielding the monstrous. No, Cornelia just finds nature interesting. She has dolls and games and educational toys, a little brother burbling toward speech, and a nanny during the day while both parents are at work. But she spends many happy hours alone in the yard, rediscovering insects, dogwood blossoms, acorns, and fungi. She likes to name the bugs—"Catty" being a favorite for caterpillars. My naming the garter snake that lives in the backyard "World Without End" clearly puzzled her, but she

---

*In the first century B.C., sundials swept the imagination. Nobility and city folk were fascinated by them. But the earliest sundial can be traced to Egypt in 3500 B.C.; it consisted of a vertical stick arranged so that its shadow showed the sun's progress across the sky. Berosus, the third-century B.C. Babylonian priest and astronomer, improved the sundial. And both Greeks and Romans had water clocks for days when the sun didn't shine.

understood my need to name it, and also that it fell to her as a friend to praise my choice, however faintly. She hasn't the knack yet of how to feign emotions, as society requires, but she's learning. She doesn't know that she's restaging Adam's task, the naming of the beasts; she just feels the powerful urge to make nature personal. She does not know that the kindergarten intrigues of the last week are versions of love she'll grapple with more fully later. Because she's one of the two oldest kids in her class, the other children woo her. It's not just that there's status in being part of her clique—one finds this same pattern of envying the in-crowd among chimpanzees and other primates— some of the boys have crushes on her. Last week, Nathan, a deeply smitten five-year-old, kicked her in the ankle a few times as a gesture of affection, and Cornelia got mad and told him he couldn't be her friend anymore. Stricken to the core, Nathan went home sobbing because his Adored One had banished him and, by evening, his mother called Cornelia's mother and together they worked out a rapprochement which involved suggesting to Cornelia that she might have been a little hard on Nathan, and taking her over to Nathan's house to play—just the two of them—which both children enjoyed. In this small drama of power, worship, exile, and reunion, Cornelia's mother, Persis, recognized the seeds of romance and sighed bitter-sweetly as she related the story during one of our early morning runs.

"Nathan's so sensitive and vulnerable," she said. "You can already see how some girl is going to break his heart later on." Just then we reached the hill leading up past the purple and gray Indian Students Center, the roughly mown baseball field, and the brick village of the freshmen dorms. We slow to a walk up the steep incline, and that gives us more chance to talk.

"What do you suppose Cornelia will be like in love?" I asked.

Looking into the middle distance, Persis smiled, her cheeks arching high, the way she does sometimes when playing with her children, and she shook her head excitedly. "I don't know," she said. A race of memories seemed to cross in front of her. "I can't wait to see."

Although she expressed it passively, as a spectacle she would stand back and behold, we both knew how emotional it would be for Persis, balancing her role as adviser and bystander. Helping a child heal the first contusions of love must be difficult. The image that comes to mind is of a harbor boat guiding ships through lanes of hidden rock and hull-snagging coral to the vast seas beyond.

Persis expects her daughter to marry a man she loves. But in the days of Cornelia Gracchus such a thought was scandal. Female children were lucky to be alive at all, since "exposing" newborns, especially daughters, by abandoning them in the wild was a father's prerogative. Horrible as this practice sounds, I can only imagine it felt elementally right to the Romans: born of the earth, a child was returned to the earth. A father could decide a child's fate at birth, depending on whether a girl or boy was born. So what must the mother have felt for nine months, holding her natural love in abeyance? Mother was the ocean carrying the child to port, but the child could only stay if the father secured it with the ligature of his name. Our word "possessive" in its most maniacal sense, suggesting bouts of jealous rage, begins to capture how Romans felt about their property. Everything a man owned increased his stature, made him seem broader and taller. As he acquired land, slaves, livestock, wealth, and wife, a man cast a longer and longer shadow on the earth. It was as if he could extend his own body through his acquisitions, and thus digest a larger piece of the planet. Perhaps a mother comforted herself that, in death, her baby girl would find, as Lucretius had written, "a sound slumber, and a long good-night." Perhaps, instead of calamity, she felt a sense of fatalistic regeneration. People who grow crops and animals are acutely aware of the cyclical processes of nature, and tend to accept that

> All things, like thee, have time to rise and rot;
> And from each other's ruin are begot.

Nonetheless, women frequently plotted to have their exposed children rescued and raised secretly by others.

It's not that the Romans felt no tenderness—one need only read their literature to discover the streams of passion that irrigated every field of action. Rome itself—the world's first large-scale city with a population of about three quarters of a million—was said to be built in the wake of a tempestuous love affair, whose stirring details every Roman knew. The poet Virgil offers an absorbing, breathless account in his epic poem *The Aeneid*.* Although the story is supposedly set

---

*The seventeenth-century English composer Henry Purcell's *Dido and Aeneas*, a magnificent, heart-wrenching opera, explores the tragedy in homespun melodies reminiscent of ballads and madrigals.

in the distant past, Virgil's audience belonged to Rome in the first century B.C., and it had to seem realistic to his readers, so it is probably a good reflection of the relationships they would recognize. The story goes like this:

DIDO AND AENEAS

After the fall of Troy, the Trojan hero Aeneas sets sail to search for another home. A storm separates him from most of his men and he lands on the African coast, near Carthage, a city being founded by Dido, who is its queen. Made invisible by magic, Aeneas and his friend Achates steal into the city and find it ambitiously under way, raising theaters, harbor, temples, and workshops, in a hive of activity. It dazzles him, and he wishes it were his home, when the radiant Queen Dido appears with her entourage. Soon Aeneas' men also find their way to the city, and approach the queen, explaining that their leader Aeneas is apparently lost at sea, and requesting shelter while they fix their "storm-shattered" vessels. Their tale of woe moves her, and she welcomes them wholeheartedly, regretting only that Aeneas is not safely there as well. Hearing this, Aeneas and Achates decide to make themselves known:

These words were hardly spoken, when in a flash the cloud-cloak
They wore was shredded and purged away into pure air.
Aeneas was standing there in an aura of brilliant light,
Godlike of face and figure: for Venus herself had breathed
His manhood and a gallant light into his eyes . . .

The queen is understandably smitten, and it's as if he's voicing her destiny when he says: "I am here, before you, the one you look for. . . ."

Actually, she wasn't looking, but he's come at the right time. A grieving widow, Dido is a fiercely passionate woman with a strong sense of self-dramatization who has pledged that

He who first wedded me took with him, when he died,
My right to love: let him keep it, there, in the tomb, for
ever.

But "for ever" is a very long time, and Aeneas seems "heaven-born" to rekindle "the old flame" that she's nearly forgotten.

Old flame. It's amazing how many metaphors for love and arousal we share with the ancients. "I'm on fire," Bruce Springsteen wails lustily in a recent rock song. In another song (also written by Springsteen), the Pointer Sisters sing "I say I don't love love you / but you know I'm a liar / because when we kiss—F-i-r-e!" Dido tells of that same delicious conflagration. Notice it's not the physical pain of burning skin that's being referred to, but stoking the invisible, primordial "fire" in each cell, which then blazes brighter. Love feeds a million watch fires in the encampment of the body. Not only does Dido find Aeneas physically appealing, and his war and sea stories enchanting, she has a lot in common with him, despite their different cultures. Both are royalty. Most of all, she identifies with his suffering:

> I too have gone through much; like you, have been roughly handled
> By fortune; but now at last it has willed me to settle here.
> Being acquainted with grief, I am learning to help the unlucky.

She translates this charitableness into hundreds of bulls, sheep, swine, and other goods for his men; a private banquet for him; and the invitation to stay as long as he wishes. Without meaning to, she falls deeply in love, and soon is "a woman wild with passion . . . wandering at large through the town in a rage of desire, like a doe pierced by an arrow." One day Dido takes Aeneas hunting; a storm hits and they find shelter in a cave, where they make love and exchange vows. To Dido and the Roman understanding of such things, it's a marriage. After a luxuriant period of marital bliss, the fickle gods decree that Aeneas' fate is to found his new city in Italy, his lost homeland, and they order him to return at once. Torn between love and duty, Aeneas plans to steal away by nightfall without telling Dido. Although this seems cowardly, the reader forgives him, because many a hero has lost his nerve in clashes of the heart. When rumor of his plan reaches Dido, she becomes unbalanced by grief. The powerful, productive, omnicompetent queen suddenly feels destitute and ragged. Her path into the future disappears behind a veil of dust, and she loses her inner compass. Without love, life is a desert night filled with wolves. After her first husband died, her heart had gone into hibernation. She joined the suspended animation of the aggrieved. If she was numb, at least she was safe from pain. Just as in the fairy tale of Sleeping Beauty, a princely hero arrives to wake her from that dreamless sleep. With Aeneas she risks all in a powerful openheartedness that makes her vulnerable. When he betrays her, she goes to pieces. Dido's lament is the timeless anthem of the jilted woman, who alternately chastises herself and begs her lover to stay. Slightly delirious, she pleads with him, using quick turns of logic and every wile she can think of. What litigant is as avid, what lawyer as skillful, as a woman in love? Here is a small sample of her anguish:

By these tears, by the hand you gave me—
They are all I have left, to-day, in my misery—I implore
  you,
And by our union of hearts, by our marriage hardly begun,
If I have ever helped you at all, if anything
About me pleases you, be sad for our broken home, forego
Your purpose, I beg you, unless it's too late for prayers of mine!
Because of you, the Libyan tribes and the Nomad chieftains
Hate me, the Tyrians are hostile: because of you I have
  lost
My old reputation for faithfulness—the one thing that could
  have made me
Immortal. Oh, I am dying! To what, my guest, are you
  leaving me?
            . . . .
If even I might have conceived a child by you before
You went away, a little Aeneas to play in the palace
And, in spite of all this, to remind me of you by his
  looks, oh then
I should not feel so utterly finished and desolate.

When none of her pleas moves him, and it's clear he's really going to leave her, she becomes angry and wishes him ill fortune, bad seas, and misery. Then she takes the bed on which they made love, gathers some belongings that he hasn't picked up yet—a sword she gave him as a present, various articles of clothing—and drags them to a court-yard, where she builds a bonfire. Climbing to the top, she falls upon Aeneas' sword and dies, knowing that he'll see her funeral pyre from his ship. Later in *The Aeneid*, Aeneas gets safe passage to the Under-world to visit his father, and there he sees the ghost of Dido wander-ing through the woods like marsh gas. Filled with pity, he begs her forgiveness, and swears that it wasn't his will to abandon her but the iron edict of "Heaven's commands." He speaks tenderly to her, "trying to soften the wild-eyed/Passionate-hearted ghost" who re-mains "stubborn to his appeal" and finally rushes away, without forgiving him, "hating him still."

THE FAMILY

The astringent rules of Roman life were set against such stories of unswerving passion and dizzying love. Hobbled by laws and social convention, its people praised monogamy, efficiency, and restraint, but indulged in carnality, intemperance, and other clandestine plea-sures, much as the upper-class Victorians did centuries later. Strict-ness, stoicism, and denial of temptation were part of an ideal father's image. His children addressed him as "Sir," and he was expected to set a rigid model of deportment. How did one withstand the entrea-ties of vice? Through hard work. Virtue triumphs more easily in exhausted limbs. It fell to the mother to be lenient now and then. Women were expected to be emotional and occasionally go haywire.

Not only marriages, but adoptions, were used to seal loyalty and wealth between families. Children were chattels who could be swapped for money or power at any moment, and parents often left it to nursemaids and servants to dispense love. Raised by a nurse, tutored by a "pedagogue," a boy would study mythology, Greek language and literature, rhetoric, and other high-toned subjects. Un-like the Greeks, who believed education should drench the whole body, Roman students didn't spend half their time at sports. A man of quality was expected to know mythology, even if he didn't believe it. And education was prized not for the openness of mind it allowed but for the prestige it bestowed. An educated man was a respected man. A girl of twelve didn't need education, because at fourteen she would be declared a woman and promptly married off. After that, it fell to her husband to educate her, if he wished. Young men were free to enjoy male lovers, frequent prostitutes, or live with mistresses; but when they married, they were supposed to put all their high spirits and mischief behind them, and become the decorous head of the family. An odd element of the Roman legal system was that a male child of whatever age or marital status spent his life ruled by an omnipotent father. If the father judged the son harshly, he could condemn him to death. Adult sons were powerless in the eyes of society, and it must have been humiliating for a grown man to need his father's consent to make business or legal contracts, have a decent career, or even marry. A son's income belonged to his father, a father who could disinherit him at any moment. By law, a woman's agreement was required when she married. But, on the other hand, she couldn't reject her father's wishes. So it is easy to understand why family squabbles too often turned vicious, and resulted in children disinherited or fathers murdered.

In the early days of Rome, slaves were not allowed to marry, and little is recorded about their lives. When respectable citizens of Rome married, they didn't involve the state. There was plenty of ritual and ceremony, but nothing legal. No justice of the peace, no papers to sign. Yet inheritance laws required that children be "legitimate," so everyone had to know that the couple was indeed married. Circumstantial evidence would do, but it was wise to have a wedding party or, at least, a couple of witnesses. Gifts were given, out of goodwill, and perhaps also to bind the guests to the marrying families. The groom gave the bride a ring, which she wore on the same finger she would today. Aulus Gellius explains why that finger was chosen:

> When the human body is cut open as the Egyptians do and when dissections . . . are practised on it, a very delicate nerve is found which starts from the [ring] finger and travels to the heart. It is, therefore, thought seemly to give to this finger in preference to all others the honour of the ring, on account of the loose connection which links it with the principal organ.

The man was said to receive "the hand" of his bride, and the ring symbolized that with her hand she gave her innermost self. Every time they touched hands, they touched hearts. The wedding ceremony was a combination of divine and human laws, a forging of the spiritual with the civic, in a total union of whole lives. The bride wore white, with a belt tied into the "knot of Hercules," which the husband looked forward to untying in private after the wedding. Her hair was carefully arranged and covered with a bright orange veil that symbolized dawn. Guests threw grain to wish the pair a good harvest of children. After the ceremony there was a reception, with toasts to the newlyweds, and then the bride was carried over the threshold for good luck. If the wedding ceremony sounds remarkably familiar, it is because many of its rituals were adopted by the Christian church, which was wise about preserving traditional customs whenever possible. Except for sacrificing animals, little has changed. Then came the wedding night, which social historian Paul Veyne sums up as less than tender:

> The wedding night took the form of a legal rape from which the woman emerged "offended with her husband" (who, accustomed to using his slave women as he pleased, found it difficult to distinguish between raping a woman and taking the initiative in sexual relations). It was customary for the groom to forego deflowering his wife on the first night, out of concern for her timidity; but he made up for his forbearance by sodomizing her.

This was not intended to be a love match. The purpose of marriage was to produce children, make favorable alliances, and establish a bloodline. But there was a new civility in marriage. It was hoped that husband and wife would be friends and get on amiably. Happiness was not part of the deal, nor was pleasure. Sex was for creating babies. Any extra kisses or touches were an extravagance, and Stoic philosophy didn't condone wasted effort. Wives were still inferiors, but they warranted respect. In ancient Greece, it had been a man's civic duty to marry. His role as citizen superseded his role as husband and head of the family. In Rome, it behooved a man to marry, but he was also expected to be a decent husband. In fact, a respectable man treated all his dependents justly—his servants, his children, his slaves, his wife. Was she cherished as an equal partner in a lifelong alliance of the heart? Did she and her husband socialize as a couple? When they made love, did they rejoice in each other's sexuality? It's highly doubtful. Romans praised harmony in the household as something precious and desirable, but it was a bonus. In exile, the poet Ovid once wrote of his tenderness for his wife and the "love that makes us partners." But he knew how rare that affectionate union was. Ovid often sought and found love elsewhere; but to discover it at home, in and among his errands and idle moments, when he awoke each morning, even when he ate or dressed—that was the luxury. Did he and his wife make love during the daylight hours? If so, they did it secretly and with the titillation that comes from breaking a taboo, because few things were thought lewder than daytime sex. Lovers were expected to be cat burglars, masked by nighttime, their flesh illuminated by the occasional shaft of moonlight.

OH, VICTORIA!

For some reason, we picture the Romans as sexual gladiators who did whatever, whenever, to whomever. Or as debauched drunkards enjoying one long fraternity party. The Romans found nothing shameful about the penis as an object of beauty or devotion. Phallic objects appear in their art as images of power, domination, and protection, as well as sex. The Latin *fascinum,* which meant "witchcraft," was associated with the phallic god Fascinus. Parents would hang a penis-shaped amulet around a child's neck to avert the evil eye. On Velia, one of the first hills of Rome, a temple was dedicated to the god Mutanus Tutunus, who was represented in the form of a penis. Priestesses and married women wreathed the god's image with flowers, and newlyweds kept an effigy of the god in their bedrooms. On her wedding day, a bride was to sit on the effigy, giving up her virginity as a sacred offering.

But, despite the banquets and spectacles and phallic gods, Romans were ruled by many puritanical prohibitions. Adultery and incest were taboo. So was sex with a naked woman. A prostitute might take off all of her clothes; a nice girl left on at least her bra,* for discretion's sake. Oral sex was tolerated between homosexual men or

---

*The word they used for brassiere was *mamillare,* and there was apparently a considerable need for them, because Latin includes two words for big-bosomed, *mammosa* and *mammeata.*

women, enjoyed by men at the hands of courtesans, but it was considered repulsive and degrading for a man to pleasure a woman with his mouth. The essence of this degradation lay in the idea of a man being servile to a woman. Roman men were obsessed with machismo. In homosexual affairs, this meant pitching rather than catching. With men or women, the key was to be active rather than passive, to be served rather than do the serving. Above all, they wished never to act like a slave to anyone or anything—including love. The ultimate class consciousness doesn't just involve one's rank with other people—but also with ideas. Passion enslaves, however willingly we may wear its shackles. Because love lured one away from the concerns of the populace, it was a kind of social treason. Because it involved dependence on a woman—a moral inferior—it lessened a man's stature. Because it made one lose control in a culture obsessed with domination, it showed bad character.

But love is an act of sedition, a revolt against reason, an uprising in the body politic, a private mutiny. Writers have always relished being its revolutionary scribes. In T. E. Lawrence's *The Seven Pillars of Wisdom,* on which the movie *Lawrence of Arabia* was based, an Arab chieftain proclaims: "I am a river to my people." In every era, poets become rivers flowing with emotion, connecting the farmhands and the city dwellers, nourishing the lovers. In ancient Greece it was Sappho, sinewy and ripe, who wrote so deliciously about female lovers that the term "lesbian" was coined from her hometown of Lesbos. Rome had many love poets, each with a slightly different complexion: the saucily neurotic Catullus, the romantics Tibullus and Propertius, the epic Virgil, and Ovid, love's scribe and laborer.

OVID AND THE ART OF LOVE

Born in the provinces to an equestrian family, Ovid moved to Rome in his teens and spent most of his life there writing frisky, sensuous poetry that reflected the raucous morals of Roman high society, which was waging an all-out war against boredom. Women had more freedom and confidence than before, but no access to a public life. As one scholar notes wryly: "They were permitted to do a great deal—as long as they did nothing constructive." So they focused much of their creative energies on beauty treatments, adornments, dinner parties, and romantic intrigues. Ovid, who was married three times, had a great many affairs, and wrote from experience about the torrents of love. From the evidence in his poems, he seems to have been in a perpetual snit. He yearned, he leered, he ached, he flirted, he bad-mouthed, he laughed, he taunted, he wooed—all in bright, rambunctious poetry. In a style personal and introspective enough to have been written today, he talks gamely about his spell of impotence, his occasional fetishism, or his jealousy. He exposes the full anatomy of his lust. His "erotic commonplaces" were often quoted by others, but when he wrote *The Art of Love,* a skillfully crafted "seducer's manual," he became the wicked darling of Rome. Here's a glimpse into it:

Love is a kind of war, and no assignment for cowards.
    Where those banners fly, heroes are always on guard.
Soft, those barracks? They know long marches, terrible weather,
    Night and winter and storm, grief and excessive fatigue.
Often the rain pelts down from the drenching cloudbursts of heaven,
    Often you lie on the ground, wrapped in a mantle of cold.

      . . . .

If you are ever caught, no matter how well you've concealed it,
    Though it is clear as the day, swear up and down it's a lie.
Don't be too abject, and don't be too unduly attentive,
    That would establish your guilt far beyond anything else.
Wear yourself out if you must, and prove, in her bed, that you could not
Posssibly be that good, coming from some other girl.

It was Ovid's bad luck to publish *The Art of Love* during the reign of Augustus, at a time when the emperor decided to get tough about the city's plummeting birthrate. Rome's formidable rates of sterility, miscarriages, and stillbirths were most likely the result of chronic lead poisoning. Each day, Romans unwittingly dosed themselves with lead through the pipes that carried drinking water, the lead-based face powder and other cosmetics women used, the cooking pots, and the syrup used to sweeten cheap wine. Another possibility is that the men's perpetually coddled testicles rendered them sterile. Men and women both spent a lot of time stewing in the baths, and we now know that raising the temperature of the testicles in hot water can reduce the sperm count. Whatever the cause of this barrenness, in 18 B.C. Augustus tried to remedy it through a system of rewards and punishments. He imposed strict marriage laws to prevent illegitimate children (because they might be aborted or killed), encourage large families, and not waste any fertile woman's womb. Adultery had been a private, family matter of grave importance. Augustus shoved it into the law courts and changed it from an act of infidelity to an act of sedition. Henceforth, he decreed, any man who discovered his wife's adultery had to divorce her or be prosecuted himself. The wife and her lover would then be exiled (in different directions). Half their wealth would be confiscated, and they would be forbidden ever to marry each other. A husband could engage a prostitute, but not keep a mistress. Widows were obliged to remarry within two years, and divorcées within eighteen months. Childless couples were discriminated against, as were unmarried men. Parents with three or more children were rewarded. Promiscuity was chastised. Augustus meant to stabilize the family, but the opposite happened. The divorce rate skyrocketed, since divorce was the only nonprosecutable form of dalliance.

All things considered, this was not the ideal climate in which to publish a guide to infidelity. But it was just the moment Ovid chose for his. Why? There's an impish, swaggering quality to Ovid. I think he saw himself as a bawdy trafficker who lived on the edge, a purveyor of contraband morals. Anyway, he created a sensation in high society, had a brisk following, and became quite a famous rogue. This shocked and irritated Augustus, and was the excuse he gave for dealing harshly with him. But evidence points in another direction, indicating that Ovid became embroiled in some mysterious high-level scandal. No one knows exactly what happened—in part because Ovid was told to choose between silence and death—but clues in his writing suggest one of two possibilities. Either he dared to have an affair with the emperor's wife, which the emperor discovered, or he was privy to an attempted coup d'état. If the empress fancied him, as well she might after reading his books, he would have been caught between a rock and a hard place, as the saying goes. He couldn't have safely said yes or no. Whatever happened, it was serious enough for Augustus to banish him to a distant, uncivilized territory where he spent the remainder of his life longing for the sophistication and gaiety of Rome.

Some classical scholars dismiss Ovid as a scoundrel and pornographer interested only in sexual conquest. It's amusing that, all these years later, people are still scandalized by his candor. Some wince at his bravado. Like Shakespeare, Ovid promises his girlfriends that they will become immortal through his poems. But, you know, he was right. We still sigh over his lover, Corinna, the heroine and temptress of his early *Loves*. Although we don't know her real identity, she may have been his first wife. They were teenagers, "two adolescents, exploring a booby-trapped world of adult passions and temptations, and playing private games, first with their society, then—*liaisons dangereuses*—with one another. . . ." In Ovid's writings one finds a full catalog of love, from chaste worship to unregenerate conniving. Although Augustus banned *The Art of Love,* it has endured through the ages, as a brilliantly insightful meditation on love, vanity, and temptation.

DECORATING LEISURE TIME

As the city of Rome grew larger, extending itself in land, variety, and the imagination of its populace, the avenues for love multiplied. This happened in part because the quest for amusement became a kind of pastime. Where the Greeks sought to perfect the body through athletics, Romans perfected the leisure life. It could be bustling and avant-garde, provided it was ample. Roman women had more freedoms, and that brought a new confidence and self-respect. Greek women were so housebound that they had little chance to meet men with whom they might strike up a romance, even if they wished to. But Roman women had time and opportunity for intrigue, and morals were flexible enough that their affairs were found understandable, even if not officially condoned. Women of the right class were obsessed with their looks, spending the morning on coiffures, makeup, and choosing the perfect accessories for their outfits. In the afternoon, they lunched and shopped, organized the household, then tidied up their makeup and later prepared for a dinner party. Fashion has always been a badge of rank, as well as a creative outlet, but they were also obsessively refining and accentuating their physical appeal. Decoration can be a form of advertising, and the new commodity they had to offer was their worth and desirability.

A government thrives on order. Love is anarchic. Chaotic and emotional, we try so hard to impose what we aren't on everything around us, and punish those who don't live up to our ideals. On a walk this morning, I passed through the perfume of a honeysuckle bush so sweet and pleasing I turned around and followed it to its source. I did not mean to be diverted from my path by pleasure; I couldn't help myself. In the same way, love distracts one from the tidiest plans, the narrowest course, the clearest goals. The Roman vision of social order grew, but so did the empire of love. Hard as Augustus tried to legislate morality, he was grappling with a seditious passion so natural for human beings that he was, essentially, warring with nature. To the Romans, love was not a good enough reason for marriage, but everyone understood its power and how, like a furious river, it could charge past hardship, law, or death.

THE MIDDLE AGES

THE BIRTH OF CHIVALRY

During the Middle Ages, France seethed with paradoxes. Plague, famine, and filth were Everyman's constant companions. So-called witches were regularly burned at the stake, and heretics of all stripes were tortured and driven from their homes. Nobles played chess by waging war with one another, in the process destroying crops, terrorizing towns, and killing legions of innocent families. Gangs of outlaws scoured the countryside, looting and burning. No one felt safe from nature or from one another. But, at the same time, a modern-feeling civilization was starting to take hold in Europe. The population was growing, and new towns were being built, improved plows and other tools gave agriculture a boost, merchants had wares to sell, craftsmen busied themselves in the cities, and pilgrims traveled the roads and rivers. The world was in motion, and as Chaucer related so well, anyone could meet anyone on the crossroads to anywhere.

It's no coincidence that spires began to appear on the churches. The entire era was gripped by the symbolism of the spire, which connected the earth and sky, the concrete with the abstract, the all-too-visible hovels—full of bodily functions, poverty, and fatigue—with the loftier realities of an invisible city. Could there be no relief from earth's sweat and decay? Was it possible that a poor life led only downward to a carnal circus underground? People aspired toward heaven, which they depicted as pure, clean, deodorized, and brightly lit. (Throughout history, women have also been associated with cleanliness, that is, they've been held responsible for keeping things clean, and judged on the basis of how clean their house is, how well laundered their family. They've been required to be "pure" and "clean" sexually. Their virginity and virtue have been extended to the home.)

Etymologically speaking, a spire is the pointed head of a flower. The cathedral spires of the era, cast in stone and outlined in tiny stone buds, promise the resurrection of spring. I've often walked beside such churches in springtime and looked up at their spires through the identically budded branches of a tree. No doubt medieval strollers did the same, reassured by the symbolism. Records tell us that on holy days peasants thronged the churchyards in celebrations so lecherous and pagan that the clergymen reprimanded them. But people yearned for transcendence. In the heaven of their hopes, they abandoned the exhaustions of daily life. The times were infused with great spirituality.

In this atmosphere of the lofty and the mundane, a ritualized code of manners, called chivalry,* arose to reconcile the worlds of warfare and religion by giving them a common enemy. "A moral gloss was needed that would allow the Church to tolerate the warriors in good conscience and the warriors to pursue their own values in spiritual comfort." By making the warriors knights of the lord, they supposedly fought for truth, goodness, piety, and the Church. In a solemn dedication ceremony, a knight would purify his soul through

*From the French for a man on horseback and, by extension, knightly behavior. *Cavalier* comes from the same source.

confession, receive communion, and take his sacred vows. Then he was free to slaughter for a holy cause.

It wasn't easy being a knight, whose sole occupation was warfare, which meant hand-to-hand combat while wearing a suit of armor that wasn't very flexible and weighed around fifty pounds. Lances, swords, and battle-axes were preferred weapons, and they were used during what amounted to traffic accidents—two riders galloping at each other at full speed. The ensuing crash usually hurled at least one rider to the ground, where getting up was like an overturned turtle's efforts to right itself. Being a knight took immense strength and energy; and, if you didn't exhibit plenty of what was called *prowess,* you were branded a sissy. Wounds were frequent, and they often became septic. Only the young could manage this lifestyle for long. Lest knights become unruly or psychopathic, chivalry's code required that they be courteous and kind when dealing with civilians. Dandies in later eras, who spread their capes over puddles so that women might pass with unsullied ankles, inherited their sense of gallantry from the knights. A knight's word was his bond; breaking it was an act of treason. This was the code, anyway. As often as not, the ideal differed from the reality. Soldiers were ruffians by trade, who settled disputes with violence, and they sometimes fought battles for lords whom they then murdered and robbed, or used the costume of chivalry to lure maidens whom they seduced or raped. According to one knight, La Tour Landry, he and his pals would ride into a village, lie like crazy to the local girls in order to bed them, then ride off like a band of armor-plated gigolos.

When they weren't at war, knights engaged in tournaments staged by nobles with time to kill and a yen for a human version of a cockfight. As much as a week might be devoted to a tournament, with all sorts of events interspersed with the fighting. A hundred or so knights would contest with one another, in pairs or in groups. Just as a horse race or soccer match is usually surrounded by parties and ballyhoo, the tournaments justified feasts and merriment. They attracted people from all classes, including gamblers, conmen, prostitutes, souvenir sellers, and groupies. If a knight died during a tournament, the Church considered it suicide, which meant direct passage to hell. Even that didn't deter the knights, who had much to gain in prizes and fame, and women to impress. Tournaments gave them a chance to win armor and horses, and rehearse the codes of chivalry in a small, safe setting. Faced with the rigors of all-out warfare, etiquette and form might be the last things on their minds.

During the first thirty years of the twelfth century, half the knights in France rode to the Crusades, joined by knights from England and Spain. The first Crusade was a blood-and-thunder success, driving the Muslims farther and farther south and out of Jerusalem. Knights returning from the Holy Land were conquering heroes. Imagine the wild temper of revelry and vindication they must have felt, not to mention divine favor. All had seen friends die savagely at sword point. Many would be suffering from what we now call posttraumatic stress syndrome. Spirited young men full of spunk and mischief, they were accustomed to bloodshed, intrigue, and new hungers. They brought back a taste for the exotic spices of the Orient; brilliant silks and sensuous perfumes tempted the western appetite. The knights sang songs of conquest, bawdiness, bravery. At their most exquisite, they praised nature for allowing them pretty fields in which to slaughter their enemies. Heroic epics such as the *Song of Roland* celebrated the warriors' brotherhood, and since castles revolved around knights and war, it was just these songs that rang from their parapets.

While the men were away fighting, it often fell to the women to manage the estates. Although both Church and society dismissed women as frail, incompetent beings who were lifelong children, women handled the estates with an aplomb that raised their image and self-esteem. When necessary, they even took disputes to court. This didn't radically alter their position in French society, but it gave them confidence, it widened their social contacts, and it improved their legal status. As new decision makers, they had greater freedom of action, of course, but, more important, they had greater freedom of thought. And with that came the fantasizing about love, the hiring of troubadours, and the indulging in affairs.

Mind you, the Christian tradition preached that erotic love was dangerous, a trapdoor leading to hell, which was not even to be condoned between husband and wife. He was allowed to kiss, fondle, and caress her—provided he didn't really enjoy it. Sexual appetite was normal and acceptable; passion was not. Any man who felt too much erotic passion for his wife was committing an act of adultery. Instead they were supposed to live together like business partners, who felt affection for each other, got on amiably, and just happened to have children. The idea of all-out love lay elsewhere.

BOOKS OF LOVE

Most ideas about love came from reading the pagan or Christian thinkers. Books were rare, but students could find some in the libraries of monasteries and cathedrals. There they might read a smattering of Greek and Roman authors, some of whom were just being translated. Plato was popular because he renounced the material world and abandoned the delights of the flesh. Distrust of the body, while seeking the spiritual, fit neatly into Christian teachings. Plato and Cicero both celebrated lofty, nonerotic love between men, and that appealed to the celibate clergy. From Virgil's Dido and Aeneas, students learned of love as a demented passion, a mix of bliss and raw danger. People could die from love, so surely it was an affliction, a deadly humour, a plague. Ovid's smart-alecky *Art of Love* introduced them to the frank country joys of lust, where every lover was a soldier in the trenches. But in Ovid's writings, they also found descriptions of the tender love he felt for women. The myth of Orpheus and Eurydice taught them about the heroics of love, which led deep into the Underworld and out again.

They learned from the Christian writers of a loving and merciful God, an idea we now take for granted; but to the ancients it was a startling thought. The pagan gods didn't waste affection on human beings, whom they often toyed with as rather peevish pets. Gigantic, alien, and magically endowed, the gods were nonetheless all too human in their sadism, whimsy, and churlishness. In contrast, the Old Testament God, obsessed with love, commands his people first and foremost to "love the lord your God with all your heart, and with all your soul, and with all your might." It is one's moral duty to feel love. This continues into the New Testament, where we learn that "God is love," that "God so loved the world that he gave his only Son," and that one must love one's neighbor as oneself. With what poignancy St. Paul describes this new importance of love:

If I speak in the tongues of men and of angels, but have not love, I am a noisy gong or a clanging cymbal. And if I have prophetic powers and understand all mysteries and all knowledge, and if I have all faith, so as to remove mountains, but have not love, I am nothing. If I give away all I have, and if I deliver my body to be burned, but have not love, I gain nothing. . . . So faith, hope, love abide, these three; but the greatest of these is love.

The Bible teaches that God's love is unconditional, a gift given by a doting parent. It needn't be won, and it doesn't go only to those who deserve it. Altruism appears as a moral good, even if loving one's neighbor does have a missionary zeal to it. No one can be saved who doesn't convert to Christianity, so converting a neighbor is the greatest gift you can give him.

Heterosexual love in the Old Testament is sometimes down to earth, very material, and deliciously sensual, as when Solomon tells his future bride:

> You are stately as a palm tree,
>   and your breasts are like its clusters.
> I say I will climb the palm tree
>   and lay hold of its branches.
> Oh, may your breasts be like
>   clusters of the vine,
>   and the scent of your breath like apples,
> And your kisses like the best wine
>   that goes down smoothly,
>   gliding over lips and teeth . . .

But, in the New Testament, sex becomes nonerotic and full of self-denial.* Paul advises that "It is well for a man not to touch a woman," but he concedes that marriage is a last resort for those who can't be celibate. Because pent-up desires can lead to fornication or adultery, "each man should have his own wife and each woman her own husband." Their duty is to use sex as a safety valve and to

---

*The word *testament* comes from the Indo-European root *tre,* having to do with triads (two deal makers and a witness). A testament was a pledge, and it concealed the idea of castration. When a man swore something was true, giving *testimony,* he put his hands on his testicles. In effect, he was saying: *You can cut off my balls if I'm lying.* In time, law courts decided that asking a man to put his hands on the Bible might be more decorous.

produce children. Divorce is forbidden. "To the unmarried and the
widows," Paul warns, "I say that it is well for them to remain single
as I do. But if they cannot exercise self-control, they should marry.
For it is better to marry than to burn." And better to marry than to
burn with desire, which he depicts as a private hell in which sin walks
one's nerves as if they were so many tightropes. In this mix of
traditions, Plato's call for sublimating one's desires blended neatly
with Christianity's, and at times celibacy seems to be enjoyed as a
reverse erotics all its own. St. Augustine describes his vow of abstinence like this: "Now was my soul free from the biting cares of
canvassing and getting, and weltering in filth, and scratching off the
itch of lust." That's rather spirited self-sacrifice.* Then something
happened that would change the course of love in the western world.

TROUBADOURS

When he returned from a spotty career in the Crusades, William
IX, duke of Aquitaine (1071–1127), began composing songs of love
and yearning, which we now recognize as the first troubadour love
songs. He may well have been inspired by Moorish writers, who sang
of love as an ennobling force and women as transcendent goddesses.
Arabia and Spain regularly exchanged artists as well as ambassadors,
and their culture spread into southern France. Best known was the
Andalusian poet Ibn-Hazm, who wrote in his classic *The Ring of the
Dove* (1022) that "the union of souls is a thousand times more
beautiful than that of bodies." His attitude was deeply Platonic as
well as Muslim, especially when he spoke about the need to become
one with the beloved. It was a natural need, common as sand but
powerful as radium, because love is the reunion of souls that, before
creation, were made from the same primordial stuffs that became
divided later in the physical universe. "The lover's soul," he says, "is
ever seeking for the other, striving after it, searching it out, yearning
to encounter it again, drawing it to itself it might be as a magnet
draws the iron."

*Compare this with a confidence offered by a twentieth-century Arabian woman,
who said that wearing a veil gave her a profound sense of relief, because it freed her
from being sexually attractive to men, a feeling that had dominated her thoughts and
bedeviled her self-esteem.

Beauty is the lure. The soul is beautiful and it feels drawn to physical beauty. But if sex is the only appeal, then the soul can't grasp the beautiful object long enough for love to take shape; it needs the glue of finding a kindred spirit. Arguing that lust is a vulgar emotion, though reveling in the other's senses is magnificent, he depicts the lover as his mistress's slave, who should address her either as *sayyidi* ("my lord") or *mawlaya* ("my master"). He cautions the lover against actually possessing his beloved, details the torment of love-sickness, and even offers this guide to help read love's facial semaphores:

> To make a signal with the corner of the eye is to forbid the lover something; to droop the eye is an indication of consent; to prolong the gaze is a sign of suffering and distress; to break off the gaze is a mark of relief; to make signs of closing the eyes is an indicated threat. To turn the pupil of the eye in a certain direction and then to turn it back swiftly, calls attention to the presence of a person so indicated. A clandestine signal with the corner of both eyes is a question; to turn the pupil rapidly from the middle of the eye to the interior angle is a demonstration of refusal; to flutter the pupils of both eyes this way and that is a general prohibition. The rest of these signals can only be understood by actually seeing them demonstrated.

Ibn-Hazm's lovers become transformed by love, growing strong and brave, dignified and generous. His countrymen wrote love stories with similar concerns, steeped in the senses; they relied heavily on natural imagery, and were usually accompanied by musical instruments. The sensuous world of the East would have been as welcome as perfume in French society, at a time when the upper class was becoming richer and idler.

On crusade, William and his fellow knights discovered harem women, beautiful but remote and unknowable, hushed behind walls, their chastity an inaccessible garden. Arab men gazed at their shy eyes and spun luxurious fantasies. With their emotions hidden, faceless as psychoanalysts, these women were blank slates for the men's imaginings. In the Mideast, knights enjoyed exotic games that sparked their senses and challenged their intellect, board games such as chess, war games with peculiar weaponry, and also games of the flesh—new sexual techniques, new varieties of desire.

William wrote his songs in the street language of Provence, and this gave them an immediacy and a certain vulgar reality that appealed to his contemporaries at court. Sassy, ribald, audacious, and a bit of a rogue, he thought nothing of snatching someone's wife when her husband was out of sight, or painting a portrait of his mistress's body on his shield. When eyebrows raised at this, he saucily replied that she had carried him often enough on the shield of her hips. He once bragged that he had bedded the wives of two well-known lords 188 times in one week. Whether or not we believe his bravado, or libido, he betrayed the rules of courtly love by boasting. It must have been tempting to rattle the abacus of one's self-regard, but secrecy was the code in courtly love, not just because it heightened the excitement, but because there was hell to pay if a wife was caught being unfaithful. For her, in the early Middle Ages, infidelity was a capital offense; and, in later years, it usually meant being banished to a convent. The husband was even within his rights to murder her and her lover, if he wished. With so much at stake, it's small wonder women put men through exhausting tests to make sure of their sincerity.

Most of the troubadours were commoners, the medieval equivalent of traveling folksingers who played other people's songs along with some of their own. If they were talented and lucky, and could find a hospitable lord or lady with money, they performed regularly at a castle. That small world could get smaller by the hour in idle moments. There were no novels of romance, no gossip magazines, no thrillers to watch at the cinema. A clever singer, full of soap-operalike stories and bloodcurdling adventures, was a welcome guest. Thanks to the troubadours, affairs of the heart became a favorite theme of poetic sagas, and so the love story first entered European literature. The compass of heroism widened, and the idea of "the couple"—two people served by a single verb—began to tantalize society.

THE HEART'S REBELLION

One of the great changes of the Middle Ages was a shift from unilateral love to mutual love. That love could be shared, that two people could feel passionate concern and desire for each other, was at first an avant-garde and dangerous idea. Because the Church taught that love was appropriate only for God, it found the idea of mutual love simply impossible. After all, one was to love God without ransom, expecting nothing in return. To the churchman's mind, love was not a collaboration of hearts, not a pas de deux, not a two-way street, not an exchange of goods and services, but a solitary state.

I don't think the troubadours believed they were being subversive by saying that the lightning of love could flow between two people, not just toward heaven. Nonetheless, by making love available on earth, between mortals, they could be charged with encouraging the worship of false idols. They introduced the image of the lovers, a society of two, as something noble and valuable. They honored pairs who felt passionate love for each other. Until then, love between men and women was thought to be sinful and vulgar. As often as not, it led to madness. And it was always degrading. To portray love as majestic, an ideal to be searched for, was truly shocking. To accept that sexual desire might be a natural part of love, but that the total feeling was more spiritual, an intense oneness, didn't jibe with classical teachings. After all, in Greek tragedy, love was an affliction, a horror that led to cruelty and death. For theologians, human love was a poor reflection of the real thing, which could be found only in spiritual rapture. Insisting that women were equal participants in love, even ennobled by it, seemed outlandish because it tampered with the natural order of feudal life, where men served their lords, and women were faithful to their men. If one's lover deserved one's total dedication, where did one's feudal master fit into the equation?

As courtly love bewitched society, the grip of the Church weakened and power began to sift from the hands of the nobles. This new concept of love radically altered how people defined themselves and sought fulfillment. Most revolutionary of all, perhaps, it introduced the idea of personal choice. In a world where hierarchy ruled, one owed one's fealty first to God and next to the lord of the manor. Choosing whom to love—expressing a preference—was an act of outright rebellion, a revolt against the morality of the age, which denied the individual. Yet this coup d'état found its leaders in the highest ranks of government.

It was in the court of Queen Eleanor of Aquitaine (William's granddaughter), and her daughter, Marie, that the tournament of love really flourished. There, troubadours wrote some of their most daring and exquisite songs, often combining love stories with tales of adventure, such as the Celtic myth of King Arthur and his knights of the Round Table. The ladies of the songs bore such names as "Beautiful Glance," "Pure Joy," and "Beautiful Hope." And the troubadours tossed them bouquets of praise and adoration. They crafted an art form from music, poetry, and pure desire. "Courtly love" it came to be called,* a phrase intentionally ambiguous. A courtship developed at court, but it was also very much a game played on a court. Just as sports are played in the confines of an arena, courtly love was played inside the small world of a castle. Its strict rules were known by all, often rehearsed in public, and viewed by many. One game that became popular was the Court of Love, which was as much a debate as a litigation. Everyone would gather in a central hall, and some love problem would be offered for consideration. Each player chose a position and had to defend it. The question might be: "Who is easier to win over, the wife of an impotent man or the wife of a jealous man?"; or "What do you prefer, warm clothing in winter or a courtly mistress in summer?"; or "If your lady gives herself to you on the condition of her spending a night with a toothless old man, would you prefer she fulfill this condition before or afterward?" Clearly no one expected solutions to these predicaments, only witty banter and the chance to enjoy love talk in public. In one such game, Queen Eleanor was asked to decide which she would rather have as a lover—a young man of no virtue or an old man of much virtue. She picked the old man, because in courtly love virtue was paramount. In the revolving worlds of court, the players knew one another, if only in passing, or by reputation. But beyond their magic circle, courtly love followed a purer path.

Castles were islands of civility and culture, where a wandering knight could pause to refresh his spirit, much as a sailor might visit a bustling port after some time at sea. It must have seemed a dazzling mirage: the lady and her damsels, the children and other relatives, and all the servingmen and -women. Encountering such an island, a

---

*Because we use the word *love* in so many ways, we find "courtly love" a useful term. However, the phrase originated in the late nineteenth century, when a French medievalist, Gaston Paris, referred to the *amour courtois* of twelfth-century France.

knight would choose a beautiful, remote, married "lady," whom he greatly idealized. At first he would hide in the bushes and worship his lady from afar, a voyeur excited by his invisible intimacy. The sweep of her skirt would make him flush. The revelation of her wrist would send gooseflesh down his neck. In time, he would present himself to her as a humble servant, pledging his heart and soul, his faithfulness and his valor. This is when cushions first appeared in the western world; a swain falling to his knees before a lady needed a soft place to land, and a lady expecting a swain always had a cushion handy. No doubt there was an enchanting coquetry in how far away she kept the cushion. Whatever trials she set him he swore to meet. Loving her would be a pilgrimage of her own devising. In a feudal world, where serfs bowed down to a lord, he would be her serfdom, she his master. With each test, she granted him an added familiarity. The stages might include her condescending to speak his name, then his being allowed to sit worshipfully beside her for a short spell, then perhaps their strolling together in the garden. Ultimately, she would grant him a kiss, and later allow him to see (but not touch) her naked body. In time, he might even be allowed to make love to her. But consummation was not part of the game. That would spoil the romance and end his quest. A plucky knight proved his worth by slaying the mightiest dragons of all—his independence, sexual hunger, and pride. Striving for self-possession, he was supposed to love without possessing the beloved. This was important in practical terms, because she belonged to her husband, and also because the whole point of the adventure was the knight's attempt to perfect himself apropos of the beloved. So the essence of courtly love was protracted excitement, a delirium of gorgeously unbearable longing. Only by staying wholly infatuated, damp with sublimated erotic passion, could one mine one's emotions inexhaustibly, and strive higher, risk more, achieve nobler ends. This game of perpetual arousal required a sensuous discipline, a voluptuous rigor that took patience and skill, and it weeded out anyone who just wanted quick sex.

The lady loved the knight only if he merited her love. This notion—of the female putting the male through tests before she accepts him as a lover—is not a supercivilized human conceit; it is a ritual played throughout the animal kingdom, from insects to bowerbirds to elks. The knight, on the other hand, loved his lady because of her innate beauty. This was not a Platonic love of beauty, which would have been familiar to the ancient. The idea of first worshiping the beloved's beauty only to learn from it how to worship the beauty of others would be anathema to a courtly lover. Nothing could pull him away from the celestial mechanics of his devotion, spinning around his beloved like a captured moon, held in check by gravity. Knights were warriors; how thrilling for a lady to force them to be gentle and refined in her name, knowing what violence was being reined in. "Service" was everything. The Romans and Greeks despised men who served anyone, especially a woman. Now we find service raised to an art form, and knights longing to be humiliated by love. If so ordered, a knight would even be willing to lose a joust intentionally, telling no one that he had thrown the fight, slinking away like a fool:

> Courtly love service by its very nature was meant to mortify male pride. In this voluntary submission of the friend to the loved one, there was a profound verity: since it was the deeply ingrained misogyny of the male which, until then, had reined in the impulse toward mutual love, it was important that such love now have as its point of departure the symbolic humiliation of male power.

What fascinated the troubadours were the first stages of love, whose flickering emotions they chronicled, the trembling moments at the beginning of an affair when two lovers were transfixed by one another, absorbed into each other's version of reality, but quivering with uncertainty. Sexual intercourse put an end to such a story, and conjugal love didn't interest them at all. It was too dull. They preferred the lying awake at night, the devoured glances, the secret codes, the fetishes and tokens, the steamy fantasizing, the moaning to one's pillow, the fear of discovery, the agony of separation, the torrents of bliss followed by desperate hours.

What a contrast there was between the values of courtly love and the world in which it thrived. Life in medieval France was brutal, violent, mercurial, vulgar, filled with the arrogant theatrics of war. Lovers, on the other hand, wished to be humble, faithful, refined, gentle, and discreet. They began to speak of "true love," not as a madness but as something wonderful, something morally good. The Church ruled with an iron will, yet courtly love was a briskly irreligious enterprise, an almost Marxist revolt against the Church. Condoning adultery, and even claiming that good could result from it (a man became nobler, humbler, more refined), elevated adultery above marriage. Celebrating passion, and defining love in natural terms, were equally sacrilegious. Yet, because France was the center of artistic, intellectual, and political life, this radical new idea of mutual love became the fashion and spread throughout Europe. From Provence, it drifted south to Italy—where Dante adapted and refined it so that it didn't quarrel with his belief in Christianity—and then north, where Chrétien de Troyes and others wrote stories of a curiously new sort, concerned with how people thought and felt.

THE ORIGINS OF COURTLY LOVE

Why did such stylized love evolve at this point in history? There are many theories. Some argue that courtly love simply mirrored the economics of the time—knights served their lady the way vassals served their lord or humans served their God. As C. S. Lewis reminds us, "What is new usually wins its way by disguising itself as the old." Feudal relationships between men might have provided a basis for romantic love between men and women. "These male affections," Lewis writes,

—though wholly free from the taint that hangs about "friendship" in the ancient world—were themselves lover-like; in their intensity, their willful exclusion of other values, and their uncertainty, they provided an exercise of the spirit not wholly unlike that which later ages have found in "love."

One thing is certain: during the Crusades, knights discovered a more elastic sense of society, and savored cultures that had a greater respect for women. Widening their horizons made them more receptive to the social changes already taking place in France while they were away. In Byzantium, they encountered the cult of worshiping the Virgin Mary. This stood in stark contrast to the age-old teaching of the Church, which held that Eve's wickedness doomed all of us. Out of Oedipal feelings, perhaps, the profane idea of "the noble

Lady" and the sacred idea of the Virgin Mary eventually became interchangeable to the point where, at one time, the worship or love of Mary surpassed the love or worship of Jesus. Churches were christened "Our Lady" (as in Notre Dame de Paris). Knights didn't serve women, they served "ladies," the elite form of the female.

However, the momentous change was the notion that women could be the objects of love. This was by no means an attitude that all of society shared. Medieval thinkers habitually depicted women as inferior beings unfit for education. They were still a land to be tilled, as they had been to the Greeks and Romans. Thomas Aquinas's explanation for such a state of affairs is that by nature

> woman is defective and misbegotten, for the active force in the male seed tends to the production of a perfect likeness in the masculine sex, while the production of woman comes from a defect in the active force or from some external change, such as that of a south wind, which is moist, as the Philosopher observes. On the other hand, in relation to the universal nature, woman is not misbegotten, but is included in nature's intention as ordered to the work of generation.

After three thousand years of subjugation, women certainly didn't mind being elevated above valiant knights. They enjoyed their higher status, and knights enjoyed the purification and nobility courtly love bestowed. In a coarse, crude society, where it was difficult to advance oneself, knights liked being part of a moral aristocracy, an elite that could be achieved by men of any class.

The seeds of courtly love were imported in part from the Arab countries, the style and sentiment of whose poetry delighted troubadours in southern France. However, there was one important way in which Frenchwomen differed from the idealized and longed-for women of the harem—Frenchwomen were available. One could bump into them in the marketplace, castles, at tournaments, or at court. This took away some of the challenge, and much of the mystery. In converting Islamic love to the freer European world, obstacles somehow had to be replaced. According to Tannahill, "Virtue was the attribute that, by elevating woman to some immaculate plane, cleansed their love of all taint of carnality and left it free to soar into the realm of the spirit. Virtue became the European harem." Notice that it's the woman's *virtue,* not her personality, that is so winning. Her reality as a down-to-earth, full-bodied woman, one with talents and troubles, allergies and brains, doesn't figure in the quest. What the knight seeks is the conquest of virtue by virtue. His lady is only a memory aid so that, on the battlefield, when weakening, he can remember what virtue is, can spell it with his pulse, embody it in his mind. She makes possible his spiritual awakening, and her reward is an improved image of herself. Later in the Middle Ages, the engagement between knight and lady became more abstract, and though knights rode to battle with talismans from their ladies, they might equally well have been fighting for colors or country.

But in the early days of courtly love, knights found ample scope in creative adultery, although adultery didn't have to be part of the game. Some men enjoyed a courtier's relationship with their wives, admiring them lavishly and being perfect swains. But they were the rare exceptions. Neither pagan nor Christian writers had discussed love in marriage, nor erotic love between a man and a woman. Such notions were thought absurd, anarchistic, and immoral. Medieval marriages had little to do with love or mutual attraction. Marriage was a business contract. Men have always exchanged their women according to carefully mapped kinship lines. This was especially true of royal marriages, which made alliances, pooled wealth, fixed status and power. A woman could refuse a marriage with someone she loathed, or secretly arrange a so-called abduction by her beau, but mainly she consented, having no real choice in the matter.

With many men away at war much of the time, women dominated court life. So there were many influential married women, thirsty for intrigue and starved for love, whose favor could be won through flirtation and flattery. This would not have been a circumstance shared by their husbands, who could bed women wherever they wished. It didn't matter if the husband fooled around, but if the wife did the husband might end up supporting a child he hadn't sired. So, naturally, husbands didn't approve of erotic love, nor troubadours think highly of husbands. Their songs often refer to a husband showing up at an inopportune moment to spoil things for the lovers, and they endorse a blatant double standard—jealousy is depicted as noble when felt by lovers, despicable when felt by husbands.

One must keep in mind that a knight's lady was a complete stranger, a pretty face encountered on his travels. The Church didn't allow marriages between even distant kin, so knights had to leave their homes and search for a mate. But it was also possible to be an unattached (or "free-lance") knight, someone who owned no land and answered to no feudal lord. Such knights defined themselves through acts of valor, and prized a good reputation, that small theater district of self-regard. Their goal was to romance other men's wives with a gusto and tenderness that contrasted sharply with the dreariness of a loveless marriage. Danger was a tonic.

Passionate devotion was possible because the lovers were abstract objects of desire, whose love was forbidden, a taboo and a novelty. Intimacy between lovers, a fairly recent idea, was not any part of the medieval mood, but it gradually arose from the pressure on lovers to be secretive. Wallowing in each other's eyes, speaking through gestures, exchanging notes and signs, they learned to be a secret society complete with passwords and ceremonies and a holy crusade, a religion of two.

So many of our novels, poems, operas, and songs are about love that we take it for granted. What else, it's assumed, should authors write about? But that fashion began in eleventh-century France. One day it is likely to change, as fashions do, into a mass obsession with something else. But, in the meantime, we still practice somewhat medieval codes of chivalry and etiquette—men opening doors for women, helping them on with coats, and so on—along with our understanding of love as a noble passion, and our taste for romance. No small change. As C. S. Lewis says so well,

> French poets, in the eleventh century, discovered or invented, or were the first to express, that romantic species of passion which English poets were still writing about in the nineteenth. They effected a change which has left no corner of our ethics, our imagination, or our daily life untouched, and they erected impassable barriers between us and the classical past or the Oriental present. Compared with this revolution, the Renaissance is a mere ripple. . . .

In the late twentieth century, while gangs riot in the ghettos, countries are craven for power, and sirens wail through the steep canyons of the inner cities and sprawling suburbs, we talk dreamily about courtly love. The twentieth-century Swiss thinker Denis de Rougemont railed against it and dismissed it out of hand as a plague, a bother, and a downright bad mistake. He despised the way it gave emotion mastery over reason. Sensible people longed for sound judgment, and romantic love left one feeling helplessly out of control. He asked: "Why does Western Man wish to suffer this passion which lacerates him and which all his common sense rejects?" He felt it made human relationships far too intense and unsettling, and he didn't like the way suffering was openly sought and enjoyed, or how it ruined one's chance for a happy marriage, which certainly couldn't compete with the remembered succulence of love. More than that, it pandered to an instinct subterranean, dangerous, and unspoken—a yearning for death. People secretly felt this attraction but could not risk acknowledging the phenomenon. It was all so chaotic and plural out there, all such a battle to stay orderly. Struggling every second of one's life against odds that would defeat one in the end, in fatigue heavy as a glacier, one secretly longed for annihilation. No one said so, but all this organized suffering and torment, wishing to die or be struck blind by the mere sight of the beloved—it felt too close to giving in to the seductiveness of death itself.

Perhaps de Rougemont was right. On the other hand, courtly love did help to raise the status of women and of many knights, granted individuals the right to make certain choices about their fate, encouraged mutual affection, and urged lovers to feel tenderness and respect for each other. As gentle-hearted friends, flushed with intimacy and regard, lovers tried to improve their character and talents, and so become worthy of love. No wonder it had such a powerful appeal.

ABELARD AND HELOISE

Another rigor of medieval love developed among the clergy, who were tormented by the conflict between church and heart. The outcome was usually calamitous, as the spiraling love affair between Abelard and Heloise illustrates so well. Of all the medieval love stories, their saga of passion, hope, despair, and pain seems especially tragic, touching people in every generation. Mythic lovers accidentally drink a love potion, and, thus biologically abducted, are not responsible for their destiny, pouring thick as cement, which they can do nothing to stop. Of the many curiosities about human intelligence, the widespread belief that things are "destined to be," that we are prisoners of fate, is one of the strangest but most widespread. So powerful is this feeling that it made sensible myth, lore, and religion, and still does. Existentialism evolved, in part, as a rebellion against such a mental straitjacket. In a typically existentialist way, Abelard and Heloise freely chose their fate, and it is this that made their drama doubly tragic; with the best intentions and the most loving of hearts, they brought about their own downfall.

Peter Abelard was born in Brittany in 1079, the first child of Lord Berengar of Le Pallet, a minor aristocrat. Tutored in both the pagan and Christian authors, he received a top-notch education and was especially fond of Ovid, whom he often quoted. An intellectual boy with a passion for learning had only one path open to him—the clergy— so he went to the local cathedral school and then, at twenty, on to Paris. There, as one of five thousand Latin-speaking students from all over Europe, he learned the fine arts of rhetoric and debate. His fame quickly grew; at twenty-two, he opened his own school, which attracted many paying students. His career leapt from one success to the next, honors mounted, and no goal seemed beyond his grasp. In time, he was appointed head of the cloister school of Notre Dame ("the chair long since destined for me"), and students rushed to his classes, the most popular in Europe. Brilliant, learned, eloquent, charming, he was a man self-besotted, ranking himself "as the only philosopher of standing on the earth." At forty, Abelard met Heloise, the seventeen-year-old niece of a neighbor.

From all accounts, she was a pleasant-looking girl ("tall and well-proportioned . . . with a high, rounded forehead and very white teeth") with a superb mind, who was well educated and vibrant. Abelard fell in lust with her, and talked her uncle, Fulbert, into letting him pay to lodge at their house, adding that he would tutor Heloise for free. This was a generous offer, since women were not allowed to attend his classes. Heloise was overwhelmed by his looks, fame, and erudition. He was the pluperfect professor, superstar, hunk. "What wife, what young girl did not burn for you in your absence or become inflamed by your presence?" she would later write. For his part,

Abelard was proud and lecherous and on the prowl. In Heloise he found quarry that was sexy, young, available. He knew he could manipulate her feelings. As he freely confessed:

> I had such celebrity at that time and possessed such graces of youth and body that I feared no refusal from any woman I found worthy of my love. I thought moreover that this young girl would yield all the more readily because she was cultivated and loved her studies. Even when we were separated, we could be in contact by letters, writing things too bold to be uttered, and thus our delicious relations would never be broken.

He himself said that Fulbert had entrusted "a tender lamb to a famished wolf." Before long, a tempestuous affair began to blaze, and they often made love all night long, with the books scattered around them. What began in opportunity ended in love. He wrote her love songs, she wrote him love letters; they became completely absorbed in each other. But their passion made them careless. One day her uncle discovered them in flagrante, and was outraged by the sight of his young niece being dishonored. He sent Abelard packing. Soon afterward, Heloise learned she was pregnant, and she and Abelard ran away to his sister's house in Brittany, where Heloise gave birth to a son they named Astrolabe. Arguing that they were deeply in love, Abelard begged her uncle to forgive them, and he even offered to marry Heloise, provided the marriage be kept a secret, since it would compromise his prospects as a clergyman. This seemed fair enough, and Fulbert agreed. Heloise did not. She knew what marriage would cost Abelard—it would produce a scandal sufficient to scorch his career. Selflessly, she urged him to stay a bachelor. Leaving the child in Brittany, the pair nonetheless went to Paris and married in secret. But, in the eyes of the world, they appeared to be unmarried wantons. Her uncle started rumors about the existence of a marriage, which Heloise violently denied. Dreadful fights ensued. To get her out of the line of fire, Abelard carried her off to her former childhood convent at Argenteuil, where she dressed in nun's clothing and they made sacrilegious love—in the refectory and sometimes even in the church itself. Her uncle fumed with rage when he discovered Heloise gone; it seemed to him that Abelard meant to hide her away like any common mistress. No doubt Fulbert was less concerned with Heloise's happiness than his own reputation. A seduced daughter (in this case a ward) dirtied the name of the household; it was a form of public cuckoldry, and Fulbert would lose face if he didn't react. For whatever reason, he and his friends plotted a monstrous revenge. As Abelard describes it:

> One night as I lay sleeping in my chamber, one of my servants, corrupted by gold, delivered me to their vengeance, which the world would learn of to its stupefaction: they cut off those parts of my body with which I had committed the offense they deplored. Then they fled.

Word spread fast, and soon Abelard's castration was known to all. He said he suffered far more from humiliation than from pain. Indeed, his humiliation tormented him. With what horror he remembered how the eunuch was depicted in the Bible as "an abomination to the Lord, forbidden entrance to church as if a stinking, unclean monster." Without his testicles, he was no longer human, no longer a man, no longer holy. In shame, he retreated to the Abbey of St. Denis, and he ordered nineteen-year-old Heloise to become a nun and spend the rest of her life in celibacy. For her, their affair had always been all or nothing. She was totally given to passion, commitment, and love. She would have followed him "to hell itself," as she said. And one must remember that, in her day, people took hell literally, as a real place of torture and damnation. Abelard waited for her to take her vows—to be certain that she did—before he took his own. For ten years, they lived in silent separation as monk and nun, not even exchanging letters. In an abstract sense, this was another form of castration. In time, Abelard recovered his equilibrium and returned to the pulpit, and once again he became a famous orator, expressing daring—some said subversive—ideas about Church doctrine. Nonconformists were not tolerated, and he was soon banished to an outlying abbey far from mischief. As abbot of the Abbey of St. Gildas de Ruis in Brittany, he had the power to help Heloise when her convent (where she was by this time prioress) was threatened with closure. So, after ten years apart, Abelard and Heloise met again. Abelard now thought of her as "my sister in Christ rather than my wife." He began writing his autobiography, his "history of calamities," which gives a blunt, at times self-mortifying, account of his life and marriage. A copy made its way to Heloise, and prompted her to write a love letter to Abelard. Filled with passion, confusion, torment, she begins by addressing it "to her master, no, her father; to her husband, no, her brother; from his servant, no, his daughter; from his wife, no, his sister; to Abelard, from Heloise." He clearly plays so many roles in her heart that she is unable to reduce him to just one. Abelard worshiped God, but Heloise worshiped Abelard:

> You know, my beloved, the whole world knows, how in losing you I lost all. . . . You alone can cause me sadness or bring happiness and comfort. . . . I have obediently carried out all your commands. Powerless to oppose you in anything, I had the courage, on a single word from you, to destroy myself. Even more, strange to say: my love was transformed into such madness that it sacrificed beyond hope of recovery that which it most ardently desired. When you commanded it, I changed myself, not only my dress, but my mind, to prove you were master of my soul, as of my body.

The letters that passed between the two lovers were so passionate and tender, so tormented and candid, that they have moved generations of readers. For Heloise, love is consolation enough; it grants peace, happiness, and freedom. For Abelard, love is a hazard along the path to truth and salvation. Love is her philosophy; it obstructs his. Even as an abbess she kept his picture in her room and often spoke to it. The only other picture there would have been of Christ.

Both Abelard and Heloise felt that love could best be expressed through self-sacrifice. In the blunt economics of the heart, what costs the most is prized the most. But, for Abelard, God was paramount. Heloise shocked him by confiding that loving him was more important to her than loving God. It is clear from her letters that love filled her with a cleansing fire and made her feel sacred, holy, baptized by an earthy pagan faith. She became a nun as an act of enslavement to her lover; she was love's martyr. Love was the real order whose vows she took. People praised her virtue and celibacy, she told Abelard, but she alone knew how wanton were her thoughts and her hands. Horrified by her confession, discovering that she was still the teenager desperately in love, Abelard wrote back reprovingly, explaining that his castration was actually an "act of divine mercy" because it brought him closer to God, and that he was glad to be rid of carnal desire, which was nothing but a bugbear and a burden and a quick ticket to sin. She stopped writing to him.

Abelard seemed to channel his erotic energy into reforming the Church, and he was accused of heresy and excommunicated. Making a pilgrimage to Rome to beg Pope Innocent II for clemency, he stopped first at Cluny, because his health was poor. And there he died in 1142, at the age of sixty-three. Told at once of his death, Heloise petitioned for, and finally received, a letter of absolution for Abelard's sins. When she died twenty years later, also at the age of sixty-three, her body was placed in his tomb as she had requested. Rumor at the time said that, as her body was being placed there, his arms fell open to embrace her. Now both bodies rest in the Père Lachaise cemetery in Paris, among the bones of other lovers. Both had believed deeply in love, courtly love—kept concealed, outside of marriage, full of quests and tests, a secret society. That is why Heloise preferred to be considered Abelard's mistress rather than his wife. In the Middle Ages, to be a mistress was a far nobler calling.

Here is one of her heartfelt letters:

... Observe, I beseech you, to what a wretched condition you have reduced me; sad, afflicted, without any possible comfort, unless it proceed from you. ... I have your picture in my room. I never pass by it without stopping to look at it; and yet when you were present with me, I scarce ever cast my eyes upon it. If a picture which is but a mute representation of an object can give such pleasure, what cannot letters inspire? They have souls, they can speak, they have in them all that force which expresses the transport of the heart; they have all the fire of our passions, they can raise them as much as if the persons themselves were present; they have all the softness and delicacy of speech, and sometimes a boldness of expression even beyond it. ... But I am no longer ashamed that my passion has had no bounds for you, for I have done more than all this. I have hated myself that I might love you; I came hither to ruin myself in a perpetual imprisonment, that I might make you live quiet and easy. ... oh! think of me; do not forget me; remember my love, my fidelity, my constancy; love me as your mistress, cherish me as your child, your sister, your wife. Consider that I still love you, and yet strive to avoid loving you. What a word, what a design is this! I shake with horror, and my heart revolts against what I say. I shall blot all my paper with tears. I end my long letter, wishing you, if you can desire it (would to Heaven I could), for ever adieu.

MODERN DAYS

THE ANGEL AND THE WITCH

During the Middle Ages, people were more intimately woven into the fabric of their society. Vassalage meant wearing many ropes of obedience and, in combination, they held one securely in check. This was doubly true for a woman, who was also bound and defined by her relationships to men, as her father's daughter, her husband's wife, her son's mother. Most of one's life was played out in public, and few people moved beyond their small community, where everyone was known and gossiped about, values were uniform, and there could be little confusion about what sort of behavior was scandalous. Some adventurous souls traveled between towns, but for most people the world ended where their land did, or at the village outskirts. Visitors from afar were unlikely, and leaving home seemed both unnecessary and frightening. Surely monsters roamed the lands beyond the hills. Knights returning from the Crusades carried stories of grand cities and silks, but also of savagery and appallingly strange and sacrilegious customs.

As the Middle Ages waned, villages grew like overspilling ponds, more large cities appeared, and it was difficult to keep track of everyone's doings. Noblemen who wished to wage war or do business needed support from the swelling class of merchants, manufacturers, and bankers. Because socializing smoothed the way for business deals, the upper and middle classes rubbed shoulders with increasing frequency and sometimes intermarried. And so the bog of social life, where one fell into a class and stayed there, began to change into a landscape that clever folk could navigate. If one dressed correctly, and knew how to speak, he could maneuver among the classes. A man always had his reputation to protect and his position to maintain, through duels or display. Since honor was paramount, the crown of one's status, requiring a fealty all its own, it became possible to invent an aura and an acceptable past. Appearances were everything.

Despite the social ambiguities of the time, artists and scholars were drawn to the ancients once again, especially to Plato, in whom they found truths clear-cut and eternal. Because their passion, though deeply religious in its intensity, was grounded in a secular vision of humanity, the focus of life shifted from the Church to human beings, who were pictured as life's architects, wardens of the good and noble. We share that sentiment today and even if we don't think angels walk the earth, we do believe in everyday acts of saintliness and heroism. Artworks revolved around symmetry and classical form, favoring the curious sleight of eye known as perspective, in which a flat, two-dimensional object creates the illusion of three-dimensional space. It's often stated that perspective was invented in the Renaissance, but this isn't true. Perspective was practiced long before—I saw it beautifully rendered in the 17,000-year-old cave paintings of animals at Lascaux—but it obsessed the people of the Renaissance, who perfected its chicaneries. All art is deceit: it cons the mind into imagining a world by showing it a kernel.* Perhaps because society was changing so quickly, they wished to know exactly where a person stood in relation to everyone else. Today we often talk about "keeping things in perspective," an idea that also preoccupied Renaissance minds. Perspective brought the dimension of time to painting; one is gradually stitched to the horizon, a distant place but also a different moment. Elements report back to key figures, they have associations and kinships, and in that sense, the painting's visual world throbs with a tribal reality.

People were painted naked and glorious like Greek gods and goddesses, and women's bodies were celebrated as temples of beauty. As

---

*An abbess was once asked what she held in her hand. Opening her fist to reveal a horse chestnut, she replied: "All that is made."

we have seen, by the Middle Ages the status of women had improved a little. The Virgin Mary as a latter-day version of Aphrodite had come to be the image Botticelli, Titian, and others preferred; they painted women whose robust flesh glowed with color, energy, and motion. Every cell resonated with life. They were sumptuously beautiful, and beauty was good, as Plato had said. Yet at precisely the same time, a loathing for women flourished that has been unequaled in any age. Some men—particularly theologians—felt that women were the root of evil in the world because they were more bestial than men, and therefore had to be stopped, punished, and killed. At no time in history were more women condemned as witches and tortured to death. Sixty thousand in Europe, and a few thousand more in New England. But twice that many were prosecuted without being burned. Two Dominican theologians, after much experience as the pope's inquisitors, offered the following conclusions:

> A woman is beautiful to look upon, contaminating to the touch, and deadly to keep . . . a necessary evil, a natural temptation . . . an evil of nature, painted with fair colors . . . a liar by nature. . . . Since [women] are feebler both in mind and body, it is not surprising that they should come under the spell of witchcraft [more than men]. . . . A woman is more carnal than a man. . . . All witchcraft comes from carnal lust, which is in women insatiable.

The twentieth century has tended to depict men as sexual carnivores, predatory by nature, out of control when their hormones blast, unable to resist acts of sex or violence. "Men are beasts," women complain; males "think with their dicks," men confess. For much of history, that sort of view described women; the depiction of them as vile, demonic creatures didn't start in the Renaissance. This toxic version of woman, identified with Eve, a fallen woman who had lured a man to his doom, one whose very name sounds like the word *evil,* was always prevalent. Father Odon, the abbot of Cluny Abbey, wrote in 1100:

> Indeed, if men were endowed, like the lynxes of Boetia, with the power of visual penetration and could see what there is beneath the skin, the mere sight of a woman would nauseate them: that femi-

nine grace is only saburra, blood, humor, bile. Consider what is
hidden in the nostrils, in the throat, in the belly: filth everywhere.
. . . How can we desire to hold in our arms the bag of excrement
itself?

Men have both despised and adored women, found them saintly and
base—the angel and the whore—but this duality was especially glaring during the Renaissance, when women's bodies were depicted as
flawless temples of beauty to be studied and worshiped, even as scores
of so-called witches were reviled, tortured, and killed in public.

The woman-as-angel produced glorious works of art in what was
essentially a latter-day fertility cult. One was surrounded by pictures
of robust motherhood, usually in the form of a sweet-faced Madonna
holding a plump, cherubic, good-natured Child. No doubt they were
the ideals; nutrition for pregnant women or infants was little understood, and sickness claimed many lives. However, such a Madonna
would have been a familiar image from daily life, since virtually every
woman one met (except the elderly or barren) was pregnant or nursing. Wealthy women didn't nurse their own babies; they hired wet
nurses, which allowed them to become pregnant again faster, and it
was their duty to produce as many children as possible. As Martin
Luther said, "Even if they bear themselves weary, or bear themselves
out . . . this is the purpose for which they exist." High fertility was
such an important feature in a future bride that a woman was sometimes encouraged to conceive before marriage, just to prove that she
could before being linked to a man's estate. Economically, daughters
were a bother unless they could produce heirs. Therefore, dowries
were important. A family had to bribe a man for taking on the burden
of its daughter. Supply and demand dictated the going price. During
the Renaissance, when there were plenty of marriageable women,
dowries soared to such ridiculous heights that it was considered a
monumental act of charity for someone to bestow a dowry on an
orphan girl, who couldn't marry without one. Single, unattached
women, who were not recognizable as someone's daughter, wife,
widow, or sister, had no definition, thus no place in society. The
literature often reveals poor young women working night and day to
earn enough money for a dowry, without which they had no hope of
marriage.

In such a milieu, a female child was simply a commodity, and marriage even more of a business contract. She had no say when it came to picking a husband. Loving parents tried to choose someone agreeable, but for most of them, their daughter, despite her handicaps, was an important form of wealth, actually a trading in futures, on which a family banked for social mobility, income, and heirs. Only an ungrateful or disloyal daughter objected. Pregnancy was a woman's life and trade. Divorce was impossible. These were truths as fundamental as mountains. But she also knew that society, while not condoning infidelity, understood that hanky-panky could take place. With any luck, she would give birth to a healthy son, better yet two or three, and then she could fall in love and have affairs, provided they were discreet. Clergymen preached that husbands and wives should be the best of companions, real chums, people who loved each other and raised their children with care. And frequently they did—wills and other legal records are filled with the affectionate phrases that come from tender hearts. But more often marriage was an emotional desert, which partners crossed by nourishing themselves elsewhere.

ROMEO AND JULIET

Arranged marriages were a hand-me-down custom known to all, but at about this time, amazingly, a significant number of people began to object. Shakespeare's plays are filled with collisions over the right to choose whom to marry, and complaints by couples who'd prefer a love match. Shakespeare didn't invent the best known of them, Romeo and Juliet, leading characters in a classic that had been told in sundry cultures and genres. In the second century A.D., Xenophon of Ephesus presented the story as *Anthia and Abrocomas,* but it may have been older than that. Over the years it fed many imaginations, and its hero and heroine changed names. In 1535, Luigi da Porto spun the tale as a slow-moving melodrama in a novel with an eighteen-year-old heroine named *La Giuletta.* The story was still being written in the latter half of the sixteenth century, in poetry and prose, and even the distinguished Spanish writer Lope de Vega wrote a drama called *Capulets and Montagues.* In telling the story yet again, Shakespeare was doing what Leonard Bernstein and collaborators did with *West Side Story,* putting a well-known, shopworn tale into contemporary dress, locale, and issues. They knew people would identify with the heartbreak of "Juliet and her Romeo,"* as it's so often described, focusing on the romantic hopes of the girl. Referring to it in that way makes "Romeo" sound less like a man than a condition or trait possessed by Juliet.

A beautiful, chaste Veronese girl, whose very name is rhyme (Juliet Capulet) encounters a boy who embodies her robust sensuality. He is passion incarnate, someone in love with love. "Love is a smoke made with the fume of sighs," he at first tells his friend Benvolio, and then decides it isn't gentle, but "too rough, / Too rude, too boisterous, and it pricks like thorn." On the rebound from a girl named Rosaline, and electric with need, Romeo is like lightning looking for a place to strike. He meets Juliet and the play's thunderstorm of emotions begins.

The story hinges on the rivalry between two noble houses, and the forbidden love of their children, Romeo and Juliet. Chance, destiny, and good playwriting ordain that they shall meet and become "star-crossed lovers" with a sad, luminous fate. Typically adolescent, the lovers feel the same bliss, suffer the same torments, and tackle the same obstacles young lovers always have. One age-old note is that they must keep their love a secret from their parents, a theme beautifully expressed in the ancient Egyptian love poems. The erotic appeal of the forbidden stranger also is an old theme, whether he's from the enemy's camp or just "the wrong side of the tracks." So is the notion of love as detachment, a force that pulls you away from your family, your past, your friends, even your neighborhood. Old, too, is the idea of love as a madness; and the fetishistic desire to be an article of clothing worn by the beloved ("O, that I were a glove upon that hand, / That I might touch that cheek!" Romeo cries), echoing, centuries later, the Egyptian love poet's desire to "be her ring, the seal on her finger."†

Shakespeare made important changes in his telling of the story. In his play, Juliet is thirteen years old; in the other versions she's older.

---

*The closing lines of the play are:

> For never was a story of more woe
> Than this of Juliet and her Romeo.

†In a secretly recorded telephone conversation in 1993, Prince Charles swore to his mistress that he longed even to be her "tampon."

In his play, she and Romeo only know one another for four days in July; in other versions, the courtship lasts months. Even if we accept the gossip of his time—that Italian girls mature faster than English ones—why does he make the couple so young and their love instantaneous? Shakespeare was about thirty when he wrote the play, and as his exquisite sonnets declare, he knew love's terrain. Indeed, in one sonnet he laments the mistake of introducing his male lover to his female lover. Apparently, they fell for each other and left Shakespeare high and dry, in double grief. I think he wished to demonstrate in *Romeo and Juliet* how reckless, labile, and ephemeral the emotion of love is, especially in young people, and especially if one compares it with the considered love of older people. Most of the heroines in his other plays are also very young.* Throughout the plays, one finds the tenets of courtly love, but with two exceptions: love always leads to matrimony, and Shakespeare does not condone adultery. The lovers have to be young, of good social rank, well dressed, and of virtuous character. The man has to be courageous, the woman chaste and beautiful. Rarely are the lovers introduced. They fall in love at first sight, the beauty of the beloved's face signaling everything they need to know. Danger usually lurks close by, but they are headstrong, powerless to resist love. The lovers are constantly obsessed with each other. They credit the object of their affection with godlike qualities, and go through religious rituals of worship and devotion. They exchange talismans—a ring, a scarf, or some meaningful trifle. A medieval lady gave her knight a piece of clothing or jewelry to protect him, a kind of love charm. Lovers still exchange such tokens today, and imbue them with similar power. During the Middle Ages, lovers were secretive, often so that the woman's husband wouldn't discover her infidelity. In Elizabethan times, lovers were still secretive, but then it was to keep the girl's father from preventing their meetings. When Shakespeare's lovers declare their love, they intend to marry. An ordeal keeps them temporarily apart, and during this lonely, dislocated time, they weep and sigh, become forgetful, lose their appetites, moan to their confidants, write elegant, heartfelt love letters, lie awake all night. The play ends with marriage and/or death. These are

*For example, both Miranda in *The Tempest* and Viola in *Twelfth Night* are only about fifteen, and Marina in *Pericles* is fourteen.

the only choices open to Shakespearean lovers, because they can only love one person, without whom life seems worthless. In Shakespeare's plays, the characters all practice courtly love, but there is one important difference: instead of craving seduction, they crave marriage. Their families might be mad as hell, go to war over it, or send the girl off to a nunnery. But the lovers don't need their parents' legal permission to marry. When love conquers all, it isn't through subterfuge or blackmail or because of pregnancy, but because the parents understand the sincerity of the couple's love.

As *Romeo and Juliet* unfolds, the main characters make it clear that there are many forms of love. T.J.B. Spencer sums this up in his commentary to the Penguin edition:

> There is Juliet's—both before and after she has fallen in love; Romeo's—both while he thinks he is in love with Rosaline, and after his passion has been truly aroused by Juliet; Mercutio's—his brilliant intelligence seems to make ridiculous an all-absorbing and exclusive passion based upon sex; Friar Laurence's—for him love is an accompaniment of life, reprehensible if violent or unsanctified by religion; Father Capulet's—for him it is something to be decided by a prudent father for his heiress-daughter; Lady Capulet's—for her it is a matter of worldly wisdom (she herself is not yet thirty and has a husband who gave up dancing thirty years ago); and the Nurse's—for her, love is something natural and sometimes lasting, connected with pleasure and pregnancy, part of the round of interests in a woman's life.

The teenagers of *Romeo and Juliet* are hotheads, or hot loins, who decide that they are mortally in love and must marry immediately, though they haven't exchanged a hundred words. "Give me my Romeo," Juliet demands, with an innocence blunt and trusting. But even she fears the speed at which they're moving:

> It is too rash, too unadvised, too sudden;
> Too like the lightning, which doth cease to be
> Ere one can say it lightens.

The use of lightning and gunpowder images throughout the play keeps reminding us how combustible the situation is, how incandescent their love, and how life itself burns like a brief, gorgeous spark in the night. Their moonlit balcony scene, full of tenderness and yearning, with some of the most beautiful phrasing ever written, shows them sighing for love under the moon and stars, vibrantly alive in a world of glitter and shadow. After such intimacy under the covers of night, their secret marriage is certain. Then comes the impossibility of living without one another. After many obstacles, a set of dire confusions leads the lovers to commit suicide. Ironically, the horror of their deaths serves to reconcile the feuding families. Thus love is portrayed as an emissary force that can travel between foes and conduct its own arbitration. On the most basic level, this is biologically true, however one expresses it, as *competing organisms join forces for mutual benefit,* or *love can make bedfellows of enemies.* Why does the world seem unlivable without the loved one? Why does a teenager abandon hope of ever loving or being loved again in the entirety of his or her life?*

Romeo and Juliet is but one Renaissance example of a radical idea spreading through the bourgeoisie—that romance might be combined with marriage. The play appealed on many levels to many classes, in part because family life had begun to change. There were fewer battles to wage, business kept men close to home, husband and wife spent more time together, and they understandably wanted it to be an agreeable union. The bourgeoisie wanted to indulge in the delights of courtly love, but without feeling sinful. By 1570, Roger Ascham was complaining:

> Not only young gentlemen, but even very young girls dare without all fear though not without open shame, where they list and how they list marry themselves in spite of father, mother, God, good order, and all.

Court life evolved an opulence and grandeur unknown even in myths and legends. Courtiers, both male and female, had special outfits for different times of day, ornate accessories, and clothing that did not conceal the body, but clung in just the right places to accentu-

---

*This belief that *there is only one person in the world for me, without whom I am lost* is a familiar part of loving stated formally by Plato.

ate gender.* Royalty staged theatrical extravaganzas for thousands of guests, which lasted for days on end. Just as in the Middle Ages the knights had rules of courtesy to follow, in the Renaissance courtiers strove for certain ideals. Ladies were not merely worshiped from afar, they were to be witty, polite, well read, conversant in politics and current events, in short, entertaining companions. Unmarried men and women were allowed to spend a lot of time together, and a lover was not obliged to prove himself through anything as antique as quests. Because love meant being preoccupied with good and beauty, it was championed as a fine and noble enterprise. Men and women were encouraged to meet often, get to know one another, talk about romance as much as they liked, desire the body, but not rush to intercourse. To that extent courtship was still medieval—a chaste period filled with the torment of waiting as long as possible before consummating one's desire. Waiting can be dull, so artful flirtation became fashionable. All the rigmarole of knights, quests, and the service cult of courtly love were considered passé. Every law has its scofflaws, and not everyone played by the rules. Men still adored their ladies, whom they professed to love, but they slept with mistresses and whores. A perpetual tug-of-war raged over virginity. Maidens connived to keep from being seduced; and men connived to seduce them. Among the marrieds, virtue was up for grabs.

BRIDLED HEARTS

In the eighteenth century's reverse tantrum of polish and decorum, neoclassicism reigned, and religion gave way to a faith in reason, science, and logic. If nature and human nature were orderly parts of a clockwork universe run by a dispassionate God, then it behooved

---

*One of the most curious, perhaps, was the codpiece, worn by European men between the fourteenth and sixteenth centuries. Somewhat like a tribal penis sheath or a jockstrap, its purpose was to protect the penis, but men exaggerated its size and shape—sometimes even decorating it with a gargoyle-like head—to draw attention to the penis and make it appear to be constantly large and erect. In 1976, the product-development department of Birds Eye frozen foods planned on calling their new fish balls "cod pieces," until someone pointed out that the term had an ancient and somewhat bawdy lineage.

human beings—lesser gods—to display equal restraint. Hiding one's true feelings was expected of all, masked balls became the rage, masked hearts the style, and elegantly stilted turns of phrase helped to keep everyone stylishly remote. Etiquette required a seesaw of elegancies, protocols, and endless verbal handshakes. Lovers were bound by these generalized rules of demeanor and deportment. The codes of courtesy included foppish bows, the taking of snuff, and a lady's use of her fan as semaphore. Ornate, mannered, it was all a form of social dressage. A woman could receive socially while in bed or bath, because she and her visitors alike were expected to hide their feelings.

While self-control was the byword, cruelty was sometimes the practice. People felt comfortable picnicking at public executions, of which there were a great many. Society was fascinated by the legend of Don Juan Tenorio, a fourteenth-century Spanish aristocrat who cut a figure as a cold, sadistic, and artful ruiner of women's reputations. Love affairs were enjoyed as a blood sport by many who thrilled to the complex battle of wills. The game was a seduction as capricious as it was feigned, in which one's partner was first utterly vanquished, then swiftly, heartlessly dismissed. Among the gifted generals in these campaigns, the sleekest, both male and female, wore invisible hearts as medals. Most rational gentlemen regarded women as large children, advising their sons, as the Earl of Chesterfield did, that

> a man of sense only trifles with them, plays with them, humours them, and flatters them, as he does with a sprightly, forward child; but he neither consults them about, nor trusts them with, serious matters, though he often makes them believe that he does both.

It was in such an atmosphere that Casanova became a dashing figure, one who lived a picaresque life of seduction, gambling, and adventure. Because he was a serious outlaw of love, remarkable for his conquests, an extreme but familiar psychological type, he gave his name to an attitude, thereby wedding him to the future. This victory would have pleased him greatly, because he was a mistreated child who spent his life seeking love, approval, and respectability. Giacomo Casanova was born in Venice in 1725, the son of two stage performers. Actresses usually doubled as prostitutes, actors as pimps, and his parents often left him with his maternal grandmother while they traveled around Europe, plying their trades. As a gutter child, he felt shame about his mother's whoring, but her constant abandonment of him hurt even more. It was as if her motherly love were written in invisible ink. Because he suffered from frequent nose-bleeds, his grandmother sent him to Padua, hoping the fresher air might restore his health. "So they got rid of me," he wrote in his memoirs fifty years later, still hurt and angry. In time, he received many forms of education (including being awakened sexually by an older woman who had helped to raise him), and finally graduated from the University of Padua with a doctor-of-law degree and his first real experience of romance.

After that, the world was his oyster. Indeed, he often ate raw oysters off a woman's breasts, which gave him a special thrill. Oysters may be said to resemble female genitalia, and it excited him to taste all the briny nooks and crannies. Risk hardened his desire, he loved a saucy intrigue, and so he persuaded women into making love with him in all sorts of unlikely places—inside a speeding carriage; with a jealous husband hovering in a nearby room; through prison bars; at a public drawing-and-quartering; sometimes while being observed by a third party; sometimes as part of a ménage à trois. His youth, good looks, and quick wit made him appealing to men and women alike, and the evidence suggests that he was bisexual, although most of his lovers were women. They tended to be older ones, about whose age he lied in his memoirs, tactfully making them out to be much younger. His gift, as a biographer writes, "was in keeping his wits and his erection when all about him were losing theirs." Understandably, he contracted venereal diseases eleven times, often took the cure, used a half lemon as a rather ingenious diaphragm, and sometimes wore a rudimentary condom made of sheep's intestine. There was a side of him that was pure rake and scoundrel. No wall was too high, no window too narrow, no husband too near, to prevent his making love to a woman he fancied, "because she was beautiful, because I loved her, and because her charms meant nothing unless they had the power to drown all reason."

Every romance was a quest for the golden fleece, so it's not surprising that he referred to his penis as "valiant steed." Always genuinely in love with the woman he was pursuing, in his ardor he became irresistible. "When the lamp is taken away, all women are alike," he once said of his occasional escapades with horny hags in the dark. But he also swore that "without love this great business is a vile thing." Over and over he lost his heart, and over and over he lost his worldly possessions. But in his private reckoning they were the same thing. Searching for respect, he conned and ingratiated and bedded his way into high society. A handsome raconteur, he devised ingenious scams, found a way under the skirts of countless women, often at crowded events (no one wore underwear, so sex in public became a special delectation), and had dozens of careers—as a military officer, spy, priest, violinist, dancer, silk manufacturer, cook, playwright, pimp, and cabalistic necromancer-soothsayer-magician, to name only a few. He rubbed elbows with emperors, popes, and guttersnipes; fought duels; relished the theater; was a cat burglar; spent years in prison and many hours carousing with royalty; translated the *Iliad* and other classical texts, wrote two dozen learned books, and enjoyed the company of Rousseau, Voltaire, Franklin, and other thinkers. He lied about his parentage, and lived in fear that the truth might be discovered. What were the feeble frauds he performed compared to the inner fraudulence he felt? Living on the edge kept his wits sharp, but it also made him notorious. When he entered a city, the police took note, as did desirable women and their husbands and lovers.

People often speak the names Don Juan and Casanova in the same breath, and they did have something important in common—both felt unwanted and dismissed as children. Discovering, in time, that their good looks and sexuality could bring the attention they craved, they instinctively relied on seduction, eroticizing every relationship, just as Marilyn Monroe would. However, the fourteenth-century Don Juan bedded women to assure himself he was a virile man, whereas Casanova needed to prove he was a desirable child. Desperate for love, respect, family, a sense of belonging, he disguised his insecurities in bravado and heartiness. He tried to hide the fact that he was drawn to mother figures, and to fleecing the rich and aristocratic just to prove that a poor boy could.

Casanova wanted to compel all women to fall in love with him, but when they did he left them, as he had been left by his mother. She was the first woman he had loved, a serious heartbreaker, and he spent his life chasing her shadow in other women. When he caught it, he discovered to his surprise that he held nothing in his hands, and so he chased the next shadow he saw, with the same result. However, there was one type of woman he found truly magnetic, whom he couldn't resist, couldn't win, and from whose clutches he couldn't escape, though she drained him of money and power and made mincemeat of his self-respect. He couldn't save himself from a tease, a woman who led him on without giving in, alternately tantalizing and dismissing him. When such a woman entered an affair with him, all she had to do was not show any concern about the outcome. The uncertainty kept him dangling over a fiery pit; he found it too much like the random love and rejection that had bedeviled him as a boy. It defused his explosive sensuality, short-circuited his lust, rotted his self-confidence, and yet he kept going back for more punishment. But he kept this secret well. For the most part he married life itself, and became so engaged in living flamboyantly, so full of randy good humor that doors sprang open for him, skirts lifted, and bosoms heaved. It is ironic that dictionaries define a *casanova* as a man who is promiscuous, libertine, and heartless in his dealings with women. The real man was an emotional risk-taker, who wagered heavily in games of love and often lost. His secret weapon was the language of scars, which drove him to do, say, become anything, in order to love and be loved. It was all illusion, shadow animals against a wall. But it was a hell of a ride, and at the end of his life he said wistfully, "I regret nothing."

Casanova was one type of eighteenth-century lover, dangerous and indiscreet. But Ben Franklin epitomized the gallant gentleman of the era, both as thinker and as lover. He knew Casanova in passing, because they sometimes met at court and talked ideas with Voltaire and others; but they were very different cats in the night when it came to love. Unlike Casanova, who was tempestuous and risky, Franklin was levelheaded, playful, and sincere. The French welcomed him into their hearts and boudoirs; indeed, they idolized him.

When we were a nation of shopkeepers, Ben Franklin was a man of the world. In a time of kings, he was proud to be a printer. Equally good at persuading monarchs, small children, and lynch mobs, he became a budding revolution's secret charmer, advancing its cause in Europe. In the heyday of abstract theories, he could turn complex facts on the lathe of a simple idea. Witty by taste and trade, he reduced life's homespun truths to the rigorous pungency of epigrams. He was as at home in the bluster and debate of open politics as in the sly innuendoes and intrigue of French salons. Though not a churchgoer, he had a great vision of universal law and order, down to waves of light, up to the perfectibility of people.

A family man, with relations sprawling over two continents, whom he tended with patriarchal devotion—especially his own illegitimate son and that son's illegitimate son—he stayed married for forty years, but spent fifteen of them living abroad without his wife. We remember him as the old, shrewd man of economy and common sense, but even in his seventies he was courting the great beauties of France in sizzling letters and wickedly witty flirtations. Well-rounded both in outlook and physique, he was a whole man whose parts worked in unison. While other men fretted over trifles, he imagined the complete experience of American life, filled with hospitals, paved streets, academies, insurance companies, libraries, fire engines, and personal freedom.

Franklin was a playful problem solver. His passion was to make the scientific theories of his day practical, to improve the daily lives of common people. When electricity was little more than a parlor trick, he used it to roast turkeys. He invented the bifocals he himself wore. He invented the lightning rod that he used in his own home, and those marvels of efficiency, the Pennsylvania furnace and the Franklin stove. A keen observer of symptoms, he diagnosed lead poisoning, suggested treatments for his private bugbear, the gout, and wrote an insightful treatise on the contagiousness of the common cold. An ace meteorologist, he predicted storms and studied eclipses, waterspouts, thunder, and the northern lights. He was the first person to try to map the Gulf Stream. In spare moments, he studied fossils, spelling reform, marsh gas, smallpox, the possibilities of manned flight, sunspots, the hot-air balloon (when asked what use it was, he replied: "What use is a baby?"), and so many other commonplace curiosities of life that it would take paragraphs to list them. "Ideas will string themselves together like ropes of onions," he wrote about his nomadic, penetrating mind that knew to the penny what each flower bulb cost, but also took pains to introduce the yellow willow to America, invent a flexible catheter for his ailing brother, and write this epitaph for a distraught little girl's dead squirrel: "Here Skugg/ Lies snug/As a bug/In a rug." His technique, in matters of science and of the heart, was to begin with general principles, then move to practical application, and finally to simple advice. To a saucy young heartbreaker, he wrote: "Kill no more pigeons than you can eat."

There was a tough, moral streak to Franklin that drove him to search out and think about virtue, debate it with friends at a philosophical club he founded, and write about it often in pamphlets and in *Poor Richard's Almanack* (which sold 10,000 copies a year at a time when Philadelphia's population was only 20,000). But, having identified and related what virtue was, he felt under no obligation to live a virtuous life. His years in France were lavish by American standards. And he was one of the great skirt chasers of all time. Legend paints him as an old lecher, but this is light-years from the truth his letters reveal. He was the lifelong advocate of women's rights, and of the dignity, beauty, and value of women of all ages and classes. One of his funniest, best-known, and also wisest letters is about the advantages of making love to older women, in which he notes among other things, "They are so grateful." Not only was he protective of his lady friends, at times providing them with money, legal help, housing, advantages for their children, and carefully thought-out advice when they presented him with problems, he also had great intellectual respect for them. Women, like lightning, were a force of nature, and Franklin loved to study both. He did so calmly, at length, and without fear.

It comes as no surprise that, in France, in his seventies, he became the symbol of ageless vitality. It was all the rage to put his portrait on things: pocketknives, vases, entire dinner services, handkerchiefs, inside chamber pots. Frenchwomen, who took the subtle roller coaster of flirtation and raised it to a high art, found in Franklin a player of exquisite mastery. Women craved his attentions, and swore their love to him for the length of their lives, in forthright and heartfelt letters. His French ladies sent mittens and dolls to his grandchildren in America. His wife sent homely, countrified gifts to his friends in France. On at least two occasions he asked Frenchwomen to marry him, and they lovingly refused. But, in all fairness, they were as much as forty years younger and already married, and they lamented their plight in letters of devotion. There were no telephones, and he enjoyed letter writing as a robust and eloquent love game, sending impish, wickedly flirtatious letters to his lady friend Madame Brillon, whom he visited at least twice a week, on some occasions playing chess with her while she bathed, on a board placed over her bathtub. His reputation was based on anecdotes such as this: Unexpectedly, one winter evening, he met a woman to whom he had made love some months before. A trifle hurt, she said, "You haven't seen me all summer. I fear you no longer desire me." "Madam, nothing could be farther from the truth," Franklin replied. "I've merely been waiting for the nights to get longer."

A WAKING SWOON

In time, the boomerang of public opinion traveled around Europe, and society changed its mind about life and love once again. Rationalism was out, Romanticism was in. A middle class, grown large enough to be powerful, could not express its worth through noble birth. Instead, it proclaimed that each individual was of value, regardless of lineage or class. Industrialism's "Promised Land" included noisy, filthy cities, from which people wanted to escape; the middle class had the money and the leisure to seek novelty and go on country jaunts. The British monarchy seemed less august; the philosophers were talking ardently about democracy; and the French and American revolutions set the world ablaze with new ideals. Eighteenth-century scientists had been dogmatic and absolute, and their rigidity made the Romantics cringe. Much of life was mysterious and unknown, much of one's experience was deeply personal. For ages, society had been suffocatingly programmatic, issuing moral laws like so many straitjackets. The Romantics wanted a free society, open to experiment and personal response. They delved into orientalism, glamorized the Middle Ages for its flights of emotion, felt that society was evolving toward some utopia, urged people to follow the heart rather than the head, adored wildest nature as a state of Edenic grace, encouraged artists to be confessional in their work, and, most radical of all, admired originality for its own sake—because something new and unheard of and untried was a precious addition to the world of sensation. Love as a board game no longer made sense. Treasuring the self, soul-searching with a vengeance, brimming with sensibility and tender feelings, the Romantic felt love as a waking swoon, an all-consuming force strong as a tidal wave.

No composer personified the passion of the age better than Beethoven, a tempestuous and defiant man who wrote avant-garde music full of majesty and organized alarm. Hampered by the rigors of traditional music, he fed his own anger, heartache, and struggle into his work. Expressing so much feeling would have been impossible in shopworn musical terms, so he invented a new vocabulary, one richer and more volatile, one closer to pure emotion. His music spurned the skillful embroidery of the past, it surged with raw feeling. Instruments were stretched to encompass a wider range of sounds, and performers had to learn new techniques to play them. As the old rules crumbled, Beethoven's music became even more personal, alive with suffering and intensely human.

He wrote thirty-eight piano sonatas, and I am especially fond of the "Pathétique" and the "Appassionata," the first written when he realized in horror that he was going deaf, the second when he resolved to fight his destiny with all the creative fury he could muster. "I shall seize fate by the throat," he vowed, "it shall certainly never overcome me." With these sonatas, piano music changed for all time, becoming huge, powerful, broad as orchestral works, deeply felt. Later in life, when he was completely deaf, Beethoven wrote his most confidential and intimate, some say his purest, music—sixteen string quartets. But it is in his piano sonatas, where hope alternates with despair, that I hear how he struggles with love.

Ludwig van Beethoven was born in 1770, the son of a father who sang for a living and whose alcoholism made his family's life a fright and a misery. Discovering his son was a musical prodigy, he decided to capitalize on it and use him as a cash cow—or calf. After all, Mozart had been paraded around Europe and made a fortune for his parents. He ordered young Ludwig to spend all day at the piano. Sometimes he returned home after all-night binges, staggering drunk, and dragged the boy out of bed, demanding that he practice in the dark. When Ludwig made mistakes, as any boy would, his father beat him. Considering the emotional Molotov cocktail of lovelessness, physical abuse, and a childhood shackled to a piano, it's a wonder Ludwig developed any regard for music at all. Add to this the fact that he was reported to be quite ugly, slovenly, and understandably shy, and it doesn't sound as if he had much chance. His mother, though devoted to her children, was brutalized by her husband and always miserable; she died young of tuberculosis. Ludwig was only eight years old when he gave his first public concert, and by fourteen he was assistant to the court organist. With his mother gone and his father out of work, this position allowed him to support the entire family, though barely. But he was no gentleman. Short, blockish, unrefined in manner, with a pockmarked face and a heart scarred by neglect, he was a bad-tempered and intolerant young man, who became easily excited and fought fiercely. He didn't put up with insults or criticism (both of which his music inspired), and he didn't suffer fools. Coming as a sequel to the deprivations of his childhood, his growing deafness was excruciating. Not because of his composing—he could hear the music in his mind whether he heard the actual sounds or not—but because of the even greater distance it put between him and the world. He became a tortured spirit, a phantom of life's opera. Just imagine in what self-eviscerating pain he wrote these words: "O ye men, who think or say that I am malevolent, stubborn, or misanthropic, how greatly do ye wrong me, you do not know the secret cause. . . . For me there can be no recreation in the society of my fellows, refined intercourse, mutual exchange of thought; only just as little as the greatest needs command may I mix with society. I must live like an exile. . . . O providence—grant me at last but one day of pure joy—it is so long since real joy echoed in my heart—O when—O when, O Divine One—shall I feel it again in the temple of nature and man—Never? No—O that would be too hard!"

As his deafness devoured him, he began to compose with even more urgency. He fell vertiginously in love, often and foolishly, inevitably choosing young, beautiful highborn women who never returned his love. The "Moonlight" sonata he dedicated to his own Juliet, Giulietta Guicciardi; but it was her cousin, Therese, who inflamed him enough to write the "Appassionata." Was she the "Immortal Beloved" he addressed in a letter found in a secret drawer after his death? "What tearful longings after you," he wrote, "you—my life— my all! farewell. Oh, continue to love me, never misjudge the faithful heart of your beloved L.—Ever yours—Ever mine—Ever each other's—" Was it an unmailed letter, or a copy of one he had sent? Or was it a fantasy written in an idle hour? We remember Beethoven as a heroic figure, triumphing over his deafness to create electrifying music of great power and passion. We remember him as a rebel and visionary, not as a moody dreamer who was at loose ends emotionally, lonely and tormented, frustrated by unresponsive ladyloves whom he idealized, terribly susceptible to rejection and slight, attuned to life's sensations, and painfully withdrawn. But Romanticism glorified just that sort of sensitive spirit.

A RETURN TO COURTLY LOVE

Reacting against the bridled hearts of the rationalists, the nineteenth-century Romantics cherished a delicate responsiveness to the world, an aesthetic readiness that at times led to physical weakness, pessimism, or despair. Love poetry flourished that was neither bawdy nor witty but shy and soulful, bursting with asexual rapture. Infatuated with the Middle Ages, when emotions were ceremonial and the Good and the True rode to battle in the name of Virtue and Beauty, poets once more unearthed courtly love. No matter that it had begun among feudal knights and ladies as an adulterous game based on born-again Platonism. In a modified form, it still fitted their needs.

Courtly love is actually a form of decoration. What's being decorated is lust. Over and over, succeeding generations have discovered courtly love as a way to cleanse sexual attraction of its carnality. In an era of shame-worship we naturally assume that social conventions exist to hide our animal origins, but suppose their purpose is the opposite—a way to draw even more attention to them? The female baboon has a rump and genitals which swell to balloonlike proportions and flush fiery red when she's in heat. *I'm ready,* she announces, *man oh man, am I ready! And here's the target.* Courtly love and other such games are similar in that they decorate the process, highlighting the ripeness and availability of the female. Consider the bee. A bee can hone in on the (to us invisible) large, bright, ultraviolet target of a black-eyed Susan, and stay on the glide path until it reaches its goal. In complex human societies, where the target isn't always clear or available, there are many distractions. Elaborate courtship guides one steadily closer and closer to mating. Many a woman has waited for her knight in shining armor to arrive from an unknown direction and treat her with dignity, worship, adoration. Like Rapunzel, she could then let down her hair and allow him to climb into her bedchamber. Her days are pitted with boredom. She feels self-doubt, and a sense of inferiority. Then a benevolent Other arrives who will heal her life, smooth it out, applaud her finest points, and crown her with garlands of praise. She has felt the arrows of sexuality being crafted inside her, a secret quiver. At last a lover arrives, his heart a target; he praises her supple, bowlike body, and he begs her to let fly.

Why do we need a duvet cover for the warm, rich, feather comforter of sensuality? Why hide it beneath artifice? Why try to purify it? Why turn it into a ceremonial stalking dance? What's wrong with good, old-fashioned, common or garden lust? Why does it embarrass and shame us? For one thing, lust can lead to love, and love is a conspiracy of two that often results in treason. When people fall in love, they break the tight bonds of kinship and leave their families to found a new family with its own bonds, its own values, its own country and kin. "I'm not losing a daughter, I'm gaining a son," a father often says with a buoyancy too automatic to be believed. He knows only too well that he *is* losing a daughter, who will relegate him to the category of fond friend, who will stop obeying him, and in whose life he will no longer be paramount.

Even if all that weren't true, love games would still appeal to us because they test our wits, and remind us of childhood. In fact, they're the principal way adults play. Humans love sports—pitting their strength, nerve, and cunning alongside a teammate or against an opponent on a field of glory, in the hope of winning and being rewarded. Love is a demanding sport involving all the muscle groups, including the brain. The goal of love games is intense physical pleasure, and its special challenge is that the rules are always changing, there is plenty of misdirection, the goal sometimes disappears behind a fog of guilt or misgiving, other players (such as in-laws or rivals) can unexpectedly appear on the field, one's advantage can reverse at a moment's notice, and power often changes hands before the game is finished. What is chess, polo, baseball, or war compared to that?

In this tournament of wills, complete with armor and jousting, control is the wager and the damsel in distress is one's self-esteem. The wilder children of Romanticism—Rousseau, Byron, Shelley, Goethe, and others—mastered and adored it, but they were the exceptions who defined the movement. Two lowercase casanovas, Byron and Shelley, fueled the literary hearts of the nineteenth century, professing free love and utter availability to whim, to the moment, and to one's unique response to life. But a large, powerful middle class had already begun making up its mind about life's important issues—religion, economics, morals, and even what and how to feel. Women were supposed to be delicate, modest, and susceptible to shock. Romantic lovers fell tempestuously in love, indeed they spoke of love in terms of torrents and gushings and floods. (There's so much liquid moving around in Romantic poems it's a wonder the games weren't called on account of rain.) But their love claimed to be nonsexual, chaste, and true. How else could it be, when nice girls were supposed to be pure, sweet, nurturing, and frail? How could they possibly defile such motherly creatures? Women no longer came with large dowries and inherited lands. And while, for women of a certain economic class, industrialism freed them from traditional labors—teaching the children, making clothes, cooking, and baking—it also made them utterly dependent on their husbands. It wasn't seemly for the middle-class wife to go out, to socialize, volunteer, or attend school. If a wife didn't need to work, and she didn't bring wealth with her, what role did she fill? Mainly a child bearer and symbol, she fitted a romanticized ideal that no one could live up to, just as medieval ladies couldn't live up to their knights' ideals. Women were to stay at home and tend the children; men returned home after work and spent time with them and the children. All the important decisions affecting the family were made by the man, the lord of the manor, whose home, modest though it might have been, was his castle. When romantic love sifted through the new dreams of the middle class, it became domesticated, simplified, tidy, sexless.

The Victorians found peace in worshiping the family itself as a living idyll, and looking to the home as a realm of freedom and stability. In that sacred state, it fell to women to be the civilizing force in the family, instilling morals, guarding the good, and encouraging spirituality. This honor was also a terrible burden. Statues to morality dare not bend. How could any woman live up to the perfection required of someone who was dispensing a moral education? Prudery reached an all-time high, because paragons of virtue could not utter or be exposed in any way to indecency. Courtly love had included the cult of the queen, and Queen Victoria herself, a prim matron, fitted the bill nicely. She became its symbol.

Calling a fig a fig was thought to traumatize a woman, so candid words were replaced by euphemisms. At dinner, a woman would be offered the "bosom" of the chicken. If she rode horseback, it had to be sidesaddle, because she dare not hold anything so lusty as a horse between her legs. Noah Webster, who canonized the American vocabulary by compiling its first dictionary, was a terrible prude and a religious fanatic who worried a great deal about delicacy. He altered offensive words, changing "testicles" to "peculiar members," for instance. Under the entry for love, the example of usage he gives is solely religious. There are many legends about Webster, but my favorite recalls the moment when his wife caught him kissing the chambermaid. "Why, Noah, I'm surprised!" she is supposed to have said. To which he replied, like the bona-fide schoolmaster he was, "Madame, *you* are astonished; *I* am surprised."

A woman visiting a doctor's office might use a doll to show the place where she felt pain. During childbirth, a doctor worked blind, his hands underneath a sheet, lest he see the woman's genitals. Since the avenues of love and evacuation are so close together, the whole area became taboo. Filth in every sense—moral and literal—was disgusting and had to be scrubbed out of the home, the body, and one's life. Romanticism had idealized women as benevolent, chaste mother figures. That made sex with them incestuous, wicked, and dirty. Any woman who tried the spirited flirtations of the eighteenth century was thought a trollop. A woman could only wait for a man to notice her, and then she could only accept him or refuse him.

Havelock Ellis, a sex researcher of the time, reported instances of couples married for years who had never seen each other naked. A wife's role as a sex partner was to lie still, act helpless, and be unaroused, while her husband performed his bestial act. In fact, many people, including doctors, claimed that women simply didn't feel sexual pleasure. To enjoy sex with a willing and enthusiastic partner, one who was allowed to act that way, a man had to visit a brothel. So it comes as no surprise that prostitution and pornography flourished during the Victorian era, as did masochism, perversion, and venereal disease. Richard von Krafft-Ebing, an Austrian psychiatrist and forensic doctor, first described masochism in his *Psychopathia Sexualis* (1886), naming it after a contemporary fellow-Austrian, Leopold von Sacher-Masoch, who wrote novels about men who liked harsh, dominating women to humiliate and physically hurt them (preferably while wearing leather or fur). In this classic scene from Sacher-Masoch's short story "Venus in Furs," the cruel but sophisticated Wanda ties up her lover Severin and then stands menacingly in front of him:

> The beautiful woman bent on her adorer a strange look from her green eyes, icy and devouring, then she crossed the room, slowly donned a splendid loose coat of red satin, richly trimmed with princely ermine, and took from her dressing table a whip, a long thong attached to a short handle, with which she was wont to punish her great mastiff. "You want it," she said. "Then I will whip you." Still on his knees, "Whip me," cried her lover. "I implore you!"

The idea of the femme fatale, the woman who wielded pain and gave the man a dose of guilt, the "beauty fresh from hell," as Swinburne put it with relish, contrasted appealingly with the submissive woman at home, the monument to sacred motherhood. Commenting on the guilt-clad morals of the time, Gustave Flaubert quipped: "A man has missed something if he has never woken up in an anonymous bed beside a face he'll never see again, and if he has never left a brothel at dawn feeling like jumping off a bridge into the river out of sheer physical disgust with life."

We use the word *puritanical* to describe a repressive attitude about love and sensuality. But it was the Victorians rather than the Puritans who dressed women in the fashion equivalent of a straitjacket and hushed up lovers' sighs. Their fiction of "the happy family," where Father rules and a grateful mother is the lady of the house, was a social ideal picked up later by the film industry and handed whole to the twentieth century.

Paradoxically, just when the moralists were adding castor oil to the tonic of marriage, militant women were fighting for the right to be equal at work, at home, and in bed. They wanted to dress comfortably, play at sports as men did, educate themselves, and do meaningful work. Marriages were little but sepia halftones. Freud, Havelock-Ellis, Balzac, Flaubert, and others recorded lives of quiet desperation, but their own lives weren't free of neuroses and marital mayhem. Despite their singular open-mindedness, I doubt they would have guessed the extent to which love and sex would fascinate and obsess the twentieth century. From our current turn-of-the-century perspective—which now includes Masters and Johnson, psychoanalytic theory, and the goals of the women's movement—this kind of obsession all seems normal, even traditional, since it's what many of our parents experienced as well. Birth control, the mass media, a growing respect for women, a greater separation between the religious and secular worlds, the sexual revolution, and biological nightmares such as AIDS have all reshaped our moral world. It may happen now that we marry for love, but for many centuries people didn't find that necessary; new generations may not find it possible. Other eras had other matters on their minds—salvation, honor, inheritance, knowledge, war, a plunging birthrate. We treasure love. It quenches, vexes, guides, and murders us. It seeps into the mortar of all our days. It feeds our passions, it fills our fantasies, it inspires our art. What will future eras make of this?

MODERN LOVE

When I think about the essence of being modern, the changes in attitude that led to the life we now know, three things come to mind: choice, privacy, and books. As a child of the seventies, I find it almost impossible to fathom a time when people couldn't make choices in their lives—whimsical choices, let alone solemn ones. Personal freedom has a long, slow history, based in part on the growing size of the world's population, which gave people a chance to be anonymous. If they couldn't be exempt from the moral law, they could at least toy with exemption in private. Despite arranged marriages, people stole the freedom to love whom they chose, without shame; then to choose whom to marry; and in time they even made the shocking leap to wishing to marry someone they loved. As wealth and leisure grew, houses began to have specific rooms for specific uses, including a bedroom where couples could be unobserved. Soon, young marrieds wanted a place of their own, separate from their in-laws. They wanted to be "alone together," a new idea based on a newly won sense of privacy.

The invention of printing aided and abetted lovers. Once people became more literate, they could take a book with them to some quiet place and read to themselves and think. Reading changed society forever. Solitary contemplation began to emerge as commonplace, and readers could discover in romantic and erotic literature what was possible, or at least imaginable. They could dare controversial thoughts and feel bolstered by allies, without telling anyone. Books had to be kept somewhere, and with the library came the idea of secluded hours, alone with one's innermost thoughts. Lovers could blend their hearts by sharing sympathetic authors; what they could not express in person they could at least point to in the pages of a book. A shared book could speak to lovers in confidence, increasing their sense of intimacy even if the loved one was absent or a forbidden companion. Books opened the door to an aviary filled with flights of the imagination, winged fantasies of love; they gave readers a sense of emotional community. Somewhere in another city or state another soul was reading the same words, perhaps dreaming the same dream.

THE HEART IS
A LONELY HUNTER

IDEAS ABOUT
LOVE

PLATO: THE PERFECT UNION

Proust's *Remembrance of Things Past* begins with a child waiting in bed for his mother to come and give him a good-night kiss. Sensitive and lonely, he grows anxious and unhinged, and the rest of the novel (more the mosaic of a life than a work of fiction) chronicles his attempts to bridge the gap between himself and the rest of humanity. He could not feel more separate, isolated, and alone. The passage shows the eternal quest of the child, who must learn to be separate from his mother even while he longs to reunite with her. One of the keystones of romantic love—and also of the ecstatic religion practiced by mystics—is the powerful desire to become one with the beloved.

This vision of love has its wellsprings in ancient Greek thought. To Plato, lovers are incomplete halves of a single puzzle, searching for each other in order to become whole. They are a strength forged by two weaknesses. At some point, all lovers wish to lose themselves, to merge, to become one entity. By giving up their autonomy, they find their true selves. In a world ruled by myth, Plato tried to be rational, often using myths as allegories to make a point. His investigations of love in *The Symposium* are the oldest surviving attempts to systematically understand love. In *The Symposium,* he advises people to bridle their sexual urges, and also their need to give and receive love. They should concentrate all that energy on higher goals. He understood perfectly well that people would have to struggle hard to redirect such powerful instincts; it would produce much inner warfare. When, almost 3,000 years later, Freud talks of the same struggle, using words like "sublimation" and "resistance," he is harking back to Plato, for whom love was a great predicament and a riddle. This was no doubt in part because Plato was confused about his own sexual identity; as a younger man, he wrote in praise of homosexual love, and as an older man he condemned it as an unnatural crime.

At *The Symposium*'s banquet staged in honor of Eros, Socrates—who was a teacher and companion of Plato—and his friends exchange ideas about love. Actually, Socrates' job is to poke holes in everyone else's ideas. The banqueters are not present just to praise love, but to fathom it, to dive through its waves and plumb its depths. One of their first home truths is that love is a universal human need. Not just a mythic god, or a whim, or madness, but something integral to each person's life. When it is Aristophanes' turn, he relates a fable—one that has influenced people for thousands of years since. He explains that originally there were three sexes: men, women, and a hermaphroditic combination of man and woman. These primitive beings had two heads, two arms, two sets of genitals, and so on. Threatened by their potential power, Zeus divided each one of them in half, making individual lesbians, homosexual men, and heterosexuals. But each person longed for its missing half, which it sought out, tracked down, and embraced, so that it could become one again—and thereby Aristophanes arrives at an astonishing definition of love:

Each of us when separated, having one side only, like a flat fish, is but the indenture of a man, and he is always looking for his other half. . . . And when one of them meets with his other half, the actual half of himself, whether he be a lover of youth or a lover of another sort, the pair are lost in an amazement of love and friendship and intimacy, and will not be out of the other's sight, as I may say, even for a moment: these are the people who pass their whole lives together; yet they could not explain what they desire of one another. For the intense yearning which each of them has towards the other does not appear to be the desire of lover's intercourse, but of something else which the soul of either evidently desires and cannot tell, and of which she has only a dark and doubtful presentiment.

Suppose Hephaestus, with his instruments, were to come to the pair who are lying side by side and say to them, "What do you people want of one another?" They would be unable to explain. And suppose further, that when he saw their perplexity he said, "Do you desire to be wholly one; always day and night to be in one another's company, for if this is what you desire, I am ready to melt you into one and let you grow together . . ." There is not a man of them who when he heard the proposal would deny or would acknowledge that this meeting and melting into one another, this becoming one instead of two, was the very expression of his ancient need. And the reason is that human nature was originally one and we were a whole, and the desire and pursuit of the whole is called love.

It is an amazing fable, saying, in effect, that each person has an ideal love waiting somewhere to be found. Not "There's a lid for every pot," as my mother has sometimes said, but that each of us has a one-and-only, and finding that person makes us whole. This romantic ideal of the perfect partner was invented by Plato. It appealed so strongly to hearts and minds that people believed it in all the following centuries, and many still believe it today. As Freud discovered, Plato took his fable from India, where some gods were bisexual. Indeed, the original human in the Upanishads is as lonely as Adam in the Bible, and like Adam he asks for company and is pleased when a female is made from his own body. In each case, all the people of the earth are born from their union. Evolutionary biologists tell us that our ultimate ancestor almost certainly was hermaphroditic, and something about that news feels right, not just in our reason but in the part of us that yearns for the other. John Donne wrote magnificently about this passion for oneness, which takes on a special piquancy in his poem "The Flea." One day, sweetly loitering with his mistress, he notices a flea sucking a little blood from her arm and then from his. Joyously, he observes that their blood is married inside the flea.

Why should the idea of oneness be so compelling? Love changes all the physics in the known universe of one's emotions, and redraws the boundaries between what is real and what is possible. Children often believe in magic and miracles, and when they grow up they naturally believe in the miraculous power of love. Sometimes this is depicted in myths or legends by having the lovers drink a love potion, as Tristan and Isolde do; be stung by Cupid's arrows; be enchanted by music as Eurydice is; or receive a reviving kiss à la Sleeping Beauty.

In many eastern and western religions, the supplicants strive for a sense of unity with God. Although this is not supposed to be an erotic coupling, saints often describe it as if it were, dwelling in orgasmic detail on the sensuality of Christ's body. Religious ecstasy and the ecstasy of lovers have much in common—the sudden awareness, the taking of vows, the plighting of troths, the all-consuming fire in the heart and flesh, the rituals leading to bliss, and, for some Christians, a cannibalistic union with the godhead by symbolically drinking his blood and eating his flesh. Whether we fall in love with a human demigod or with a deity, we feel that they can return us to a primordial state of oneness, that then our inner electric can run its full circuit, that we can at last be whole.

How bizarre it is to wish to blend blood and bones with someone. People cannot actually literally become one, of course; it's a physical impossibility. The idea is preposterous. We are separate organisms. Unless we are Siamese twins, we are not merged with another. Why should we feel incomplete, anyway? Why believe that uniting our body and thoughts and fate with another person's will cure our sense of loneliness? Wouldn't it make more sense to believe that when love brings two people together they are a community of two, not a compound of one? The idea of merging is so irrational, so contrary to common sense and observation, that its roots must strike deep into our psyche. Because a child is born of a mother, and lives as a separate entity, we think of the child as an individual. But in biological terms that is not precisely true. The child is an organic part of the mother that is expelled at birth, but it shares much of her biology, personality, even scent. The only and absolute perfect union of two is when a baby hangs suspended in its mother's womb, like a tiny madman in a padded cell, attached to her, feeling her blood and hormones and moods play through its body, feeling her feelings. After that perfect, pendent, dependent union, birth is an amputation, and the child like a limb looking to attach itself to the rest of its body. I am not saying this consciously occurs to anyone, but that it may explain the osmotic yearning we all feel, at one time or another, to blend our heart and body and fluids with someone else's. Only the thinnest rind of skin stands between us, only events slender as neurons. Only the fermenting mash of personality keeps us from crossing the boundary that organisms cherish to become one appetite, one struggle, one destiny. Then, when we finally reach that pinnacle, we feel more than whole: we feel limitless.

STENDHAL MEETS THE DEEP SOUTH

A special irony in the history of mind and heart is that wise people don't always act wisely in their own lives. Novelists, blessed with insight about the psychology of their characters, may not be equally intuitive with friends, or with themselves. Lofty thinkers often become petty and obsessive when they're at home. Even charismatic and inspiring world leaders sometimes secretly suffer from depression, or enjoy being degraded and dominated in the boudoir. We credit famous people with unwavering moods, good character, and a lifestyle defined by their genius. The usual truth—that they are as human, insecure, and neurotic as the rest of us—always comes as a shock, which public opinion rarely forgives. To my mind, it doesn't matter that Freud was part of a ménage à trois, or that Havelock Ellis liked women to pee during sex, or that Churchill used to get down on all fours, pad over to his wife's bedroom door, and meow like a tomcat. But I may be unusual in this. Most people expect their heroes to be flawless. I feel greatness is something that otherwise normal people rise to. Although their genius separates them from the rest of humanity, only their genius is different. Indeed, they may well have devised an intricate web of coping mechanisms to deal with that genius. We forget that highly attuned people are also highly sensitive to slight, self-doubt, and rejection.

Marie Henri Beyle (Stendhal) was just such an artist. Insightful as he was about human nature in his novels, in real life he plunged deeper and deeper in love with a woman who just toyed with him. Her rejection was a constant knife wound. And yet he couldn't break his obsession. Mathilde Viscontini Dembowski was, at twenty-eight, a beautiful Milanese mother of two, who had separated from her Polish husband, and was active in Italian revolutionary politics. In 1818, Stendhal fell vertiginously in love. She never returned his feelings, or understood him. During the winter of his discontent, she grew colder and colder; even rationing him to one short visit every two weeks. She didn't refuse him entirely; she saw him just often enough to keep his hopes alive. Her power over him must have excited her beyond measure. In time, Stendhal fled to England to avoid arrest, and Mathilde died at the age of thirty-five. He wrote about her longingly for the rest of his life, and during her lifetime went to extraordinary lengths to deal with his ill-favored love for her.

In his famous book *On Love* (*De l'Amour*), Stendhal used a code name for Mathilde, and attributed to other men what in fact had happened to him. Not even his friends knew that he was writing about himself, or that he was limbering up his heart and focusing his creative energies in an effort to win Mathilde's esteem. Perhaps he also felt that by analyzing his passion, by trying to understand the nature of love, he might be able to break its stranglehold. Before you can exorcise demons you must name them.

He begins the book by explaining that there are four kinds of love: "Mannered Love," "Physical Love," "Vanity-Love," and, the highest of all, "Passionate Love"—a romantic, all-consuming, death-defying feeling that doesn't need to be returned. This was a state Stendhal knew only too well. Mathilde kept him so off balance that, on the rare occasions they were together, he felt too much pressure to be charming. As a result, he would as often as not become clumsy and tongue-tied, or gabble ridiculously, or say something tactless. He must have seemed pathetic to her. His desire for her was hopeless, even mortifying at times, fed by the illusion that somehow she would ultimately return his love. One November day in 1819, he decided to reveal himself to her in a poised, artful way—as he never could do in person. He would write a novel called *Métilde*. A few weeks later, he hatched a different idea, something bolder, to write a "physiology of love" which would speak on several levels. To the general reader, it would be a profound work of intuitive perception; to Mathilde, it would be a personal appeal. In it, he calls her Léonore, and refers to himself as "a young man of my acquaintance," but she would recognize both of them, since he quotes her word for word and refers to events in her life. So, although millions of readers have turned to the book for general truths about love, and found it illuminating, it was written about one tormented man's unfulfilled love for one woman.

Mary Shelley's *Frankenstein* had been published the year before, and there was something of that sensitive, underestimated freak in Stendhal, who lived on the outskirts of Mathilde's bungalow and would stare longingly through the window at her cheerful hearth, knowing that he was repugnant in her eyes.

Stendhal is also reminiscent of a character in Carson McCullers's *The Heart Is a Lonely Hunter*. McCullers was only twenty-four when she wrote her novel filled with lonely hearts. The main character, Mr. Singer, though deaf and dumb, is loud with love he can't make anyone hear. The adolescent heroine, Mick, is desperate for acceptance from her peers, but feels isolated. Everyone in the novel hunts for love in one form or another—stalking it, misfiring at it, sitting quietly in wait behind a carefully constructed blind. Some fire at shadows. Some have infallible aim. But most are like planets in orbit around others—bound together by the gravity of the human condition, trailing in one another's wake, but doomed never to touch. Many of the characters are invalids or handicapped in some way, as McCullers herself would become five years later, when, at twenty-nine, muscular dystrophy imprisoned her in a wheelchair, where she would remain until she died at the age of fifty. She was relegated to the bleachers for most of her life, watching the able-bodied on the field of play. It made her especially sensitive to hidden infirmities. Her characters are consumed by their own private cancers, or severed from life. None can see the suffering of the other. Each is on a lonely trajectory through life, which they long to share, long to explain, but they can find no one with whom to connect. Mr. Singer appears the sanest, yet is the most alienated because he cannot even speak with other humans. He is like a trapeze artist swinging out over an abyss; ultimately he gives up hope of finding another pair of hands waiting to catch him, and he just lets go. Stendhal would have felt right at home in this circus of high-wire loneliness and lovesickness.

His investigation of love is a small anatomy of obsession. He talks about the paralyzing shyness one feels in the presence of the beloved; how important it is to act naturally—but also how difficult; the way the beloved's kind words can render one speechless; how the alternating current of hope and despair can fry one's nerves; the way the most trivial gesture or word can devastate a lover one moment and cause bliss the next; how music can convey the wordless depths of love; love's power to whitewash the true nature of the beloved; and the pitilessness of self-doubt and self-consciousness that savage one's heart. Ever the taxonomist, he describes seven stages of falling in love: First one admires. Then one hopes the feeling will be returned. When hope combines with admiration, love is born, and the senses awaken to the joy of touching, seeing, talking with the beloved. The next stage includes one of his key ideas, what he terms "crystallization," the tendency for someone in love to idealize the beloved, imagining him or her to be finer and nobler than any other human being. It is "a mental process which draws from everything that happens new proofs of the perfection of the loved one." He labels it crystallization because it reminds him of the way crystals form on twigs in the salt mines. The miners throw a bare bough into an abandoned shaft and when they pull it out two or three months later they find it encrusted with glittering salt crystals. "The smallest twig, no bigger than a tom-tit's claw, is studded with a galaxy of scintillating diamonds. The original branch is no longer recognizable." After crystallization, doubt creeps in, and dreadful misgiving, as the lover demands proof after proof of affection. (Men and women doubt different things, he explains. The man doubts if he can attract the woman and cause her really to love him. The woman doubts the man's sincerity and reliability; perhaps he is just interested in sex and will quickly desert her.) When doubt is overcome, "the second crystallization" occurs, with the mind imagining every act as a proof of love. At this stage, the opposite of being in love is death. If the idealized person should leave, the mournful lover assumes it was his fault, and that, through his own bungling, happiness is lost forever. There is no consolation. Depression deadens every light thought. The mind can no longer attach the idea of pleasure to any pleasurable activity. Stendhal writes: "This is the optical illusion which leads to the fatal pistol shot."

Stendhal also details the role played by the involuntary memory.

An object or sensation can unexpectedly remind one powerfully of the beloved. The reason for this, he argues, is that when you are with a lover you are too focused and wrought up to notice the world around you; instead all you are aware of are sensations. At a later time, encountering an object you'd forgotten was relevant, you relive the sensations. Pretending to be reading from a friend's diary, a man for whom "passion was the first real course in logic he had ever taken," he relates his own torment:

> Love has reduced me to a condition of misery and despair, and I curse my very existence. I can take no interest in anything. . . . Every print on the wall, every stick of furniture, reproaches me for the happiness I dreamed of in this room, and which is now lost for ever.
>
> I strode through the streets under a cold rain; chance, if you can call it chance, led me past her windows. Night was falling, and as I walked by, my tear-filled eyes fixed upon the window of her room. Suddenly the curtain was lifted for a moment, as if for a glimpse of the square outside, and then it quickly fell back into place. I felt a spasm at my heart. I could no longer hold myself up, and took refuge in a neighboring portico. My feelings were running riot; it might of course have been a chance movement of the curtain; but suppose it had been her hand that lifted it!
>
> There are only two miseries in life; the misery of the unrequited passion, and that of the DEAD BLANK.
>
> In love, I have the feeling that boundless happiness beyond my wildest dreams is just round the corner, waiting only for a word or a smile.
>
> Without a passion . . . I can find no happiness anywhere, and begin to doubt whether it is in store for me at all. . . .

Growing sour, he laments that it would be better if he had been born without passion, merely possessing a mild heart in calm weather. But like a dog circling and circling before it can peacefully lie down, he returns again and again to the addictive, replenishing power of love, which gives to life a "mysterious and sacred glow." As he leaves his "friend's" diary, he continues on with his treatise, inventing such wise adages as: *Sixteen is an age which thirsts for love and is not excessively particular about what beverage chance may provide.* Or:

A long siege humiliates a man, but ennobles a woman. Or: *Glances are the big guns of the virtuous coquette; everything can be conveyed in a look.* His psychological wisdom weathers well today. He understands, for instance, how the past molds our choice of a partner: "You have conceived an ideal without knowing it. One day you come across someone not unlike this ideal; crystallization . . . consecrates for ever to the master of your destiny what you have dreamt of for so long." He notes that "The loves of two people in love with each are seldom the same. Passionate love has its phases, when first one partner and then the other will be more in love." Some people, "loving on credit," as he puts it, "will hurl themselves upon the experience instead of waiting for it to happen." Women didn't have much control in his society, and he writes, from personal experience: "A woman's power lies only in the degree of unhappiness with which she can punish her lover."

For Stendhal, the essence of love is fantasy. We fall in love with gods and goddesses of our devising. We never see them clearly. We never know the forces that drove us to them, but we are predisposed to love them. Indeed, one's choice of lover is formed by the early experiences of one's life, and it is but a matter of time before one meets someone who fits the preexisting mold.

Fear, too, is crucial to love. Certainty, familiarity, complacency—they all lead to pleasant relationships of companionship and goodwill, but not to the feverish adventure of being in love. Unlike many later thinkers, who describe love as an emotional event that takes place between two people, Stendhal argues that love is a solitary feeling, which exists whether it is returned or not. An ardent feminist, Stendhal didn't condemn all women for Mathilde's cruelty, or even blame her overmuch. It was his own fault that she didn't love him. Yet he didn't regret the mad catastrophe of his feelings. Even in its unrequited form, love rewarded him with ambition, imagination, and vigor. It gave a sense of enterprise to each day, filling his daydreams with beauty and hiding his worst nightmares behind a veil of possibility.

DENIS DE ROUGEMONT:
LOVE AND MAGIC

On this cold November morning, the snow is blowing sideways in a hard white artillery, and ice-jacketed trees have begun rocking back and forth like keening women. The winds drop. Slow-motion flakes fall silently and knit together on the lawn. Suddenly the winds blast up a frenzy, and a great commotion of snow funnels fast into the sky.

All that power, euphoria, frailty, and destruction fits with the music surging through my study: Wagner's *Tristan und Isolde*. A pure, white-hot tempest of sensuality that is prolonged, savored, and explored, the music recreates the physical passion of a love so fierce that it exalts its lovers only to destroy them. The cellos moan with longing; the oboes yowl with desire. Now restless, now ecstatic, voluptuous and tense, the prelude begins in gloom, reaches a feverish crescendo and climax, and then unravels itself utterly, ending with a whisper. From that emotional summary, the opera unfolds an ancient tale of love and death:

Long ago, in the days that troubadours sing of, the Beautiful Maiden Blanchefleur fell in love with a Brave Handsome Knight who, in time and after many obstacles, she married. He was summoned to battle and killed while she was pregnant. The shock was so great that Blanchefleur fell desperately ill. She lived long enough to name her newborn son Tristan, or "Sadness," and after her death the orphan was adopted by Blanchefleur's brother, King Mark of Cornwall, who took him to live at Tintagel castle. The boy grew up heroically, and at puberty, the age of knighthood, he performed the required acts of bravery. He killed the Morholt, for example, a monstrous Irish giant. But in the process the Morholt wounded Tristan with a poison barb and, thinking he would surely die, Tristan asked to be set afloat with his sword and harp. In a small boat with neither sail nor oar, he drifted for some while and at last drew near the coast of Ireland. This was doubly good fortune because the queen of Ireland, as well as her daughter Iseult the Fair, possessed powers of healing, and they had a remedy to save him. He went to them straightaway and told his tale, carefully concealing how he got his wound (because the Morholt was the queen's brother), and Iseult nursed him back to health.

Some years later, King Mark was standing at a castle window when a bird landed on the stone sill. It was carrying in its beak one beautiful golden hair that shone in the sunlight. King Mark was so enthralled that he decided then and there to marry the woman whose hair it was. Tristan was sent to find her. En route, a storm shipwrecked him once again in Ireland, where he vanquished a dragon that had been plaguing the locals, and again his wounds were nursed by Iseult. But this time she learned the truth about his past, and when she realized that he had slain her Uncle Morholt, she grabbed a sword and went to kill him in his bath. Tristan leapt to his feet, Iseult saw him in all his naked glory and was impressed, Tristan explained the mission that King Mark had sent him on, Iseult said that she was the very woman he sought and that she would indeed like to be queen, and with one thing and another she put down her sword and spared him.

The pair set off at once for Cornwall, but at sea the doldrums hit, the air felt loose and hot, and they asked Iseult's maid for a drink. Rummaging around in a nearby cabin, the maid grabbed a small flask of wine from one of her mistress's bags and poured an equal measure for both. What she didn't realize was that the flask contained a powerful love potion made from grasses and herbs, which the queen had brewed as a surefire wedding-night gift for Iseult and Mark. Thirsty and unaware, Tristan and Iseult drank the potion, and then reacted very strangely: they sat bolt upright and stared rivers of fire into each other's eyes. From that moment on, their destiny was fixed and inescapable, for they had "drunk their destruction and death." According to the original version of the myth, the love potion had an expiration date of three years, but for the time being they were absolutely joined by love, inseparable at heart, soul, and flesh.

Despite this obvious and catastrophic betrayal, Tristan was still a knight, with knightly codes of conduct to follow, and thus duty bound to complete his mission and bring Iseult to King Mark, which is what he did. On the wedding night, Iseult's maid, under cover of darkness, crept into the royal bedroom and secretly consummated the marriage in Iseult's place. Apparently, King Mark didn't detect any significant difference in body type, or look too closely at her face, or talk much during lovemaking. The following day, the king's barons reported that Tristan and Iseult had been lovers. Although the king banished Tristan, the lovers continued to meet on the sly, and through a series of colorful escapades and tests King Mark became only too aware of their continuing adultery. At that point, he sentenced Tristan to die at the stake and handed Iseult over to a mob of lepers. En route to his execution, Tristan managed to escape, then he rescued Iseult, and they ran away to hide in the forests. This might have been bliss, a green thought in a green shade, but the myth specifically characterizes their life together as "harsh and hard." One day, King Mark found them sleeping, with Tristan's drawn sword lying between them. The king was so moved by their apparent chastity that he forgave them, left his own sword in place of Tristan's as a sign, and crept away.

After three years, the love potion wore off, and suddenly the lovers began to feel guilty and to have second thoughts. Tristan said he missed the excitement of court life; Iseult missed being queen. First visiting an ogre, then enduring magic rituals and ordeals, and at last lying preposterously to both the king and God (Iseult swore that she had never been held in anyone else's arms except those of the king and the peasant lad who just carried her ashore—however, the peasant was Tristan in disguise), the couple ingratiated themselves back into the good books of gullible King Mark.

Reinstated as a knight, Tristan set out again on adventures, some of which carried him a great distance from Tintagel. Alone for some while, he missed the company of women, and missed in particular Iseult the Fair, whom he concluded was happy at home and didn't love him anymore. In a moment of nostalgia, he married a beautiful woman with Iseult's name—"Iseult of the White Hands"—but, out of loyalty to the original Iseult, could not bring himself to consummate the marriage. The rigors of battle finally took their toll, and one day, wounded by a spear and about to die, he sent word for Queen Iseult to hurry to him with her medicines and save his life. She set out at once, sending a messenger to Tristan saying the ship carrying her would bear a white sail. But Tristan's wife, Iseult of the White Hands, saw the ship arriving with her rival and, consumed by jealousy, told Tristan the sail was black as doom. Tristan died as Iseult the Fair landed. Rushing to the castle and finding him dead, Iseult was so tormented by grief that she fell down next to her lover and died beside him.

Fatal love is the oldest theme in song and legend. As Denis de

Rougemont points out in his classic study of the Tristan myth, *Love in the Western World,* poets seldom sing about happy, tune-whistling, untroubled love. History doesn't bother recording eternally happy lovers. "Romance only comes into existence where love is fatal, frowned upon, and doomed . . . not the fruitful contentment of the settled couple; not the satisfaction of love, but its *passion*. And passion means suffering." Passion is something we dream about, want for our children, cheer in others, admire as a blinding bright jewel of emotion, secretly long for. Every person needs passion, a song by Rod Stewart tells us, listing some of the people who do, from farmers to diplomats, saints to thieves. "Even the president needs passion." But, as de Rougemont rightly points out, passion by definition includes suffering. It is in essence a calamity. Then why do we prize it? Because caring and suffering make us feel more alive, they give us a frisson, a jolt. Passion whips us into a frenzy of feeling so intense we crave it, even though it pains us. Passionate love elevates, but it also afflicts us, and for that carnal thrill—feeling all of our senses on red alert, the sun always at noon, each hour a small forever—we would gladly suffer.

The Tristan myth swelled up like water from the ground of public morality. Many hands shaped it, many voices uttered it. Myths tend to be cautionary tales about the rules of conduct one is expected to follow in society, but they also express taboo thoughts and a people's secret fears. This myth reflected the concerns of twelfth-century Europe, when people were trying to grapple with moral contradictions and hard truths. On the one hand, the codes of chivalry said that strength rules, and also that a knight must first and foremost serve his lady as her vassal. Accordingly, no one would have faulted Tristan, who was much braver and stronger than King Mark, from running away, with Iseult as his prize. On the other hand, the codes of feudal society ordained that he obey his lord as a vassal. So Tristan returned Iseult to his king. There are many kinds of allegiance and devotion. Whom should one be true to, the myth asks, when faced with different and conflicting forms of duty?

Once Tristan and Iseult drank the love potion, they lost their free will and were prey to nature, which gave them the right to be smitten and run off together. But the ideals of courtly love are based on flirtation, romance, and longing. The knight is not supposed to actually possess his lady. In fact when the lovers go to see a powerful ogre in the forest, they claim they're in love because of the potion, but that in truth they don't even like each other! Love happened to them against their will, when they weren't looking, without being their fault. It was a double abduction. Something magical happened that hurled them outside the realm of guilt or sin, good or evil, above morality, into a kingdom of two, with its own edicts and physical laws.

There, in exquisite anguish, they both rule and serve, not because they are in love, but because they are in love with love. As de Rougemont astutely observes, "Their need of one another is in order to be aflame, and they do not need one another as they are. What they need is not one another's presence, but one another's absence." That's why there are so many obstructions in the story. When finally together, living as a married couple in the forest, with one day like the next, they become bored with life and bored with each other. De Rougemont argues that the need for obstruction is what this myth is all about; it is what is *required* to feel intense passion. The lovers "are seeking peril for its own sake. But so long as the peril comes from without, Tristan's prowess in overcoming it is an affirmation of life." That is why, when they're living together in the forest, he puts a drawn sword between them as they sleep, to add a little cozy peril of his own.

De Rougemont notes that three years is about as long as ardent but unthwarted love can last, which is why the love potion's expiration date was well chosen. After that, couples develop a different, quieter form of companionable love. For the love to stay tantalizingly hot, it has to be fueled with new perils.

In addition, de Rougemont says, the Tristan myth conceals a dreadful, secret, shameful yearning in all of us, something so awful we cannot utter it except as a sort of emotional hieroglyph. So we talk symbolically about ancient lovers in a distant time. The truth we cannot speak is that we long for death.

> Magic comes in because the passion which has to be depicted has a fascinating violence not to be accepted without qualms. . . . The Church proscribes it as sinful, and common sense looks upon it as a morbid excess. It is thus not open to admiration till it has been

freed from every kind of visible connexion with human responsibility. That is why it was indispensable to bring in the love-potion, which acts willy-nilly, and—better still—is drunk by mistake.

The love-potion is an *alibi* for passion. It enables each of the two unhappy lovers to say: "You see, I am not in the least to blame; you see, it's more than I can help." Yet thanks to this deceptive necessity, everything they do is directed towards the *fatal fulfillment* [italics added] they are in love with, and they can approach this fulfillment with a kind of crafty determination and a cunning the more unerring for not being open to moral judgement. . . . Who would dare admit that he seeks Death . . . that what he longs for with all his being is the annihilation of his being.

Only in death do we stop posing, struggling, and resisting, only then do we cast off the impediment of reason, the mind games of politics and religion, all the human frets and bothers, and become part of life at its essence, its most organic. In that ultimate state, where even the power of love evaporates, the senses reach heights of glory as they die. Paradoxically, it is in that moment of annihilation that we become most open to life. Dylan Thomas has a beautiful sonnet on this theme:

> When all my five and country senses see,
> The fingers will forget green thumbs and mark
> How, through the halfmoon's vegetable eye,
> Husk of young stars and handfull zodiac,
> Love in the frost is pared and wintered by,
> The whispering ears will watch love drummed away
> Down breeze and shell to a discordant beach,
> And, lashed to syllables, the lynx tongue cry
> That her fond wounds are mended bitterly.
> My nostrils see her breath burn like a bush.
>
> My one and noble heart has witnesses
> In all love's countries, that will grope awake;
> And when blind sleep drops on the spying senses,
> The heart is sensual, though five eyes break.

Passionate love means giving up the notion of free will and ceding one's sunlit life to the powers of darkness. As de Rougemont reminds us, it means secretly cherishing hardship, welcoming death as a possibility, and mining pain and suffering for a special lode of deeply erotic satisfaction:

> To love love more than the object of love, to love passion for its own sake, has been to suffer and to court suffering. . . . Passionate love, the longing for what sears and annihilates us in its triumph—there is the secret which Europe . . . has always repressed.

Despite its tragic, even lugubrious, plot, in which everything goes wrong, and the lovers die in misery, the Tristan myth has been wildly successful through the ages. The ancients, the nineteenth-century Romantics, and we at the turn of the twentieth century all swoon over the beautiful melodies created by their passion. We like unhappy stories. We find it organically right that the lovers die. Why are passion and death so closely connected? Because we become most alive, most aware, on the brink of death—and we find that erotic. "The approach of death acts as a goad to sensuality," de Rougemont writes. "In the full sense of the verb, it aggravates desire."

Few things are as heady as an ordeal survived. The mind paints the sensory memory with lavish details, caressing each obstacle, savoring the mix of panic, hope, and dread. In crisis, emotions don't replace one another, but exist side by side like the notes in a musical chord. *Come alive!* the brain instructs the terror-stricken body. When the calculations of defeat suddenly begin presenting themselves one by one, as hard evidence, every jot and iota matters. The color of the heaving swells, the burn of the rope running through one's fingers—any part of it may figure in survival's final frantic arithmetic. Questing for detail, the mind shifts to a state of heightened sensitivity in which the air becomes savory and sound is a forest. It is a kind of rapture to feel so alive, regardless of what prompted the awakening.

Even afterward, having survived, the mind remembers the ordeal almost lovingly, with obsessive delicacy, relish, and pinpoint awareness. That theme of *here's what it felt like when I nearly died,* restaged in slow, horrific detail, has fed many works of art, from the Tristan myth to *The Tempest* to *Moby-Dick*. There is something about the sea that lends itself especially well to such accounts, maybe because the sea's dark coma reminds us so much of the unconscious mind, a shadow world where irrationality lurks and motives are hidden.

When Tristan was campaigning, something about all those years' worth of vivid sensory memories, left behind on a distant island, as if they were dreams he knew he had had but couldn't quite remember, disturbed him viscerally. The loss was too great. He became obsessed all over again with his love for Iseult. Can one excavate the past? Is it possible to become reacquainted with our forgotten selves? At what point should one allow them to be castaways? Never, if what we really seek is not a person but a state of the most intense excitement, receptivity, and awareness. Even if it means death. As poet Wallace Stevens writes, "The pensive man . . . He sees that eagle float/For which the entire Alps are a single nest." Without hurdles, the mind doesn't take wing, and there can be no flights of passion. One of the best avenues to passion is adultery, whose timeless appeal shines in the ancient myth of Tristan and Iseult and other tales of forbidden love. We know the delicious bonfire that a dangerous love affair can ignite, and we long for that steep arousal. When we hear the Tristan myth, we dream the lover's dream, crave the lover's fire. We long to be every player in that violently thrilling hunt—the tracker, the wild animal, and the hunter—because we know it would take a drama that electrifying to drive the partridges of passion up into the open air and set the pulse running and dodging like a rabbit. Then we could use ourselves in every pore and cell, feel breathtakingly alive, be rocketed right out of our skins and hurled into a state of supernatural glory, where we feel as lusty and powerful as gods.

MARCEL PROUST AND THE EROTICS OF WAITING

To wait. To feel her ribs pressing against the walls of the chest and a hollow ache, as of someone knocking, in the vault of the stomach. The minute hand of her watch seems frozen. All of life's processes stop; there is no birdsong or car engine. The world grows slack. Silence reigns. Yet her pulse is leaping like a frightened stag. She sits at the window, searching every movement on the street below, atomizing each face for the resemblance of her beloved. A flash of light hair sends her into ripples of delight, then disappointment, as she realizes it belongs to a stranger. A moss-green raincoat turns the corner—at last!—but no, it is only a businessman stopping by the bakery on his way home from work. Time after time, her senses signal and then betray her. By midmorning, when her lover finally arrives, she is exhausted from the sheer strain of anticipation. An old Chinese proverb warns: you should not confuse the sound of your heartbeat for the hooves of approaching horses.

A teenage girl, sitting beside a telephone, her back stiff with worry, her fingers twisting a strand of hair, nervously waits. A Victorian girl, doing embroidery or crochet of the most laborious kind—intricate eyelets and laces on napkins, pillowcases, petticoats, doilies, afghans, and nightgowns—passively waits. In theory, she is assembling items for her "hope chest," but the real purpose is to fill the vacant hours of adolescence with busy work while she waits for the real work of love to begin. A contemporary woman hanging out in singles bars, placing romantic personals in a newspaper, joining a dating service, or going to a church dance, actively waits. Waiting for love is something we all do, and badly. The essence of waiting is that it makes us suffer. But suffering, remember, is a prerequisite for passion. Waiting for "Mr. or Ms. Right," the "one true love," that "special someone," the "significant other" to enter your life has always preoccupied people and inspired works of art. In Charles Dickens's *Great Expectations,* we find the pathetic, dried-up Miss Havisham sitting among cobwebs in a decaying bridal gown, still waiting for the groom who left her standing at the altar . . . decades before. In a fairy tale which has appealed for generations, Sleeping Beauty waits in suspense for a hundred years until the handsome Prince arrives with an invigorating kiss. Then, at last, she can wake, breathe deeply, and start to live a meaningful life.

In the past, it was usually women who were depicted waiting for love, and as Stephen Kern points out in *The Culture of Love: Victorians to Moderns,* "Victorian art reveals the limits of women's preparation for anything but love." It is obsessed with the "iconography of waiting," such as:

> the sleeping women depicted all over Victorian art—under trees, at the edge of lakes, and on hammocks, beds, sofas, benches and grass. . . . Endlessly waiting women in voluptuous preparations were depicted in Roman baths or Middle Eastern marriage markets, slave auctions, and harems.

For most of history, women have spent so much time under lock and key as chattels that they were unable to leave home and search for love as men could. The fair maiden had to wait for the knight in shining armor to ride by, be wowed by her, and start courting. In that sense, they were starlets sitting at the counter of a Hollywood drugstore, hoping and praying to be discovered by a handsome mogul. Girls used to wait to see whom their family would choose for them. These days, both men and women wait for "karma," "fate," "destiny," or some other temporal god to send a likely partner their way. Not for Cupid's arrows exactly, but for time's. They still believe in a magic force that commands the saga of one's life.

The essence of waiting is wishing the future to be the present. For a slender moment or string of moments, time does a shadow dance, and the anticipated future is roped by the imagination and dragged into the present as if it really were the here and now. The here and now is made to last beyond its mortal limits. What can be controlled this instant, and only for this instant, is magically generalized into a sea of instants in the uncharted world of the future. The thrill of waiting comes from the pretended breaking of irrevocable boundaries. It is like being privy to life after death. Some people fear a high-speed future racing toward them, beyond human control, a mindless missile full of explosives. Others anticipate but do not fear the future, assuming it will be filled with both good and bad surprises. Both types of people wait for love, one more feverishly than the other. Most often, waiting becomes a delicious prelude to love, as two people reunite in a flurry of reassurances and kisses.

For Marcel Proust, waiting had an erotics all its own, a delectation made all the sharper if the beloved never appeared. "The Midnight Sun," his Parisian friends called him, because his hours were reversed:

he slept by day and wrote or socialized by night. Chic, witty, wealthy, cheerful, dressed like a dandy, full of gossip, obsequious in the extreme, he moved among the highest echelons of Paris society, had crushes on older matrons, and wrote wonderful long letters to his friends; but he spent most of his life under covers in the cork-lined bedroom of his sumptuous apartment. He was frail and ill (he died of asthma at fifty-three), but he was also emotionally in retreat. Almost a hermit, he lived in a night land remote as deep space. It was there, in his palatial rut, propped up against exquisite pillows, eating mashed potatoes delivered from a favorite posh restaurant, that he created his masterpiece of embellished recollection, *Remembrance of Things Past,** in which he tried to remember everyone he had known, every self he had been, every thing he had seen or done in his entire life. How can one convey the ampleness of being alive—all the people and emotions, animals, skies, sensations, and thoughts, as well as the subterranean life of the mind itself? His fictional frieze sprawls for three thousand pages, whole sections of which sing with the gorgeous music of the mind and heart, and are, appropriately, unforgettable. "He was a dream analyst," Paul West writes in a homage to Proust, "a trance-conjurer, a scandal-savorer, a girl fondler, a boy cuddler, a matron stroker, a snob maven, a dealer in smart remarks, and a prodigious theorist of love, memory and imagination."

Marcel Proust was born in Paris in 1871, at the climax of the Franco-Prussian War, a time of hideous deprivation, short rations, and disease. In desperation, the citizens of Paris ate dogs, cats, and rats to survive, and cholera epidemics blighted one neighborhood after another. Unable to get the nutrition she needed during pregnancy, his mother blamed herself for the child's frail start in life. Soon she became pregnant again, and Marcel had a brother and a rival whom he resented and with whom he squabbled nonstop. But his mother coddled and fussed over him, lavishing special attention if he seemed ill, and each night reading grown-up books to him before he went to sleep, taking care to skip over the romantic passages. In time, he began to associate books with his mother, but he also learned that

---

*The accepted English translation of the title (which Proust hated) comes from one of Shakespeare's sonnets. A more accurate translation would be something like: *In Search of Lost Time*, but even that fails to catch the subtleties of the original: *À la recherche du temps perdu*, which implies a sense of study and capture.

being ill extracted the most attention from her. It was as if, fearing that she had produced a diseased child, Jeanne-Clémence instinctively treated him as one, and her increased attentions as nurse-devotee led Marcel to act even more infirm. Mother and son formed this pact early on, and each identified powerfully with the other, excluding everyone else from their tight symbiotic circle. Nowadays we would perhaps describe Jeanne-Clémence as an "overprotective" mother, and wonder if Marcel's asthma had psychological origins. Freud would most likely have suggested—as he did about Leonardo da Vinci—that Marcel's evolving homosexuality had its origins in too close an identification with his mother, so that he ended up loving boys as she had loved him. In any case, Marcel was bedridden much of his childhood, often missing school, and it was his mother who nursed him during the time his father, a doctor, spent at the office. Throughout his life, Marcel and his mother exchanged frequent letters—even when they were living in the same house—and hers often end with ornate endearments of the sort shared by lovers. These were golden days of love and discovery for young Marcel, whom his mother teasingly called "my little wolf" because he devoured her care; it was a time when the sun always stood at noon, and he monopolized the love of the only perfect creature on earth.

The adult Proust didn't search for childhood memories to mine. They came unbidden as manna, and he referred to them as "involuntary." That is, they weren't drafted for novelistic service, they just happened. But once they did appear, he turned each into a small forever, a mini-universe of inexhaustible study, a carousel of sensations. In *Swann's Way,* to use the famous example, on a cold winter day, Marcel's mother offers him some *petites madeleines*—scalloped-shaped little cakes—and tea. He soaks a morsel of cake in a spoonful of tea and raises it to his lips. When he tastes it a shudder runs through him, a gong sounds in his memory, and he is transported to his childhood visits with his aunt, who served him *petites madeleines* and lime-blossom tea. He retastes those plump little cakes, resmells those cups of fragrant tea. A dam has opened and a river of textures, atmospheres, sights, and sounds flows in. Blessed with a photographic memory and a passion for accurate detail, he is able to paint his sensations onto the reader's mind so powerfully that each reader feels he has slipped into the room with Proust's aunt and her maid, and become an intimate part of the scene, all alone, as if no one else on earth had ever read or imagined it. A voluptuous animist, Proust believed that memories hid like demons or sprites inside objects. One day you taste something special—or pass a tree, or see a bow tie— and the memory leaps out at you. When it does, it unlocks the door to all the memories surrounding it, and a sensory free-for-all ensues. The past is a lost city of Inca gold—complete with fabulous temples, quixotic rulers, mazy streets, and sacrifices—that can be discovered in all its grandeur.

You'd think such a sybarite would fare well in love, savoring every moment, celebrating small pleasures. As a boy, waiting for love, Marcel is as ready as an archer with a full quiver of arrows, when to his amazement a target suddenly appears in the form of a red-haired, freckled girl holding a trowel. She is standing beside a hedge of jasmine, and he's overwhelmed by her succulent, fragrant aura. They exchange a glance deep as a long kiss, and he experiences her with all of his senses open. He can feel his soul swim to her and blend with hers, experiencing what Freud would later call the "oceanic feeling" of love,* and he wants to possess her, though he knows full well that nothing—not even sexual or mystic union—can solve the problem of how alone and separate we all feel.

As an adult, the narrator falls in love with a certain Albertine, a dark-haired, unremarkable-looking girl of the lower middle class ("let us leave pretty women to men devoid of imagination") whom he adores, and who ultimately decides to leave him. She is fickle and runs off to carouse with both male and female lovers. He tries to entice her back by offering to buy her a Rolls-Royce and a yacht. She agrees, only to be thrown by a horse and killed before she has chance to return. In much of *Remembrance,* the narrator obsesses about Albertine with a fascination as disquieting and automatic as a hacking cough. She is the central planet in an unknown solar system. Every object she touches offers a glimpse of a bright new world. Fixated on her bicycle, her "pale cheeks like white slugs," the dust that she stirs when she moves, he becomes consumed with possessive jealousy and grief. Every face reminds him of hers. Every object is a

---

*Freud thought it was a carryover from the infant's wishing to merge with its mother, or, indeed, a memory of being one with its mother in the womb.

trip wire to an explosively painful memory. She is perpetually present in her absence. And that really is Proust's point about love, that it doesn't exist in real time, only in anticipated time or remembered time. The only paradise is the one that's been lost. Love requires absence, obstacles, infidelities, jealousy, manipulation, outright lies, pretend reconciliations, tantrums, and betrayals. Meanwhile the lovers fret, hope, agonize, and dream. Torment whips them to a higher level of feeling, and from that mental froth comes love. Love is not a biological instinct, not an evolutionary imperative, but a feat of the imagination which thrives on difficulty. In *The Sweet Cheat Gone,* the narrator remembers how Albertine delicately cuddled with him face-to-face, entwining her eyelashes with his, and he nearly swoons at the memory of such intimate, delicate togetherness. But he also recalls feeling utterly powerless and trapped at that moment.

When the narrator confides that his passion for Albertine is really a reshaping of his childhood love for his mother, he sounds classically Freudian. He even confesses that none of his mistresses has loved him as dearly or made him as happy as his mother, whose love was absolute and dependable, a fixed point on the compass rose of his childhood. There are many parallels in *Remembrance* to Freudian thought, and though Proust may have encountered Freud's work, there is no suggestion in his letters or other writings that he did. What makes his obsession with his mother so fascinating today is that it was an innocently occurring—if extreme—example of a child's total fixation on one parent, what Freud labeled the Oedipus complex. But Proust's general views about love differ greatly from Freud's. Whereas Freud believes sublimated sex is the origin of love, Proust does not see love as a warped or disguised or reconstituted sex drive. For him, sex is an integral part of love because it encourages intimacy—but love springs from a need all its own. Love is not something you inherit; you must search for it. Why is it precious? Because it is the great enabler that allows us to commune with every aspect of being alive, with people and objects, animals and cities. One needs love to feel harmonious, to feel part of the rich landscape of one's life. That's why, when the narrator most appreciates the natural world, he simultaneously yearns for a woman to love. By loving a person and nature at the same time, he is able to heighten his passion for both. It puts his senses on active duty, smacks him to attention, and makes him ultrareceptive to every nuance around him. A forest is never drab, but when one is in love it throbs with even more color and sound. The beloved becomes an embodiment of that forest, and one can transfer all one's sexual energy, devotion, and sheer rapture to the forest itself. It's as if sexual excitement were a hard currency of the brain that you can spend wherever you wish.

Ecstasy is what everyone craves—not love or sex, but a hot-blooded, soaring intensity, in which being alive is a joy and a thrill. That enravishment doesn't give meaning to life, and yet without it life seems meaningless. This results from the treachery of habit, a particularly insidious thug who chokes passion and smothers love. Habit puts us on autopilot. Proust uses the example of walking through one's house in the dark—one doesn't actually see the furniture in the hallway, but one knows where it is and instinctively avoids it. When we finally possess someone we start to take them for granted, and passion soon wanes. Only the inaccessible and elusive is truly alluring. Each person is attracted over and over again to a predictable "type" of lover. Each has a habitual pattern of loving, and of losing: "The men who have been left by a number of women have been left almost always in the same manner because of their character and of certain always identical reactions which can be calculated: each man has his own way of being betrayed . . ."

For Proust, human love is not a cameo of divine love. Rather, it is a conscious, deeply creative act of communion with the beloved, reaching into and through that person to all of life. As he says, "The fact is that the person counts for little or nothing; what is almost everything is the series of emotions, of agonies which similar mishaps have made us feel in the past in connexion with her . . ." Each time the narrator looks at Albertine, he summons his full powers of taste, smell, and touch, using her as the vehicle of his senses. She is merely "like a stone round which snow has gathered, the generating centre of an immense structure which rose above the plane of my heart." Albertine becomes a means to extend himself, a magnifying lens that widens and refines his sensitivity. We do not love people for themselves, or objectively; quite the contrary, "we alter them incessantly to suit our desires and fears . . . they are only a vast and vague place in which our affections take root. . . . It is the tragedy of other people that they are to us merely showcases for the very perishable collections of our own mind." It is only because we need people in order to feel love that we fall in love with people.

For that matter, the mistresses whom I have loved most passionately have never coincided with my love for them. That love was genuine, since I subordinated everything else to seeing them, keeping them for myself alone, and would weep aloud if, one evening, I had waited for them in vain. But it was more because they had the faculty of arousing that love, of raising it to a paroxysm, than because they were its image. When I saw them, when I heard their voices, I could find nothing in them which resembled my love and could account for it. And yet my sole joy lay in seeing them, my sole anxiety in waiting for them to come. It was as though a virtue that had no connexion with them had been artificially attached to them by nature, and that this virtue, this quasi-electric power, had the effect upon me of exciting my love, that is to say of controlling all my actions and causing all my sufferings. But from this, the beauty, or the intelligence, or the kindness of these women was entirely distinct. As by an electric current that gives us a shock, I have been shaken by my loves, I have lived them, I have felt them: never have I succeeded in seeing or thinking them. Indeed I am inclined to believe that in these relationships (I leave out of account the physical pleasure which is their habitual accompaniment but is not enough in itself to constitute them), beneath the outward appearance of the woman, it is to those invisible forces with which she is incidentally accompanied that we address ourselves as to obscure deities. It is they whose good will is necessary to us, with whom we seek to establish contact without finding any positive pleasure in it. The woman herself, during our assignation with her, does little more than put us in touch with these goddesses.

But love is also a titillating bout of agreed-upon suffering. If love requires difficulties to thrive, and torment is its dynamo, how could it be otherwise? "Love is a reciprocal torture," Proust concludes. Proustian lovers tend to be tragically insecure, clinging and masochistic, as Proust was himself. They don't start a love affair to avoid suffering; a state of privileged suffering is what they seek. It's what we all seek, Proust says, because it makes shamans of us, allowing us to peer into life's sacred and hidden heart.

Insecure about how likable he really was, Proust used to overtip waiters, give embarrassingly large presents to friends, and generally try to buy affection and win acceptance from people. He did it with such wit, intelligence, and style that people thoroughly enjoyed his company; but love was another matter. His parents kept telling him that he was "weak-willed" for not overcoming his illness and taking a serious job. They thought this tactic of severe criticism would inspire him to prove them wrong, but it had the opposite effect—in time he simply came to believe what he was told. Was it his low self-esteem that caused him to be such a snob? One of his biographers, Ronald Hayman, thinks so:

> If snobbery is defined as addiction to the pleasure of associating with an elite, Proust was undeniably a snob. His desperate need for love made it impossible for him not to envy the aristocrats whose birth ensured them a place at the centre of other people's attention and admiration.

A related compulsion was

> the lifelong habit of trying to buy good will. Even when making love or when having love made to him, he couldn't believe he was lovable.

So, as he aged, to play it safe, he forged

> liaisons with footmen, waiters, and male secretaries, but in his friendships with young men who were socially his equals or superiors, jealousy was integral to the pleasure, even when sexual intimacy wasn't integral to the friendship.

These were useful emotions for a novelist. "Even while living it," Hayman points out, "Proust was developing his possessive jealousy into a work of art."

In later years he enjoyed frequenting a brothel, where his habits were jotted down in a notebook by one of the young men who worked there. He preferred for the man to stand naked beside the bed and masturbate. Watching him, Proust would also masturbate. If

Proust had trouble reaching a climax, the man was obliged to bring in two savage rats in cages, and "Immediately the two starving animals threw themselves at each other, emitting heart-rending cries and tearing at each other with their claws and teeth." Proust once told André Gide about this sexual peculiarity of his, explaining it simply as his sometimes needing intense sensations to achieve orgasm, including watching warring rats. In any case, repeatedly wounded by rejection, he grew to prefer his sex partners anonymous and emotionally unappetizing, who made no demands on his heart. Otherwise he knew he'd be launched into a stratosphere of possessive jealousy, where the air was thin and unbreathable. Through a lifetime of illness and facing an early death, believing that his masturbation would shorten his life even if his asthma didn't, lamenting the loss of his mother and others he loved, he understandably wondered if time was irrevocably lost.

Proust's outlook on love is so negative and masochistic he finally concludes that only love of one's art is worth the heart-wrenching effort, and it was in this way, in the closing years of his life, that he tried to sublimate his doting and insatiable passion. No doubt he would have agreed with Baudelaire's definition of love as "an oasis of horror in a desert of boredom." But he replayed love voluptuously in his mind, caressed the memories with his pen.

Although he claimed that *Remembrance* was not autobiographical, most scholars believe it is, and that the narrator's entanglements with Albertine echo Proust's doings with his lover, Alfred Agostinelli, for whom he bought not a Rolls-Royce but an airplane. It was one of the first, and Alfred died in it, spinning into the Mediterranean where he drowned, which gave him the dubious honor of being one of the first people to die in an airplane crash.

Despite Proust's pessimism, he contributed profoundly to our understanding of the psychology of love. He traced the patterns of relationships, and showed how each fresh heartache resonates with past ones, making our "suffering somehow contemporaneous with all the epochs in our life in which we have suffered." We long to be loved in earnest, he argued. Otherwise we are as alone in life as if we were walking upon an empty beach. Otherwise the world would seem as flat as a postage stamp. Once the beloved is gone, through death or abandonment, grief fills all the seams of one's life. But ultimately, if we wait long enough, grief will become oblivion. How should one wait? It's best to develop a passion for the world itself, a revolving rapture that is both poetic and scientific. Natural and manmade objects can anchor one to the world, where we seem to have so little mooring. We enter into them, pathically, lovingly, and grow sturdier. Indeed, one can lose one's self and become an Everyman, an artist who is powerful and keen-eyed and full of joy. Waiting for love to emerge, waiting to rendezvous with a lover, waiting for the lover to feel the same love in return, waiting jealously when the lover is out of one's sight, waiting for the ex-lover one hopes will reappear. For Proust, each stage of love bridges time and is colored by a sensuality all its own, especially the final stage—waiting through grief for oblivion—which is perhaps the most welcome of all, since it restores one's sanity until the next emotional uprising. As Virgil wrote in the *Eclogues,* "Time bears away all things, even the heart."

FREUD: THE ORIGINS OF DESIRE

A few years ago, a neighbor of mine was summoned to a frightening scene. Jack, a Presbyterian minister and one of the founders of Suicide Prevention and Crisis Service, learned that a man was holding a loaded gun on his family, threatening to kill them and himself and anyone else who got in the way. Jack hurried into the man's house, sat down beside him, and said quietly: "Tell me your story." Ten hours later, the man gave him the gun. The truth buried in this drama gets to the very heart of Freudian thought: each of us has a story, each of us has a loaded gun that we aim at ourselves. After hours, or years, of guided talking, the story can at last be told in its fullness, and the gun can be laid down.

Freud was trying to map the war zones of the heart, where air-raid sirens wail and bombs blast, and furtive souls scurry around in the half-light, frantically searching for a way back home, to where loving parents wait with food and open arms. In a world filled with psychological land mines, he thought, any step might trigger a memory that explodes one's self-esteem, and a small trip in the psychic rubble may lead to badly sprained emotions. We belong to our past, we are its slave and pet, though the leash is invisible.

But we also belong to our time. "The key to the period," Ralph Waldo Emerson wrote about the era he and Freud shared, "seemed to be that the mind had become aware of itself. . . . The young men were born with knives in their brain, a tendency to introversion, self-dissection, anatomizing of motives." Freud first was drawn to medicine and actual knives, but in time he became more and more fascinated by the workings of the mind and the scalpel of persistent talk. Although he was confident in his discoveries relating to dreams, sexuality, and neurosis, he was less comfortable delving into love. "I do not think," he wrote to Jung, "that our psychoanalytic flag ought to be raised over the territory of normal love."

But he did tackle the problem, and his intuitions sparked a world of strong opinions. Before Freud, people thought of love as something that evolved at puberty, when the body busily roused itself for courtship and mating. Freud searched for clues to love in the unexpected— even taboo—reaches of early childhood. At once provocative, influential, and shocking, much of his theorizing was based on the idea of infantile sexuality. He didn't mean that babies want to have sexual intercourse, but that they feel pleasure in all their sexual zones, especially around the mouth and anus. The height of infantile sexuality occurs in what he called the Oedipus complex, when a baby longs for one of the parents and wishes to murder the other, who is seen as a rival. In a knot of ambiguity, the baby loves both parents and hates both parents, and its heterosexual and homosexual instincts clash. A helpful amnesia takes over later in childhood, and the child represses its sexual feelings. When the child reaches adolescence and begins looking for a nonincestuous love partner, it unconsciously chooses one that reminds it of the parent with whom it was so smitten, the first love of its life. This isn't a conscious awareness, or it would be short-circuited by the incest taboo. Adult lovers, indulging in kisses, caresses, oral sex, and other forms of foreplay, Freud saw as recapturing the pleasure of nursing at Mother's breast. As he wrote in *Three Essays on the Theory of Sexuality:*

At a time at which the first beginnings of sexual satisfaction are still linked with the taking of nourishment, the sexual instinct has a sexual object outside the infant's own body in the shape of his mother's breast. It is only later that the infant loses that object, just at that time, perhaps, when the child is able to form a total idea of the person to whom the organ that is giving him satisfaction belongs. As a rule the sexual instinct then becomes auto-erotic, and not until the period of latency has been passed through is the original relation restored. There are thus good reasons why a child sucking at his mother's breast has become the prototype of every relation of love. The finding of an object is in fact a refinding of it.

If one extends Freud's image, from Mother's breast to many of her attributes, then his devastating conclusion that "all finding is a refinding" makes fuller sense in terms of current psychoanalytic thinking. This could not be more Platonic, or more Proustian. Love is a remembrance of things past, a refinding of lost happiness. According to Freud, in order to love freely and unneurotically one must retain a strong attachment to one's parents, but cast one's net elsewhere when it comes to passionate love. If this doesn't happen, it is difficult to focus all of one's desire on a romantic partner, and neurosis ensues. Freud wrote epigrammatically of such people: "Where they love they do not desire, and where they desire they cannot love." They may become obsessive about unobtainable people who don't return their love, or they may feel the need to humiliate and debase a sexual partner. Why does this happen? Freud argued that an overly (or overtly) seductive parent could awaken a child too early to genital sexuality, as a result of which the child becomes completely fixated on that parent. Unable to loosen its grasp on the parent, it cannot find someone else to love. Freud saw problems at both extremes—excessive sexuality leading to perversion; repressed sexuality leading to neurosis. Some people can become aroused only by unusual love partners—men in uniform, much older women, other men's wives, for example—and Freud explains such behavior as a compulsive desire for reunion with one's father or mother. Such a specific, rigid search leaves no room for free will. One carries an old, worn family photograph in one's unconscious, and is attracted only to people who resemble that yellowing image.

This notion—that we have a preconceived image of the person we mean to love—also comes from Plato, who said that there are perfect universal forms, and humans are constantly searching for facsimiles of those forms. Just as airplane designers first build prototypes, people spend their lives building and rebuilding relationships according to one set of blueprints. But can we find peace and satisfaction loving what are, essentially, surrogates? In *Civilisation and Its Discontents* (1930), a brooding, disillusioned Freud thinks not. Freud's idea of "refinding" has spoken to many people, as have Plato's ideal forms. There is something deeply human about the need to believe in landmarks, ancient figures, and fundamental laws and attachments.

When people fall in love, Freud said, they regress to a childish state and idealize their partner in much the same way they once idealized their parents. Their self-esteem lies in the other's hands. If the love is returned, they feel like the adored child again, majestic, prized, and reassured; and they experience the head-over-heels, swept-away, cloud-nine bliss of love. The nature of this theory is essentially economic—the lovers transfer self-worth to the person they love, who is seen as an ideal self. The beloved, in turn, feels richer, nobler, finer.

Some of Freud's best ideas were not wholly original. Nietzsche had already written that "Every man keeps in himself an image of the woman deriving from that of his mother, and according to the image he will be prone to respect or despise women." Schopenhauer had written of the symbolic relationship between the womb and death. Indeed, the Elizabethans often used the euphemism "to die" to mean feeling sexual pleasure. The ultimate reunion with one's mother would have to carry one back to the perfect safety of the womb, which would mean not yet being born. Plato had written about prototypes, sublimation, resistance, and merging. Many philosophers and poets had written about the meaning of dreams. But it took Freud to amplify such ideas, explain their underlying mechanisms, draw general conclusions, and devise a workable therapy based on them. Freud was also a ruthless analyzer of his own past and motives. (Allowing the one to stand for the many, the part to imply the whole, was also an ancient Greek idea.) His theories were based on sometimes painful personal experience, and delivered in the context of nineteenth-century values about women, and the fin-de-siècle revolution in culture and ideas that lasted for about twenty years into the twentieth century. A self-proclaimed philistine when it came to the talents of Picasso, Braque, Schiele, and the many other cubists and expressionists popular in the Vienna of his day, he was nonetheless working in a parallel vein, dealing with interlocking planes of experience, and the warping and distorting of images to better express one's emotional state and the role people play in one's life. Relativity theory had begun to subtly influence novelists like Virginia Woolf and Thomas Hardy, linguists like Benjamin Lee Whorf, and a host of poets and painters, philosophers and theoreticians. Its verdict, that perception was relative, and the world freshly minted by each pair of eyes, began seeping throughout society and contributed to Freud's deterministic outlook. Above all, he believed in chance and choice. The world was full of accidents; the mind was not.

Freud was born poor and Jewish above a blacksmith shop in Freiberg in 1856, and given the name of "Sigismund Schlomo," which as a teenager he shortened to the more Germanic-sounding "Sigmund." His father, Jacob, was a wool merchant. His mother, Amalia, was a young, beautiful woman whom he remembers being astonished to glimpse naked when he was about four years old. It made him so uncomfortable, even thirty-seven years later, that he could only describe the event in Latin. A third wife, she was twenty years younger than her husband; and as a child Freud often felt she would have been a more suitable wife for his young uncle or half-brother. His complex, somewhat confusing relationship with his parents, siblings, half-siblings, and large extended family formed the foundation of his theories about everything from the Oedipus complex to artistic creativity. Bravely, he used himself as raw material. As biographer Peter Gay describes the situation:

Such childhood conundrums left deposits that Freud repressed for years and would only recapture, through dreams and laborious self-analysis, in the late 1890's. His mind was made up of these things—his young mother pregnant with a rival, his half brother in some mysterious way his mother's companion, his nephew older than himself, his best friend also his greatest enemy, his benign father old enough to be his grandfather.

In his twenties, Freud married an unexceptional woman, Martha Bernays, who raised their six children. She was not consulted in his intellectual life. He had been determined to marry her, and though they remained chaste for the four years they were engaged, he obviously richly desired her. Once, in Paris, he wrote her about his climb up the Eiffel Tower: "One climbs up three hundred steps, it is very dark, very lonely, on every step I could have given you a kiss if you had been with me, and you would have reached the top quite out of breath and wild." Although he wrote Martha many tender, impulsive, revealing love letters while they were engaged, once they were married the love letters stopped. At one point he apparently had an adulterous affair with his sister-in-law. When he was thirty-seven, he wrote to a close friend about his worrisome troubles with impotence. A heavy cigar smoker, Freud was lavishly addicted to what he knew would kill him, and in time it did, abetted no doubt by his growing use of cocaine. Before he was married, he once wrote to Martha that "smoking is indispensable if one has nothing to kiss," and he later claimed that all addictions were a replacement for masturbation. His was in many ways a typical bourgeois home, very tidy and orderly, in which Father ruled and everyone else served. He alone named his children, and he chose for them the names of his personal heroes, mentors, or friends.

In 1980, participants of the annual meeting of the American Psychoanalytic Association received a rare treat: Freud's eighty-five-year-old daughter, Anna, narrated a thirty-minute film of her father, captured in home movies by several of his friends (who were also his patients). At times unaware of the camera, Freud seemed relaxed, an affectionate patriarch, playing with his dogs in the snow, looking for goldfish in a pond with his two grandsons, whom he tenderly embraced. "Here my father didn't know he was being photographed," Anna Freud explained, as the camera showed Freud sitting in a garden talking peacefully with an old friend. "He didn't like to be photographed and often made a face when he knew the camera was on him." Another, more formal, twenty-minute film followed, which included scenes of his fiftieth wedding anniversary, and his flight from Vienna and the Nazis. Freud posed with his brothers and sisters, some of whom would die in concentration camps, and his children, including little Anna, smiling proudly in an attractive dress. This latter film was made by his one time patient Philip R. Lehrman; Freud went along with the filming, but thought Lehrman's need to photograph him probably qualified as a compulsion. Peeking through the keyhole of the camera, the APA members got a small, tantalizing glimpse into Freud's private hours. It seemed a thoroughly conventional home life.

A systematic collector of Egyptian, Greek, and Roman antiquities, which crowded his waiting room and office like a dreamscape of past lives, he claimed to have read more books on archaeology than psychology. It was his enduring fascination. His patients often commented on all the statues, carvings, bits of ancient rubble, and reproductions of ruins that met their gaze. Whatever did they make of that necessary vigil in the waiting room, where they could not avoid staring at a reproduction of Ingres's *Oedipus Questioning the Sphinx*, or mysterious fragments of almost recognizable faces, limbless beings, puzzles cast in stone? Sitting at his desk, Freud would often pick up one of the objects and caress it thoughtfully. It was always in eyeshot, this caravan of partial truths, whose riddles spanned time and countries. It was a powerfully symbolic obsession, which reminded him of his work—the rudimentary excavation of souls—and probably also of his mideastern heritage, his boyhood fantasies of exploration, and the simple faith that shapes, even when slightly mutilated, retain a timeless dignity and beauty. If anything, he found them more mysterious because of their injuries. He saw his work as a layer-by-layer excavation through the sediment of the past and deep into the lost cities of the heart.

Freud was very much aware of the revolution in thinking he had started. It was like throwing a ball into the air with such force that it would take some time for it to land; meanwhile, everyone kept looking upward. He lived long enough to see his disciples achieve renown, which clearly thrilled him.

Much of the last years of his life were spent at the center of a political whirlwind, in which the budding profession of psychiatry squabbled with itself. He was bad at keeping secrets about the sexual perversions of his patients and friends, and often became embroiled in father-son relationships (most notably with Jung), which led to monstrously painful breakups. Actually, his relationship with male friends and acolytes was always complicated. His life was such a checkerboard of adoration and petty quarrels that he himself wondered if he had some inner need to sabotage the relationships that mattered most to him. As he confided in *The Interpretation of*

Dreams, "An intimate friend and a hated enemy have always been necessary requirements of my emotional life." The whole enterprise of psychoanalysis was fraught with problems, not least of which were the questions of whether or not a patient could be cured by it, and how to put the sessions' truths to work in everyday life. Even if Freudian analysis didn't always cure or rehabilitate, it gave a patient something remarkable and precious: a sense of one's life as a narrative. It was to Freud's credit that he tried to tackle every phantom and underpinning of the mind, no matter how shameful or opaque or embarrassing, in terms of his own life.

Freud always meant to write a large book about "man's love life," but he never did, although he often delivered important papers on the topic. For example, at a meeting of the Vienna Society in 1906, he said:

> In the final analysis, the treatment accorded the child is decisive for his love life. People in love, for example, use for each other pet names by which they were called during childhood. Man becomes childish when he is in love. . . . Love is said to be irrational, but its irrational aspect can be traced back to an infantile source: the compulsion in love is infantile.

It is one thing to maintain that we search for lovers reminiscent of our parents, but quite another to say that love itself is an agreed-upon return to infancy. It suggests that grown-ups so much miss being children that they join forces with one another in a subversive act, which allows them to tunnel backward in time to where each becomes the other's child. In this quest, love is a search for the golden days of childhood, the blissful tyranny of being the center of attention, and a mother-child relationship which one has lost forever.

ATTACHMENT THEORY

Many great thinkers followed Freud into the labyrinthine mine of the psyche, holding one sort of lamp or another, eager to cast light into the dark corners. It would take pages just to list all the psychoanalytic theories about love that have amplified, contradicted, or borrowed Freud's insights. Because many minds have contributed to the field, questions such as "What exactly is love?" have elicited ingenious answers. Some think of love as a ballistic escape from oneself, a sort of spine-tingling, rip-roaring, druglike addiction. Some swear love is a learned vulnerability, agreeing with François de la Rochefoucauld when he said: "There are people who would never have fallen in love if they never heard of love." Some argue that love is all self-delusion and fantasy. As John Barrymore once put it, ungallantly: "Love is the delightful interval between meeting a girl and discovering that she looks like a haddock." Some see love as a narcissistic enterprise, in which people who feel inadequate use others to perfect themselves. Some differentiate between infatuation and "real" love. Some ask if love is a behavior or an attitude. Some chart the varieties and stages of love. Some distinguish between the fever of young relationships, and the more enduring "companionate" love felt by longtime spouses. Indeed, love has been surveyed from so many perspectives, gauged in so many ways, one would think by this time we would have compiled a useful atlas or relief map, showing its coasts and mountain ranges, borders and hinterlands. Instead, it is still a frontier for those who study it, and for those who cross it still a newfound land.

One currently popular line of thinking, "attachment theory," sets love against an evolutionary backdrop. While British psychiatrist John Bowlby was studying the behavior of human infants and children, he came upon the work of animal behaviorists Konrad Lorenz and Harry Harlow, who were observing infant behavior among birds and monkeys. Bowlby was struck by the similarities. Most baby animals need to form passionate attachments with their primary "caregiver" (usually the mother). Once an attachment has developed, they become depressed, desperate, and emotionally disturbed if they are separated from that caregiver. This makes good biological sense, because a youngster in the wild cannot afford to lose its family—it would swiftly die of hunger or be eaten by a predator. So, for individuals to pass on their genes to the next generation, family members must feel powerfully bound together,

> and this requires that every separation, however brief, should be responded to by an immediate, automatic, and strong effort both to recover the family, especially the member to whom attachment is closest, and to discourage that member from going away again. . . . The standard response to loss of loved persons are always urges first to recover them and then to scold them. If, however, the urges to recover and scold are automatic responses built into the organism, it follows that they will come into action in response to *any* and *every* loss and without discriminating between those that are really retrievable and those . . . that are not. It is an hypothesis of this kind, I believe, that explains why a bereaved person commonly experiences a compelling urge to recover the person even when he knows the attempt to be hopeless and to reproach him or her even when he knows reproach to be irrational.

When infants are separated from their mothers, they respond in predictable ways: first they protest loudly and search frantically for her; then they become sad, passive, and despairing; and at last they become quite detached, even defensive, and refuse to go to Mother when she does return. Loss is a weed whose roots strike deep into our evolutionary past. Seen from this perspective, most psychiatric illness is a form of mourning for lost or inadequate love. Bowlby, who clinically observed people for over twenty years, found many links between disturbed adults and broken attachments in childhood. He argues that the making of a strong bond of affection is what we call "falling in love"; steadily sustaining that bond is what we call "loving"; and breaking up or in some other way losing a love partner is followed by what we label "grieving."* But all are biologically necessary functions. Out of convenience, and confusion, and perhaps a bias not to think of ourselves as being under nature's thumb, we use

---

*Darwin writes that the facial expressions adults use when they feel grief seem to be the result of two warring emotions: wanting to scream like an abandoned child, and trying not to let that scream out.

these terms as a shorthand for what, in reality, are elaborate emotional dramas that have evolved because they were strategic for survival.

Bowlby says also that conflicts in loving, especially in courtship, are not only healthy but easy to explain in evolutionary terms: "All animals are constantly beset by impulses which are incompatible with one another, such as attack, flight, and sexual approach." In the stealth and slash world of nature, an armistice must happen when animals are ready to mate; each has to be sure that it won't be beaten or eaten, and each has to suppress the instinct to fight or devour the other. This usually calls for a minuet as elaborate as two eighteenth-century fops standing in unctuous mock-graciousness at the doorway to a dining room, one saying "After you," the other insisting, "Oh, *no,* after you"—repeated until the two are pushed headlong through the door by a hungry crowd. Bowlby offers the example of the European robin: both male and female have red breasts, and come springtime the male instinctively wars with any other male that enters his territory. Seeing a female's red breast, a male's instinct is to attack her, and hers is to fly off. Instead, at courting time, she stands fast, becomes coy, showing him just a little interest, then none, then a little again, and this allows the male to control his wrath long enough to begin wooing. "In the early phases," Bowlby writes, "both sexes are in a state of conflict, the male torn between attack and sexual advance and the hen between flirtation and flight." Conflicts are normal in romance as in all other glades of life. Governing them makes love, family, and society possible. The mentally ill are people who cannot regulate the conflicting emotions they feel.

Our attachments are strongest during childhood, when we are utterly dependent on our parents for survival, but in adulthood we also form strong attachments, to a lover and perhaps to such authority figures as an employer or a teacher. We choose someone who seems to cope with the world better than we do. Knowing such a person is "there for us," in case of emergency, helps us feel safe and secure. The need strikes especially hard when one is frightened, sick, or alone, and it's an instinct that is perfectly normal and healthy. A child needs a "secure base" to return to after its small forays into a bustling world filled with marvels and frights and strangers. As Mary Salter Ainsworth discovered, in her four-year study of children in

Uganda, infants regularly use their mother as a home base to which they return after miniexpeditions. Ainsworth conducted a parallel study with American children in Baltimore, with similar results. She identified three patterns of attachment. If a caregiver is responsive to a child's need for contact and comfort, it explores happily and will probably develop into a self-reliant adult. If the caregiver rebuffs the child's bids for closeness, the child learns to keep its distance, distract itself with nonsocial activities, and become compulsively self-reliant. If the caregiver acts inconsistently—at times responsive, at other times neglectful or intrusive—the child becomes clingy, and expresses its distress more urgently, which tends to preclude exploration. Self-reliance correlates very highly with reliance on parent. That is, children who have a trusting relationship with a parent, using that parent as a safe harbor, turn out to be more stable and self-reliant adults.

Freud assumes that the mother-child bond is so strong because of the food the mother provides. But Bowlby argues that the human infant's need for attachment is all-consuming, has little to do with food, and is the same drive that later on in life leads one to seek a love partner. Crying, calling to, following, and clinging are all part of the routine, whose purpose is to elicit nurturing. With adults, we see this behavior most clearly when a person is worried, ill, upset, or afraid. Being separated from a loved one—say, when a child goes off to school or college—isn't necessarily dangerous, but it very slightly increases the risk of danger, and that is enough to produce a gut-wrenching pang.

Freud concludes that when lovers act irrationally what they're really doing is regressing to the needs, insecurities, and obsessions of childhood. Using an archaeological metaphor, he pictures the mind as the many-layered city of Rome, where different eras and societies rub shoulders. Right below today's bustling metropolis lie other cities, and each one has its own set of morals, principles of justice, punishments, customs, rulers, piety, and red tape. In contrast, attachment theory looks at Rome and sees, in the remnants of the past, more than artifacts:

> . . . some of the important historical landmarks, bridges and crooked streets are still there. But few of the ancient structures exist unaltered or in mental isolation, so simple regression and fixation

are unlikely. There is continuity in attachment behavior, but there can also be significant change.

Accordingly, romantic love is a biological ballet. It is evolution's way of making sure that sexual partners meet and mate, then give their child the care it needs to be healthy and make loving attachments of its own. This isn't a simple or fast process. The human brain is so complex, the mind so ingenious, that biology and experience work hand in hand. People usually undergo a series of crushes, infatuations, and loves between infancy and adulthood. They learn to make magnetic attachments, whose power they feel in their cells, in their bones. Thinking about the loved one steers their every thought, and they would die rather than break the force field of their devotion. It is as if they were two stars, tightly orbiting each other, each feeding on the other's gravity. Because nothing and no one in time or creation seems to matter more, a broken relationship rips the lining from the heart, crushes the rib cage, shatters the lens of hope, and produces a drama both tragic and predictable. Wailing out loud or silently, clawing at the world and at one's self, the abandoned lover mourns.

How do we learn to grieve? Society provides customs and rituals, but it's a behavior the body knows by heart. First we protest and refuse to accept the truth; we keep thinking the loved one will magically return. Next we sob a torrent of tears. Then we sink into despair; the world sags under the dead weight of our pain. And at long last we mourn. In time, we gather our strengths like so many lost buttons and begin searching for a likely attachment once again.

But suppose a child is orphaned or abused? When, through malevolence or circumstance, the early bond between parent and child is damaged, the psychological repercussions are profound. Such a person may end up with marital problems, personality disorders, neuroses, or difficulty in parenting. A love-thwarted child spends its life searching for that safe, secure relationship and absolutely loving heart which is its birthright. As an adult, missing cues that might lead to just such a relationship, it judges people harshly, trusts no one, and becomes exiled and alone. A child that's unsafe, or rejected, or deprived of affection, feels anxious, becomes obsessively clingy, and doesn't take many chances. Assuming that it will be spurned, *that it is the sort of person one could only reject,* it may try to be self-sufficient and disinherit love, not risk asking anyone ever to truly care. Such a child becomes afflicted with itself, and needs no other accuser, no other lynch mob. It feels as if it has been caught red-handed in the midst of a felony—its life. Is there no salvation for such a damaged child? Studies show that even one continuously sympathetic caregiver in childhood can make the difference between a seriously disturbed adult or someone who is nearly invincible. Ideally, there would be a parent whom the child perceives as its partisan, apologist, patron, devotee, grubstaker, well-wisher, and admirer rolled into one. But the minimum is one reliable guardian angel—not necessarily a parent, just someone who is always there, cheering in the dugout, steadfast through both strikeouts and home runs.

Cornell psychologist Cindy Hazan and her colleagues have gone so far as to chart the direct parallels between the many stages of childhood attachment and adult romantic love. What they found is that childhood experiences do trigger, and sometimes garble or distort, the love relationships made later. But nothing is cast in stone. As the child grows, it forges new attachments and some of these may dilute bad childhood experiences. This is an important conclusion, because it suggests that abused children—who are, essentially, loving disabled—may still be helped later in life. As anyone who has received or dispensed psychotherapy knows, it's a profession whose mainspring is love. Nearly everyone who visits a therapist has a love disorder of one sort or another, and each has a story to tell—of love lost or denied, love twisted or betrayed, love perverted or shackled to violence. Broken attachments litter the office floors like pick-up-sticks. People appear with frayed seams and spilling pockets. Some arrive pathologically disheartened by a childhood filled with hazard, molestation, and reproach. *Mutilés de guerre,* they are invisibly handicapped, veterans of a war they didn't even know they were fighting. What battlefield could be more fierce, what enemy more dear?

$\mathcal{A}$LL FIRES THE FIRE

THE NATURE
OF LOVE

THE LOVING IMPAIRED

DISABLING LOVE

Among the many handicaps that can befall human beings, few are sadder than the inability to feel love. Because we imagine love to be wholly psychological, we don't even have a word for people who are biologically unable to love. But there are some unlucky souls who, through trauma to part of the brain, cannot feel emotion. For this minority of misfits, there are no telethons, no acronyms, no government agencies. We sometimes think of loving as a luxury, little more than a high-thrill hobby like bungee jumping. So why lament its absence? Veterans of bad breakups and torturous affairs might even envy people who aren't vexed by love.

Antonio Damasio, a neurologist at the University of Iowa College of Medicine, reports a curious case, in which a man we'll call John had been living a normal life as accountant, husband, and father. At thirty-five, John had a benign tumor removed from the front of his brain. The operation was a success, but soon afterward his personality changed dramatically. He divorced his wife, became involved with a prostitute, acted irresponsibly at work, lost one job after another, became penniless—all without feeling anything, not even bewilderment or concern. It was his brother who finally sought medical help for him after a decade of worry.

Using magnetic resonance imaging to peer inside John's brain,

Damasio found that the ventromedial region of the frontal cortex was damaged. This injury had most likely occurred during the tumor operation, and it leads us to a small portion of gray matter between the eyebrows, which seems to be a factory for emotions. At this crossroads in the brain, we find incoming sensory information and outgoing messages to the autonomic nervous system that controls the involuntary workings of the body: heartbeat, breathing, sweating, pupil dilation, and blood pressure. Sweaty palms, racing pulse, and labored breathing, as well as other sensations, often combine to signal that an emotion is taking place. If you're scuba diving at night for the first time and become separated from your dive buddy, the emotion might be fear of death. If you meet someone special whom you're desperate to know better, the emotion might be fear of acting stupid and being rejected. In effect, this region of the brain acts like a city in the jungle, connecting the dark interior of our lives to the civilized strain of the outside world.

Damasio hooked John up to a machine similar to a lie detector, and presented him with a barrage of emotionally charged slides, sounds, and questions. Some were violent, some pornographic, some unethical. John had *no response* to any of them. A field of flowers registered no differently than a murder.

When I learned of this study, I thought immediately of the film *Blade Runner,* directed by Ridley Scott. Suffocating, ferocious, poignant, its musical and visual melodies stay with one for some time. In the film's futuristic megacity that Los Angeles has decayed into, the streets are dripping with split water mains, pools of grease, and waves of blowing newspapers. Overhead, electronic billboards fill the sky with visual racket. In Chinatown, the press and stench of people and smoke and sin rival any hell anyone has ever imagined. Civilization has stopped evolving. Society is a corpse watching itself putrefy and decay. None of them realize they're decaying, but when they kiss their bones rub. The streets are full of fluids that belong inside bodies. The streets swarm with the unknowingly embalmed. Anything can be bought or sold. People live there because they have something to hide or mischief to make, and so many throats are cut daily that an industry of knife sharpeners has arisen.

Harrison Ford plays a down-and-dirty police assassin, who has been sent into this underworld to locate humanoid robots that have escaped from the offworld and come to earth to find their inventor. The humanoids have learned they are programmed to die at a specified point and, though savage, bloodthirsty, and maniacal, they also think, form attachments, and don't want to die. They need to know how long their lifespan will be. They need to confront their cold-blooded creator. In a large sense, *Blade Runner* is a movie about the terrifying quest for one's humanity and soul, about facing one's creator with hard questions about love, death, good, and evil.

How do Harrison Ford and other bounty hunters recognize the humanoids? By testing likely suspects, asking them a list of loaded questions in a monotone. Only human beings struggle with issues of compassion or morality or social responsibility. During this exam, Ford monitors the size of their pupils for involuntary clues. The autonomic nervous system makes the pupils swell when a human being faces (or even imagines) such piercing emotions as horror, sex, or violence. To be human is to be emotional, to have a body that is regularly ransacked by emotions of many kinds, including love. To lose all that is to lose the cauldron of one's humanity, which is why John's brother—in a typically human way—worried over the fate of his loved one.

THE HORROR OF THE IK

Trauma takes many forms. It can be as obvious as a blow to the head, or as subtle as long-term damage to a child's self-esteem. If love is a natural, even essential human emotion, an automatic response to family that is crucial in child rearing, then it should be impossible to obliterate it in whole populations, right? One of the most curious accounts of the loving disabled was reported by anthropologist Colin Turnbull. In the 1970s, Turnbull spent two years living with the Ik (pronounced *Eek*), a small tribe of hunter-gatherers in a remote, desolate mountain region of Uganda. He knew little about them beforehand, except that there were only two thousand of them left, and the odd fact that their language was more similar to classical Middle-Kingdom Egyptian than to any living language. Indeed, they were not his first or even second choice for research. But he settled happily among them, because it's easier for an anthropologist to observe the workings of a society that is both small and isolated. He brought with him some expectations, based on anthropology's understanding of how hunter-gatherer societies work. Usually the women gather the roots, berries, and other vegetables that are a crucial part of everyone's diet, while the men go off on hunting parties from which they may or may not return with meat. Although the hunt figures magically in the life of the tribe, because it's fraught with danger and excitement as berry-picking is not, the women's foraging is regarded as equally important because it provides most of the daily food. Cooperation is vital for all, both in hunting and foraging. Depending as they do on the land for sustenance, such tribes usually have a deep mystical relationship with their environment. They display the sorts of qualities we treasure most in ourselves: hospitality, generosity, affection, honesty, and charity. In fact, these mean so much to us that we call them "virtues," and if asked to define the highest hallmarks of being human, we would refer to them, perhaps adding compassion, kindness, and reason.

To the hunter-gatherers, these "virtues" are not carefully appraised ethics or options, or even preferences, but instinctive strategies for survival. They make it possible to coexist in a small closed society that would crumble without them. Even though we have evolved from bands of hunter-gatherers, and retain their instincts and traits, those virtues don't help us as much now in the sprawling societies we've invented. But we still cherish them. Living among the Ik, contrary to everything he expected to find, Turnbull was first saddened, then angered and horrified to conclude that love of one's children, parents, and spouse, "far from being basic human qualities" are merely "superficial luxuries we can afford in times of plenty." For the Ik had become truly monstrous. They had lost their ability to love.

Once upon a time, the Ik had been prosperous hunters. But when the Ugandan government forbade them to hunt in the Kidepo National Park, which was part of their homeland, the Ik had no choice but to frantically attempt to forage and farm in the neighboring mountains, which were parched and lunarlike. The mountains were so fissured and barren that one couldn't walk more than a hundred yards without stumbling into a ravine several hundred feet deep. But there was nowhere else to go. After only three generations of drought and starvation, the Ik became hostile, selfish, mean. They had abandoned love along with other so-called virtues because they could not afford them. It was simple economics. Every waking second—squatting at their toilet, performing sex (a rare act), eating—was spent scanning the horizon for possible meals:

> On one occasion I saw two youths on a ridge high up on Kalimon masturbating each other. It showed some degree of conviviality, but not much, for there was no affection in their mutuality; each was gazing in a different direction, looking for signs of food. . . .

Competition for scraps of food was constant, sadistic, conniving, and cruel. The most basic social currency became worthless. People greeted family, tribe members, or strangers alike with the imperative "Give me food" or "Give me tobacco." Schadenfreude became the highest form of humor; the Ik would hurt, deprive, or in some way cause misfortune to others—even their own child—then roll around laughing about it. One of their favorite pastimes was to lie convincingly to or successfully exploit another. Pulling off that con was a rich delight, but even more pleasure came from then telling the victim he or she had been duped and watching the pain it caused. The old were not fed, because that was considered a waste of food; they were left to die painfully and alone. Indeed, "It was rather commonplace, during the second year's drought, to see the very young prying open the mouths of the very old and pulling out food they had been chewing and had not had time to swallow." The young were turned out of the house at the age of three, and expected to look after themselves by joining an *ad hoc* band of children.

People felt no loyalty or emotion toward relatives, even immediate family. If children died, the parents were thought to be lucky. Turnbull tells of the time he saw a new mother set her baby down on the ground and go about her business, only to discover later that a leopard had carried it off. This thrilled everyone, including the mother, because it meant that she didn't have to continue nursing, but it also suggested that an animal was nearby that they might be able to kill more easily, since it was bound to be sleepy and sedated from eating the baby. This indeed turned out to be the case, and they tracked the leopard, killed, and cooked it, "child and all."

Anyone who found food ate it fast and in secret. The word for "want" was the same as the word for "need." People wanted only what they needed; and if they wanted to help someone, it was only because they needed to. All rituals had been abandoned. Rituals required feasts, and no food could be wasted. Perhaps most eerie was that the Ik no longer even made eye contact with one another. If they sat together, idly whittling wood to splinters, they watched the action of one another's hands, but not the face. If their eyes met by chance, they looked away in embarrassment. They dared not show or feel any interest in one another as people.

"It was hard to detect emotion anywhere," Turnbull writes, because all compassionate feelings had been replaced by self-interest:

> I had seen no evidence of family life such as is found almost everywhere else in the world. I had seen no sign of love, with its willingness to sacrifice, its willingness to accept that we are not complete wholes by ourselves, but need to be joined to others. I had seen little that I could even call affection. . . . There simply was no room, in the life of these people, for such luxuries as family and sentiment and love. So close to the verge of starvation, such luxuries could mean death. . . . It was all quite impersonal. . . . Children are useless appendages, like old parents. Anyone who cannot take care of himself is a burden and a hazard to the survival of others.

With a despair vast as Africa, Turnbull left the Ik and traveled back to civilization. When he returned a year later, after a flood season that had produced many plants, he discovered to his horror that, despite the abundant crops now rotting in the fields, the Ik had not changed. It was too late. Lovelessness had taken root and spread like a virulent weed, crowding almost all else out. The family did not matter anymore, neither emotionally nor economically. Neither did friendship nor respect for life. His grief over the Ik includes the pessimistic conclusion that they made the same sort of choice we all might make, if we were faced with their hardships.

The Ik saga is chilling. If love can vanish so quickly from the life of a tribe, then surely love is not a necessity but a luxury, maybe even an invention. This could be an awful truth. Awful because of the doubts it raises about the ruggedness of love. Awful because of how quickly love vanished among the Ik, for whom love became silly and dangerous, a spillage of energy. Love did not conquer all. Like a complicated melody no one had sung for a while, it was lost forever.

What can the plight of the Ik teach us? Are there parallels in western society, where the old are shut away in nursing homes and the young in day-care centers, where cooperation has been replaced by self-interest, when we speak wistfully of the extended family, and friends are disposable? Can it be that the values we treasure most are not inherently human values but a by-product of one form of survival strategy called Society? In the two preceding examples, we've seen love destroyed by a blow to the head and love surrendered to adaptive evolution. In both cases, love was lost through a great trauma to the nervous system, and that should make us think hard about the hidden evils of child abuse, mass starvation, and malnutrition. For example, few are asking what will happen to the IQ and sanity of the children of Somalia, *if they live*. Malnutrition has been associated with poor brain development, and an absence of nurturing with lawlessness. Love provides an insulation from the harshness of the world. What the Ik show us is how human beings look with their raw nerves exposed and love amputated.

If the ability to love is something that can be so destroyed, then it has a physical reality, it is matter. Where does love reside in the body? When W. H. Auden writes of the mystery

> Where love is strengthened, hope restored,
> In hearts by chemical accord

he's poking fun at romantic love, and reminding us of the organic chemistry of mutual attraction. Throughout history, people have located love in the heart, probably because of its loud, safe, regular, comforting beat—that maternal two-step babies follow from before birth. We can find the heart as the seat of love and other important emotions in the ancient Egyptian language. *Ab,* the hieroglyph for heart, was a dancing figure. The heart quickens at the sight or thought of a loved one. Having no idea where love grows, we suppose it must be the noisiest and most rambunctious part of us, that gabby inmate of our ribs. But isn't it odd that many people think fondly of one of their internal organs? The image of the heart adorns greeting cards, blood banks, coffee mugs, bumper stickers, and paintings of the Crucifixion. A real heart, viewed during open-heart surgery, seems a poor symbol for so much emotion. "In my heart of hearts," we say, making a *matryoshka* doll of it: in the innermost cave in the labyrinth of my feelings. The heart is vital to being alive, the unstated logic runs, and so is love. Furthermore, love seems so tyrannical and opinionated, it must have one source—if not a god or goddess, or Wizard of Oz–like character issuing edicts, then a single factory of cells, an undiscovered organ. Does love happen in the brain? In the hormones? Are pheromones love's messengers? What biological mechanism allows us to feel love? And, for that matter, how did love begin?

BRAIN-STEM SONATA: THE NEUROPHYSIOLOGY OF LOVE

Because humans give birth to so few young, nearly every infant has to live to adulthood. If love had not evolved as a binding force between mother and child, and between men and women, we would not have endured. A mother puts up with a lot of pain to give birth, and risks her own life, health, freedom, and leisure to look after a baby. Love makes it feel worthwhile. However, a baby is born with much of its brain still developing—in fact, most of a baby's neuronal pathways develop *after* birth. How they develop depends on what happens in the first few years of the baby's life, during which time it learns the fine art of being human, including how to give and receive love. More and more evidence supports the conclusion that what a child learns during those early years programs it emotionally for the rest of its life.

Psychophysiologist Gary Lynch has found that deeply emotional events stimulate the brain cells more than usual. Those neurons then become sensitized to similar events. Whenever the experience is repeated, the neurons become more and more responsive. This happens because with each repetition of the experience an enzyme signals more receptors to become available at the synapse, which in turn allows in more and more information. This would explain why "practice makes perfect," and why one can learn a foreign language, or how to perform dentistry, if one applies oneself long enough. Children learn languages fast and easily when they're very young, while adults find the same task nearly impossible. This is also true of emotional vocabulary and grammar. As Anthony Walsh wisely remarks,

> The information communicated to children during the critical early years of life regarding their self-worth and lovableness contributes strongly to their later evaluations of their own worthiness or unworthiness. One study of self-esteem showed that early parental nurturance completely overshadowed all other factors examined in explaining levels of self-esteem among college students. If love is so tremendously important to us throughout the lifespan, it is imperative that the brain's "love trails" be well and truly trodden during this period. Deeply etched love trails in the brain will strongly predispose the infant in later life to respond to the world with caring, compassion, and confidence.

Why is this so important? Because "later communications, even if they are positive, will tend to be relayed along the same negative track as though some mischievous switchman were stationed at a crucial neurological junction ready to derail any train of pleasurable thought or feeling." To love, one needs to have been loved. Unloved children often grow into adults for whom love is a foreign land, and sometimes their fate can be even more calamitous than that. Without love, a person can sink through the quicksand of depression. Without love, a person can wither and die. The lovability message is delivered in many forms other than verbally, including touching and caressing, which is one reason that breastfeeding should be encouraged if at all possible. Hugging a child, giving it enough reassuring touches, is so crucial to its development that untouched children don't grow as tall, and they often have lower IQs, learning disabilities, and many allergies and immune system disorders. At the most basic level, they assume that mother will not protect them, that they are disposable, so there is no use wasting energy by continuing to grow. Infants reason with their bodies; they can only feel. So if they are not touched, they naturally assume they have been abandoned, or will be shortly, and they don't feel safe in the world. Studies done with rats, monkeys, and humans show clearly that those that are stroked and loved develop normally, and those that aren't become stunted physically and psychologically. Even well-fed babies can suffer from a syndrome called "failure to thrive" if they aren't being lovingly handled. A nursing baby will sometimes stop and wait for his mother to cuddle him, soothe him, talk to him, before he starts sucking again. To prevail, a child must feel valuable and loved, and much of that information comes from cuddling, kissing, and close body contact.*

When we rack our brains to fathom the existence of evil in the world, we should keep in mind the role that lovelessness plays. Our instincts can teach us only what is normal and life-affirming for our species. They can't prevent us from acting in ways that will produce neurotic or even criminal behavior in our children. Many studies highlight the connection between crime and lack of love, and show that criminals tend to issue from love-deprived childhoods. When a child's experiences of love have been negative, abusive, and rejecting, he or she will have difficulty forming friendships and romantic relationships later on; in effect the "switchman" will misread the signals and send them down the only love tracks he can find, the ones built on pessimism, rejection, pain, and lack of trust. Love will not be associated with pleasure; and it may even trigger frustration, rage, violence. A Harvard study of ninety-four men, observed over a thirty-five-year period, found simply that those who had been happy children were happy adults, and those who were unhappy children were unhappy adults. Add to that the ever-increasing evidence of the high correlation between child abuse and criminal behavior. As Ashley Montagu observes:

> Show me a murderer, a hardened criminal, a juvenile delinquent, a psychopath, a "cold fish" and in almost every case I will show

---

*For a lengthier discussion of this phenomenon, and how it relates to prematurely born infants, see my *A Natural History of the Senses*, pp. 71–80.

you a tragedy that has resulted from not being properly loved during childhood.

On two occasions I've met men I would characterize as psychopaths. Both were brilliant, inventive, wealthy, powerful, and famous. They had august power over the lives of all around them, courted danger, were publicly insulting to underlings, and committed acts most people would describe as heinous. Each invited me to stay longer, to spend a few days with him, and I declined on both occasions. Something was wrong with their voices, so wrong that I felt unsafe being around them. Their voices lacked all emotional fiber, and a crucial ability to identify with others was missing from their conversations. They did not seem to feel any sense of morality or guilt or fear of punishment. They could as easily marry as murder. I do not know if they were abused, love-deprived children, but they fitted the psychological portrait perfectly.

Unteaching the incorrect, inadvertent lessons of childhood is one of psychotherapy's hardest tasks, made all the more difficult by the way in which the faulty information was laid down in the brain. According to Daniel Alkon, a researcher at the National Institutes of Health specializing in memory, traumatic childhood memories are probably not erasable. Recorded on the thick trunk of the dendritic tree, they occupy a central position. Later memories are recorded in peripheral areas, and therefore are less powerful or permanent. This is not to say that adults cannot unlearn bad habits or master new skills. They certainly can (hence the popularity of the T-shirt that says *It's never too late to have a happy childhood*). But there is a big difference between learning how to keep a kayak afloat in rough seas or mastering the fine art of social dressage, and in reaching emotional equilibrium if you didn't start out with any. It's possible, but no picnic. You have to change your patterns of behavior and how you interpret experiences; and that means changing the brain itself, which can be a soul-wrenching process. The brain is flexible and does change, but it does so most easily when we are young. Though love is a natural tonic that all infants crave, it must be fed to them and thus taught. As the lyrics to a pop song warn: *Teach your children well . . .*

THE EVOLUTION OF LOVE

Children often draw cavemen and dinosaurs in the same picture, and they love to play games with lilliputian models of the unthinkably large beasts with razory teeth. A child's capacity to be charmed by the monstrous is one of life's little imponderables. But in truth there weren't any people around when dinosaurs ruled, since dinosaurs predated humans by millions of years. Only the misanthropes among us should lament their passing. For if the dinosaurs had not died out, we would not be here. Their extinction made room for the small, timid, squirrel-like mammals that would lead to us. Actually, there weren't ever a lot of dinosaurs roaming around, but they were big bruisers with big appetites. In contrast, there were great herds of smaller mammals. Either strategy will work: a few giants most of which survive, or swarms of dwarfs most of which perish.

Whatever catastrophe befell the dinosaurs left enough of our mammalian ancestors alive, and with the dinosaurs gone mammals spread throughout the planet, thrived, evolved, grew in size, changed shape, developed more refined brains. You are reading this because the dinosaurs died. That happenstance of evolution startles me, because it underscores how precarious our humanity really is. In my travels, I've seen some wondrous landforms and animals, but nothing more surprising or awe-inspiring than human beings. We are not different or separate from other animals. We are not gods who have the right to destroy our world or other worlds, but we are rare and remarkable creatures to have evolved on this planet. We are amazing bursts of dream and matter. Our minds as mazy as the Grand Canyon. Our needs as stark as warmth in winter. Our wants as murky and voluptuous as oceans. We are natural wonders.

The death of the dinosaurs was only one piece of luck that allowed humans to evolve. There were important others, and one of them was love. By "selecting" the ability to love as a crucial part of our biology, evolution made us what we are. Contrary to what philosophers, moralists, theoreticians, in-laws, and counselors have always argued, love is not a choice. It is a biological imperative. And just as evolution favored human beings who were able to stand upright, it favored human beings who felt love. It favored them because love has great survival value. Those who felt love made sure their offspring survived, those offspring inherited the ability to love, and they lived longer and had more offspring of their own. In time the tendency to love became part of our genetic endowment, and then it became more deeply ingrained than a mere tendency, aptitude, or bequest, and its richness began to subsidize every enterprise of our lives. Humans became emotional venture capitalists.

Matter inherits matter. Emotions, personality, desire all spring from flesh and chemicals. The brain is only three pounds of blood, dream, and electricity, and yet from that mortal stew come Beethoven's sonatas. Dizzie Gillespie's jazz. Audrey Hepburn's wish to spend the last months of her life in Somalia, saving children. It's not surprising that we have created a host of machines (such as stereo receivers and radar) that are transducers—apparatuses that translate sensations into electricity. Not surprising because we ourselves are transducers. Walt Whitman was accurate when he wrote "I sing the body electric." Every one of our cells is sheathed in electricity, even our brain cells, crackling with energy, surging like a network of tiny lightning storms. Many of our machines are merely cartoon versions of us, simple versions of the hand, eye, and so on. The world confronts us with its awkward languages of shape, color, movement, sound wave and smell, and we translate all of them into the electric lingo our bodies speak, sending messages by Morse code and semaphore to the brain. When we love with all our heart, all our soul, all our might, it is an electric passion. Love develops in the neurons of the brain, and the way it grows depends on how those neurons were trained when we were children. Evolution hands out a blueprint for the building of the house of one's life, but, as with a house, much depends on the skill and experience of the builders; the laws and codes of society; the features or quality of the materials; not to mention the random effect of tornadoes, landslides, or floods; plumbing catastrophes; and the caprices of inspectors, supervisors, hooligans, or neighbors. How we love is a matter of biology. How we love is a matter of experience.

If the need for love is instinctive, built-in, a part of the wiring, how can it also be molded? Humans are great ad-libbers. We revise, we create, we invent new strategies. If food becomes scarce, we navigate to where there's more, or we change our diet, or grow food, or synthesize it, or build vehicles to transport distant food to us. The reason we are so flexible is that we cannot create many offspring. With animals that lay numerous eggs or have big litters or give birth often, there is a good chance that some of their genes will survive into the next generation. Life, for them, is cheap. Frog spawn coats a moonlit pond only briefly before most of it is devoured by predators. If but a few eggs survive to become tadpoles, and a few tadpoles frogs, everything is working right. Frogs don't travel much anyway, and when they do they choose a similar environment. So frogs follow strict rules of behavior. They have no need to do otherwise.

But humans give birth to very few young, only one a year in most cases. If that child dies, there are no backups. And the human species lives in various environments. To get their offspring safely to adulthood, humans must make many decisions, depending on the obstacles and threats they encounter from day to day. This requires a subtle and flexible brain, a brain driven hard by basic instincts, but also adaptable to novelty. Individuals and tribes have different experiences, and so they evolve individual strategies, emotions, beliefs, habits, preferences. We call this "culture" and "personality," and we say it is something one "develops," as if it were a photographic image emerging from the darkroom of one's past. It could not be more natural, or more animal, an enterprise. Faced with a hectic environment, a life-form has the best chance at survival if it can evaluate new experiences, make quick decisions about them, and learn from those decisions. Our genius is our ability to adapt and change. We are nature's great generalists. We sample. We change our minds. We bend to pressure. We persuade others. We are persuadable. We avoid danger. We court disaster. There is an irony in this, a self-fulfilling prophecy. The more we respond to environmental pressures by changing our way of doing things—living in houses with furnaces to keep us warm, for instance—the more we create our own problems (garbage, pollutants, and the like) for which we must then devise a solution. This combination of rigid behavior on the one hand and the ability to improvise on the other is why all people are basically alike but everyone is very different. Beethoven inherited a sensitivity to music from his parents, who were musical, but it was the hard luck of his childhood that shaped his career as a composer. As Anthony Walsh describes the physical process in *The Science of Love:*

> The human infant greets the world óverflowing with slumbering potentialities. The awakening, development, and actualization of these potentialities depends considerably on experience. These experiences that make us what we are and may become are perceived, processed, and acted upon via an intricate electrochemical maze of interactions among roughly 10 billion brain cells (neurons). . . . Neurons, the complex building blocks of the nervous system, are units of communication. . . . Projecting out from the body of the neuron are axons, which transmit information from one cell to another in the form of electrical signals of constant strength but varying frequencies, at infinitesimal junctions or gaps called synapses ("to clasp").
>
> The information is transmitted across the neuronal synapses by chemical "handshakes" in the form of tiny squirts of chemicals called neurotransmitters. Neuroscientists have identified approximately 60 different kinds of neurotransmitters thus far. . . . At the molecular level, neurotransmitters are what make us happy or sad, enraged or quiescent, anxious or relaxed.

Endorphins are one brand of neurotransmitter, especially pleasurable because they're natural opiates that can kill pain, produce a druglike high, or calm someone down. When a mother cuddles her newborn, endorphins pour through the baby's body and make it feel happy, peaceful, and secure. The baby learns to associate affection with pleasure.

A baby zebra can scramble to its feet and walk soon after birth, and indeed most other animal babies hit the ground running. But human babies are born helpless and unformed. In our distant past, as we evolved our big brains, women did not evolve big hips to go with them. Evolution faced a dilemma. Big-brained humans had a better chance at survival. Small-hipped women died in childbirth. Big-hipped women were too slow on their feet and couldn't escape predators. It was not the only possible solution by any means, but the one that happened was that women evolved *slightly* bigger hips and babies were born while they were still essentially fetuses. Thus a mother could protect her infant while it continued growing and developing, now outside her body but sheltered by the womb of her obsessive concern. And if a father could be persuaded to stick around, he would protect both the mother and the baby during this dangerous period. It was a rather clumsy, iffy, and complicated solution, true, but evolution proceeds by barter and handshake, not by proclamation.

It's tempting to think of evolution as a sort of city planner, laying out all its designs at once. This reverse logic is terribly seductive, because we crave meaning and anyway we prefer tidy explanations of things. But to describe the actual events would require a rambling sentence with many contingencies and semicolons, something like this: bigger-brained babies survived better and created offspring who also had bigger brains; but many of the mothers died in childbirth, except for those few who happened to have bigger hips; and, despite the awkward features of bigger hips, in time big-brained and big-hipped females had a better survival rate; especially those who protected their infants best, that is, those who were chemically rewarded when they felt a powerful drive to nurture and sacrifice all for their young; especially if they were aided by males who felt similar urges, thus making sure that the male's genes would survive, even if that required a long-term payoff—his genes reaching into future generations—rather than the short-term goal of not being encumbered by a dependent mother and child.

NEW-AGE SENSITIVE GUYS

These days, we expect men to be more sensitive, vulnerable, loving, sympathetic, and supportive; to be less competitive, territorial, and violent; to be monogamous and to share the child rearing fifty-fifty. Actually, what we're asking is that men be more like women, and for some that's a tall order. Their biology protests *You're joking, right? I'm not programmed for this.* And yet, without such mutual concern and equality modern life would be intolerable for both men and women. An ironic footnote is that, as men become the New-Age sensitive guys women want, some women are less able to find them sexually attractive because they strike too many feminine chords. I find this amusing because it reminds me that we're dealing with ancient hungers, ancient drives, and trying to adapt them to a society for which they weren't designed.*

To their credit, many men do soften their instincts. Indeed, in a world plagued by war, this is essential. We no longer live in small bands, armed with spears and rocks, where words like "anger," "revenge," and "hate" result in violent, tragic, but limited destruction. We have raised the ante until everything is at stake. Evolution cannot keep up with our passion to invent new ways to possess, rule, or destroy. We have changed the world, but not ourselves. How are we supposed to use ancient attitudes to solve contemporary problems? You can't teach an old dogma new tricks. Our patterns of behavior didn't evolve to deal with life in a teeming metropolis or with weapons of mass destruction. But that is why love means so much to us. As Konrad Lorenz has pointed out, only truly aggressive species would need to evolve love. Our violent nature is what makes love possible. Totally peaceful creatures would not need the balm of love.

Glance in the mirror, and a predator stares back at you. Prey animals—antelopes, horses, cows, deer—have eyes located at the sides of the head, so that they can watch for danger creeping up behind them. In contrast, a tiger has eyes facing front, so that it can use its stereo vision to precisely pinpoint the whereabouts of the next meal, run it to the ground, and leap upon its neck or flank with bared teeth. Humans have the eyes of a predator, a tiger's eyes, and that tells us something about our ancient origins. But we also have colossal brainpower. We are not just dangerous, we are ingenious. Without mechanisms for subduing our violent, craven, and predatory appetites, we would have wiped ourselves out, adding our name to the long roll call of extinction. But evolution gave us a powerful peacemaker. Our ability to love has saved us from ourselves.

*Some women I know are thinking of marketing a New-Age Sensitive Guy doll. Pull a string in his back and he says: "You look great without makeup." "Relax, I'll do the dishes." "Have you lost weight?" "Let's just concentrate on *your* pleasure."

If we voyaged to a distant star and observed our kind there—naked with a big tuft of hair on the head—we would probably refer to them as "crested primates." And we would be fascinated by their paradoxical home lives. Humans throughout the world flirt, fall in love, and marry. Ninety percent of American men and women marry, and many societies prize monogamy. Some have even built it into their religious and legal laws. Emotionally, the same sort of law exists—men and women are perpetually searching for their "one true love" with whom to form a lifelong bond. Despite that, humans are deeply unfaithful. Unfaithful even if the risks to life, limb, and family are high. In one of many polls on the subject, 72 percent of married American men say they've been unfaithful, and 54 percent of American women. However, adultery is reported as a constant in all cultures. If evolution's plan is for us to meet and mate, then what part does adultery play in the equation?

There are many reasons why female adultery may have evolved over the millennia. Females could barter sex for extra food. Having a backup male to help raise the kids might come in handy if a female's mate ran away or died. If a female chose a mate who turned out to be unfit, she stood a better chance of passing on strong genes if she mated with someone else. Genetic variety is always a safety net—when a female has offspring by different fathers, each child receives a slightly different genetic inheritance, and the chance that one of the children will survive is all the stronger. A savvy female might have made friends with many males so that they wouldn't hurt or kill her offspring. If the males couldn't be sure which of them was the father, they would *all* look after her child.

Whatever the cause, women with a strong sex drive who were unfaithful to their "husbands" produced more children who survived, and thus the genes for that tendency to cheat were passed on. Men and women who felt powerfully devoted to each other as "husband" and "wife" also produced more children who survived. Men who impregnated as many women as possible also produced more children, even if they didn't stay to help raise them. It was in this way that our contrary sexual urges probably evolved, with the result that we now have men and women who are happily, gratefully monogamous, and yet chronically unfaithful.

If men and women are designed to fall in love, mate, and bear young, then why are they always fighting? Because their biological agendas are different. An average man's ejaculate contains only five calories, and is mainly protein. It shoots out at twenty-eight miles per hour, roughly the speed limit on my street, which suggests the colossal pressure men must feel when they're erect. But one ejaculation contains about 200 million sperm. In theory, the neighbor boy could populate his own planet. If he wants his genes to survive, he should impregnate as many girls as he can. Parents of girls sense this and are worried about his "intentions" toward their daughters. After all, a female can produce only one egg a month and not many in her entire lifetime. If she becomes pregnant, she will be weaker and more vulnerable for nine months, less able to support herself, and then will have to nurse the baby and look after it for years. The male's investment is a bit of spunk on a romantic evening. The female's investment is many years of self-sacrifice. It's in her best interest to choose someone who will stay by her and help support her child. Biologically, it's in the male's best interest to love 'em and leave 'em. A T-shirt prominently displayed in the window of a beachfront shop in West Palm Beach summed up the male imperative perfectly, if crudely. It showed three hot young women from the rear—mainly blond hair and buns in thong bikinis—you couldn't see their faces at all. Underneath were the words *Jump 'em, Pump 'em, Dump 'em.*

The battleground is minute. The time limit is roughly thirty years of life. Both adversaries are generals. Both desire the same goal—the perpetuation of their genes. What differs is their strategy. She wants a man who will stick around, and because that's never a surefire thing she becomes very choosy. She hopes to fall mutually in love with somone protective but nurturing, faithful and fit. She tests his sincerity, grills him about whether or not he really loves her, if he would go through fire and water for her. She uses words like "always" and "forever." She's jealous and possessive, but with a twist: it doesn't matter if he screws around, provided he's not in love with those other women. She knows he's driven to sow his seed in other fields. What she cares about is his practical fidelity, his staying with her to make sure she and her offspring survive. So, angry and tearful, she forgives him once or twice, or pretends not to know, but puts her foot down if it's chronic or seems serious. He's also jealous and possessive, but he allows her no slips. If she becomes pregnant by someone else, he'll end up supporting a child with none of his genes. To him, that would be catastrophic. So, if she even looks lasciviously at another man, he goes on the rampage. This is not true just for individual men, but for whole countries.

For example, reports of rape and infanticide in Bosnia-Herzegovina fill today's newspapers. Overwhelming an enemy is not enough. Bloodthirsty warriors want to murder unborn generations, making sure that only their own genes will survive. Perhaps the most obvious example of this was in 1300 B.C. A monument at Karnak, Egypt, chronicles King Menephta's revenge on the Libyan army, which he vanquished. It lists the severed penises that his army brought home: *Phalluses of Libyan generals—6. Phalluses cut off Libyans—6,359. Sirculians killed, phalluses cut off—222. Etruscans killed, phalluses cut off—542. Greeks killed, phalluses presented to the king—6,111.*

Men and women have trouble understanding each other because their bodies speak slightly different dialects of survival. Some of the words are the same, but the meanings vary, each gender has its own slang, and at times the grammar can be different. As Deborah Tannen has demonstrated so entertainingly in *You Just Don't Understand*, when men and women speak the same sentence they often mean totally different things. When men get together, regardless of what they're discussing, there is always a subtle element of competition, a jockeying for position and power. When women get together, regardless of what they're discussing, there is always a subtle element of making connections and bonding. For example, if a couple is out driving and they get lost, the man is unlikely to ask a passerby for directions. He wouldn't want the stranger to think he isn't masterly enough to navigate. It infuriates him. It makes him lose face, and in his reckoning there are few crimes as disturbing as another man's laughter (a form of manslaughter). The woman, on the other hand, has no trouble asking for directions, and she would gladly provide help to a stranger who was lost. For her it is not a question of status, but connection. Most often, the man drives around getting more and more lost, and the woman yells at him for being too stubborn to ask for directions.

A woman spins out a web of forevers, which she finds reassuring and cozy. She tries to build an extended family in the community, give parties, do things together as a couple. The man says he needs his space, doesn't understand her mania for socializing, and doesn't want to feel tied down, or that she's smothering him. They compromise by developing their own private time and public time. He goes out hunting hoops with the boys. She goes out gathering at the shops with the girls.

The purpose of ritual for men is to learn the rules of power and competition. Watching sports together, for example, they see the formal enactment of ritual, become loyal to a team, learn to conceal their vulnerability. The purpose of ritual for women (going to lunch together, sharing a favorite salon, etc.) is to learn how to make human connections. They are often more intimate and vulnerable with one another than they are with their men, and taking care of other women teaches them to take care of themselves. In these formal ways, men and women domesticate their emotional lives. But their strategies are different, their biological itineraries are different. His sperm needs to travel, her egg needs to settle down. It's astonishing that they survive happily at all. Love provides many remedies in this battle: a no-man's-land where both are safe, a messenger between the lines, an island of bliss in a fen of misgiving.

THE CHEMISTRY OF LOVE

MOTHER LOVE, FATHER LOVE

One day my friend was packing for a business trip when her five-year-old son went into a paroxysm of despair. She reassured him that she would soon be back, and, in any case, that his father would be home to look after him and his sister. "It's not the same thing," her son moaned. "You hatched us."

As any five-year-old knows, mother love and father love are different. In general, young children go berserk when separated from their mothers, but not necessarily when separated from their fathers. Harry Harlow has shown in classic studies with monkeys that fear of losing one's mother is not just a human phobia. Other young animals feel a special attachment to the mother, too. How could it be otherwise? A tiny hobo in its padded cell, the baby spends nine months sharing mother's food, blood, air, hormones, angers, and joys. At birth, it still cannot construe the world; it is a totally vulnerable sensing machine. It does not know that mother left briefly to run errands while it slept, or went shopping for her own food, or bought the blankets that keep Baby warm. Mother is physically intimate with her baby, obsessively kissing it, rocking it, caressing it. Mother herself is food, is warmth, is safety. A soft, fragrant reservoir of life, her breast seems but an extension of the baby's body. The baby continues to be attached to her by the umbilical of its need. Loving mother is really a form of self-love. Beginning as one loving whole, a single world, mother and child will in time become separate beings; just as lovers, beginning as two separate beings, in time become one world, one whole.

Nothing is more absolute or unquestioning than a mother's love, which is a gift freely given, a last of last resorts to a troubled soul. Even serial killers have mothers who love them. Erich Fromm explains this visceral feeling in *The Art of Loving:*

> Mother is the home we come from, she is nature, soil, the ocean. . . . Mother's love is unconditional, it is all-protective, all-enveloping; because it is unconditional it can also not be controlled or acquired. Its presence gives the loved person a sense of bliss; its absence produces a sense of lostness and utter despair. Since mother loves her children because they are her children, and not because they are "good," obedient, or fulfill her wishes and commands, mother's love is based on equality. All men are equal, because they all are children of a mother, because they all are children of Mother Earth.

A father's love, on the other hand, is more distanced, and often has conditions attached to it. Fromm characterizes it as earned or deserved love, pointing out that fathers subconsciously say to their children: "I love you *because* you fulfill my expectations, because you do your duty, because you are like me." Fatherly love tends to punish and reward, to set limits, make demands, expect obedience. A child may or may not deserve his or her father's love. It is a love that judges, and therefore a love that can be lost. Mother love is the love of the ancient earth-ecstasy religions, when people worshiped the fecundity of the wide-hipped land, the sultry heat of the summer sun, the all-embracing spirit of the earth. They worshiped a goddess who poured forth her love as she poured forth her children, nursing them with water from her breasts, cradling them against her flowing haunches. But, by the time of the Old Testament, god had become a father figure who issued demands, expected obedience, and judged his children, punishing or rewarding them according to their actions. We admire monarchies and crave political leaders because it's impossible for us not to wish to return to childhood and certainties. We seem to yearn eternally to recover that parenting. Part of the nature of being a child is being ruled by tyrants and obeying laws that aren't tailor-made.

Of course, both are important to a child's well-being—feeling that she will always be completely loved, no matter how foolish or ugly or sinful she may be; and feeling that she's worthwhile and valuable as an individual. From mother's love, a child learns how to love; from father's love, a child feels worthy of love. This doesn't mean that a deeply loving single parent can't raise an emotionally healthy child, or that abuse doesn't sometimes happen in a two-parent home, but it strongly argues in favor of both parents helping to shape a child's sense of self.

Throughout much of the animal kingdom, fathers guard or provide food for their young but are not intimately involved with child rearing. The idea of "motherhood" and "fatherhood" as roughly equal roles is a human invention. In our early evolution, Mother needed to stay with her infant, nursing and protecting it. Father needed to be free to hunt and fight to protect mother and child. This was a major part of his job description. Violence was an important element in his life; combat was one of his trades. What kept the ancient family in balance was a division of tasks. Females evolved a greater drive to nurture and make peace, males evolved a greater drive to battle and dominate. Contemporary men still feel those dammed-up urges. I suppose it shouldn't surprise us to learn that 85 percent of all violent crimes in the United States are committed by males. Indeed, there is a strong link between males and crime in cultures throughout the world. Females enter the crime statistics in a big way only when their hormones change during and after menopause. I know many unwarlike men who feel great tenderness for their children and friends. I know single fathers who are raising their children with sensitivity. But, in general, men continue to commit most of the violent crime in the world, and women do most of the nurturing and loving.

In one study, researchers took women of various ages, some of whom had children and others not, and showed them photographs of babies. Their pupils automatically dilated, signaling interest and emotion. The same physiological response did not happen in men—*unless* they were fathers with small children. This is even the case with rats—the fathers become more attentive parents after they've spent time with their pups and gotten used to them; mothers respond instantly. Such studies as these suggest that females are predisposed to feel an instinctive, automatic concern for children; but men learn to feel that way only when they have children of their own. Even so, fathers desert their infants twenty times as often as mothers do. Unlike expectant fathers, pregnant women undergo hormonal upheavals that prepare them for child rearing. Bathed in a chemical glow, they don't need to think about how or why or when to love their babies. The sky is blue. The ground is underfoot. They cherish their babies. What could be simpler?

THE CUDDLE CHEMICAL

Oxytocin, a hormone that encourages labor and the contractions during childbirth, seems to play an important role in mother love. The sound of a crying baby makes its mother's body secrete more oxytocin, which in turn erects her nipples and helps the milk to flow. As the baby nurses, even more oxytocin is released, making the mother want to nuzzle and hug it. It's been called the "cuddle chemical" by zoologists who have artificially raised the oxytocin level in goats and other animals and produced similar behavior. Oxytocin has many functions, some of them beneficial for the mother. The baby feels warm and safe as it nurses, and its digestive and respiratory systems run smoothly. The baby's nursing, which also coaxes the oxytocin level to rise in the mother, results, too, in contractions of the uterus that stop bleeding and detach the placenta. So mother and baby find themselves swept away in a chemical dance of love, interdependency, and survival.

Later in life, oxytocin seems to play an equally important role in romantic love, as a hormone that encourages cuddling between lovers and increases pleasure during lovemaking. The hormone stimulates the smooth muscles and sensitizes the nerves, and snowballs during sexual arousal—the more intense the arousal, the more oxytocin is produced. As arousal builds, oxytocin is thought to cause the nerves in the genitals to fire spontaneously, bringing on orgasm. Unlike other hormones, oxytocin arousal can be generated both by physical and emotional cues—a certain look, voice, or gesture is enough—and can become conditioned to one's personal love history. The lover's smell or touch may trigger the production of oxytocin. So might a richly woven and redolent sexual fantasy. Women are more responsive to oxytocin's emotional effects, probably because of the important role it plays in mothering. Indeed, women who have gone through natural childbirth sometimes report that they felt an orgasmic sense of pleasure during delivery. Some nonorgasmic women have found it easier to achieve orgasm after they've been through childbirth; the secretion of oxytocin during delivery and nursing melts their sexual blockade. This hormonal outpouring may help explain why women more than men prefer to continue embracing after sex. A woman may yearn to feel close and connected, tightly coiled around the mainspring of the man's heart. In evolutionary terms, she hopes the man will be staying around for a while, long enough to protect her and the child he just fathered.

Men's oxytocin levels quintuple during orgasm. But a Stanford University study showed that women have even higher levels of oxytocin than men do during sex, and that it takes more oxytocin for a woman to achieve orgasm. Drenched in this spa of the chemical, women are able to have more multiple orgasms than men, as well as full body orgasms. Mothers have told me that during their baby's first year or so they were surprised to find themselves "in love" with it, "turned on" by it, involved with it in "the best romance ever." Because the same hormone controls a woman's pleasure during orgasm, childbirth, cuddling, and nursing her baby, it makes perfect sense that she should feel this way. The brain may have an excess of gray matter, but in some things it's economical. It likes to reuse convenient pathways and chemicals for many purposes. Why plow fresh paths through the snow of existence when old paths already lead part of the way there? New fathers feel gratified by their babies, too, and their oxytocin levels rise, but not as high.

How about cuddling among other animals? At the National Institute of Mental Health, neuroscientists Thomas R. Insel and Lawrence E. Shapiro have been studying the romantic lives of mountain voles, promiscuous wild rodents that live alone in remote burrows until it's time to mate, which they do often and indiscriminately. Mother voles leave their pups soon after birth; father voles don't see their pups at all; and when a researcher removes a pup from its nest it doesn't cry for its mother or seem particularly stressed. They have nothing like what we might call a sense of family. What the researchers have found is that mountain voles have fewer brain receptors for oxytocin than their more affectionate and family-oriented relatives, the prairie voles. Despite this, but just as one might predict, the oxytocin levels of the mountain voles do climb steeply in mothers right after birth, while they're nursing their pups. Such a study makes one wonder about the complex role that oxytocin plays in human relationships. Are oxytocin levels lower in people characterized as "loners," in abusing parents, in children suffering from the solitary nightmare of autism?

THE INFATUATION CHEMICAL

First, a small correction of something we take for granted. The mind is not located in the brain alone. The mind travels the body on an endless caravan of hormones and enzymes. An army of neuropeptides carries messages between the brain and the immune system. When things happen to the body—like pain, trauma, or illness—they affect the brain, which is a part of the body. When things happen in the brain—like shock, thought, or feeling—they affect the heart, the digestive system, and all the rest of the body. Thought and feeling are not separate. Mental health and physical health are not separate. We are one organism. Sometimes hunger pangs override morality. Sometimes our senses wantonly crave novelty, for no other reason than that it feels good. Sometimes a man does indeed *think with his dick*. Because we prize reason and are confused about our biology, we refer to our body's cravings and demands as our "baser" motives, instincts, or drives. So it is craven to yearn for sex, but noble to yearn for music, for example. Depraved to devote hours to finding sex, but admirable to devote hours to searching out beautiful music. Perverted to spend an afternoon fantasizing and masturbating repeatedly, but wholesome to spend the same afternoon enraptured by music. When love becomes obsession, the whole body hears the trumpet blast, the call to arms.

"The meeting of two personalities is like the contact of two chemical substances," Carl Jung wrote, "if there is any reaction, both are transformed." When two people find each other attractive, their bodies quiver with a gush of PEA (phenylethylamine), a molecule that speeds up the flow of information between nerve cells. An amphetaminelike chemical, PEA whips the brain into a frenzy of excitement, which is why lovers feel euphoric, rejuvenated, optimistic, and energized, happy to sit up talking all night or making love for hours on end. Because "speed" is addictive, even the body's naturally made speed, some people become what Michael Liebowitz and Donald Klein of the New York State Psychiatric Institute refer to as "attraction junkies," needing a romantic relationship to feel excited by life. The craving catapults them from high to low in an exhilarating, exhausting cycle of thrill and depression. Driven by a chemical hunger, they choose unsuitable partners, or quickly misconstrue a potential partner's feelings. Sliding down the slippery chute of their longing, they fall head over heels into a sea of all-consuming, passionate love. Soon the relationship crumbles, or they find themselves rejected. In either case, tortured by lovesick despair, they plummet into a savage depression, which they try to cure by falling in love again. Liebowitz and Klein think that this roller coaster is fueled by a chemical imbalance in the brain, a craving for PEA. When they gave some attraction junkies MAO inhibitors—antidepressants that work by disabling certain enzymes that can subdue PEA and other neurotransmitters—they were amazed to find how quickly the therapy worked. No longer craving PEA, the patients were able to choose partners more calmly and realistically. Other studies with humans seem to confirm these findings. Researchers have also found that injecting mice, rhesus monkeys, and other animals with PEA produces noises of pleasure, courting behavior, and addiction (they keep pressing a lever to get more PEA). All this strongly suggests that when we fall in love the brain drenches itself in PEA, a chemical that makes us feel pleasure, rampant excitement, and well-being. A sweet fix, love.

The body uses PEA for more than infatuation. The same chemical soars in thrill-seeking of any kind, because it keeps one alert, confident, and ready to try something new. That may help explain a fascinating phenomenon: people are more likely to fall in love when they're in danger. Wartime romances are legendary. I am part of a "baby boom" produced by such an event. Love thrives especially well in exotic locales. When the senses are heightened because of stress, novelty, or fear, it's much easier to become a mystic or feel ecstasy or fall in love. Danger makes one receptive to romance. Danger is an aphrodisiac. To test this, researchers asked single men to cross a suspension bridge. The bridge was safe, but frightening. Some men met women on the bridge. Other men encountered the same women—but not on the bridge—in a safer setting such as a campus or an office.

The men who met the women on the trembling bridge were much more likely to ask them out on dates.

THE ATTACHMENT CHEMICAL

While the chemical sleigh ride of infatuation carries one at a fast clip over uneven terrain, lives become blended, people mate and genes mix, and babies are born. Then the infatuation subsides and a new group of chemicals takes over, the morphinelike opiates of the mind, which calm and reassure. The sweet blistering rage of infatuation gives way to a narcotic peacefulness, a sense of security and belonging. Being in love is a state of chaotic equilibrium. Its rewards of intimacy, warmth, empathy, dependability, and shared experiences trigger the production of that mental comfort food, the endorphins. The feeling is less steep than falling in love, but it's steadier and more addictive. The longer two people have been married, the more likely it is they'll stay married. And couples who have three or more children tend to be lifelong spouses. Stability, friendship, familiarity, and affection are rewards the body clings to. As much as we love being happily unsettled, not to mention dizzied by infatuation, such a state is stressful. On the other hand, it also feels magnificent to rest, to be free of anxiety or fretting, and to enjoy one's life with a devoted companion who is as comfortable as a childhood playmate, as predictable if at times irksome as a sibling, as attentive as a parent, and also affectionate and loving: a longtime spouse. This is a tonic that is hard to give up, even if the relationship isn't perfect, and one is tempted by rejuvenating affairs. Shared events, including shared stresses and crises, are rivets that draw couples closer together. Soon they are fastened by so many it becomes difficult to pull free. It takes a vast amount of courage to leap off a slowly moving ship and grab a lifebuoy drifting past, not knowing exactly where it's headed or if it will keep one afloat. As the "other women" embroiled with long-married men discover, the men are unlikely to divorce, no matter how mundane their marriages, what they may promise, or how passionately in love they genuinely feel.

THE CHEMISTRY OF DIVORCE

"Philandering," we call it, "fooling around," "hanky-panky," "skirt chasing," "man chasing," or something equally picturesque. Monogamy and adultery are both hallmarks of being human. Anthropologist Helen Fisher proposes a chemical basis for adultery, what she calls "The Four-Year Itch." Studying the United Nations survey of marriage and divorce around the world, she noticed that divorce usually occurs early in a marriage, during the couple's first reproductive and parenting years. Also, that this peak time for divorce coincides with the period in which infatuation normally ends, and a couple has to decide if they're going to call it quits or stay together as companions. Some couples do stay together and have other children, but even more don't. "The human animal," she concludes, "seems built to court, to fall in love, and to marry one person at a time; then, at the height of our reproductive years, often with a single child, we divorce; then, a few years later, we remarry once again."

Our chemistry makes it easy to follow that plan, and painful to avoid it. After the seductive fireworks of first attraction, which may last a few weeks or a few years, the body gets bored with easy ecstasy. The nerves no longer quiver with excitement. Nothing new has been happening for ages, why bother to rouse oneself? Love is exhausting. Too much of anything feels overwhelming, even too much thrill. Then the attachment chemicals roll in their thick cozy carpets of marital serenity. Might as well relax and enjoy the calm and security, some feel. Separated even for a short while, the partners crave the cradle of the other's embrace. Is it a chemical craving? Possibly so, a hunger for the soothing endorphins that flow when they're together. It is a deep, sweet river, just right for dangling one's feet in while the world waits.

Other people grow restless and search for novelty. They can't stand the tedium of constancy. Eventually the ghost of old age stalks them. They are becoming their parents. Elsewhere, life is storied with new horizons, and new flanks. Everyone else seems to be enjoying a feast of sensual delicacies, and they want to smother themselves in a sauce of sensations. So they begin illicit affairs or divorce proceedings, or both.

One way or another the genes survive, the species prevails. Couples who stay together raise more kids to adulthood. When couples part, they almost always marry again and raise at least one child. Even when the chemical cycle falters and breaks, it picks itself up and starts again. Both systems work, so both reward the players. As Oscar Wilde once said, "The chains of marriage are heavy and it takes two to carry them—sometimes three."

APHRODISIACS

In the second half of the nineteenth century, French doctors wrestled with a strange dietary mystery. Soldiers stationed in North Africa, after dining on frogs' legs, developed severe cases of priapism, a prolonged and painful érection of the penis. In 1861, Dr. M. Vezien, making his rounds in a field hospital, was impressed by the *"érections douloureuses et prolongées"* with which several legionnaires returned his salute, and he questioned them about their menu. Could these men have been poisoned? Frogs' legs are a popular French delicacy, and the soldiers had eaten a local variety of frog that lived in a nearby swamp. When Dr. Vezien collected some of the frogs and dissected their stomachs, he found remnants of meloid beetles. In 1893, another military doctor in North Africa reported a similar case: same steely erections, same frogs, same frog guts filled with same beetles.

Cornell biologists have solved the mystery of the erect penises and the aphrodisiac frogs. Meloid beetles contain cantharidin, a urinary-tract irritant otherwise known as "Spanish fly." Many men—most notably the Marquis de Sade—have dosed themselves with it to boost their virility, and dosed ladies with it to win their consent.

When a man's potency flags, he's willing to try almost anything as a pick-me-up. Oysters, caviar, powdered rhinoceros tusk, cocks' combs, figs, eggs, "Love Potion Number Nine," ambergris, bull's blood (drawn from the testes), camel's milk, phallic-shaped fruits, or such "lascivious"* vegetables as asparagus. These remedies sometimes work, either because the user *thinks* they will or because they provide a vitamin or trace mineral the person lacks. People don't feel very sexy if they're unhealthy. For example, oysters contain zinc, and men with diets low in zinc tend to have a low sperm count. That doesn't mean that a plate of oysters will make a man feel sexy . . . unless the texture of the oysters excites his imagination, suggesting a woman's nether petals, as well it might. In the grand opera of the imagination, everyday foods may suddenly become succulent and magical. If he is dining with his ladylove, and the oysters remind him of a bicycle trip they took along the windswept dunes of Cape Cod,

*Sir Richard Burton's term for such foods.

and an afternoon when they made love on a secluded beach, their skin lightly scoured by the sand, the surf loud as a freight train, and the briny smell of the ocean rich in their nostrils, then simply eating the oysters will touch off a sensual circus.

Ginseng, a nutrient plant native to Korea, Russia, and China, is reputed to be a tonic for the nervous system in general and thus a boon to potency. A spicy bowl of bird's nest soup, also said to be an erection special, is made from the nests that sea swifts build in caverns along the coast. The nests provide much phosphorus and other minerals. Asparagus is a rich source of potassium, phosphorus, and calcium—all of which are essential for energy—and it stimulates the urinary tract and kidneys, which may be why seventeenth-century herbalist Nicholas Culpepper advised that asparagus "stirreth up bodily lust in man and woman." The Japanese claim that *unagi,* raw eel, makes a fine aphrodisiac, and there are thousands of restaurants in Japan that specialize in eel. The dish is often served with some form of pickle, the most expensive and prized coming from a phallic-shaped plum.

Men have often presented women with flowers, chocolates, perfumes, music, and other pleasurable treats to put them in a romantic mood. "Awaken her senses first" seems to be the unstated motto of suitors. In any case, flowers are the plants' sex organs, and they evoke the sex-drenched, bud-breaking free-for-all of spring and summer. Chocolate contains mild central nervous system stimulants, as well as an amphetaminelike chemical the body produces naturally when we're in love. Montezuma drank fifty cups of chocolate a day, to boost his virility before he visited his harem of six hundred women.*

Most perfumes contain the essences of flowers mixed with secretions from wild animals (musk, civet, ambergris, and the like), or laboratory versions of them. Smelling a randy pig might not sound sexy, but we are sometimes remarkably simple about what turns us on. Seeing or hearing or smelling other animals having sex can be inspiration enough. Truffles contain a chemical similar to the male pig sex hormone, which is why hot-to-trot sows eagerly dig them up. But the chemical is also similar enough to a human male hormone

*See "The Psychopharmacology of Chocolate," in *A Natural History of the Senses,* p. 153.

that its mustiness appeals to human diners, too. It has even been used in various popular perfumes.

Although the celibate Capuchine monks invented cappuccino, that exquisite frothy typhoon of whipped hot milk and espresso, coffee drinkers are statistically more sexually active than other people. But then, they're more active about everything. Tried and true, alcohol works well at the outset, by relaxing inhibitions, but then it depresses the nervous system just when it should be jubilant. It was Shakespeare (in *Macbeth*) who warned that alcohol "provokes the desire, but takes away the performance." The ancient Egyptians claimed radishes were aphrodisiacs. Ovid swore by onions, perhaps because of Martial's epigram: "If your wife is old and your member is exhausted, eat onions in plenty." But a more popular Roman aphrodisiac was a sauce made from rotting fish entrails, and prettied up under the name of *liquamen*. Travelers to Pompeii bought it at a famous factory owned by Umbricus Agathopus. They relied on live snails cooked in peppery liquamen sauce; mushrooms coated in a honey-and-liquamen sauce; roasted venison eaten with a caraway, honey, vinegar, and liquamen sauce on the side; soft-boiled eggs stewed in a pine kernel, honey, and liquamen sauce; wild boar basted with liquamen sauce; and, for variety, a sort of shish kebab of truffles dipped in liquamen sauce.

Medieval men and women preferred a concoction of the flowers and leaves of myrtle marinated in wine. Eighteenth-century women used "angel water"—a mixture of one pint of orange flower water, one pint of rose water, and half a pint of myrtle water. The mixture was shaken well, and mixed with musk and ambergris. Then they applied it to their bosoms, which were pushed up and displayed by a bra which hid only their nipples. Sometimes they also attached a jeweled brooch to the center of their décolletage, to make sure a glance fell between the hillocks. This was the era when gems were cut in facets for the first time, revealing the brilliant fire we now associate with gemstones, and they were bound to waylay the eye. Similarly, a dab of perfume on the slopes, giving off vapors as it warmed on the brazier of the skin, would lure a wayward nose.

The ancients believed in the magic power of the purplish-flowered mandrake root, probably because its branched shape was thought to resemble the human body. In *The Odyssey*, the sorceress Circe drops mandrake into her potent brew, and as late as the seventeenth century it was used in love potions. That's why John Donne, in his sad, despairing "Song" about the infidelity of women, all of whom seem bound to betray him, says to a confidant:

> Go and catch a falling star,
>   Get with child a mandrake root,
> Tell me, where all past years are,
>   Or who cleft the Devil's foot;
> Teach me to hear mermaids singing . . .

Even if his friend can do these miraculous things, and travel far and wide, he will not return from his travels having met even one woman who was true, or at least, if she was true when he left her, by the time John Donne meets her she will be false. His anguish, though soul-sapping, is temporary. One day, he'll be finding a little Eden in Twickenham Garden, where he longs to be the stone fountain, "weeping" all year so that lovers may come with crystal vials and drink his tears. Next, he blasphemes "Love, any devil else but you"! Another day, he's celebrating a new affair, and eloquently revealing, in "Love's Diet," how he restricts himself to one sigh a day, to stay somewhat in control of that ever-alert, transcendent, black-angel raptor, his "buzzard love."

Catherine de Médicis's love diet included many artichokes, and Paris street vendors used to cry their commercials: "Artichokes! Artichokes! Heats the body and the spirit. Heats the genitals!" Another incendiary food, garlic, is universally celebrated as an aphrodisiac because, as Culpepper wrote, "Its heat . . . is vehement." Because they create minifireworks that arouse the lower organs, black beans have always been a favorite aphrodisiac of Italian peasants. The fourth-century cleric St. Jerome would not allow the nuns under his spiritual direction to eat black-bean soup for that reason. But sometimes a concoction of rarities is the best stimulus of all. Here's a surefire aphrodisiac from the medieval "Black Book" of "venereal pastimes":

Burdock seeds in a mortar pound them. Add of three-years-old goat the left testicle and from the back hairs of a white whelp one pinch of powder, the hairs to be cut on the first day of the new moon and burned on the seventh day. Infuse all the items in a bottle half filled with brandy. Leave uncorked twenty-one days to receive astral influence. Cook on the twenty-first day until the thick consistency is reached. Add four drops of crocodile semen and pass through a filter. Rub mixture on genitalia and await the result.

Crocodile semen? I may be willing to travel far and endure hardship for a great aphrodisiac, but masturbating crocodiles is where I draw the line. An article in *The Aphrodisiac Growers Quarterly* (yes, it really exists) analyzed over five hundred seduction scenes in literature and found 98 percent of them preceded by a stimulating meal.

When it comes to high-tech pharmaceuticals, cocaine is reported by many to be a sexual stimulant, albeit one with grave side effects. Errol Flynn, who claimed to have slept with women on 13,000 of his swashbuckling nights, liked to apply a touch of cocaine to the tip of his penis as an aphrodisiac. Some prescription drugs seem to work well with people suffering from impotence or aversion to sex. Wellbutrin is recommended for both men and women, and is most often used in conjunction with psychotherapy. Yocon or Yohimex, made from the bark of the African yohimbine tree, restores erections for some impotent men. There are various drugs being studied that affect the levels of dopamine and serotonin in the brain. Men can also get pumped for sex by using a tiny inflator implanted in the penis. Perhaps a man stepping into the next room for minor hydraulics sounds unromantic, but no more so than a woman taking her leave briefly to insert a spring-loaded diaphragm or inject spermicide from a plastic caulking gun. Lovers might even pump up together as a part of foreplay.

The "goat's eyelid" favored by the Mongols of the Yüan dynasty in China (late thirteenth century) was more of a sex aid than an aphrodisiac. Also known as a "happy ring," it was literally the eyelid of a dead goat, with eyelashes still attached. It was first placed in quicklime, then steamed and dried until it reached just the right texture. A man would tie it onto his erect penis, so that it tickled his lover during intercourse. In many parts of the world, it's still common for men to scar or insert objects into the penis to excite their women. For instance, men in Borneo pierce the end of the penis with a piece of bamboo or brass wire; and men in Sumatra make holes in their penises and press small stones into the wounds—the flesh grows over the stones, leaving a knobby and presumably enticing texture.

But let us quickly return to the mystery of the French legionnaires. Spanish fly is a sexual stimulant, a proven aphrodisiac, but it's a dangerous one. When the biologists fed meloid beetles to frogs and then measured the amount of cantharidin in the frogs' legs, they were shocked to discover 25 to 50 milligrams of cantharidin in each gram of thigh muscle. That's more than enough to cause priapism, and a man feasting on 200 to 400 grams—a mere half pound to a pound—of such food could die from cantharidin poisoning. "Cantharidin, when taken internally, acts as an inflammatory agent with drastic, irreversible effects on the urogenital system," entomologist Thomas Eisner said. "This is very toxic stuff. When cantharidin is applied topically, as little as a tenth of a milligram can blister the skin. The lethal (internal) dose to humans is somewhere between ten and a hundred milligrams, and one meloid beetle can contain several milligrams of cantharidin."

Such beetles live in many locales around the world, including the United States. Any bird or other animal that eats them saturates its body with the poison; then any humans who eat such infected animals could be poisoned just as the legionnaires were. In fact, horses are occasionally poisoned by eating meloid beetles in alfalfa. One Australian man has the honor of being the only person known for sure to use cantharidin as a murder weapon. Feeling especially randy one day, he hid a dollop of it in his girlfriend's ice cream, which she licked with gusto. She died soon afterward.

By the way, Spanish fly is not a sexual stimulant for the half-inch-long meloid beetle but a form of chemical warfare. The beetle exudes drops of cantharidin-spiked fluid from the knee joints when disturbed by a predator (or a biologist with tweezers). I should add that the researchers did not concern themselves with whether or not large doses of cantharidin produced priapism in the frogs.

A NECESSARY PASSION

THE EROTICS
OF LOVE

FIRE FROM THE FLESH:
WHY SEX EVOLVED

Room 53, Ambassade Hotel, the canal district, Amsterdam: the white marble bathroom, redolent of vanilla soap, with a shower door that opens like the hinged wings of a cricket; a flesh-pink rug, parquet writing desk, and silk-upholstered armchairs; the bed whose wooden headboard is six large quotation marks, lending silent testimony to all its couples have said; in an old print, a man fording a wild stream on a frightened horse whose eyes are bright linens; a low marble table holding a vase of roses, carnations, yellow euphorbia, and trumpeting red amaryllis that spill pollen everywhere and lift small white anthers in reply to the simplest interrogations of sunlight; four long chintz-covered windows, freckled with rain, beyond which the canal quivers—all oil prisms and tangoing light; the tall, slender, many-paned houses across the water (from one, the husky twang of Captain Beefheart singing "Stud Puppy Blues"); a cloud-clotted sky like the lit sapphire of an Indian sari; two lovers idling down the brick street, arms entwined, aswim in each other; as they pass, a tinkling sound, as of glasses clinking, or a bicycle on cobblestone, or the bright coins in their hearts, while they stroll home to a love-crumpled bed.

If those lovers were asked about their passion, they might say simply that sex is pleasurable, that it satisfies a wolflike need, that it leaves them feeling content and sweetly exhausted. They would not be thinking that they were acting out an ancient drama whose sole purpose was to make sure that his sperm could unite with her egg. Pleasure is their motive, not evolution. Yet they're bound by social rituals, courtesies, and protocols whose design is to make the meeting of sperm and egg possible. And also palatable. We are suave, fussy creatures. We clothe the primal act of evolution in the latest fashions.

Humans, like other primates, are obsessed with touching and attachment. We are colonial animals who yearn for family, friendship, community, and a loving partner. To be sociable, we've had to master certain skills: compromise and negotiation, organizing behavior according to rules, being competitive but not too competitive. Feeling close is not absolutely necessary for mating, but it's a key part of lovemaking's lure. Compared to other animals, men have very long penises for their body size. A man tends to penetrate a woman deeply during sex, which means holding her tightly in his arms. Couples mainly make love face-to-face, looking into each other's eyes, kissing, sharing endearments. So much of having intercourse is not simply sex that we don't even call it mating. Birds, which meet once a year for ten seconds or so, to swipe cloacas against each other, "mate." Most people prefer to describe it as something more intimate. Sperm hurtles toward the egg just the same, but the ambiance and emotional investment are different. For us, the drug of closeness is a powerful hypnotic and sedative. We are touchoholics, we are attachment junkies, we are affectopaths. Thank heavens.

Evolution is not a mass hysteria, not a team effort; it happens one by one, single organism by single organism. Those two lovers outside know only what's right for them, and they require delicacy. Crude sex would not work. Whether her lover is Mr. Right or Mr. Right Now, they require romance to feel properly aroused. They are haunted by life, they are a ventriloquist's dummies. *Breed,* their bodies command, *pass on your genes.* They gaze into each other's eyes, their mouths open, and they sigh *I love you.*

None of this surprises us. We are tangled up with the male and female forces of the planet in our actions, in our desires, in our agriculture, in our societies, in every aspect of our lives. One example is the habit of labeling words as either male or female. Why is the Spanish word for chair feminine, but the word for couch masculine?

Some cases undoubtedly have to do with ease of pronunciation, but most hide a historic notion of that object's innate masculinity or femininity, based on its use or form. Sex obsesses us, as it must if we are to procreate. So it's only natural that some cultures dub everything they encounter male or female. It's only natural, too, that tribespeople in New Guinea who had never seen an airplane (or even wheels) before, ran up to a bush plane just after it landed, and asked its pilot two critical questions: What does it eat? Is it male or female?

When we see a person of ambiguous gender walking down the street, we instinctively struggle to read the clues. Is it male or female? That is the oldest question, one posed by children, shamans, and poets alike. No division is more ancient or responsible for more mischief. As Dylan Thomas writes,

> Shall it be male or female? say the cells,
> And drop the plum like fire from the flesh.

In his free-associative lament, "If I Were Tickled by the Rub of Love," he goes on to argue that, if he were in love, despite the torments all lovers feel, despite the disruption of one's schedules and plans and the general "muscling-in of love," he would be fearless, he would feel invincible. He would act as life's barrister. He would subdue the sinister. He would not fear God, civilization, nature, carnality, or his own death, not "the apple nor the flood/Nor the bad blood of spring" . . . not "the gallows nor the axe/Nor the crossed sticks of war." . . . Not "the devil in the loin/Nor the outspoken grave." The world would be horizonless and personal, and yet as old and probable as the sun. As Thomas understands, love bridges the genders, the one and the many, the individual and society, the lonely soul and the vast plurality of life. Love is a messenger, a meddler, a statesman, an oracle. Love answers questions people don't have to raise. The body asks its own basic question, and proceeds from there:

> Shall it be male or female? say the fingers
> That chalk the walls with green girls and their men.

What poets don't ask is why there should be two sexes at all. Or only two. That question has troubled scientists for some time, and there are several possible answers. If the prime directive of evolution is to pass on one's genes, why not clone oneself? Identical twins give us an idea of what the world would look like with human clones. Some plants and animals reproduce themselves in that way, and it seems to work just fine. Our technique is to combine our genetic material with someone else's, and the offspring gets half from each parent. This is by no means a flawless system. A healthy person can't be sure if the partner's genes will be healthy. Males are needed for their sperm, but only females give birth and nurse, and that leaves a lot of extra males around. With so much variety, it's easy to inherit weak or faulty genes. Yet sexual reproduction is the preferred form for most creatures, so it must offer powerful advantages.

At the dawn of life, simple cells dwelt on earth. They reproduced by making identical copies of themselves. Sometimes they were destroyed by hunger or by the rigors of the elements. In time, some stumbled on a dramatic solution—they became cannibals. In eating a neighbor, they fed themselves, but they also incorporated the neighbor's DNA into their own. So, in the plainest sense, it was a sexual union. But that resulted in too much DNA being crammed into too tiny a space, so they divided, sharing the DNA among the daughter cells. Because this cannibalistic system worked, allowing cells to pass on their genetic cargo, evolution encouraged it. And the rest is history.

This version of the origin of sex sees it as a kind of auto-repair shop, where the mechanics cannibalize some cars to fix others. Whatever did happen, one thing is certain—sex offers variety, and variety is salvation in an unpredictable world. Mongrels are stronger, healthier, better equipped to deal with unusual struggles. In life's wilderness, survival rates are higher if an organism gifts its offspring with the genetic version of a bulky Swiss army knife. Just in case of emergency, there is a saw, a Phillips screwdriver, a fishhook, a knife, a scissors, a magnifying glass for starting fires, and so on. Toss in a map, some antibiotics, and a flask of water, and its chances are even better. That gives the offspring a fighting chance to stay alive, stay healthy, and stake out new territories. Using this metaphor, it makes sense for two parents to barter with the goods they possess, so that each can give their young a knapsack full of survival tools.

So variety is life-giving. Then why not more sexes? Because two are plenty for mixing genes. More aren't necessary, and, anyway, two complicates things royally. More would just get in the way. We call those two male and female, by which we mean that one produces sperm and the other produces eggs. The sperms are tiny, the eggs are big. A sperm moves fast, like a souped-up sportscar. An egg moves slowly, like a cantering horse. Males and females aren't attracted to sperm and eggs, of course; they fall deep into the well of each other's eyes, bowled over by a lovable face.

THE FACE

Close your eyes and picture the face of someone you love. Without meaning to, you will begin to smile, your eyes will squint a little as you savor the image, and a warmth will flood your heart. As poets have said, one face is enough to launch a thousand ships, another to stock a private armada of rejection and woe.* Lovers can sit and stare for hours, soldering their hearts together with a white-hot gaze, finding in the other's face a view of paradise. This is likely to happen, too, when a mother looks at her child. Hypnotized by the baby's face, gladdened by the tonic of her love, she could happily sit and stare at it for days on end. The baby smiles at her, and she melts. The smile triggers her devotion and it's absolute in its subtle tyranny. A newborn baby is the most powerful pitchman on earth. Although it can't walk, or even roll over by itself, it controls the lives of all around it. Even children born blind know how to smile.

Visitors to foreign lands, who know nothing of the customs or

---

*"Was this the face that launch'd a thousand ships,/And burnt the topless towers of Ilium?" Christopher Marlowe asked. A joke making the rounds is that scientists now have quantified beauty into units called "helens." A millihelen is just enough beauty to launch one ship.

language, know instinctively how to flirt with the natives. It doesn't matter if they're in Holland, Taiwan, Indonesia, or Amazonia. When humans feel, they register emotion on their faces, and to do that they use the same bag of tricks. People all over the world use nearly identical facial idioms when they flirt. Practice isn't necessary. They know just how to tempt an onlooker with a glance. For children, flirting elicits care from adults. For adults, flirting begins the mad tango of romance. But the technique is the same. To flirt with a man, classically, a woman lifts her eyebrows a little and flashes him an eager, wide-eyed look. When she has his attention, she shyly turns her head away, lowering her eyes and lifting her cheeks into an almost imperceptible smile. Then she tilts her head back toward him again, seeming to touch him once more with her eyes. Sometimes she giggles while she does this, or grins, or hides her face in her hands. This flirting drama—a combination of modesty and blunt sexual inter-est—is a universal behavior, one that women apparently evolved long ago to alert men that they were available for sex.

The face is usually the first thing we notice about a person. A face reminds us of our parents, or an old lover, or someone who hurt us. A face sometimes tells us how a person feels, whether they're anxious, playful, confident, or sullen. Eventually, a face records in its fine lines a lifetime of easy laughter or stubborness. Character may come from within, but a face gives one a sense of identity. Other animals can recognize and greet their kin and friends by smell, but we recognize a person by face. When a new baby is born, the first question asked is: Whom does he or she look like? We have to be able to recognize faces quickly to weave through all the relationships in our complex society, and we're especially good at spotting a face in a sea of warring stimuli, of recognizing a familiar person from just a few lines of caricature. Actually, we're better with caricatures. Robert Munro and Michael Kubovy, researchers at the University of Oregon, showed drawings of faces to a group of students. When the students saw the same faces again later, they recognized them, but were faster and more certain about it if the faces were distorted, the features elongated or exaggerated. "Why should a distortion of a face be remembered better than the face itself?" Munro asked. He and Kubovy believe it's because the brain remembers faces in the same shorthand way, fixing on the features that make one face different from another. Because a caricature is closer to the brain's version of a person, it's easier to recognize than a complete portrait. Some brain-injured people suffer from a condition known as prosopagnosia, which leaves them unable to recognize faces. In severe cases, they cannot even recognize their own reflections in a mirror.

A fascination with faces is a human trait. Portraiture goes back at least sixteen thousand years, to the days of the Cro-Magnons, who carved the profile of one of their people on a limestone plaque, which was discovered in a cave at La Marche, France. Pliny thought that the first painting was probably a silhouette made by tracing someone's shadow on the wall; and he may have been right. Throughout history, humans have associated identity with faces—the faces we find on ancient coins, in Ice Age carvings, in death masks, on the shrunken heads of enemies, outlined in ocher on Paleolithic walls, painted in three-quarter view (known as "eye and a half") on canvas by fifteenth-century Venetians, carved in gems as cameos, etched on copper to make cheap daguerreotypes, collected in photo albums. In his portraits, Leonardo da Vinci strove to reveal what he referred to as "the motions of the mind."

The word *face* probably came from the Latin *facere,* to make or shape, and the Indo-European root *dhe-k-,* to set or put. The etymology hints at artifice. A face is something we revise to fit the occasion. Or, as T. S. Eliot writes in "The Love Song of J. Alfred Prufrock": "To prepare a face to meet the faces that you meet." *The Oxford English Dictionary* records the word *face* being used first in A.D. 1290, to denote the front part of the head. By the fifteenth century, it could also be used as a verb, meaning to brag. In the English Midlands, I once heard a woman in her eighties refuse a second helping of cake by saying: "Don't overface me." We face off, face the music, interface, lose face, do an about-face, face up to, fall flat on our faces, talk face-to-face. We regard the face of the clock or of a building, and remark how the face of the city has changed, and how life may vanish from the face of the earth. On the face of it, we are obsessed with faces.

Look at a child less than a year old, and you'll see a face that's ancient. Every bone in it can be traced back through the fossil record to a creature that roamed the primitive seas. The human face began 350 million years ago with the Crossopterygii, a lunged fish that was driven by drought or hunger to leave its ocean home and leap into the thinly linked realms of air and water, flopping from pond to pond. As it settled along riverbanks and streams, it evolved strong fins with which to propel itself, a larger brain, better lungs. In time its gills became excess baggage that, along with the gill muscles, evolved into a jaw and the rudest beginnings of a face. Every face we now meet on land, whether it belongs to a pet cat, or our grandmother, or this new child, can trace its ancestry to that one species of fish.

Amphibians evolved much later, then reptiles, and at last mammals, the class to which humans and many land animals belong. As each developed its own needs and habitat, its face changed. At home on the jungle floor, the first mammals hunted insects and had whiskers and long sharp noses. Over a period of thirty million years, they evolved into horses, elephants, whales, and other higher mammals. As discussed earlier, those with widely spaced eyes had a better chance of survival, bore more young, and passed along their vigilance to their offspring. Predators, on the other hand, needed eyes set right in the front of their faces, for good depth perception and stereoscopic vision. One glance at a human face tells all about our origins: we were not the prey but the predator.

When our primate ancestors began living in trees, about sixty-five million years ago, their eyes changed. Swinging from branch to branch required even better depth perception. Color vision made it possible to judge ripening fruit, and to recognize dangerous plants and animals. Their teeth became larger and blunter, good for grinding plants. At first the primate face was almost expressionless, a mask that could only show fear or rage by rolling back the lips and baring the teeth, but in time the eye sockets migrated around to the center of the face, the mouth developed an arching roof, and the lower jaw widened into a sweeping curve. A long caravan of hominids rose and fell, with some lines dying out and others prevailing. Then, two million years ago, a small-bodied, brainy ape appeared, *Homo habilis* ("handy man"), who made simple tools. A social being, *Homo habilis* probably had a range of facial expressions. Because *Homo habilis* switched from a strict vegetarian life to the habits of an omnivore, its teeth changed—a diet of plants requires teeth with large grinding surfaces and strong muscles and jaws to hold them. But meat-eaters can have more delicate faces. Then, about a million years ago, *Homo erectus* appeared, an upright hominid with small teeth, a big brain, and prominent eyes. After they tamed fire, they not only cooked food (making it easier to chew), they gathered around fires to eat and keep warm, sat and looked at one another face-to-face, engaged in social activities. Cro-Magnon man, the next stage in human evolution, appeared on the scene around 35,000 to 40,000 years ago, with a large forehead that housed a colossal brain, a rounded cranium, a rather delicate jaw, and a tongue, mouth, and larynx capable of speech. The original Cro-Magnons were a relatively small group of people and, as they grew and split up and migrated to different parts of the world, each group adapted to a new environment and passed along unique traits through natural selection. For example, some African blacks developed a gene that protects them against malaria (unfortunately, it also causes sickle-cell anemia); some northern Asians developed stout, squat bodies to prevent heat loss and slitted eyes to keep out glare from the snow; some tribes living in hot, humid regions grew tall, lanky bodies with greater skin area to prevent overheating.

Extrapolating from such evidence, our common sense, our science, and our folk wisdom all tell us that people have evolved different "looks" as a way of adapting to the rigors of their environment. People who live in the tropics are said to need more melanin, a dark brown or black pigment that helps them withstand the brutal onslaught of the tropical sun, which can cause skin cancer. Some scientists even claim that dark skin acts as better camouflage in the jungle, or prevents beryllium poisoning, or helps to maintain the right level of folic acid. Kinky hair is said to protect the head and allow it to perspire more freely. The plump, padded skin on the faces of the Inuit supposedly helps to provide insulation in subzero temperatures. Desert dwellers are said to have large hooked noses that serve to humidify the dry air before it enters the lungs, Scandinavians to have pale skin so that they can absorb more sunlight and vitamin D.

But does this make sense? Living as far north as they do, Inuits should have ultra-pale skin, but they don't. Although Tasmania receives little light, which should result in fair skin, its peoples have very dark skin. None of the original inhabitants of the Americas had black skin, even those who lived at the equator. In the Solomon Islands, people with black skin and white skin live on islands close by. Although one sees much blond hair among Scandinavians, one also finds it among Australian aborigines. Blue eyes supposedly see better in the dim light of northern climates, but the peoples of regions with even lower light levels, such as the mist-shrouded mountains of New Guinea, have dark eyes. If we consider skin and eye color in connection with the amount of sunlight received, it becomes clear that no simple correlations can be made. Over a hundred years ago, Charles Darwin said the same thing. In *The Descent of Man and Selection in Relation to Sex,* he points out that there are many human traits—especially facial ones—that natural selection cannot explain fully. It is more likely that hair and eye color, shape of lips and eyelids, skin color, amount of facial hair in men, the form of the penis, and the color of a woman's nipples and shape of her buttocks have nothing to do with adaptation to environment, but, instead, have evolved through "sexual selection." According to this line of reasoning, only the sexiest survive. People choose mates they find attractive, and we find people most attractive if they look like us. This may be because children imprint on the people they see around them—especially their parents and siblings, the people they see most. So, fair-skinned, brown-eyed brunets, who grew up in a family of people who looked the same, would find fair-skinned, brown-eyed brunets beautiful and be attracted to them as mates. This narcissism could work on quite a large scale: in a group of curly haired people, people with straight hair would have fewer mates and fewer offspring. In time, the gene for straight hair would either die out or the curly-haired people would tend to mate with their own kind and the straight-haired people with theirs, thus forming distinct groups and creating separate gene pools.

SURVIVAL OF THE CUTEST

Small children naturally develop plump, bulging cheeks, a large forehead, big eyes, a small round chin, and, often, dimples. Just looking at them makes the heart melt, and studies strongly suggest that such a response is biologically based. Cuter babies are handled more, and smile more often, which elicits even more smiles and affectionate touching from adults. Cuteness triggers a protective response in both adults and children. Studies show that when adults retain these childlike features, they're also thought to have attractive personalities. As researchers Diane S. Berry and Leslie Zebrowitz-McArthur report: "People with an infantile craniofacial profile, low vertical placement of features, a small, and rounded chin, large round eyes, high eyebrows, smooth skin, or a short nose are perceived as warmer and more submissive, weaker, more naïve, and less threatening than those with more mature versions of the same features." This may help to explain society's double standard of beauty when it comes to aging. People who are shown photographs of men and women choose younger women but older men as the most attractive. As Konrad Lorenz first argued, this is because men are attracted to women in their childbearing years, knowing that they will be healthy enough to bear children and raise them; whereas women are attracted to men who have the status and power to protect those children.*

What physical features of a woman's face do we find attractive? Society reads childlike, even infantile, facial features as "cute." Women tend to retain those features as adults, and that works well at first. In order to find a woman attractive, we need to see her as feminine, and a key ingredient of femininity is being a little childlike in appearance. Unfortunately for a woman, those facial features change as she grows older. So aging hits women harder than men, because older women can sometimes seem less feminine-looking to us, while older men tend to grow more masculine-looking as they age. This contributes heavily to the double standard of beauty we find so unjust.

Fortunately, beauty's power isn't absolute in every case. The equation of looks and personality runs in both directions: we credit attractive people with being superior in other ways; but we also credit good/talented/superior people with being more attractive. Consider

*Interesting local theory: Irene, who runs Isadora's, a lingerie shop in my town, tells me that she's noticed something curious among her male clientele. Unlike the women, they respond voluptuously to the feel of the softest fabrics. They spend a long time choosing just the right nightdress or slip, but once they touch something that's silky and soft they buy it, regardless of price. She thinks this may be because men have evolved to relish the softest-fleshed women, the young fertile ones, and thus instinctively respond to skin-soft frillies.

the sometimes dissonant features of many famous and talented actors and actresses thought to be beautiful—Marlene Dietrich, for example. She was a beautiful woman, with an angular face and quite sunken cheeks. To achieve that caved-in look, she had her upper rear molars removed when she was a young starlet. To look wide-eyed and innocent, she plucked her eyebrows into very high, thin, rounded arches that made her look as if she were always on the verge of asking a question.

When one is in the throes of an affair, it's easy to believe one's lover an Adonis. Then, years later, bumping into the same man in a bookshop, you may think: *I never noticed how short he was,* or *Did he always have that broken capillary in his eye?* Anaïs Nin describes beauty's fickle current in her notebooks. When a gorgeous woman strolls by, she's instantly smitten, but then she discovers the woman's inner face, and that completely changes how she perceives the outer one:

> As June walked towards me from the darkness of the garden into the light of the door, I saw for the first time the most beautiful woman on earth. A startlingly white face, burning dark eyes, a face so alive I felt it would consume itself before my eyes. Years ago I tried to imagine a true beauty; I created in my mind an image of just such a woman. I had never seen her until last night. Yet I knew long ago the phosphorescent color of her skin, her huntress profile, the evenness of her teeth. She is bizarre, fantastic, nervous, like someone in a high fever. Her beauty drowned me. As I sat before her, I felt I would do anything she asked of me. . . . By the end of the evening I had extricated myself from her power. She killed my admiration by her talk. Her talk. The enormous ego, false, weak, posturing . . .

FACING OUR BIASES

As both Dietrich and Nin understood, we often judge someone's character by their looks. Attractive criminals receive lighter jail sentences; suspects with ugly or coarse features have a harder time proving their innocence, and are dealt with more harshly if they're guilty. And if people look alike, we suspect they may act alike. Prompted by these simple truths of human nature, Galen, Hippocrates, and many other ancient doctors believed in physiognomy, the practice of deciphering a person's character and condition from his face. Formal treatises on face-reading abound in medical literature, from the Greeks to the Chinese. Aristotle claimed that if a person looked at all like an animal he shared that animal's essential nature. Someone with a beaky nose and angular face would be eaglelike—bold, brave, and egotistical. Someone with a horsey face would be loyal and proud. A broad face indicated stupidity, a small face trustworthiness, and so on. In medieval Europe, astrologers read faces as well as the stars. The Elizabethans believed that eye color revealed one's character. Honest people had blue eyes, ne'er-do-wells had medium brown, the innately jealous had green, people of mystery had the darkest brown, and those with loose morals had blue eyes ringed in a slightly darker blue. In his "Moral Diseases of the Eye," Cotton Mather, the Puritan minister, went so far as to correlate virtue with health of the eyes. Someone with inflamed eyes was proclaiming how "unchaste" they were, a truth that must have been especially disillusioning during allergy season. If a person squinted, it proved they had a base nature, a myopia of the soul. Along with face-reading, phrenology arose, the art of reading the shape of the head and any bumps it might have. In time it became so fashionable that instead of telling someone "You need to get in touch with your feelings," the usual line was "You need to have your head examined!" Although, intellectually, we may dismiss such customs as claptrap, to some extent we do judge people by their faces. So it's no surprise that reconstructive surgery is an ancient practice.* Or that a beautiful face is enough to start the engines of love.

---

*The fifteen-hundred-year-old Sanskrit *Rig Veda* speaks of nose repair, and the Egyptian Papyrus Ebers offers instructions for repairing noses, ears, and other parts disfigured by war or accident.

THE HAIR

When lovers describe their sweethearts, they usually mention the color and length of their hair. One may love the whole person, body and spirit, but hair becomes the fetish of that love. Yielding and soft, sumptuous and colorful, decorative and dangling, it invites a lover's touch. It's fun to fondle, play with, and disarrange. Messing it up is the symbolic equivalent of undressing the other's body. A woman quickly learns that cutting her hair without warning her lover first is a bad mistake. Even a becoming change of hairstyle can be shocking and disturbing.

A boyfriend, on the verge of breaking up with me, once exclaimed with a wince, "Your hair!" "What's wrong with it?" I asked, suddenly vulnerable as a trembling fawn. "Well, there's just so much of it . . ." he said. I knew then that everything was over between us. Hair is the caressable plumage of love, a feature individual as the shape of one's chin or the size of one's fingers. If he had said: "I no longer like your mouth," it wouldn't have been more wounding. I once tucked a perfect curl of my hair, tied with a lavender ribbon, between the pages of a poetry book I was returning to a friend. The curl marked my favorite love poem, and I felt as if I were charging the book with my life force. I knew I was giving him a powerful talisman. Hair is sacred to lovers, but also to society.

In the late sixties, a white woman was nowhere if she didn't have straight hair. Straight hair suggested a nonethnic (and therefore upper-class) bloodline; the cheerleaders all wore their blond hair straight. And among the rebels who yearned to be like Judy Collins and Joan Baez, it expressed a sincerity based on contempt for society, hand-me-down values, and the coiffed generation's ideals. However, I came into this world capped in black curly hair—deep-night black with real corkscrew curls—and you could no more straighten it than you could hold back the sea. But I tried. I used to iron my hair; get it temporarily denatured in a reverse permanent; or set it on jumbo orange-juice cans. In fact, most of my teen years were spent sleeping on rollers of one Inquisitional design or another. "Beauty sleep" was an oxymoron. What self-imposed tyranny! For short spells, my hair did look "tamed," "tidy," "controlled." Society was exploding in all directions, but my hair was in place. Lack of control was scary, and suggested the lawlessness of murder, bank robbery, or having sex—all equally criminal for "nice girls" when I was sixteen.

Then, sweet miracle, one day many years later I walked into the Lexington Avenue salon of Richard Stein, whose pretty, vivacious styles I had seen on a number of fashionable women. He looked compassionately at my country-western hairdo, which had taken two hours under a hair dryer to achieve, and said indignantly on my behalf: "Why do you do this to yourself?" Then he turned the anima in my hair loose, shaping it into a long thick shag—the waterfall of curls it always yearned for—and for the first time in my life I had simple, wash-and-wear hair. The years of setting, drying, and vanity-rich fussing were over. So was a special kind of bondage to one rigid ideal of beauty. A symbolic freedom came from accepting my hair on its own terms, relishing its eccentricities instead of trying to disguise them. Now, once every three months or whenever I begin to feel like a sheepdog, Richard tames what he refers to as my "Queen of the Amazon" hair. He has often been the last person I would see before setting out on an expedition, or the first when I returned. This does not surprise him. Scissorwise and insightful, he knows well how symbolic hair is, particularly to women.

And especially for me, since my hair sometimes seems to have a life of its own. "Just look for a weather system of black hair," I say, "and you'll find me." A poetry student of mine (who was also a professional cartoonist) once did a series of drawings about a woman with my kind of hair. It was her hair that a beau introduced to his parents, her hair that chose from a menu, her hair that streamed out of a car window like Spanish moss. Recently, when I was having the house enlarged to accommodate a room that's a combination bathroom and astronomical observatory (one telescope), a twinkling-eyed woman whose job it was to help design that sensory marvel, said: "I don't know what your taste is . . . but I presume it's like your hair." Then she suggested a harem tent fluttering over the tub, its flight propelled by small strategically placed fans. Once, stricken by despair, I phoned a girlfriend and, when I calmed down enough to speak, sobbed out my woes. "Oh, boy trouble," she said in a tone of voice that meant *Hell, we can deal with that.* "I was afraid you'd got a bad haircut."

When her daughter was born, she cradled the baby in her arms and swore: "I promise I'll never give you a hard time about how you wear your hair."

This is the crux of the matter. Mothers and daughters are always confronting each other on the battlefield of a daughter's hair. I know so many women whose mothers would greet them—sometimes before even saying hello—by pushing their hair straight back and exclaiming, "You'd look so much better with the hair off your face, dear!" They say this for years, regardless of how hairstyles change, and it's always accompanied by yanking the hair back severely, as if it should be held by an Ace bandage.

It's as if a daughter were seen as the incarnation of the pure side of a mother's being. An important moment comes when a mother tells her daughter that she likes her hairdo, which often occurs late in life and signals an armistice of larger dimensions. There is something too sexy about out-of-control hair, or hair falling over the face. Something too competitive. Remember how Glenn Close in the movie *Fatal Attraction* is always seen with psychotic blue eyes under a blond whitewater of hair. When long-haired women have children, they frequently cut their hair short. Pleading convenience, they explain it merely as a practical move. But it is, I think, more symbolic. In various cultures and religions (among nuns and some Jewish wives, for instance) women are expected to cut their hair short so that they will no longer be attractive to men. A freshly bobbed new mother might be saying, in essence, I'm going to focus my life now on nurturing my family; I'm not available for flirtation. At the end of World War II, collaborators were de-sexed and shamed by having their hair chopped off in what was, essentially, a form of social circumcision. Mothers often wish a daughter to cut her hair short when she reaches puberty, but fathers want a daughter to keep her hair long forever. A friend tells me that when she turned fourteen her mother talked her into cutting her waist-length hair, much to the horror of her father who, in a melodramatic and ritually symbolic gesture, insisted that he alone be allowed to cut it.

Throughout history, hair has been considered not just ornamental but magical. In ancient Egypt, a widow would bury a lock of her hair with her husband as a charm and, possibly, as a vow that her love went with him. The goddess Isis used her hair as a rejuvenating fabric to bestow life on her dead lover, Osiris; and even the shadow of her hair, spread like the wings of an eagle, protected her child from harm. The constellation Berenice's hair—a pretty cascade of stars lying between Boötes and Leo—is said to be the hair of an Egyptian queen who lived in the third century B.C. and was married to her brother, Ptolemy III Euergetes. Soon after the wedding, Ptolemy III went off to war in Asia, and Berenice swore that if he returned alive and victorious she would sacrifice her hair to the gods. I don't think her motive was that the gods needed chignons, but the all-too-human belief that nothing good happens without the requisite amount of sacrifice or punishment. On Ptolemy's safe return, she offered up her long hair in the temple of Aphrodite near present-day Aswan. But the next day, mysteriously, the hair vanished. Soon the Alexandrian mathematician and astronomer, Conon of Samos, alerted the king to a swarm of stars he had seen near the tail of the constellation Leo, and his conviction that they were the queen's hair, set in the heavens to commemorate Ptolemy's victory. What really happened to Berenice's hair, we will never know. (Perhaps Conon secretly had a crush on Berenice, and wanted at least to possess her hair, an intimate part of her.) But his discovery certainly was timely.

Although I haven't always been happy with my hair, I never thought of it as literally demonic. Now and then I might have hoped it would beguile, but I didn't suppose it was supernaturally evil, the devil's circuitry, the whips of hell. In more superstitious days, however, people associated horror with women's hair. During the Middle Ages, the unruly hair of "witches" was thought to control the weather. All manner of hail, hurricanes, or windstorms could be unleashed by a woman allowing her hair to fall wild. Of course there was always some woman somewhere who didn't give a fig for the reputed evil in her hair, and unbraided her long tresses to have a good wash. This was considered highly uncivic-minded, since, as everyone knew, a thunderstorm occurred solely because a woman somewhere was combing out her hair. In Corinthians 11:10, St. Paul warns that good Christian women should cover their heads because demons leap like sparks from female hair and enter the world to do mischief. The tradition of a woman covering her head in church originated with this belief, that any mild-mannered woman could poison the church building with her licelike demons.

Pagan superstitions about hair ran riot during the Middle Ages.

One example: bury a snippet of hair from a menstruating witch and it will become a snake. Reminiscent of the Medusa myth, this one combines many suggestive images—witches, the temptation of Eve, the supposed filthiness of menstruation, the power that came from secretly possessing a lock of someone's hair. But there was also good magic associated with hair, especially when strands were braided and given as amulets. Lovers often exchanged locks of hair, and knights rode to battle with a precious twist of their lady's sacred hair to keep them brave.

But hair symbolizes more than romance; it can also serve as a political placard. Each generation, needing to feel a sense of identity, sets itself apart through hairstyle. Because there are only so many things one can do with one's hair to shock society, styles seem to reappear after a decade or so. Those who lived through love-ins and antiwar rallies probably find it as strange as I do to see construction workers now wearing ponytails and headbands or a policeman with long sideburns. Or a corporate man in a conservative suit wearing a ponytail. It makes me do a double take: the look is hippie, but the politics and philosophy are different. History, myth, and literature are filled with dramas in which hair plays a central role. Most often it symbolizes strength, as in the story of Samson and Delilah; or sexuality, as in the fairy tale about Rapunzel; or selfless love, as in the famous short story by O. Henry; or fetish magic, as in American Indian lore; or a religious portent, as in the Aztec myth from which Cortes profited—that a god would appear from afar and be recognizable by his blond hair. I won't argue that hair brought down the monarchy in eighteenth-century France, but it may have helped to focus society's rage. At Marie Antoinette's court, both men and women were said to use barrels of flour to whiten their elaborate wigs. Reputedly, this waste so outraged the common people, who were starving for want of bread, that they cut their own hair short in protest and, ultimately, condemned royal hair and heads to the guillotine.

Merely thinking about the eighteenth century's huge, cloudlike wigs and the matted, rarely washed hair beneath makes my skin crawl. I like to wash my hair every day, unless I'm far from running water. At times, I go on expeditions into perfect wildernesses. Then I braid my hair, leaving my fluffy bangs loose. Yet my hair sometimes disturbs male scientists enough that they feel obliged to comment on it. For example, when I was making arrangements for a recent trip to the Brazilian rain forest, the project director took a hard look at me and said, "You'll have to do something with your hair." "I can pull it back," I assured him, trying not to smile. Most people understand the concept of long hair—that it can be braided, put in a ponytail, or in other ways subdued for hot weather or dense foliage. But he instinctively remarked on it, as others in his position sometimes have, because long hair is suggestive. It implies excess, extravagance, rampant sensuality—literally, a lack of restraint. Expedition work tends to be unisex, and it's tough to work efficiently if there are man/woman distractions and complications. So people are often fearful of accentuating gender differences by wearing sexy clothes and loose hair, of setting free the "demons" of temptation.

The same seems to be true on the electronic frontier. This past year, with much hoopla, four of network television's anchorwomen bobbed their hair. What I find fascinating is all the ruckus it caused. Deborah Norville, then of the *Today* show, said: "My hair was never my own on television." After her *20/20* interview with Boris Yeltsin, Barbara Walters received compliments, but she was amazed to find that some were just about her new haircut. There is a tacit assumption in the media that long hair looks vampy, not authoritative or sincere, and that changing the length of hair changes the sexual message. It also changes the sexual message at home. "Now I have a whole new life," Diane Sawyer, of *PrimeTime Live,* said to *Newsweek,* "I do a year doing investigative reporting, and you call about my hair!" Her husband is reported to have complained that he went to bed with a sex symbol and "woke up with Peter Pan."

Human lovers aren't the only ones fixated on hair. Other primates devote a lot of time to mutual nit-picking and grooming—not just for cleanliness but as a way to weave relationships. Most mammals adore mutual preening. Perhaps that's why we can fuss with a loved one's hair for hours in a state of hypnotic rapture. Hair care is a task one rarely performs alone. We require others to tend our hair at beauty salons. We obsessively prepare our hair for our loved ones. Yet hair is not the most vital part of us. It shimmers and moves, but it is composed of dead cells. We may harvest it from time to time, carve or color it, but it will grow again and return to its weedy ways. In this, it echoes the sheer disarray of nature. People so often complain that their hair is too "wild," that they "can't do anything with it," that it's nothing but "split ends" and "strays," that it's hopelessly "fly-away." Perhaps we fear that, like ourselves, and like our feelings of love, despite our constant efforts, it will always be just a little bit out of control.

WOMEN AND HORSES

"Lorenzo, my beautiful, handsome boy," a woman in jodhpurs says, kissing the nose of a tall, swarthy male. She exhales deeply, and he inhales her breath as naturally as if they were two sleeping lovers. She runs her fingers over his soft lips. Letting her leather crop fall gently to her side, stroking his shoulder with one hand, she moves slowly down his ribcage and tightens an array of leather cinches and belts, and with each tug he murmurs a halfhearted complaint. Then she mounts him, frets his flanks lightly with her heels, and they begin to move together, as one rhythm, one power.

We are in Claremont Riding Academy, at Eighty-ninth Street and Amsterdam, in a residential area of Manhattan where even horses live in condominiums. What makes the ceiling flex and rattle as if a ghost were afoot is a horse walking down the hallway overhead. In one corner, a pungent drizzle falls between the planks, then stops. Lorenzo and his rider break into a slow, swinging canter. Six young girls, taking a weekly lesson, also begin cantering around the small arena. Few things are as beautiful as the faces of ten-year-old girls deep in concentration. Despite shadows cast by the brims of the black riding hats, their faces glow from the inner electricity of enthusiasm. Their bodies quest for discipline and control, but their eyes burn like tungsten. It's as if someone has doused them in buckets of pure light.

"The week I started Freudian analysis I bought a horse," Jane Marie tells me as she mounts a bay thoroughbred named Kahlúa. I swing one leg over a chestnut named Crunch, adjust the stirrups, and we set out through the traffic for Central Park. An expert in Japanese shamanistic puppetry, Jane Marie divides her life between teaching religion and training horses. She grew up in Montana, went to school in Colorado, and cannot remember a period of her life that wasn't made whole by horses. An ambulance wails past us at speed, its red light flashing. Pedestrians stop and follow it with their eyes, but the horses neither flinch nor shy. They are used to the concrete mayhem of the city, and the two blocks of crowds and cars between Claremont and the park. Three little girls carrying rucksacks on their way home from school run up to us and plead: "Can I pet him?" Each passes a small hand over a soft leg and then stands back in awe. When the light changes, we cross the street, step onto the bridle path, and pick up a slow trot.

"How did analysis go?" I ask Jane Marie.

"I spent a lot of time talking about training my horse, and for the few first months, the analyst probably thought, 'Well we're bound to get down to some real stuff pretty soon, so I'll just humor her.' But you know, it never did stop. I always talked about how the horse was progressing. For example, a horse has a stiff side and a supple side, just like some people do—in psychoanalytic terms that would be called a resistance—and you can't just beat a horse over the head to get to its resistance. You have to figure out how it came about. People form things into mental concepts, but if a horse has a traumatic experience, it will register it in its body. In time, I discovered that someone had been abusive with my horse while turning him into a cow pony."

As Kahlúa steps across stones hidden beneath the sandy earth, his hooves sound like flint scraping on flint. That biting rasp in a slurry of soft sand is part of what makes riding horses so thrilling. It's filled with seemingly irreconcilable sensations and conflicts. Instead of canceling one another out, they occur together, side by side, like the notes in a musical chord. The hard and the soft. The wild and the tame. The restraint and the panic. The grace and the power.

"As a trainer," Jane Marie continues, "you try to reconstruct primary experiences with the animal to unlock the horse's potential of graceful movement, and also to make a happier horse, one not afraid of other horses and people or of being ridden. So, in analysis, I was always talking about resistance—the horse's resistance—but I was also talking about my own life."

Tossing his shoulders and flattening his ears in the visual equivalent of a growl, my horse shows a bit of temper, and I romance him, as it's called, using hands, legs, and balance to gently persuade him to behave. As Crunch settles down, I speak soothingly and rub one hand affectionately along his mane. Jane Marie's dark thoroughbred breaks into a fast fly-away trot, and tries to hurl itself against some invisible foe, pulls and coils itself up for escape. Her hands gently reason with the reins, her hips settle deep into the saddle, and she holds the horse in a long extended trot in which its legs hyperextend and pump like pistons. Its neck curves the way Austrian Lipizzans' do, and then it settles into an exaggerated prance. The visual effect is that the horse seems to be pacing out of time, suspended between the tock and tick of life. It's the same effect as when a diver, reaching the highest arc of a dive, achieves the still point and hovers for one breathless moment in the air.

"What people don't realize about horseback riding," Jane Marie says, "is that you have to bring into harmony two beings that both have their own centers of gravity. People think that training horses is molding them to a human form, when really what you're doing is helping the horse recenter himself with a rider on his back. That recentering into a relationship is something that human beings are doing when they're developing intimacy with people. They find that a person on his own has a different center of gravity than a person who is in a relationship."

Unconsciously, she shifts slightly in the saddle, finding the best spot. For the first time, I notice the brand name "Patagonia" on her teal-green jacket. When I was in Patagonia, years ago, I saw a woman riding a black Andalusian stallion along the beach. Its tail hung to the ground and its long, silky mane blew in the wind like a rippling flag. The woman's long, dark hair blew like a mane, too, as she cantered slowly over the jasper pebbles of the beach. Riding bareback, with only a strap around the horse's neck, she seemed locked in an intense private dream.

"The irony, the wonderful thing, is that women can have substitute human relationships with horses," Jane Marie went on. "There's a whole repertoire of types of intimacy that are possible, and our society is fixated on just one—the sexual. When I first bought my horse, how scruffy he was! But after I worked with him for a while, how really graceful and beautiful he became! His whole shape changed. His posture changed, his conformation changed. Even the way this horse carried himself changed, because his inner self was restored."

"What did the horse restore in you?"

"Having a horse was having a pair of legs that were faster than a boy could beat up on a girl. I grew up in northwest Montana, and there violence against women starts when girls are very young. For me, having a horse meant I could escape. I could outrun them on a horse. But it's more than that. I escaped the puberty doldrums because I had a horse. Other twelve- and fourteen-year-old girls were standing in front of their mirrors doing their hair and wondering whether boys were going to notice them or not. I was polishing my horse's coat and making its tail pretty. Consequently, I wasn't overly concerned about how my hair looked, and whether or not I had pimples on my face. I was terribly worried about the condition of my horse's hooves and what his coat looked like. I would carefully braid his mane at night so that not a single hair would get caught, and I would brush out his tail.

"I think the notion that horses are surrogate lovers is wrong. They're surrogate selves."

Fall leaves litter the bridle path, and the horses' hooves make a dry, rhythmic *shushing* sound. Antique street lamps, winding down several lanes through the park, have come on with a golden glow. Birds throng overhead and among the bushes. Sparrows, finches, blue jays, and cardinals feed on the wild seeds and berries. Crows, pigeons, gulls, and other scavengers ransack the garbage bins. Woodpeckers and chickadees pull hibernating insects out of the trees. So much of the city is brick and steel that every bird for miles crams into the park, which also teems with bat and insect life. In this huge oasis, where wildlife clusters, the ancient dramas of nature play themselves out with simplicity and daring, as they would in any Alpine meadow, or deep in a New Mexico cavern. It is November, *wint-monat* or "wind month," to the Anglo-Saxons, a time to light bonfires and worship ancestors, a chilling time, a killing time. Clouds curdle overhead, and the sun slices through in wide swords of light. Somewhere far away the city guns its giant engines, launches its new perfumes, aims its bright-red lasers, creates and computes; and love, like the stock market, rises and falls. As we canter along some of the paths, we can see the minarets of that high-tech mecca, but on others we are enforested, enmeadowed, and all alone, rustling through the fall leaves on a country lane.

"At my local stable in Colorado," Jane Marie says, "the riders were almost all women, and what I noticed was that, for all those women, horses were metaphors of complex inner processes. For example, there was one woman in her fifties, an enormously fat woman who rode enormous horses. She was a nurse, someone trying to help people get in touch with their inner health. I noticed that she expressed that with everyone's horses, too. Whenever a horse got injured, she would nurse it. When she talked about health and horses, she put it in terms of what she was teaching her nursing students at the university. She worked with disturbed children, and I noticed that she was really good with horses that were disturbed."

As we trot briskly along a narrowing trail, bushes whip us like small wire whisks, and we tuck in our chins to protect our eyes.

"There was a sixteen-year-old girl, Kim, who had the best horse in the barn—a horse that had been a big-time show horse before she got it. Her aunt, who was not much older than she was, had been born badly handicapped—with one very short leg—but she got interested in horses, and her parents were wealthy, and they put a lot of energy and money into her riding, and she went all the way to becoming one of the top riders in the country. She simply rode with one stirrup short on one side. When she died, her niece, Kim, inherited a horse trailer, all the tack, and all the horses from this aunt who had made it to the nationals. Kim had wonderful horses and all this fantastic gear, but behind her horseback riding there was a sorrow at having lost an aunt she loved and felt compassion for. That sadness was never far from the surface; she often spoke of her aunt. So, for her, keeping up these horses was also a way to keep up the memory of her aunt. Everyone at the barn had good reasons to be riding, which sometimes meant an injured part of themselves that needed to be healed. I think a lot of people were constructing identities through their relationship with horses."

"What kind of relationship did you form with your horse?" I ask, as we trot into the clear once more. A small flock of birds appears overhead like a shake of pepper, and a half-moon rises among the clouds. Still low in the sky, the moon seems to be caged in the branches of the trees. A familiar sight, it is the Chinese pictogram for "leisure."

"He was three, an adolescent, and very much like a playmate. I named him Boo Radley, after the character in *To Kill a Mockingbird*. We had great adventures together, some of which were religious in their intensity. For example, I remember one evening I was riding him on top of a hill in Colorado, and suddenly this storm moved in quickly. Of course, everyone's got a story about someone on a horse being struck by lightning. You're riding around on this animal, you're the tallest thing on the landscape, and you've got metal on the bridle and saddle. So I'm up on my horse, this storm moves in, and I know I am the highest thing on the horizon for a long ways, and I know that we are basically done for if we don't get out of there. The horse wants to get out, and I decide I should just give the horse his head and hope for the best, and we start galloping at dead breakneck speed. And let me tell you, galloping down steep hills is dangerous. I've never been on a horse that moved so fast in all my life—and I used to ride racehorses when I was a kid—we were *flying* off the ground. When we got back to the barn at last, we were both sweating, and there was a sense that we had had an adventure together. We had a lot of adventures together, Boo and I."

A nightjar planes low over the trees as we leave the bridle path and head back to Claremont Academy. Flying with its mouth open, it sieves the air for insects just as a baleen whale sieves the ocean for krill. Any day now, when the last insects vanish from the sky, the nightjar will start migrating south.

"Galloping a horse in a lightning storm—that gives me a sense of what religious mystics are talking about," Jane Marie says.

Yes, I think, so does going into a barn in the middle of the night, when the horses are sleeping, sitting down next to them, and waiting for them to wake up. Or seeing a horse die. When you have these experiences, there's some sort of opening between your world and theirs, and their world, the animal world, suddenly becomes available.

As we pass one brownstone, a young man in a leather jacket, leaning insouciantly in a doorway, leers at us, at our riding crops and shiny black boots. Rolling a toothpick around in his mouth, he says, with a toss of the chin, "Hey, baby, now you know how to treat a husband."

Farther along, three little girls gush with excitement as we pass. Even girls in big cities dream about horses, as do girls in a variety of cultures, whether or not they have contact with real horses. They fantasize about unicorns, or play with horse toys, the most recent of which are long-haired ponies they can brush and groom. There is an ancient connection, hidden deep in the collective unconscious, a place where horses fuel some of our most powerful obsessions and leave us gasping in religious ecstasy.

Ancient horse worship was practiced throughout Europe, and thrived into the Christian era. In the twelfth century, Irish kings were still practicing ceremonies of symbolic rebirth from the callipygian body of their goddess Epona, the White Mare. Her chalk effigy, 350 feet long, surveys a hillside in Berkshire, England, and is much visited by tourists. In the Iron Age, people worshiped her throughout the western world. The Jutish king and queen (who ruled what is now Kent) were named Hengist and Horsa, that is, stallion and mare. Male, female, and androgynous horse gods bewitched the imagination with their explosive sensuality. Ripe, voluptuous-hipped, and intuitive, arriving in a cloud of dust as if conjured into being, accompanied by the rhythmic drumroll of their hooves, horses seemed possessed of magic. With a sense of smell more highly attuned than humans', they could bolt in panic before the thunder ripped, foretell an earthquake, flee from an advancing but still-unseen predator. It made them seem prescient as wizards. A prey species, horses panic by design. Anything out of the ordinary alerts their senses, detonating a complex bomb of responses: shrieking, shying, rearing up, bolting away. They don't wait around to analyze the threat. Reacting to dangers only they perceive—something as harmless as a wind blown leaf or a shadow flickering in moonlight—horses are flightiness on the hoof. In touch with invisible demons, they must have seemed to our ancestors four-legged emissaries from the ghost world. Humans are prone to feel unworthy, even in the eyes of animals they control. What could be more powerful an ideal than the courageous, ever-alert, heavily sexed horse, pawing the ground in defiance, its hooves all declaratives?

Sometimes votive horse heads decorated homes, for good luck, and religious dancers in Europe and Asia pretended to ride horse-headed sticks. Holding the horse god erect between their legs, shamans said they took flight and galloped across the sky until they reached heaven. When a warrior died, a horse in the funeral procession carried his ghost. His boots were arranged backward in the stirrups because ghosts supposedly had backward-facing feet. Throughout antiquity, horses carried the dead to the netherworld, as they do symbolically in state funerals today. Even the Norse god Odin figured in a vast horse cult that stretched all the way to India. Hindu gods took the shape of horses when they died; and, in an important fertility ritual, a Hindu queen pretending to be the mare goddess Saranyu would take the penis of a dead horse and dramatically plant it between her legs, while urging "the vigorous male" to "lay seed." According to *The Woman's Encyclopedia of Myths and Secrets,*

> This ancient ceremony explains one of Odin's more puzzling titles, Völsi, meaning both "Son of God" and "Horse's Penis." The penis was the "son" worshipped by Iron Age equestrian tribes calling themselves Völsungs, descendents of Völsi. The cult was not confined to Scandinavia. The Welsh had the same ancestral horse-god, Waelsi or Waels. Slavs also worshipped him as Volos, a sacrificed horse whose entrails and blood were supposed to produce the water of life. . . . Volos was still incarnated in a ritually castrated and slaughtered stallion every spring, up to the eighteenth century A.D. Since the people insisted on worshipping him, he was converted into a Christian saint, Vlas, who had no real existence except as a pagan horse god. . . . Ancient Rome knew him as the October Horse. . . . The Taurians sacrificed to Artemis horses from whom "the member was cut off."

From the union of the bloody Horse Penis and the Earth Mother came a race of centaurs: gods half man, half horse. Indian myth called such beings Gandharvas, and both cultures credited them with wizardry, light-footed dancing, and perpetual lust. In Greece, Pegasus the winged horse carried heroes to heaven, while centaurs roamed the land, full of hot-blooded mischief, looking for new brides to abduct and rape. In Sweden, kings could be ripped apart by horse Valkyries, or by their witchlike priestesses, called Volvas, who wore horse masks.

As late as the sixteenth century, Europeans were bleeding horses on the day after Christmas, as a token sacrifice to the White Mare, and straddling "Old Hob" at New Year's. Indeed, we still give our children "hobbyhorses" to ride, without realizing that it's a carryover from the frenzied dancing of the pagan horse cult. The horseshoe we hang over a door for good luck symbolizes the vulva of the mare goddess. Ancient peoples, from the Celts to the Hindus, heeded this symbol, which they wore as amulets, and in whose shape they designed their temples. In fact, the earliest engravings known in the western world—Paleolithic carvings in the rock shelters of Castelmerle—are of vulvas. In Greece, the horse vulva shape became the omega, the final letter of the alphabet, which led around again to the alpha, completing the life sentence of rebirth. If decorating one's house with images of mares' genitals sounds odd, remember that ancient Romans dressed their children in penis amulets to ward off evil spirits, and medieval churches displayed symbols of female genitals (called "sheela-na-gigs") on their doorways for the same purpose. "Horseshoe" was a slang term for the female genitals in eighteenth-century Europe (a seduced girl was said to have "lost a horseshoe"). Horses have always tantalized a wild and ancient part of us that worshiped the White Mare, symbolized by her genitals; in her secret cave, the male and female life forces united to restore nature with nuts and berries, herds of animals with young, and humans with the possibility of rebirth.

Some women embrace horses as a psychological prosthesis or as a mystic guide; for them, riding has to do with the perfection of the soul. For others, the connection is earthier and more sensual. But, for all, the infatuation begins early, in the foothills of adolescence.

After leaving Claremont Academy, I catch a flight upstate into deep country, to visit a psychologist whose practice includes adolescent girls. She lives in a lakeside town with a bird sanctuary threading through it and farmlands surrounding it, where horses are so familiar that signs along the highway forbid horseback riding through the four lanes of catapulting traffic.

The towns of upstate New York are like railway stations, where at any moment hundreds of lives converge—people carrying small satchels of worry or disbelief, people racing down the slippery corridors of youth, people slowly dragging the steamer trunk of a trauma, people fresh from the suburbs of hope, people troubled by timetables, people keen to arrive, people whose minds are like small place settings, people whose aging faces are sundials, people desperate and alone who board a bullet train in the vastness of nothing and race hell-bent to the extremities of nowhere. At the edge of the town I live in, a converted depot restaurant called The Station reminds us of the time when train cars shuffled in a long conga line to Manhattan. In earlier days a clock outside the restaurant was frozen at 6:22, when the last iron fury left town. But the trains have never stopped running. People meet often in their narrow trembling cars. They hear the sleep-thick breathing of their neighbors in the next compartment. In time, everyone meets everyone, either by repute or in person in Ithaca's equivalent of a dining car.

Downtown, in the center of a red-brick junior high school that has been converted to shops, the Café Dewitt consists of a scatter of bistro tables in a large open corridor; and it's the place where everyone goes for lunch, because diners can watch and greet passersby on their way to errands. One day, I meet Linda there for lunch. A vibrant, pretty woman of fifty, with short, wavy blond hair and large penetrating eyes, she is a clinical psychologist who sees many girls and women in her practice. Over mozzarella-and-tomato salads and whole-wheat bread drizzled with honey, we discuss horse love. I grew up completely enraptured by horses. Although Linda didn't, she has seen that rapture often among the girls she counsels.

"Horse love rarely strikes girls until they're around nine or ten," Linda says. "Before that they have little plastic ponies and unicorns; but the intense passion seems to be in prepubescence. So I see horse love on a primitive level as a girl's recognition of her sexuality, without a focus for it in the genital area. The boys they know don't begin to embody all that a girl's young body is starting to feel."

"So they're bursting with a sexuality that they have not yet identified by name or form, a free-floating sexuality?" I ask.

"Yes, and the horse is androgynous. It has all this phallic power, even if it's a mare, because of its speed and muscles and suppleness and its size next to a little girl or woman. But also it has this incredible elegance of line and beauty, which a little girl responds to aesthetically."

"When I was a girl," I confide, "I felt a powerful urge to transform myself into a horse."

"Yes," she says slowly. "There are two little girls in my neighborhood that I've been watching. They ride, collect toy horses, pictures of horses. But what they do on the weekend in the yard is become horses. They rein each other up and they ride around and they jump. But the way it looks to me is that it is a kind of ideal representation of the self, before the self is identified with the world of men, or sexuality between men and women. The girl becomes free and strong and wild and sexual and powerful. I can remember feeling some of this myself, although I never became obsessed with horses."

As I hear her describe the horse-girls in her neighborhood, my mind floods with memories of the deepest devotion. When I was twelve, the target of my love was horses. Although it felt like a secret passion, unique and nameless, I was not alone in my equinomania. Child psychologists don't offer horse love as a formal stage in a pre-adolescent girl's development, but I've taken an informal survey over the years, and found that eight out of ten girls go through a stage of horse idolatry. Boys like horses, and often feel a shared sense of magic, but they don't yearn for horses with the same magnetic devotion that girls do. This operatic longing, as powerful and obsessive as a love affair, fills every corner of a girl's life, sending her into raptures, mobilizing her daydreams, giving her life meaning. Even girls who can't draw can at least draw a horse, and they often fill the margins of school notebooks with horse heads. They usually have plastic horses and riders to play with, books about horses, and they invent games in which they ride (or become) spectacular horses. As a budding writer, I started a horse newspaper for the kids in my neighborhood, but stopped when I realized how time-consuming it would be to write out every copy in longhand. Then I began writing a novel about a horse named Stormy and a girl who loved him. A surprising number of girls keep horse scrapbooks. I still have mine, begun on my twelfth birthday, and it's the diary of a typical horse maniac. It begins with a copy of "The Horse's Prayer," an anonymous, Dickensian appeal for the fair treatment of horses, which ends with "You will not consider me irreverent if I ask this in the name of Him who was born in a Stable. Amen." The yellowed pages that follow contain an array of black-and-white photographs of people and their horses, cartoons about horses, newspaper clippings about horses for sale, postcards of horses, famous cowboys and cowgirls posing beside their horses, young equestrians at horse camp sitting astride their horses, a playing card (the eight of spades) with a horse head on the picture side, newspaper stories about horse shows or horse owners, a Christmas card from a girl named Gayle posing happily beside her white horse, many photo-portraits of Arabian stallions whose owners were standing them at stud, a movie-magazine shot of Clark Gable and Carole Lombard playing with two foals, and—my prize possession—a snapshot of me standing beside Gallant Masterpiece, a horse I thought the pinnacle of beauty and power. My ecstatic smile is because, at that moment, just touching so magnificent a creature, I had entered the gates of paradise. Sometimes the owner allowed me to brush the huge thoroughbred's head. On one occasion, in the paddock, he lifted me onto the horse and nearly fainted when the horse bolted with me aboard, and I slipped all over its back, down its neck, and around its withers, without actually falling off. A few minutes later, the owner caught up to us, and he was shaking with panic and worry, but I had hung on to the mane and was having the time of my life. The scrapbook also contains the first poem I ever memorized. I had to recite it in front of the class in sixth grade, and I stumbled badly over the word *convulsively*. It was "The Ballad of the White Stallion," a tale of primal fury, ghost horses, gutty hunters, lots of decorative imagery, and a big-hearted stallion, both godlike and unyielding, described as "A lonely spirit—/But free. . . . " I can recite it to this day.

Early human history is saturated with horse worship, but for women the relationship goes even deeper, to the core of their psychology. It also goes sideways into sociology. As I discovered growing up in the sixties, girls didn't have high-adrenaline sports to jolt the nerves and make the heart stampede. Swimming was one acceptable "girl's sport," but it didn't produce a hard sweat, let alone the roller coaster of excitement that adolescents crave. Boys had football, wrestling, track, basketball, and motorcycles—ways to use themselves with exhilaration and power. We girls were forced to boil with the lid on tight. Some took up ice skating and ballet, but many more rode horses.

Athletically, horseback riding is an apparatus sport, like driving a racing car or skiing: you magnify your body's strength and agility through the horse, which becomes a part of your anatomy that you can teach and perfect. The shy and introverted, who might be turned off by team sports, were never alone on horseback, where they could leap high fences, race the wind, and lead a secret life as a superhero. A horse will exhaust you as royally as a football scrimmage, but at its highest level riding becomes an abstract art form: dressage on the ground, haute école (what Lipizzans do) in the air. It demands the discipline of Zen, the taut muscles of dance, and the timing of gymnastics. Then, too, one has the sense of learning a craft, as well as belonging to a club complete with esoteric grips and special lingo. The uniform—jodhpurs, blue jeans, or riding britches—fits the calf snugly and accentuates one's gender. When, only a few decades ago, women rode sidesaddle, they had to struggle with long culottes, under which they wore doeskin pantaloons, under which they wore satin trousers. It was considered indelicate for a woman to have a massive horse between her legs. So women went to dressmakers, where they sat on a mock-up sidesaddle, so that inseams of different lengths could be measured. It wouldn't do to have an extra yard of doeskin, pantaloon, and satin dangling from the leg that's wrapped around the pommel. What an awful business it must have been to walk in that getup. How on earth did they sit comfortably at prehunt breakfasts, with their underclothes down to the ankle on one leg and above the knee on the other?

About the time a knack for coping with life becomes essential (that is, before a girl can drive a car), she can at least hop onto a horse and jog out into the woods, or dawdle chorelessly along a country road. Because she finds an escape route that hurts no one and works, it sticks with her lifelong. Many a girl has learned how to give affection by being around horses, living creatures she can talk to and caress, and trust with fragile ideas or unrepeatable secrets. Something that has real personality, but does not demand or censor, something big and strong that sweeps her off her feet, and carries her at a lope (a word perilously close to *elope*) out into the raging surfeit of summer, or the death wish of autumn, or the bud-breaking chaos of spring.

Older, married perhaps, a woman discovers how many frustrations can be left at the stable door. She can groom, take warmth from, and ride a horse, which doesn't complain, or get acne before the prom, or need a car, or stint her sexually, or cheat on her. Although it's bad form in riding to accentuate the pelvis, the hips roll with deep sensuality, and though riders of both sexes hotly deny it, during a slow trot or a canter the body moves a lot like it does in intercourse. The simple truth is that a horse is a big, powerful, mobile thing between a woman's legs, a half ton of snort and lather. Most people prefer not to think of riding in that way, but, throughout history, riding has been associated with pagan sensuality. Even etymologically, if one just considers the technical terms for the parts of the saddle, one discovers that a rider is seated between the male (*pommel,* knob at the hilt of a sword, slang for penis) and the female (*cantle,* wedge-shaped slice, slang for vulva). It has always been tacitly understood that when a rider mounts up she rocks between the male and female life forces.

Eyebrows raise when one mentions women and horses, because the sexuality of horses is so obvious, fiery, and dramatic. The huge creatures called horses have in their shape and the way they move more than a suggestion of virility. When a mare comes into estrus her personality changes, and that is something a child quickly notices. Stallions have enormous penises, and they mount mares with a great commotion of hooves, flying manes, bared teeth, and screaming. But, despite our use of the word "stud" to identify a lusty male, most women don't fantasize about mating with horses, although I'm sure a small number do, the most famous being Catherine the Great, who supposedly had a special harness created to restrain the reach of her favorite stallion. It isn't that women wish to have sex with horses; it's the horses embody their sexuality.

"Havelock Ellis suggests that girls may ride as a form of masturbation. What do you think?" I ask Linda.

"When you're astride a horse, racing across the field, you are riding this giant phallus, and it can have a masturbatory quality to it, when your little clitoris is rubbing right against the horse. That might, for a girl, be an unnameable experience, because very few little girls have mothers who tell them about orgasm or sexual feelings in the vagina and the clitoris. Even today, that's not information usually given to young girls. And that sense of a secret sexuality is important.

"When I was in seventh grade, that is, when I was about twelve or thirteen years old, there were two pastimes that were my very private things that I never spoke about to another soul, not to another girl, certainly. I thought they were my feelings and experiences alone. One was that we had in our backyard a giant T-bar that was part of a clothesline. Children like to do acrobatics. I used to climb this pole, and the reason I would climb it is because I would usually have an orgasm when I did. The motion would arouse me, and I felt powerful sexual feelings that were dizzying and scary but also wonderful. So I sought them out again, though I didn't want anyone to know what it was about—I didn't know myself what it was about. I had absolutely no name for those feelings because I didn't know they were anything other girls had ever had happen to them. We had to climb ropes in gym that year, and I could never get to the very top because halfway up I would have an orgasm. It was the same motion. So it occurs to me that young girls who ride horses may have similar experiences on horseback that they can't tell anyone. First, because they wouldn't know how to describe it; and second, because it's in that part of the body you don't talk about.

"When I was young, I was quite a tomboy, and I felt tremendous pride about this because I thought it meant I was more like a boy, and I wanted to be because boys had more fun. I know that women who are absolutely committed to the most feminist position feel that we're no different from men. But I think we're very different—in our psychology, our interests, the way we relate to our bodies and other people. There is this whole inner life, this sexual self that you cannot see directly unless you take a mirror to it or probe inside with a speculum. You're hidden inside. Boys have all this equipment. It's right out there. They can control it. They can show it off to other boys, to girls. Imagine doing that with your vagina. What are you going to look at? Until you get a partner who wants to look at it and explore it, and then it's fabulous."

"Because you're introduced to almost invisible parts of yourself," I add.

"And then you discover it's interesting and beautiful. So I think that sense of mystery about sex is very real. And there's a difference in male and female stances toward the world. Men penetrate, take hold of, go into . . ."

"Play golf . . . put balls into holes?"

She laughs. "Exactly. Women wrap their legs around horses. For a lot of girls, the horse love disappears once the sexual energy gets transferred to men. There's a certain age at which one seems to outgrow horses. I think horses may be more common to little girls who are rejecting the way society wants to define their femininity, which has now changed, so there may be a difference between girls now and how they were when I was growing up. But I remember that, in addition to horse stories, I read incessantly about wild animals, the lone wolf, the dogs that got separated from their masters and had to live in the wild for years. I loved the wildness and the independence of the animals. Once the beast became an ordinary man the story was changed for me, and it lost its power. I always felt that transformation at the end—which somehow brought everybody back to a normal state of reality—was such a betrayal of what the story was supposed to be about. Part of what you love about the craggy beast is its deformity, roughness—the grotesqueness and the tender heart within. Once he becomes beautiful and grand and looks like Dan Quayle, who gives a damn?"

Laughing, I tell her about the framed double photographs beside my bed—stills from Jean Cocteau's classic film *Beauty and the Beast*. Fairy tales are full of women who marry animals, not all of whom change to princes.

"Why do you think women are attracted to that beautiful beast?" I ask.

"The obvious answer is the sexual power of the beast, which promises to be enormous and terrifying, which is very exciting and stimulating. Socially and sexually, there's something deeply gratifying to most women about being swept away, and not just because it allows you not to feel responsibility for it—although that was certainly important in the fifties. When you stand at the ocean and see all that raging power—it's a thrill. To this day, when I fly in an airplane and it sets down and throws those engines in reverse and the whole plane trembles and roars, it thrills me, I love it. There may be fewer avenues for women to assert their sexuality. The beast is that sexual power, along with the sense that somewhere deep inside him lurks a vulnerability which she can see, she can touch. That gives her power. Look how many women fall in love with cowboys—whether he really is a Marlboro man on the ranch or not—someone who is tough and silent; and she alone is going to find her way to his heart.

There's something seductive about taming the wild beast in him, which, of course, makes for an unhappy love affair, because if you're a cowboy you just have to ride off into the sunset. Or, if she does tame him, then he wasn't a real cowboy after all. So she loses either way."

Throughout time, there have been stories about conquering a minotaur or dragon or some other fearsome force of nature. We have soft, penetrable skin, we are so fragile in this world. Earlier cultures were terrified of thunder; through the halls of lightning walked the gods whom humans needed to appease or vanquish. Men have traditionally faced the monster during hunts. A woman on horseback alternately masters and is mastered by that part of her nature which is a wild, snorting, powerful, mane-tossing beast, full of swerve and beauty. No one understood this better than D. H. Lawrence. In *St. Mawr*, a novella about women and horses, the main character is bewitched by a beautiful stallion, whose nerves are like rockets. Intending to buy him, she thinks of the world he represents:

It was another world, an older, heavily potent world. And in this world the horse was swift and fierce and supreme, undominated and unsurpassed. . . . There was, perhaps, a curious barbaric exultance in bare, dark will devoid of emotion or personal feeling. . . . He was so powerful, and so dangerous. But in his dark eye, that looked, with its cloudy brown pupil, a cloud within a dark fire, like a world beyond our world, there was a dark vitality glowing, and within the fire, another sort of wisdom. She felt sure of it: even when he put his ears back, and bared his teeth, and his great eyes came bolting out of his naked horse's head, and she saw demons upon demons in the chaos of his horrid eyes.

What lures me still when I ride is the disciplined panic of a horse flirting with a tantrum at every turn, the delicate, voluptuous play of muscles, the grace-sprung power. This became especially clear to me one cold winter day a few years ago, when I rode an Appaloosa mare bareback, trotting her swiftly through tight hairpin turns, and for the first time I really stuck, without sliding or jiggling. My legs hugged her belly like a cinch, and her heart pounded against my knees as she paced. Deeply I sat, fixed to the *slap, slap, slap, slap* of her trot, and the counterpoint *thud-plod, thud-plod* of her heart, enchanted by a soft percussion I felt part of, floating above the syncopated rhythm like a melody. A sweet, leathery steam rose from her chest and neck. When I fretted her belly lightly with my calf, she rolled into a long rippling, and I felt at home in the pumping of her shoulders, the sweet dank odor of hot fur, the rhythmic gesturing of her head. My legs tingled with half a dozen pulses, some of them my own. Reckless with exhilaration, I jumped her bareback over several low fences, gripping her steamy hide as we sprang over fence after fence, leaving earth for a moment between the blunt stanchions, and leaping through the gristly winter light toward the sun, now setting right at the end of the valley like a hot yellow liquid pouring out. As my legs began to reason gently with her body, we rose over a fence like a fogbank, below which lay the world of humans. For those slender moments, I felt heart-poundingly creatural, and reveled in the thrill of speed and sunlight, part of an earth-ecstasy as old as the runes. Life blew through my veins as the wind charged through the winter trees. Huge, oily-looking ravens sounded as if they were choking on lengths of blanket. And then night began seeping over the hillsides like a long spill of black ink, erasing everything civilized and safe.

As we are finishing lunch, Linda's former husband strolls by, with his new wife and his two small children. Linda is remarried, too; and she and her ex live only a few houses away from each other, so that all the children in both families have become part of one extended family. Their arrangement is often lauded by local folk as sensitive and enlightened. His nine-year-old daughter, Hannah, rushes to Linda and gives her a hug, then shows off her brand-new white western boots.

"Those are pretty boots!" she tells her.

The girl squirms shyly and says, "I got them to wear riding horses." Just saying that excites her, and she adds, "You know what, I go to Four-H, and we brush the horses and then ride them!"

"Look what *I'm* wearing," I say, pulling my feet from under the table to show her a pair of black western boots. Around the ankle of the right boot is a red leather strap studded with small silver hearts. "Mine are for riding horses, too."

Her eyes catch fire. She looks at me more intently. Then she smiles with the secret understanding of a fellow Freemason. After lunch, I hurry home to watch show-jumping finals on television, while I pack for a journey that will carry me across time and distance to where horse love began.

Flying across New York State, I look down on the evergreens, sharp as arrowheads, the forested hills, and the green-and-brown corduroy of farm fields. Last week I rode through the deserts of the Southwest, where at night the sobbing of wolves twists deep into your dreams, and by day eagles show their feathered bloomers to the world as they fly. In only a few hours I have galloped into another climate, another ecosystem, another culture, thanks to that modern-day horse, the airplane, whose energy we even define as "horsepower." Sailing aloft in a sheath of gleaming steel, while the planet turns gently below, I move forward in time by means of a pocket miracle even children take for granted. We can throw a switch and make sunlight dawn in a dark room; turn a knob and change an icy porch to summer. After such marvels, why should it surprise us that we have taught metal to fly? Or that we can gallop on the wind like the horse gods of old? Or that we can make a pilgrimage at 25,000 feet? Our planes go back and forth, but time goes only one way in nature, and in clocks, with each moment becoming a greater state of disorder than the one before it. Everything decays. Even we, who will become old and may betray our dreams. Even the living, breathing, many-laked Adirondacks below me, ablaze with what we have come to call autumn. Then I finally see JFK in the distance, flickering with haze. In some ways, time is the least plausible of our fictions. Trying to corral time is like trying to hobble a ghost, but horses have helped to make that ghost visible.

At JFK, stepping forward again in time, I climb aboard the fastest metal horse commuters ride, and in minutes leap straight up into the sky, bank briefly, and head east. We pass quickly through "Indian land"—what pilots call the altitudes where Senecas, Navajos, and other light twin-engined planes fly—and before long leave everything, even the weather, beneath us as we enter a purple sky. At cruising speed—1,000 miles an hour—we are traveling almost as fast as the earth turns. The sea below looks black, and the sun showers glitter onto the waves. Although the water appears flat, still, and silent, I think of all the dramas unfolding in every direction, and how the whole sea is sloshing up and down, like a pen inking across a chart, while the land moves, too. When they move in concert, a reef forms. Through the small porthole, I can see the curvature of the earth. Somewhere below and far away, hidden from view, is everything I've ever known, everyone I've ever loved.

In time, the purple sky gives way to blue, and we land at Orly Airport, outside Paris. There I change planes and head south, to Périgord in the Dordogne, a region famous for its truffles, goose-liver pâté, and ancient history. From Périgord's small airport, a taxi drives me for nearly an hour through small towns, past rambling châteaux, and around jagged hillsides, to a simple forest of sycamores and limestone caves. Heading back 30,000 years, I can feel the old bones of my longing to know who and what we were millennia ago. Sometimes the past is more knowable than the present, and it's easier to glimpse what we were than what we have become. This valley once burgeoned with junipers and hazels, limes, walnuts, and oaks; flowers coated its grassy prairies; strawberries, blackberries, and currants grew on its bushes; salmon filled its rivers, along whose banks wading birds fished. Bison, aurochs (ancestors of the Spanish fighting bulls), wild boars, deer, rabbits, horses, ibex, lions, bears, and rhinoceros roamed the valley. Reindeer herds poured across the grasslands, and the Magdalenian hunters feasted on their flesh, wore their hide for warmth, and used their fat to make smokeless lamps of a kind still used by the Inuit. The so-called cavemen didn't live in caves, but in hide tents close to running water, and sometimes outside a cave, using its overhang as a protective porte cochère. Journeying far into the caves, on magical expeditions to the Unknown, they began smearing the damp walls with ocher, manganese, and charcoal, organizing the dreamlike chaos of their experience into what we have come to call art.

For the past twenty-four hours, thanks to supersonic horsepower, I have been rushing eastward into the dawn-stalking earth, following a trail backward in time to see the cathedral-like walls of the Lascaux cave. There, depicted more often than any other animal (including humans) is the horse. The horse-worshipers of Lascaux most likely lived about 17,500 years ago, in a world climate similar to ours today. The mild weather filled the living larder of the hills. We picture the people as crude, but they already had perforated sewing needles, were masterful hunters, fishers, and spelunkers. They sang and danced, beat drums made of hide, and played music on bone flutes and whistles. Seminomadic, tribal, few in number, they visited the cave often, presumably for religious and initiation rites. We are the heirs of such folk. In the attic of our genes lie curios and costumes, uniforms that no longer fit, envelopes filled with photographs of relatives we have never met. They bequeathed to us much of our personality as a species—not just the blunt fury of our moods, blood lust, and territoriality, but our curiosity and awe and feeling for family. If there is a crevasse of understanding between us, it's partly bridged by art—that need to create works of numbing beauty—which speaks to us just as powerfully today. They felt a voluptuous passion for horses, along with a thirst to celebrate and praise nature. We have inherited their sense of worship.

The original Lascaux cave is sealed and protected, because the irreplaceable artworks, since their discovery, have been disturbed by air, moisture, and human exhalations. Realizing that a fungus had begun to devour some of the drawings, the French government wisely closed Lascaux to the public and built a replica cave nearby (the drawings are laser-perfect). But for many years I've longed to stand where the cavemen stood, to touch their brush strokes with my eyes. Five researchers a day may enter the original cave, very briefly, following strict rules; and I have the privilege of being one of them.

In a small office aboveground, five of us gather to be briefed by an official guide; then we set off. Walking down the swollen belly of a hillside, down a flight of steps, and through a thin vent, we enter an anteroom where a shallow basin of disinfectant waits for us to dip our feet. That completes the purification ceremony. Then, passing through a steel door, we climb down another flight of stairs to a womblike opening, through which we creep in darkness. The guide groups us together, by feel and flashlight, in the perfect blackness. The damp tastes gritty and salt-sweet. No one speaks. A quiet fan blurs the sounds of breathing. In this group of five initiates, four of us are women.

Then a whisper breaks my reverie; I return to the present in the black womb of the cave, to hear the faint sound of footsteps. Suddenly an explosion of light hits the ceiling and walls, and brightly colored animals leap out at us. I flinch, blink hard, then find myself in motion. Everywhere I turn the animals are stampeding around and over us in a great galloping helter-skelter array of flashing hooves and horns. There are bison and aurochs and ibex galore. But dwarfing them all are the horses, a floodtide of horses drawn over and around and underneath one another, horses leaping into alcoves, galloping through stone valleys, kicking and rearing and fighting and grazing. They are round-bellied, pear-hooved horses with stiff, bristly manes. Keenly observed horses, with pale bellies and swarthy flanks, sometimes in shaggy winter coats, sometimes snorting breathy clouds. On one wall, a stallion nuzzles the nether petals of a mare. On another, a russet-flanked mare is grazing, her belly round as an apple. But every horse is flowing, full of rhythmic strokes, wild and dynamic. They're not just pictures, but breathing beasts in motion. Many appear to be pregnant, so their bellies are wild with motion, too.

Drifting slowly through the rooms, we seem too well behaved, watching the pageantry as if it were a static mural in a museum. The horses were not meant to be seen like this, but at speed, fleetingly, at a run, while tribal elders held lamps. In the flickering light, our pupils would be jumping, the horses would be crashing down through our dreams, and our sacred hearts would be wild as tinder.

MEN AND CARS

What horses do for girls, horsepower does for boys. Was there ever a love affair as loyal or obsessive as that between a sixteen-year-old and his first shiny car, even if it's an old rattletrap? Something about the quivering power of the car excites him. Something about the rounded curves of its flanks, and its headlights, which protrude like bosoms. Something about the grumbling moan of the engine, which responds to his touch when he "turns it on." He spends hours rubbing, grooming, and polishing it. And even more time cruising around town, slow enough to ogle girls and be ogled back, loud enough to impress other males, or fast enough to slay the more pedestrian of life's demons. In both senses of the word, cars *express* a young man, by rushing him through time and space at the sexual high speed he feels gushing through his mind and limbs. Cars are fast and furious, dangerous and alive, ready to spin out at a tight curve or a hairpin. It's how he feels sometimes—all revved up and ready to explode. Many teenage boys find in cars the embodiment of their surging sexuality. Older men are so often seen trading in sensible, affordable family cars for brightly colored sports cars that it's become a cliché. They leave their wives for sexy young women, and they leave their station wagons for sexy new cars with loud mufflers and only room enough for two. Cars are hot, fast, hard, phallic objects that hurtle through space. Cartoons sometimes show a middle-aged man riding on a steel-plated erection. The caption restates the obvious.

Men of any age and state of marital happiness can be counted on to look admiringly if 1) a beautiful woman walks by, or 2) a beautiful car zooms by. Cars arouse men on many levels, so it is not surprising that there is a festival devoted exclusively to cars, men, and masculinity. It is held in the spring, with attendant rites and ceremonies. Drunkenness is preferred. Men race and awards are given to the victor. Fast cars and women's breasts are worshiped in an orgy of pure decibel and testosterone, a celebration of male sexuality unlike any on earth.

THE INDY 500

Seven drunken, bare-chested teenage boys drape themselves across the windshield of my car as I wait for the light to change. Squirming, they relayer themselves like slabs of bacon, and their mirrored sunglasses send blinding jets of light in a dozen directions. The stoplight probably changed some minutes ago, but all I can see is flesh tanned to the color of walnut oil, cans of beer, hairless chests, and lascivious leers. A rhythmic pounding on the car roof tells me that at least one young man is trying to get in feet first. Out of the back window, I watch six more trying to lift the car by its bumpers and cart it away. Another, with a video camera perched like a falcon on his shoulder, zooms in for a close-up of my chest. Just as I begin wondering if this can possibly be for real, I decipher what they have been chanting maniacally for the past few minutes: "Show us your tits! Show us your tits! Show us your tits!"

When the light changes, they melt off the car and surge around a young woman reckless enough to take a stroll in a bikini through what appears to be the largest fraternity party on earth, a party that began miles from the Speedway in all directions and now, the day before the race, is building to a crescendo that only tomorrow morning's auto-eroticism will satisfy.

Sixteenth Street, the main drag that leads to the Speedway, looks like a war zone. Swarming around an armada of recreational vehicles and pickup trucks, half-clad young men guzzle beer, grill hamburgers, compare their muscles, preen themselves. Some carry brown bags of hard liquor. Some carry placards that say WE NEED GIRLS. At the doorway to one trailer, a large papier-mâché sculpture of a woman, naked from the waist up, wears a sign that says OFFICIAL INSPECTION STATION. Unhinged by the sight of females of all ages, body types, or dress, they chant until they're hoarse, and then make breast-juggling motions with their hands. At odd moments, a girl will leap atop a trailer and pose with her blouse held open like the Ark of the Covenant, turn so that binocular-slung oglers in each direction will get an eyeful, then button up and disappear into the rowdy mob hanging out by the thousand around the souvenir kiosks and the drive-ins that line the sprawling mid-American strip. Monstrous inflatable cans of Budweiser and Miller beer, Valvoline motor oil, and Champion spark plugs float above the ruckus like patron deities. Radios blare, people caterwaul, car engines rev, and the combined smear of low drama and teeth-rattling noise becomes fiercer the closer you get to the Speedway itself, that sacred arena of male sexuality, the still center of the carnival. Carnival, from the Latin *carnis,* "flesh," and *levo,* "to take away." A tub-thumping, earthy, hell-for-leather orgy of male puberty before life's fun has to stop.

By 6:00 A.M., when the gates open on race day, people are already in line to find the seats they purchased right after last year's race. Next to them stand fans from all over the country and the world: shoe salesmen from Switzerland, computer distributors from Germany looking for "atmosphere and action," bartenders from Detroit, autobody workers from Phoenix, carloads of young men, a few women dressed in brightly colored flame suits that hug the body tightly and suggest they might, at any moment, be called upon to leap into the pits and take charge.

People begin buying hot dogs and relish at about 8:00 A.M., and washing them down with lukewarm beer. Fire trucks choose their spots just off the raceway. Television stations set up camera booms on a spiderweb of wires. Souvenir stands are already hawking Indy 500 air fresheners, place mats, Frisbees, coffee mugs, miniature cars, black-and-white checkered victory flags, pot holders, and T-shirts. I can't resist buying a turquoise-and-pink T-shirt with an Indy car zooming off the chest, which vows LIFE BEGINS AT 220 MPH. As I slip it on over my sundress to check the size, and then off again, a TV announcer doing a remote nearby pauses to comment on my body, a platoon of men yell from their girl-watching spot on the top row of the bleachers, and a large, dusky man wearing a black Harley-Davidson T-shirt walks straight up to me, ogles my breasts, and groans, "Oh, mercy." By now this is old news, and I've learned that the men don't actually touch you; their assaults (or compliments, depending on your point of view) are strictly verbal.

Inside Gasoline Alley, wide boulevards of combed cement separate rows of garages, and life is serious as a bank balance. The winner will zoom off with half a million dollars. Just being in the race guarantees about $30,000. Companies donate dozens of miscellaneous awards, from $5,000 to $75,000 for being the oldest driver, youngest driver, fastest qualifier, leader of the first ten laps, best chief mechanic, driver with the least pit time, and so on. Champion spark plugs awards the winner a cool $68,000 provided he uses that brand during the race. You can guess which plugs all the cars start with.

Bustling around the tense streets of Gasoline Alley, young men dressed in Flash Gordon jumpsuits make sure their cars are fit. They tow each one up to the fuel pump with a long blue ribbon. Some of them carry helmets. Others have grimy gloves sticking out from their knee pads. A high-wing Cessna airplane flies overhead, towing a banner that reads: OLD INDIANA FUN PARK—ZOW!" (It recalls the Kenneth Fearing poem in which he describes a man's brief, high-speed, cartoon life as "Zowie he lived, and zowie he died.") Newsmen patrol the garage area, balancing cameras like small children on their shoulders. More cars emerge from their garages, towed by long blue canvas ribbons that look like the lunge lines trainers use when exercising thoroughbreds. Parts of the cars are often covered with black blankets, as well, to keep their flanks warm. A low-slung sulfur-yellow car belongs to Al Unser, whose son will be racing against him today, and it contains the power of over 700 horses, though it's only fifteen feet long and weighs only about 1,500 pounds.* Unser climbs inside the cramped car, which has been molded to the eccentricities of his bottom and back, and stretches his legs far into the nose. He will drive the race lying down.

Enclosed entirely in armor, with only a narrow visor open across their eyes, the drivers are all modern knights, riding horsepower. Speed is their lance. Despite the comradeship of the crews, this is not a team sport. Everyone else out on the track will be an opponent. Medieval knights had allegorical names like Sir Good Heart or Lancelot, and these latter-day knights walk around the grounds and drive cars plastered with slogans. (Some call them the fastest billboards on earth.) How eerie it is to see a man with LIVING WELL emblazoned on his helmet and DIE HARD stamped on his back. On his shoulder may be the words GOODYEAR or CHAMPION or SOUND DESIGN or TRUE VALUE. What are you to make of the apparition of a glossy red car driving toward you with SLEEP CHEAP (the slogan of Red Roof Inns) on both sides of its nose?

Cars, drivers, and pit crews all push through the crowds and take their places on the racetrack. At some point, the crews and officials withdraw a little, and the men are alone with their machines. The steering wheels have been put in *after* them. Sealed now in their narrow cockpits, each adjusts the knitted flameproof Ninja mask over the face, fixes the rub of the helmet strap, checks the buckles that hold helmet and flame suit together so that the neck won't sprain in the terrible g-forces of the turns. You can see the loneliness in their eyes, the squinting concentration with which they erase every one of the half million people from the raceway. The crowd may cheer, but the drivers hear nothing, see nothing but track.

---

*It was James Watt, an eighteenth-century engineer, who decided to compare the power of his new invention—the steam engine—to a team of horses. Measuring how much weight a single brewery horse could pull, he concluded that, in one minute, one horse could move 33,000 pounds one foot.

Unser's brow, with its accordion of worry lines, shows through his helmet and balaclava. His eyes are dark pyramids of concentration. You cannot see the lids at all, only the creases fanning out beneath them like dunes on the tanned Sahara of his face. Then he slides the Plexiglas visor down and becomes completely entombed. Tightly swaddled in cloth, steel, fiberglass, and foam, he will already be sweating in the 80-degree midwestern heat. Soon he will breathe speed, and he will become a trajectory, a single long rush, a hymn to male sexuality.

The national anthem is followed by a Memorial Day invocation by clergy, and it's no coincidence that the race takes place on Sunday morning at 11:00 A.M., church service time, with a somewhat premature prayer for the dead and injured, and then "Taps," while the stands fall silent. Jim Nabors sings about going back home to Indiana. Thousands of multicolored balloons spiral like DNA into the blue. "Gentlemen," the frail voice of the Speedway's chairperson ritualistically intones, "start your engines."

"The magnificent machines," the announcer cries, "are ready!"

A heaving and soughing of engines. Pace cars roll away to lead a warm-up lap or two at over 100 mph, as the crews sprint back to their pits to get ready for action. On the electronic scoreboard high above the stands, silhouetted fans leap and cheer and wave small flags. A crowd stretching thickly around the two-and-a-half-mile oval twitches and yells, rising like the prerace balloons as the cars roar into sight again around the far turn. The pace cars peel off and the drivers take flight, with Mario Andretti in the lead.

Immediately, three cars collide, metal parts arcing high into the air, and the race stops briefly. The cars pause at speed, and aren't allowed to change position relative to one another until debris is cleared from the track and the yellow flag is lifted. Suddenly the race restarts, with Andretti still leading. His new Chevy engine is fast, but is it as reliable as the Cosworth engines that have won so many races? Not until lap fifteen do the fans sit down in their seats. Andretti's a sentimental favorite, and they're berserk with excitement.

The speed at which the cars pass the onlooker is sense-bludgeoning. Whining, they catapult around a corner and into the straightaway, while their engines growl and gnaw in a thirty-megaton buzz. You need peripheral vision to see the cars arrive, flash past, vanish around the next turn. They move so fast that unless you fix on one car and track it, a loud blur of color whizzes past. Fans seem to shake their heads no, no, no, no, thirty-three times as the field rushes by. People dropping empty beer cans into the jungle of scaffolding underneath the bleachers make a constant drizzle of tin. When cars pull into the pits at speed, the crews come alive, changing treadless tires ("skins"), pumping methanol into the forty-gallon well, tinkering, adjusting, putting out small fires, handing the driver a drink, then shoving him back onto the track—all within ten or twenty seconds.

Not only mechanics and engineers, but aerodynamic specialists work with each driver. As the orange wind sock atop the tower reminds you, this is really an air race. How do you keep a light piece of metal going over 200 mph on the ground? Though the men inside are called drivers, they sit in a *cockpit,* they worry about the cars' *wings,* and they are obsessed with *wake turbulence.* Small canard fins at the *nosecone* up front pay homage to Burt Rutan's Challenger and all the other canard designs he's made famous over the years. The rear wing functions like an upside-down airplane wing. An airplane wing is rounded on top, but car wings are rounded on the bottom instead. Air whooshes all around the wing, but has farther to travel across the bottom, becomes thinner, and produces an area of low pressure. On top, the higher pressure presses down and the car holds the ground. The car's curved underside holds the ground, too. But the combined ground effects churn up small tornadoes, and the swirling whirlpools of wind that each car trails behind it puts the next car in peril.

When the drivers talk about the air being "dirty" or "squirrelly," turbulence is what they mean. Just as an airplane's controls become almost useless in such a wake, so do a winged car's. The car was "loose," they say, meaning that for a few hair-raising seconds at colossal speed in a turn they had no control over the car at all; its bronco horsepower had broken loose. So they search for clean air, smoother lanes to travel. Andretti spends most of the race low down the track, almost off it, in a less-traveled lane where the air is sweeter. At over 200 mph, they are driving faster than most commuter airplanes fly, in severe turbulence, in blast-furnace heat of about 110 degrees in the cockpit, with their heads jiggling unstoppably and their bodies thrust hard against the side of the car in the g-force-pulling turns, in constant fear of hitting a brick wall head-on, or bouncing off another car and splintering as they cartwheel. Two-time Indy winner Bill Vukovich once said cavalierly, "All you have to do to win at Indy is keep your foot on the throttle and turn left." But as Indy driver Dennis Firestone describes the feel of turbulence: "The effect on you is violent. You're shaking around in the cockpit. Your vision is blurred. It feels as if the air could rip your helmet off." Sometimes the pressure jams the helmet up over the eyes so its owner can barely see. And concentration is crucial. If your mind wanders for one second, the car will travel the length of a football field.

Beating, banging, fighting the steering wheel, pulling g's, the furious cars slide in and out of corners. Drivers need to be aggressive, but at a controlled pace. They must be mentally relaxed, but there is constant battering to their neck and muscles. Few sports stay right on the edge of life from start to finish. Not just speed, but a passion for the extreme must be what fuels drivers and fans alike: a dizzying, all-out, pedal-to-the-metal, death-defying effort for as long as life allows. Exhaust pours from the cars and, from the drivers, *exhaustion*. The fumes and the bone-shaking noise rattle them. Spectators in the front rows have the most sensory spot to watch from, but also the loudest and most dangerous. Cars have been known to leap into the stands like frightened deer. Today a wheel will spiral off one of the cars, bounce into the stands, and kill a spectator. At such gigantic speeds, a projectile acts like a shotgun blast, so when anything falls onto the track the race stops momentarily, then the drivers resume, occasionally farting a bouquet of sparks as if a blast furnace were melting the metal of their concentration. Weaving a little under the brake pressure, and actually out of control at times, when dirty air vexes them, they stagger on.

Andretti swerves all over the crowded lanes, roaring down to the grass, zooming up to the wall, blasting ahead, trying to break what superstitious fans and drivers call his "Indy jinx." Since his 1969 win, he's started twenty-one times, but never won again. Some malicious genie of speed and metal always seems to thwart him, and today is no exception. After he leads for 177 laps, right up to the closing minutes of the race, his engine backfires, and he slows up to 100 mph and steals into his pit. Wails of disbelief from the outspoken fans. When the next sure-winner stalls his car twice, the race suddenly passes into the veteran grip of Al Unser, whose son is driving the fourth-place car. In car racing, age matters so little that fathers and sons often compete against each other. In this Indy, Mario Andretti's son, Michael, also races.

Two black-and-white checkered flags swirl above Unser's car as he finishes first. The cheering fans sound like nonstop detonations. Slowing down, he drives a victory lap while waving ecstatically to the crowd. His son pulls up beside him, salutes, says later, "It gives me goose bumps when I think of Dad winning." In a blue flame suit, with flaming yellow hair, his wife jogs up beside his glowing, sweating, finally still car and kisses him. The crew yanks off the steering wheel and straps, struggles to pull him out of the cockpit. Like an endorsement of his future, his yellow-and-black knight's helmet says GOOD-YEAR. The epaulets on his flame suit remind you that for the past few hours he was a pilot. Someone hands him an old-fashioned bottle of milk that looks fresh from a country doorstep, and he tilts his head back and drinks long from the lip of the bottle. Tears well in his eyes as he talks to his brother Bobby, a previous Indy winner and now a race announcer for ABC-TV. "The family's proud of you," Bobby says, choking with emotion, and meaning all the menfolk: his own son, Robby, lying in the local hospital with a broken leg from a crash earlier in the month; Al's son, Al, Jr., only a few yards away; Al and Bobby's brother Jerry, who died in a crash a few years before.

Long after the race is over and the cars have crept back to their garages, the spectators will linger in the bleachers. It makes you wonder why half a million people—mainly adolescent boys—would choose to celebrate the beginning of summer by picnicking beside the scene of such death-defying drives. The atmosphere of the race may startle, but the terms of the race we know only too well. Who hasn't referred to someone living life "in the fast lane," or being "revved up," or needing "a pit stop," or being "in the pits," or "getting into gear," or "up to speed"? The green flag that means go-for-it is the color of grass, and the red flag that stops everything because of a crash is the color of blood. This is just another Saturday afternoon drive at over 200 mph, by men carrying the advertisements with them instead of passing them on the highways. It is just another blood sport indulged in by men who have always been obsessed with arenas and making things run around in them. The Speedway is more an oval than a circle, but men have always liked to corral things, be it wild animals or ball bearings in roulette wheels or Christians. Bullfighters taunting the brutality of Nature with their cunning do so in a golden circle. Accidents are described as "spectacular" and the "spectators" confirm how gripping the element of sheer spectacle is.

I don't believe most race fans come to see crashes. They come to see their gods parading at speed before them. You can't really love cars without disowning the preindustrial world. But the scorpion of progress has a wicked sting in its tail. Nature may thwart us at every turn, but the machines we've created and endowed with superhuman power sometimes terrify and thwart us even more. When men are injured in crashes, the fans sound truly aggrieved. When men walk away from devastating smashups, the fans shriek with joy. They have come partly to see Man vs. Machine, urgently hoping that man will prevail. An unconscious metaphor works on the reproductive level, too, where men are speed demons, whose souped-up sperm zoom like hot rods.

The last fans to amble out of the Speedway linger in the 500 Museum, talking animatedly about the race and admiring the array of cars. And why not? When we think of "the romance of the automobile," we forget how much courtship takes place in cars. As John Steinbeck wrote in *Cannery Row,* "most of America's children were conceived in Model T Fords and not a few of them were born in them." Many rites of passage happen in cars, especially for young men (getting drunk, picking up girls, and so on), so it's not surprising that many men find in cars something closer to transport than transportation: a mythic, animal relationship. Not only have cars changed how we live, they've changed the world in which we live, changed the look of cities, changed our health problems, changed our marital and work habits.

As for why humans crave speed, and are obsessed with watching people achieve it on land, air, and water—that would take more time to contemplate. Longer than the Indy 500 itself, the last of whose rowdy spectators have now gushed into the streets for a post-race party every bit as out-of-hand as the pre-race one.

Al Unser and his team will be heading for a victory dinner in downtown Indianapolis, with the purse in his pocket. The winner doesn't get to keep the huge gleaming silver trophy on display at the

Speedway. But a three-dimensional bas-relief of him will be added, Mount Rushmore style, to the hat-wearing, bespectacled, detailed caricatures of all the previous winners. The Indy 500 is so much a celebration of male sexuality that the male figure atop the trophy is naked—no coy drape or fig leaf hide his realistic genitals. At the ticket windows, long lines begin forming so speed-zealots can buy their tickets for next year's Indy 500. Mainly bare-chested teenage boys, wearing mirrored sunglasses that look like rearview mirrors. They seem the sort who might agree with Walt Whitman's "Oh, highway . . . you express me better than I can express myself."

THE LIGHTEST LONGING: SEX AND FLYING

The remarkable thing about St. Joseph of Cupertino, a mentally and physically retarded seventeenth-century monk, whose infirmities drew him the name of "Open Mouth," is that he could fly. "With approximately one hundred levitations ascribed to him," one scholar writes, "Joseph is the most aerial of the saints." When Joseph's ecstasies made his blood leap in his veins and his whole body soar, he supposedly carried the sick, fellow monks, startled civilians, an eighteen-foot cross, and even animals aloft with him. According to legend, he once even sailed around the refectory while waving a sea urchin. Other times, he contented himself with hovering above the treetops while he prayed, oblivious of amazed spectators below. The patron saint of fliers, Joseph believed his ability to fly his great defect; but hagiographies discreetly suggest that his real temptations were sexual, stemming from an excessively carnal response to Mary.

Flight is one of the oldest themes in myth, religion, and art, one of the first words ever spoken, a relentless longing in earthbound creatures. And it's often linked to sensuality. There is something erotic about flight, the dreamy abandonment of all sorts of gravity, including physical and moral law, while one is simply "swept off one's feet." Roman matrons collected bronze amulets shaped like erect penises with bird or bat wings, which they sometimes wore as brooches, or hung around the house and garden as charms. Reproductions of first-century winged penises show bizarre hybrids that can walk or fly, having both wings and legs. In the sixteenth century, when church elders declared the idea of flying females to be Satan's doing, Jacob van Amsterdam painted *King Saul and the Witch of Endor*, in which a naked woman straddles a fiery, rocket-driven goat that zooms across the sky. Throughout the ages, witches have been portrayed as aerial evil (they applied hallucinogens to their vaginal mucosa with a broom handle, which is how witches came to be associated with flying broomsticks).

The idea of flight has thrilled, terrified, inspired, and deeply affected people from the beginning of human history. The airplane itself is only ninety years old, still marvelous and puzzling as a pterodactyl, but it's changed our lives from sunup to forever, especially our love lives. We no longer conduct romances as people did before planes, now that we can date over many time zones. Our relationships with our parents have changed: we see them often; good-bye is not forever; there's no need to divorce them when we marry someone from a far-flung state or country. We no longer fight wars mainly with our neighbors, and feel each battle on our pulses. Now it's abstract, global, predicated on aerial surveillance. Because individuals from Australia, Puerto Rico, Japan, or Nome can now easily meet and marry others from California or Peru or China, the gene pool is changing; we won't look the way we do now for long. How we earn our living has changed, how we educate our young, how we vacation, how we choose our leaders, how we think of news, how we raise crops, conduct police work, and give emergency aid. All because of flight. It's changed our notions of privacy, observation, and pollution. Stonehenge was first deciphered from the air, as were many other prehistoric dwellings and artifacts. Flying has changed how we imagine our planet, whose most exotic barrios are now as close as a Maupintour, and which we have seen whole from space, so that even the farthest nations are political and ecological neighbors. It's changed our ideas about time. When you can gird the earth at 1,000 mph, how can you endure the tardiness of a postman or delivery truck? Most of all, it's changed how we picture our bodies, the personal space in which we live, now elastic and swift. If I wished, I could leave Manhattan and be in Calcutta for afternoon tea. My body isn't limited by its own weaknesses when it comes to moving rapidly through space. Lovers can fly to a romantic city just for atmosphere. It has changed our notion of a pilgrimage. It has redefined "the date."

People often fly in their dreams. In my nightmares, when I am being chased by villains, I escape at the last excruciating second by suddenly lifting off the earth and flying just out of reach. I don't flap my arms or assume a Superman pose, I just become lighter than air, my chest arches like the bow of an antique sailing ship, and I float up with a buoyancy both powerful and safe. In these dreams, my fright is so palpable that I awake with my pulse running and the relief of a getaway by mere inches. Freud felt that flying was dream code for sex, and for all I know my nightmares, with their flying escapes "inches" away from harm, might give a dream analyst a good old-fashioned smirk.

Flying in airplanes fills up one's senses, massages the body with low-level vibrations, sometimes scares one enough to keep adrenaline flowing, and at its most peaceful and serene can feel like a soft, voluptuous dance among the clouds, even if you are seated in a hard metal "cockpit." But sex and flying have more in common than exhilarating sensations—they're both taboo. Flagrant sex is socially taboo. Flying is the biological taboo of our species. Humans are land creatures who can walk, run, swim, but cannot fly. Except in our dreams, we are forbidden from entering that Eden. So it's small wonder that we long for the forbidden gift, that we crave flight, and imagine our gods waltzing across the sky. The grave is where we will end, and we feel that gravity tugging us for the length of our lives. We begin by falling down from our mother's womb, and we end our years by hunching closer and closer to the ground. But in sexual ecstasy, as powerful chemical rivers gush through our limbs, we become deliriously transcendent, dazed and drunk as shamans, and feel strong enough, exempt enough, to explode right out of the body and fly. Sex is a form of naked flying in open air—you lose touch with the ordinary, let go of all restraints, and release your grip on earth and reality. You do this, paradoxically, through an even more height-ened sense of touch. Perhaps this is, in part, why men found a woman pilot like Beryl Markham so irresistible. She was an archetypal siren, *woman flying.* Her ability to fly seems to have haunted them as much as her beauty. It was not enough for them simply to know or befriend her; they needed to conquer the wilderness (of Africa, and of promiscuity) that she symbolized. Even though she was a femme fatale, a gold digger, a female casanova whom they should not on any account have trusted with life, wallet, or heart, something about her relationship with the forces of wind and weather, desert and danger, clothed her in a sensuality they craved.

WINGS OVER AFRICA

The local bookstores are doing a roaring trade in femmes fatales this season. New tell-all books are emerging by or about Cleopatra, Mata Hari, Marilyn Monroe, Alma Mahler, and other queens of the heart. In our passion to understand their soft weaponry, we pore over their diaries and letters, we stare through the peephole of a camera into their bedroom eyes. We become their swains. But biographies are doomed to fail. If even corsages lose their color pressed between the pages of a book, what hope has a life? Lying in state, in print, a life can look formal, orderly, and planned. But suppose the life was in many ways a mess, albeit a fascinating, courageous, picturesque, and emotionally intense mess?

Beryl Markham lived such a life. Along with such colorful figures as T. E. Lawrence or Sir Richard Burton, Markham was one of the most extraordinary of explorers. But she was also an emotionally deprived child and, as an adult, a serious outlaw of love. She died in 1986 at the age of eighty-three; that year was the fiftieth anniversary of her historic solo flight across the Atlantic. Not much remains to shed light on her. There is her beautifully imagined memoir, *West with the Night,* published in 1942, when she was forty years old, a triumph of adventure writing, set largely in Africa, which Hemingway called "bloody wonderful," and praised at great length, conceding "this girl can write rings around all of us." He also called her a "high-grade bitch" because she wouldn't sleep with him when he was on safari in Africa. She had been hired to spot elephants from the air for him, and she was just the sort of woman who would rattle his heart. Markham wasn't too choosy about the men she slept with; rejecting Hemingway's advances must have given her a certain kick, and it clearly insulted him. But he was right about her being able to capture the effect of Africa on the senses, and write about it in voluptuous detail, in a way he never could.

The best evidence suggests that Markham had help on *West with the Night* from Antoine de Saint-Exupéry, who was her lover in Hollywood for a time. So Hemingway really hadn't a competitor's chance. Markham later also had help on her book from Raoul Schumacher. A charming, handsome man with an encyclopedic mind, Schumacher did writerly odd jobs around Hollywood, but was not having much success as a fiction writer himself. They met at a party in 1941, and married about a year later. Markham's modest royalties from *West with the Night,* along with what her short stories brought in, augmented their income. Her name was marketable, so Schumacher wrote some stories based on her experiences, and published them under her name. Throughout her life, Markham advanced herself by becoming the paramour of talented, wealthy, or powerful men. Their secret help launched her career and kept her reputation alive. Denys Finch-Hatton, Isak Dinesen's lover, who appears in *Out of Africa,* was also Markham's lover, and he taught her about music and literature. Not surprisingly, some people question the extent to which her lovers' polishing and editing of her manuscripts became more than that: her astounding experiences retold in their better-groomed words. When words failed, she was supported by tycoons and British royalty.

One recent memoir of Markham opens with a scene of heart-sinking poignancy: a frail, elderly woman sits in a small bungalow on the grounds of the Kenya Jockey Club. She is chair-ridden, poor, and spends her days drinking vodka and orange squash, which, unbeknownst to her, her servant has been watering down. She has an open wound on her arm where a flap of skin has been torn away, exposing nerve and muscle, but she's not much aware of it. Occasionally her mind wanders and, groping for a word in English, she finds it in

Swahili instead. Cataracts prevent her from reading. And, when she manages to rise from her chair and walk a few exhausting steps, it becomes an act of courage as great as any in her past. A woman comes to interview her each day, and she insists that the woman act as a lady's maid, applying makeup and doing her hair as they talk. Markham also asks for a hairdresser from the city to tint her gray hair blond again. Much of her past seems lost to her. She is quarantined in the present, old age, poverty, photographs of past loves, and her trunk of mementos.

That scene of frailty is the tail end of a roller-coaster life charged with action and intensity, and the contrast is unnerving.

She had grown up wild in Africa, living close to the land and animals, and spent most of her childhood in the constant company and under the tutelage of local tribes. She was the only white woman permitted to hunt with them, and could handle a spear as well as a rifle. She may have looked like Alice in Wonderland, with her smocked European-style dress and long, beribboned yellow hair, but she spoke a number of African dialects and sat around tribal fires listening to the tales of the elders, while learning the survival skills of a young male warrior. Abandoned by her mother before she was five, she made a childhood career of being "best lad" in her father's racing stable, subduing savage and unruly thoroughbreds. At sixteen, she married a local farmer twice her age. At eighteen, when her bankrupted father fled to South America, she took his remaining racehorses, applied for a license, and began training them herself. In her twenties, her passion swerved from horses to horsepower, and she became smitten with flying. Aviation was a thrilling new marvel; it was as young and high-spirited as she was; and she had romances with some of the early flying aces, despite having divorced her first husband and remarried a wealthy aristocrat. She partied in England and Africa with the moneyed, the glamorous, the titled, and the brave. It was the heyday of record setting, and she longed for a chance to prove herself, and to skyrocket from notoriety to fame.

Markham was a woman of diabolical beauty, with china-blue eyes, symmetrical features, a long, leggy figure, and absolutely no inhibitions. A lonely, love-starved child, she grew up mastering the arts of survival, and sometimes that meant dealing with people in ways cold-blooded and amoral. She used her beauty as a lure and as a weapon, bartered with it, flaunted it, was always aware of the hypnotic effect it had on people, and played it for all it was worth. She stole from friends, ran up huge accounts on their credit, married for money and power while telling everyone outright that she wasn't in love, and poached husbands and lovers from women friends. All her life she was penniless, but it never kept her from wearing chic gowns, dining in the poshest restaurants, traveling first class, and moving in the highest strata of high society. A "blonde bombshell" was the way many referred to her. Isak Dinesen described her as "pantherine."

Despite eventually being married three times, Markham had no real gift for marriage. Her infidelities were legendary, unrepentant, and extremely public. She never understood or forgave her mother for deserting her. She lacked a role model and female confidante; she had no one with whom she could discuss her budding femininity. There were few white women in Africa, and no African women she felt close to. Without a mother figure, she simply had to invent herself as a woman. This was especially confusing, since she socialized with, and acted like, the African men. Her father had raised her in a laissez-faire sort of way, and she idolized him so fervently that no man could live up to his example.

Imperious, ravishingly beautiful, and fluorescent with life, she charmed her way from one continent to another. Though men balked at her flagrant promiscuity, it didn't stop them from being drawn to her. Her lovers included some of the most famous artists, adventurers, and scoundrels of her day. But then, she herself was a scoundrel. She never let a lie stand in the way of what she desired. She envied lives of fame and adventure; the irony is that she couldn't see how packed with color, adventure, and accomplishment her own life was.

A pioneer of aviation, she was the first person to fly solo from west to east across the Atlantic, in September 1936, and the details of the flight are hair-raising. It was the only way she could think of to impress a pilot who had jilted her. An older man who reminded her of her father, he was the one serious love of her life, she said, but he married someone else; and to the end of her days she never stopped reliving that heartache. But on her transatlantic flight, bound for fame and glory, she was sailing on pure exhilaration. Not one man at a time but the whole world would have to worship her. When her engine quit, she made an emergency landing in a rock-strewn peat bog in Nova Scotia which, from the air, had looked like a safe green field. Amazingly, she walked away from the nose-in crash with only a small head injury, though the plane was destroyed. New York City, her original goal, gave her a ticker-tape parade, and she was lionized for her daring and skill. It seemed impossible that so beautiful a woman could be so masterful. What they didn't realize is that she had had a lot of practice flying around Africa, often at night, always with no radio or air-speed indicator and very few instruments. Bush flying at that time, over such wilderness, in such primitive planes, was unthinkably dangerous. A forced landing often meant death from the crash or from starvation, thirst, or wild-animal attack. At the age of thirty-one, she was the first woman to hold a commercial license in East Africa, and that required her to be able to strip down and repair an airplane engine. She ferried people to distant farms, acted as a game spotter for some of the great hunters, and ran an informal aerial-ambulance service. She carried mail to the gold miners in Tanganyika. She often rescued pilots who had crashed. Thinking they were doomed, they would see a plane land brilliantly in the bad terrain, then a willowy figure climb out, dressed like a *Vogue* model in the white silk blouse that was her trademark, pale trousers, a silk scarf at the neck, her hair coiffed and her fingernails carefully painted, handing them a flask of brandy and grinning.

In the 1940s, bored in London, she sailed to the United States, and was immediately invited to work in Hollywood at Paramount Studios, as a consultant on a film called *Safari*. Columbia Pictures planned to make her a movie star, since they said she was "pretty enough to be in the talkies." By then, her own adventures were widely known and she became a regular at Hollywood parties, where she attracted attractive men nonstop. For a while she lived in a Malibu beach house with the world-famous folksinger Burl Ives. One of her divorces even named a member of the British royal family as co-respondent. Her love life was notorious. But the most interesting period of her life was far behind her, in Africa in the 1920s, when a web of tempestuous and eccentric relationships arose.

Theirs was a time and place of great youth and innocence, and they were intense young dreamers drawn to Africa's wilderness. Cut off from the stultifying urbanity of Edwardian England, they kept some of its moral codes but ignored many others. The women were unusually independent and concerned with personal freedom. Finch-Hatton was an adventurer, but he was also an aesthete. And Bror Blixen was a dashing and impetuous white hunter. In these sometimes sad and decadent days, our sense of ourselves as innocent pioneers, brave and young and full of adventure, in a land defined by its promise, seems remote. We may be spiritual beings, but what greater rapture is there than living a life hot on the senses, one augustly physical? With vicarious longing, we search their lives for the outlines of what we have lost: risk, passion, curiosity, exuberance.

Bror Blixen, whom Markham described as "the toughest most durable white hunter ever to shoot a charging buffalo between the eyes while debating whether his sundown drink will be gin or whiskey," was her occasional bedmate and good friend, although she was never in love with him. They often worked safaris together—Markham flying in supplies and spotting game from the air, Blixen doing the brilliant hunting, feats of heroism, tireless partying, and indiscriminate womanizing he was known for. Married to Isak Dinesen for a while, he lived a wild, colorful life, and taught many people the details of hunting technique, such as how to tell the distance of a fleeing elephant by reading its dung (stick your finger in and judge the heat). Together, they blazed a trail of broken hearts through the wilderness. But when all was said and done, it was Markham who seemed to have lost her way. A woman of finely tuned observation, as well as courage, cunning, and vulnerability, she never trusted those strengths. Instead, she merchandised herself until her youth and beauty ran out. A bartered heart may be the currency and trade of casanovas, but in the end she became a lonely and tragic figure who lived more and more in the grand ballroom of her memory. Despite her solo flight from lover to lover, love itself had somehow eluded her.

MEN AND MERMAIDS

One tranquil afternoon on French Frigate Shoals, a wildlife refuge in the Hawaiian archipelago, I sat at the dining-room table with my traveling companion, underwater photographer Bill Curtsinger. He pulled out a folder containing photographs of a nude woman, swimming underwater in caramelized light. A gallery in Portland, Maine, soon would be showing this "mermaid" series, and he had brought them along for a final once-over. Her face obscured, the mermaid swam with full breasts spilling above a belly rise, and a pubic delta edged by shadowy vines. Her curly hair rose like smoke through the water, and in some frames she floated below a reflection of herself, embattled by light. All sway and undulation in an aqua lagoon, her solidness made the water more transparent, her nakedness shone from the dim rooms of her past, as she became the sprawling sand and gushing waves. For some time, I sat searching these images for the lure they held—not just to Curtsinger, a fortyish man, his skin salt-cured from all the years he has spent underwater—but to men everywhere.

For the remarkable thing about mermaids is that seafaring men all over the world have invented them. They are not the mythic handiwork of one culture, exported like a religion, tantalizing cuisine, or new fashion. Men in Norway, Newfoundland, New Guinea, the South Seas, Mexico, Africa, Haiti, and other lands all have ancient mermaid myths. In these fantasies, women with long hair, large breasts, small waists, graceful arms—but fish scales from the hips down—enchant men out of their wealth, sanity, heartbeat, and soul. Yet they generally aren't regarded as evil, witchlike, or savage. Quite the opposite. They are innocent assassins, feminine and alluring. Drugged by their dangerous sensuality, men long for them as a sort of sexual heroin, even though they know the romance will end badly. At best, they will be oddities in each other's world and produce children fit for neither land nor sea. At worst, the men will drown erotically in the mermaid's arms.

In the earliest religions, the world was divided into fire and water, with phallic lightning representing masculinity and the womblike sea representing femininity. Often the male gods held lightning bolts or scepters. Some of the oldest mermaid lust springs from tales of fish deities, such as the Semitic moon goddess Atergatis, whose very name steals one's breath and sends one's tongue to the front of the mouth. She had human arms and breasts and a beautiful human head; but, from the thighs down, a shimmering, golden fish's tail. Though gifted with supernatural powers, she ruled by using so-called feminine wiles. She was beautiful, vain, proud, cruel, seductive, and yet utterly unavailable to the human men who fell in love with her. Some while later, Aphrodite—a goddess who also rose from the sea—became popular, and she had mermaid minions to serve her. The Greek Sirens were at times pictured as mermaids, too, and they added much to the notion that mermaids were a fatal attraction. Supernatural lovers who lured mariners to their deaths, they sang songs so eerie and rapturous—melodic waves upon sea waves—that sailors leapt overboard and swam toward the music. Or they hypnotized captains with their charms and sent ships crashing on the rocky shore. The Germans call a mermaid *meerfrau;* the Danish call her *maremind.* The Irish *merrow* have small webs between their fingers. (What are we to make of otherwise normal women afflicted with webbed fingers?) The Finnish *nakinneito* have big breasts and long curly hair.

Breasts are a key element in all mermaid tales, but perhaps that shouldn't surprise us. In the eighteenth century, Linnaeus, a physician with a devastatingly tidy mind and a passion for labeling, decided to name our class of animal "mammal," which means "of the breast." Not just any breasts, mind you, but the breasts of a mature woman who can suckle her young. This was understandably on Linnaeus's mind, since he had watched his own wife suckle seven children and was privy to this most natural of acts for over a decade. There was a big to-do in his day about the developmental evils of wet-nursing. But by choosing a woman's breasts as the official symbol of the highest and most noble class of animal, he wasn't thought to be doing anything shocking. Breasts have always fascinated and obsessed men. (Freud says it's because their earliest pleasure was sucking at their mothers' breasts). However odd a sea creature might look—and some, such as the cleft-faced dugong, look powerfully nonhuman— it's the womanly breasts that tip men off to their status as mermaids. "Look, she has breasts!" the sailors cry, and somehow ignore the flat, walruslike face of the sea cow.

Why do fish gods appeal to us as fantasy lovers? Look at Earth from space and we see that it's mainly water, with small wafers of land floating here and there. Our planet is poorly named. We should call it Ocean. We ourselves are little lagoons in which fluids and jellies pour over a reef of bones. Our veins contain salt water, a hand-me-down from the primordial seas; our blood ebbs and flows; women have monthly tides. A fetus floats for nine months in a snug watery womb. We are born water creatures, true amphibians, mermaids and mermen, our bodies 97 percent salt water. That's why we must drink water to survive. Water also flowed through our ancestors, and they sailed the arteries of the land. People navigated on water, raised crops with water, baptized in water. We slosh when we walk. Sometimes we can hear the fluids in our ears or stomachs. We are water sculptures, vessels of water. If you removed the water from a 150-pound human being, only about four and a half pounds of matter would remain. In that sense, the "essence" of a person is not so different from the essence of a flower, and personality is the perfume of being human. Small wonder that fishermen looked at the mysterious, unpredictable ocean, which nonetheless held their food, escape, and destiny, and assumed that deities ruled the waves.

Lapping at their lives, the ocean reaches a hundred tongues into the rocky mouths and harbors where men gather and drink. But I don't think it's just coastal men who have created mermaids as a sexy version of the earth mother. Mermaids seem, in part, to echo the conflict men feel about women in general. They are beautiful, mysterious, idealized creatures whom men long to possess. But they also arouse feelings that make men vulnerable, irrational, and crazed. They can enslave the most powerful men. And they don't fight fair. The more beautiful they are, the more power they have, and when they know it, and act remote and unconquerable, they can be truly frightening. However weak of limb, they're strong enough to send a man to his doom. That age-old idea of the gorgeous and deadly woman has powered much myth and art. Mermaids crystallize the fear.

In medieval times, Europeans assumed that mermaids were as common as fairies or sprites. They had magical powers, and lived long, but were mortals without souls. During the seventeenth century, fishermen frequently sighted mermaids off the coast, and travelers returned from foreign lands with much corroborating evidence.

One of the most famous sightings was reported by Henry Hudson, and it caused quite a stir when it was published in London in 1625. While searching for the Northwest Passage, he jotted down the following in his diary:

> This evening [June 15] one of our company, looking overboard, saw a mermaid, and, calling up one more of the company to see her, one more of the crew came up, and by that time she was come close to the ship's side, looking earnestly on the men. A little after a sea came and overturned her. From the navel upward, her back and breasts were like a woman's, as they say that saw her; her body as big as one of us, her skin very white, and long hair hanging down behind, of color black. In her going down they saw her tail, which was like the tail of a porpoise, speckled like a mackerel. Their names that saw her were Thomas Hilles and Robert Rayner.

Despite the eighteenth century's passion for reason, people adored mermaids, which captains were forever encountering, and monarchs believing in. Each age adapted the mermaid to fit its notion of femininity. In the age of chivalry, the mermaid was depicted as a princess; in the early nineteenth century, a romantic ideal; in the twentieth century, a femme fatale.

European mermaids are often shown carrying combs and mirrors, because they pass endless hours sitting on the rocks and combing their long hair in the sunlight. Hair has always been a sexual symbol, one of the mermaids' lures, and by letting it fall loose and ostentatiously combing it out in front of men, they are advertising their sexuality. They rarely speak, but they can sing sounds more emotional and penetrating than mere words. In some Celtic legends, they grow monstrously large. They delve in magic herbs. They crave human lives, frolicking near coastlines and ships to provoke humans who cannot resist their sensuality. As a result, sighting a mermaid came to be an omen of storm or disaster. How to overpower a mermaid: steal one of her possessions—a comb or belt will do. Then hide it; the mermaid will live subserviently with you. But if she locates her lost belonging, she will regain her powers and return to the sea. In myths, she rarely stays with a man, because neither can live in the other's world, far from friends, families, and familiar ways.

There have been mermen, as well, especially in the legends of Scottish fisherfolk, who called them "Silkies." *The Arabian Nights* offers "The Tale of Abdullah and Abdullah," in which a poor fisherman named Abdullah finds a benefactor in a merman also named Abdullah. Legends from such unrelated places as Ireland and Syria tell of mermen who came ashore to take human wives. In Matthew Arnold's poem "The Forsaken Merman," the wife dooms him to the utmost despair. Queen Atergatis had a male consort, Oannes, who was also half-fish, half-man. As an outsider, he had the perspective to teach humans how to be more human. He was generous enough to give humans insight into their arts, sciences, and letters. At first, he was depicted with a man's head beneath a fish-head cap, and he wore his fish scales as a cloak; but that representation soon evolved into a creature that was man from the waist up, fish from the waist down. In early myths, he was associated with the sun, an important deity for Paleolithic people. He crawled onto the land at dawn and plunged back into the sea at night. In between, he offered civilization. But Oannes was worshiped in a godly way by the ancients, not pictured as a love object. Historically, women have not been much turned on by the idea of fish-men. Men, on the other hand, have been obsessed with fish-women. In the mermaid fantasy a man can penetrate a beautiful woman-child, and through her the entire ocean, which she represents. He can step outside human manners and society, which play no role in her world. She will believe everything he tells her, do whatever he asks, be his sea-geisha. As innocent-looking and beautiful as a mermaid is on top, she is a wanton animal below, untroubled by guilt or inhibition, eager for his pleasure.

Drawn on maps, tattooed on sailors' arms, printed on cans of tuna, carved on figureheads, painted on pub signs, the mermaid blurs the distinction between human and animal. Strictly speaking, she offers little reward: not enough woman to love and too much fish to fry. In a sense, she is monstrous, but hers is a sweet monstrosity, like love. For men of the sea, mermaids combine the self-destructiveness of the ocean, to which they are nonetheless wedded, with their loneliness for the women they've left behind. They find the ocean—fertile, curvy, womblike, velvety, tempestuous—all female. Its rhythms are ancient and mysterious, as are a woman's. It has monthly tides and an eternal languorousness. Rolling its hips, first one way then another, it turns gently as a sleeper does: the ocean is a woman dreaming. A man enters the water as he enters a woman, giving himself up to the liquefaction of her limbs, losing himself willingly to her soft, lucid grip. The ocean becomes mortal and embraces him, just as a loving woman, when she embraces him, in that moment becomes horizon-less as the sea.

SEXUAL CHIC: PERVERSION AS FASHION

Many lessons about whom and how to love, and what's sexually chic, bombard us from the media. Whenever I open a magazine these days, I half expect steam to rise from the pages. Perfumes war in the visual Amazon of the ads. To make their zest more potent, one rips a slit open, smears the all-but-invisible, exploded beads of scent along one's wrist or inner elbow, and inhales the aroma. We crave sensory experiences. In that, we're no different from most peoples. Locals visiting the voodoo market in Belém, Brazil, would feel at home on the first floor of Bloomingdale's. True, they wouldn't find heaps of river-dolphin vulvas, or rhinoceros-beetle horns (indeed, they wouldn't be able to identify much of what they saw), but the phantas-magoria of color, smell, and texture would delight their senses; and the bustling crowd caught up in the idea of "market day" would be perfectly familiar. World is extravaganza enough, one might think. Why add to the sensory uproar? Yet humans do, obsessively, creating art, cuisine, fashion, myths, and traditions, adding even more sensa-tions to the spectacle of living. Advertisements are only flickers amid that mania.

But what is one to make of all the recent ads offering unsubtle sex and bondage? Opening up an issue of *Details,* for instance, I find an ad showing phallic-looking shoes, and a woman down on all fours, tongue out, getting ready to lick them. In another ad, a tattooed man wearing a leather bracelet is performing oral sex on a woman outside a city building. Then the same pair are shown apparently having intercourse on the rooftop. What product is the ad selling? Shirts? Skirts? At the end of the magazine, a forty-six-page advertising pamphlet is devoted entirely to Request jeans. Most of it shows sultry, sneering, half-naked men and women caught in a film-noir escapade while enjoying miscellaneous erotic encounters with one another—straight sex, bisexual, ménage à trois, violence, bondage. Jeans don't appear in all the photos, but we do find lots of stiletto heels, fishnet stockings, leather, skirts with whiplike fringes, and phallic champagne bottles. In one shot, a man wearing underpants, boots, open shirt, and a cowboy hat sprawls on a bed with his legs wide apart, a bottle arranged like a huge erection at his groin. He is grasping it suggestively with his left hand. One full-page photo shows the back of this same man, his face turned to us in a savage snarl, as he urinates. You can see that his trousers are open and the ground in front of him is damp. In the final photo, the bare-chested man (wearing Request jeans, of course) is pegged out with ropes, his face contorted by pain, his crotch offered to the viewer, as he prepares to die in the desert sun.

Shot entirely in black-and-white, the photographs reveal a world of vice and shadows, a film-noir landscape held at a safe distance from the Ektachrome reality of everyday life. Their sex is as separate from love as it can be. The advertising sex is angry, mean, and sad. Everyone looks bitter, as if recoiling from something too horrible to name. Heavy, stylized, vulgar, the ads are perversely attractive in a slick way. But instead of the buoyant, life-affirming free-for-all sex of the sixties, one finds in this "erotica" a deadness.

Even subtle sexuality sells completely unrelated products. So, why these extremes? One answer is that, as subtle sex has become more prevalent, and even unsubtle sex appears regularly in respectable magazines, the sexual sell has had to become less subtle, too—or so advertisers assume. Hence the sex on display has become tougher and more perverse. As with real sex, a surfeit leads to a search for fresh stimulation, more exotic kicks. It used to be that gas stations offered drinking glasses or ice scrapers and snow brushes as lagniappe, a small gift to lure customers. The gas station may have been across town, but we couldn't resist getting "something for nothing," even if it really wasn't for nothing, since it cost more to drive farther and the cost of the "free" premium was factored into the price of the gas. Makeup companies do that today, and it works nicely. If you buy some products, you receive sample sizes of others. Self-esteem is now being used in the same way. If you purchase a "green" product, you can think of yourself as morally responsible. If you buy certain athletic shoes, you can think of yourself as self-confident and strong. If you Guess right or Request the right jeans, you can think of yourself as sexually desirable. The bonus is a small infusion of worth, a homeopathic remedy for self-doubt, which may indeed make one feel good—or may simply disappear into the bottomless drawer of the psyche, along with other elixirs. The question is why we find sadomasochism, exhibitionism, voyeurism, and other so-called perversions so attractive right now.

Perhaps, in part, this comes from our meandering return to Victorian morals. In that era, society was so repressive and filled with mother-worship that men felt guilty about defiling the "angel" at home, and were driven to subterranean avenues of pleasure and perversion. When societies try to stifle sexuality, they often produce a yen for acting out. In our own turn-of-the-next-century culture, as magazines remind us, soft-core pornography has gone mainstream. Fashion is filled with naked sex and bondage images. Tattoos, once associated with rednecks and underworld characters, are worn by models. (Women sported them in the twenties also, but mainly as permanent makeup—tattooed lipstick, eyebrows, and rouge—although tattoos of scarabs and other Egyptiana became popular when they were discovered on a mummy in one of the tombs.) Calvin Klein ads offer dream-scene sex at the level of slow-motion libido. Remember, these are magazines read in waiting rooms and libraries, subscribed to by teetotalers and wine tasters, delivered to one's doorstep, devoured in the agreed-upon sanctity of one's home, read in bathtubs and over coffee, left lying around the house for guests to riffle through and children to scissor up for school projects.

We are a fin-de-siècle culture, confused about our morals, with one foot planted squarely in our puritanical past and the other feeling its way into the future. We lust for extremes, a perfectly human trait. People always want some scandal beyond the scandal they're allowed. Rock stars perform fellatio on the microphone and, by extension, on the crowd, which responds in waves of screams. Porn stars show up at charity events and model clothes on haute-couture runways. Now that sex has risen to the surface of society, what does this suggest about our private habits? I suspect they may seem mild, even boring, by comparison. Private has become public; but public has not become private.

Why? In these plague years, when we cannot be promiscuous without worry, voyeurism has hit an all-time high. The ultimate safe sex is abstinence, we're warned. "Ecstasy," the current drug of choice at discos, is a sexual depressant. "The nice thing about masturbation," a cynical female friend once confided, "is that you meet a nicer class of men . . . and you don't need to dress up." Sex shows may make one think of the tenderloin area of a city, frequented by moral vermin. But, to some extent, we've taken sex shows on the road, polished them up, and made them fashionable. It's as if we were all watching the same peep show on television, in the separate cubicles of our lives, unobserved. This version of safe sex caresses the optic nerve, giving everyone a small taste of soft-core pornography. Sometimes it crosses boundaries into sadomasochism and exhibitionism. Sometimes it toys with the definition of gender. Sometimes it challenges the notions of taboo and scandal. Some of the most blatant sexual acts have nothing to do with sex per se, but rather with power, anger, and domination. Rape is an extreme example. A milder one is rock stars grabbing their genitals onstage. Look at the way we use sexual defilement as a socially acceptable threat. I've heard many heterosexual men and women say they fear prison not because of its isolation but because of rape. In their minds, prisons exist to punish heterosexuals in a homosexual way—by forcing them to change their sexuality and endure the horror of countless rapes. But public perversion always aims to shock. If you want to sell someone a CD or an idea, first you have to get their attention.

Habit is a great deadener. Nudity is so familiar that it takes wilder and wilder ways to excite us. Still, it is possible to shock us, to push the edge of the envelope, as test pilots say. And then to lick the envelope and savor the piquancy of the glue. Consider Madonna's much-publicized masturbation scene in Truth or Dare, performed in front of multitudes, and, perhaps more important, as her father watched. After seeing the film, I thought of the bad-girl syndrome, of the need to do outrageous things, and, when those are condoned, to find ones even more outrageous, questing for some absolute acceptance, asking in effect: *Will you love me now? Even if I'm a holy terror? Oh, yeah? How about now?* Madonna's follow-up book, *Erotica,* includes sexually explicit stills.

For perversion to be erotically exciting, the person has to feel like he or she is committing a sin. Some moral code has to be transgressed, someone has to be hurt or humiliated, physically abused or degraded, or reduced to an inanimate object. A shoe. A breast. A knife. Most perversion is heterosexual, and practiced by or for men, using women as sex objects. Some women are fetishists, exhibitionists, or voyeurs, but they seem to be rarer. Psychoanalyst Robert Stoller, who spent his clinical life studying perversion, interviewing and observing the habits of a great many people, including a New Guinea tribe obsessed with semen, learned that the crucial ingredient that "makes excitement out of boredom for most people is the introducing of hostility into the fantasy." A tincture of hostility works very nicely during sex—a little slap on the bottom, a pretend rape, perhaps even a pair of easily removable scarves binding the wrists. The merest pretense suffices.

Why human beings require taboos—which almost always involve eating; eliminating; death; covering the sex organs; whom to associate with; and where, when, how, and with whom to have sex—is a subject for endless contemplation. Presumably, taboos are intended to guide us (especially the young) to act in ways that are healthy or socially expedient. Once, priests were the taboo-police. Guilt, shame, and blame for supernatural revenge was the punishment that kept people in line.

Everyone has seen two-year-olds happily eating sand. Yet "Dirty!" is a negative term that can be applied equally to persons, words, ideas, or even jokes. Why don't we like dirt? We are far from biologically pure. Quite the contrary—our bodies crawl with mites, bacteria, and other organisms. Why do we worry about polluting, soiling, dirtying ourselves? And, given that fanaticism, what inspires some people—whom we recoil from and call "perverts"—to be coprophiles? In various cultures, mothers used to clean their babies by licking away the urine and feces, as other animals do. Balinese mothers carry their babies in cloth slings and frequently have a pet dog whose job is to provide "diaper service" by licking the baby and mother clean after the baby soils. The Masai drink cow urine as part of their diet, and several cultures dress their hair with dung. According to sex researcher John Money, somewhere in our primitive wiring lies the memory of drinking urine and eating feces as a natural part of behavior; and in a few people—the ones we call coprophiliacs—the wiring gets crossed with sexuality's.

Sex may seem spontaneous, raw, true, and of the moment, because the sensations are so hotly felt that the body screams out its own version of *Eureka!* But every sex act, no matter how casual, is a tangled drama, a piece of pure "theater," says Stoller, "the result of years of working over the scripts in order to make them function efficiently—that is, to ensure that they produce excitement . . . rather than anxiety, depression, guilt, or boredom." One grows more excited the more one is at risk, or pretends to be at risk. Stoller speculates that excitement happens only when we perceive two opposite possibilities—alive/dead, love/hate, strong/weak, control/out of control, succeed/fail, and so on—and manage to navigate between them:

> The poles . . . are markers limiting a territory within which the energy vibrates. Beyond the poles are experiences not of anticipation but consummation, either present or guaranteed. Excitement is uncertainty; certainty brings pleasure, pain, or no response, but not excitement.

This echoes Oscar Wilde's observation that "the essence of romance is uncertainty." Ultimately, the two poles one steers between "are risk and safety." In fantasies, pornography, or perversions, Stoller says,

> the whole business is a fraud, an act, a performance, a masquerade, a disguise—no matter how much the author . . . proclaims about truth. . . . What shall we do with daydreaming, where we know that one is quite consciously deceiving oneself, inventing a story known to be untrue, embellishing it. . . . Yet for all that falsity, tissues swell. Fantasy converts to physiology. . . . Excitement, then, is a continuum of anxiety/fear into which has been poured the possibility of pleasure, especially mastery. . . . True excitement . . . occurs when we are weighing the odds between danger (trauma) and safety.

Of course, there is nothing wrong with exciting daydreams; they serve us in countless therapeutic ways, and sometimes inspire romance, love, works of art. "For most of us," Stoller continues, "unadorned reality would boil our eyeballs. . . . Who, of those who buy tickets to war movies, would also buy a ticket to the war?" It's when sexual fantasies of hostility, debasement, and harm enter the picture that the emotional lighting changes. Why is it hostile to need perversion to become sexually excited? Because perversion is the "erotic form of hatred."

Let's consider exhibitionism. One version of it, the one that most often springs to mind, is of a flasher. Most flashers are male, and repeat offenders, because being caught is essential to their satisfaction. Typically, a man goes to a park or some other public place, approaches a woman sitting on a bench, and yanks open his coat to reveal his penis. The woman shrieks and runs for a policeman. What happens next sheds some light on the man's motives. The flasher rarely runs away. Flashing the woman fills the smallest part of his need. His real goal has many aspects, including the woman's upset and disapproval; the police coming; the bystanders gasping in a fit of shock and anger; the humiliating arrest; the appearance in court; the embarrassment to his family; the risk of losing his job. These are the critical elements of exposure for the flasher. A flasher is nearly always someone with low self-esteem, a bankrupted vision of his sexual worth, and a deep sense of failure as an individual. In his own eyes he is the unmanliest of men, a limp member of society, a worthless male. By hauling out his penis in public and causing consternation, shock, and chaos, he proves to himself how important his penis is after all, important enough to stop traffic, to make a woman faint, to get him arrested, to ruin his career. That's a mighty powerful penis; so he must be quite a man after all.

Love is an act of union or merging with a beloved, which is sought greedily by most, but there are some for whom that is a frightening thought. What if they get suffocated, swallowed up, dismantled? Intimacy takes high-wire courage; it's dangerous. One could be humiliated, lose face, be forced to relive old traumas. Perversion is a defense against that intimacy. Instead of facing the vulnerability and complexity of a real relationship, where everything is at stake, one invents a fantasy that is violent and taboo enough to be erotically exciting, but where people are dehumanized. People can't be trusted, only parts of them, or fetishes like knives and whips, or people offering themselves as fetishes. The sexual theater is exciting, not the partners. Once they're dehumanized, the would-be partners pose no threat. But there is still the sexual excitement. Most often, unknown to the players, this is a revenge drama. The exhibitionist is typically someone who was humiliated as a child and feels driven to humiliate or dominate others, usually strangers, in public. Perversion is what people resort to when intimacy fails.

Why should intimacy be so frightening? When you tell the truth about your life or feelings you give someone kryptonitelike information about you that can be translated into any language, converted into any currency; you never know when it may be used against you, or how far it may travel, or in whose unfriendly hands it may end up. Compared to that, donating an organ is impersonal. Family members risk being more intimate with one another, but they still keep a simmering portion of their lives private. Children discover that they have little privacy about their bodies and sexuality, both of which are open to view and discussion, whereas their parents' bodies and sexuality are mainly hidden. Their parents—who happily teach them how to eat and act, how to pee and reason—do not teach them how to be erotic. That equally natural activity is just too shameful and embarrassing to discuss. They learn it haphazardly from friends, books, movies, spying on elders, television, magazines, advertisements.

After being shocked, the mind adapts. A certain psychic numbing comes from repeatedly seeing sexuality as fashion. We are not unique in this. The codpiece, as we've seen, became a fashion statement for generations. One might glance at an especially fashionable Elizabethan young man and discover an upturned, mightily erect leather codpiece with a gargoyle face staring back. Somewhere underneath, a normal member was hanging with the homeboys. This is like being cowed by the big booming voice of the Wizard of Oz only to discover a modest-sized man with a megaphone hiding inside the wizard's costume. Ultimately, that is what we will find underneath all the sawdust: another glimpse of our humanity, one more piece of a huge jigsaw puzzle. The puzzle piece I'm holding at the moment, trying to fit into place, shows the bare thigh of a man or a woman and, in the background, something unsettling and mysterious—a pair of dark, fascinated eyes.

· · ·

Let's look at the most commonly practiced act of love, in public or in private, for contrast. The following section, "Kissing," first appeared in *A Natural History of the Senses* in somewhat different form, but belongs here, too, as kissing must in any contemplation of love.

KISSING

Sex is the ultimate intimacy, the ultimate touching when, like two paramecia, we engulf one another. We play at devouring each other, digesting each other, we nurse on each other, drink each other's fluids, get under each other's skin. Kissing, we share one breath, open the sealed fortress of our body to our lover. We shelter under a warm net of kisses. We drink from the well of each other's mouths. Setting out on a kiss caravan of the other's body, we map the new terrain with our fingertips and lips, pausing at the oasis of a nipple, the hillock of a thigh, the backbone's meandering riverbed. It is a kind of pilgrimage of touch, which leads to the temple of our desire.

We most often touch a lover's genitals before we actually see them. For the most part, our leftover puritanism doesn't condone exhibiting ourselves to each other naked before we've kissed and fondled first. There is an etiquette, a protocol, even in impetuous, runaway sex. But kissing can happen right away, and, if two people care for each other, then it's less a prelude to mating than a sign of deep regard. There are wild, hungry kisses or there are rollicking kisses, and there are kisses fluttery and soft as the feathers of cockatoos. It's as if, in the complex language of love, there were a word that could only be spoken when lips touch, a silent contract sealed with a kiss. One style of sex can be bare bones, fundamental and unromantic, but a kiss is the height of voluptuousness, an expense of time and an expanse of spirit in the sweet toil of romance, when one's bones quiver, anticipation rockets, but gratification is kept at bay on purpose, in exquisite torment, to build to a succulent crescendo of emotion and passion.

When I was in high school in the early sixties, nice girls didn't go all the way—most of us wouldn't have known how to. But man, could we kiss! We kissed for hours in the busted-up front seat of a borrowed Chevy, which, in motion, sounded like a broken dinette set; we kissed inventively, clutching our boyfriends from behind as we straddled motorcycles, whose vibrations turned our hips to jelly; we kissed extravagantly beside a turtlearium in the park, or at the local rose garden or zoo; we kissed delicately, in waves of sipping and puckering; we kissed torridly, with tongues like hot pokers; we kissed timelessly, because lovers throughout the ages knew our longing; we kissed wildly, almost painfully, with tough, soul-stealing rigor; we kissed elaborately, as if we were inventing kisses; we kissed furtively when we met in the hallways between classes; we kissed soulfully in the shadows at concerts, the way we thought musical knights of passion like The Righteous Brothers and their ladies did; we kissed articles of clothing or objects belonging to our boyfriends; we kissed our hands when we blew our boyfriends kisses across the street; we kissed our pillows at night, pretending they were mates; we kissed shamelessly, with all the robust sappiness of youth; we kissed as if kissing could save us from ourselves.

Before I went off to summer camp, which is what fourteen-year-old girls in suburban Pennsylvania did to mark time, my boyfriend, whom my parents did not approve of (wrong religion) and had forbidden me to see, used to walk five miles across town each evening, and climb in through my bedroom window to kiss me. These were not open-mouthed "French" kisses, which we didn't know about, and they weren't accompanied by groping. They were just earth-stopping, soulful, on-the-ledge-of-adolescence kissing, when you press your lips together and yearn so hard you feel faint. We wrote letters while I was away, but when school started again in the fall the affair seemed to fade of its own accord. I still remember those summer nights, how my boyfriend would hide in my closet if my parents or brother chanced in, and then kiss me for an hour or so and head back home before dark, and I marvel at his determination and the power of a kiss.

A kiss seems the smallest movement of the lips, yet it can capture emotions wild as kindling, or be a contract, or dash a mystery. Some cultures don't do much kissing. In *The Kiss and Its History*, Dr. Christopher Nyrop refers to Finnish tribes "which bathe together in

a state of complete nudity," but regard kissing "as something inde-
cent." Certain African tribes, whose lips are decorated, mutilated,
stretched, or in other ways deformed, don't kiss. But they are
unusual. Most people on the planet greet one another face-to-face;
their greeting may take many forms, but it usually includes kissing,
nose-kissing, or nose-saluting. There are many theories about how
kissing began. Some authorities believe it evolved from the act of
smelling someone's face, inhaling them out of friendship or love in
order to gauge their mood and well-being. There are cultures today
in which people greet each other by putting their heads together and
inhaling the other's essence. Some sniff hands. The mucous mem-
branes of the lips are exquisitely sensitive, and we often use the
mouth to taste texture while using the nose to smell flavor. Animals
frequently lick their masters or their young with relish, savoring the
taste of a favorite's identity. (Not only humans kiss. Apes and chimps
have been observed kissing and embracing as a form of peacemaking.) So we may indeed have begun kissing as a way to taste and smell
someone. According to the Bible account, when Isaac grew old and
lost his sight, he called his son Esau to kiss him and receive a blessing.
But Jacob put on Esau's clothing and, because he smelled like Esau
to his blind father, received the kiss instead. In Mongolia, a father
does not kiss his son; he smells his son's head. Some cultures prefer
just to rub noses (Inuits, Maoris, Polynesians, and others), while in
some Malay tribes the word for "smell" means the same as "salute."
Here is how Charles Darwin describes the Malay nose-rubbing kiss:
"The women squatted with their faces upturned; my attendants stood
leaning over theirs, and commenced rubbing. It lasted somewhat
longer than a hearty handshake with us. During this process they
uttered a grunt of satisfaction."

Some cultures kiss chastely, some extravagantly, and some savagely, biting and sucking each other's lips. In *The Customs of the
Swahili People,* edited by J.W.T. Allen, it is reported that a Swahili
husband and wife kiss on the lips if they are indoors, and will freely
kiss young children. However, boys over the age of seven usually are
not kissed by mother, aunt, sister-in-law, or sister. The father may
kiss a son, but a brother or father shouldn't kiss a girl. Furthermore,

when his grandmother or his aunt or another woman comes, a
child one or two years old is told to show his love for his aunt and

he goes to her. Then she tells him to kiss her, and he does so. Then he is told by his mother to show his aunt his tobacco, and he lifts his clothes and shows her his penis. She tweaks the penis and sniffs and sneezes and says: "O, very strong tobacco." Then she says, "Hide your tobacco." If there are four or five women, they all sniff and are pleased and laugh a lot.

How did mouth kissing begin? To primitive peoples, the hot air wafting from their mouths may have seemed a magical embodiment of the soul, and a kiss a way to fuse two souls. Desmond Morris, who has been observing people with a keen zoologist's eye for decades, is one of a number of authorities who claim this fascinating and, to me, plausible origin for French kissing:

> In early human societies, before commercial baby-food was invented, mothers weaned their children by chewing up their food and then passing it into the infantile mouth by lip-to-lip contact—which naturally involved a considerable amount of tonguing and mutual mouth-pressure. This almost bird-like system of parental care seems strange and alien to us today, but our species probably practiced it for a million years or more, and adult erotic kissing today is almost certainly a Relic Gesture stemming from these origins. . . . Whether it has been handed down to us from generation to generation . . . or whether we have an inborn predisposition towards it, we cannot say. But, whichever is the case, it looks rather as though, with the deep kissing and tonguing of modern lovers, we are back again at the infantile mouth-feeding stage of the far-distant past. . . . If the young lovers exploring each other's mouths with their tongues feel the ancient comfort of parental mouth-feeding, this may help them increase their mutual trust and thereby their pair-bonding.

Our lips are deliciously soft and responsive. Their touch sensations are transmitted to a large part of the brain, and what a boon that is to kissing. We don't just kiss romantically, of course. We also kiss dice before we roll them, kiss our own hurt finger or that of a loved one, kiss a religious symbol or statue, kiss the flag of our homeland or the ground itself, kiss a good-luck charm, kiss a photograph, kiss the king's or bishop's ring, kiss our own fingers to signal farewell to someone. The ancient Romans used to deliver the "last kiss," which custom had it would capture a dying person's soul.* In America we "kiss off" someone when we dump them, and they yell "Kiss my ass!" when angry. Young women press lipsticked mouths to the backs of envelopes so all the imprinted tiny lines will carry like fingerprint kisses to their sweethearts. We even refer to billiard balls as "kissing" when they touch delicately and glance away. Hershey sells small foil-wrapped candy "kisses," so we can give love to ourselves or others with each morsel. Christian worship includes a "kiss of peace," whether of a holy object—a relic or a cross—or of fellow worshipers, translated by some Christians into a rather more restrained handshake. William S. Walsh's 1897 book, *Curiosities of Popular Customs,* quotes a Dean Stanley, writing in *Christian Institutions,* as reporting travelers who "have had their faces stroked and been kissed by the Coptic priest in the cathedral at Cairo, while at the same moment everybody else was kissing everybody throughout the church." In ancient Egypt, the Orient, Rome, and Greece, honor used to dictate kissing the hem or feet or hands of important persons. Mary Magdalen kissed the feet of Jesus. Kissing the pope's ring is a near-miss kiss. A sultan often required subjects of varying ranks to kiss varying parts of his royal body: high officials might kiss the toe, others merely the fringe of his scarf. The riffraff just bowed to the ground. Drawing a row of XXXXXs at the bottom of a letter to represent kisses began in the Middle Ages, when so many people were illiterate that a cross was acceptable as a signature on a legal document. The cross did not represent the Crucifixion, nor was it an arbitrary scrawl; it stood for "Saint Andrew's mark," and people vowed to be honest in his sacred name. To pledge their sincerity, they would kiss their signature. In time, the "X" became associated with the kiss alone.†

Perhaps the most famous buss in the world is Rodin's sculpture *The Kiss,* in which two lovers, sitting on a rocky ledge or outcrop-

---

*Last-kiss scenes appear in Ovid's *Metamorphoses* (VIII, 860–61), Seneca's *Hercules Oetaeus,* and Virgil's *Aeneid* (IV, 684–85), among others, and in a more erotic form in the writings of Ariosto.

†It used to be fashionable in Spain to close formal letters with QBSP (*Que Besa Su Pies,* "Who kisses your feet") or QBSM (*Que Besa Su Mano,* "Who kisses your hand").

ping, embrace tenderly with radiant energy, and kiss forever. Her left hand wrapped around his neck, she seems almost to be swooning, or to be singing into his mouth. As he rests his open right hand on her thigh, a thigh he knows well and adores, he seems to be ready to play her leg as if it were a musical instrument. Enveloped in each other, glued together by touch at the shoulder, hand, leg, hip, and chest, they seal their fate and close it with the stoppers of their mouths. His calves and knees are beautiful, her ankles are strong and firmly feminine, and her buttocks, waist, and breasts are all heavily fleshed and curvy. Ecstasy pours off every inch of them. Touching in only a few places, they seem to be touching in every cell. Above all, they are oblivious to us, the sculptor, or anything on earth outside of themselves. It is as if they have fallen down the well of each other; they are not only self-absorbed, but absorbing each other. Rodin, who often took secret sketch notes of the irrelevant motions made by his models, has given these lovers a vitality and thrill that bronze can rarely capture in its fundamental calm. Only the fluent, abstracted stroking and pressing of live lovers actually kissing could capture it. Rilke notes how Rodin was able to fill his sculptures "with this deep inner vitality, with the rich and amazing restlessness of life. Even the tranquility, where there was tranquility, was composed of hundreds upon hundreds of moments of motion keeping each other in equilibrium. . . . Here was desire immeasurable, thirst so great that all the waters of the world dried in it like a single drop."

According to anthropologists, the lips remind us of the labia, because they flush red and swell when aroused, which is the conscious or subconscious reason women have always made them look even redder with lipstick. Today the bee-stung look is popular; models draw even larger and more hospitable lips, almost always in shades of pink and red, and then apply a further gloss to make them look shiny and moist. So, anthropologically at least, a kiss on the mouth, especially with all the plunging of tongues and the exchanging of saliva, is another form of intercourse. No surprise that it makes the mind and body surge with gorgeous sensations.

ON THE SENSUALITY
OF LOOKING

What the eyes caress, the memory fondles. As infants, using our fingers as eyes, we learn the world has depth and all of life a quirky topography, a three-dimensional feel. Then the merest glimpse of a clamshell or a shoulder is enough to kindle the touch-memory for *curve*. Then seeing a naked man lying in a shallow riverbed is enough to recall the feel of *round, hard, flat, bulging, knobbly, interflowing*. Then a woman holding a photograph of a large airy feather applied to an anonymous woman's nether parts can't help but imagine the feel of the feather. Then a photo of a woman's face, her eyes closed in carnal reverie, her cheek muscles limp, blissed-out by love, as a man's thumb gently presses open her bottom lip, is enough to make one utter a vicarious sigh.

The hands have already been where the eyes long to go, and we can imagine the terrain in painstaking or delight-taking detail. That is enough. Indeed, it is the all some people desire. PET scans show that it makes no difference whether we experience an event or *imagine* it—the same parts of the brain light up. No wonder we are ardent voyeurs, savoring the visual Eden of photograph and film. They offer us homeopathic doses of love, exhilaration, mystery, sexual adventure, and violence—all enjoyed from a safe remove. To feel but not feel. To gamble but not risk. To undress and unravel and penetrate with mere thought. These are heady thrills. A creative brain makes its own virtual reality every day. In a certain frame of mind—that of a devoted paramour—all of life is erotic. To love the world with the eyes, one uses them as hands; to love the world with ideas, one uses them as eyes.

Visual images are sticky. They attract meaning and emotion, and then quickly become unforgettable. No image is an island; it includes much that lies unseen. The lithe, giraffe-like woman nakedly feeding a real giraffe had to take her clothes off somewhere. Soon enough the giraffe, with a long insinuating tongue, will reach for the leaf she offers. And what is her relationship to the clothed person standing in the shadows behind her? Images work somewhat like pictograms. For example, in the scrapbook of my own memory, the image of a man holding a woman's face in his hands means "tenderness."

I remember the time a friend picked a ripe apple from his tree, took a bite from its firm flesh, and offered it to me to sample. We were not lovers. But, biting into the crater his teeth had just left, I joined him in the apple's flesh, which tasted sweet, sex-wet, and open. In that small oasis, our mouths met. Now when I see a photograph of such an apple, I don't think of Mom, Country, and Apple Pie. The image is tinged with the erotic. I think *kiss*.

Someone may find a telephone receiver sensuous, because it reminds him of the hot calls that inflamed an entire summer, and the delicious hours he held a phone's smooth, plastic knob as if it were his beloved's hand. Someone else may have more straightforward tastes, and be set atingle by a curvaceous back, a mischievous smile, or a ravenous glance.

What is erotic? The acrobatic play of the imagination. The sea of memories in which we bathe. The way we caress and worship things with our eyes. Our willingness to be stirred by the sight of the voluptuous. What is erotic is our passion for the liveliness of life.

PASSING STRANGE
AND WONDERFUL

LOVE'S CUSTOMS

PATTERNS IN NATURE

In the diamond quarter of Amsterdam, where hearts are cut every day, I sat on a bench during the violet hour, watching the sun drain out of the sky and a half-moon rise like an Inca god. A woman in a blue scarf, hurrying home with a net shopping bag full of produce, swerved awkwardly to avoid something in the road. A moment later she swerved again, and it wasn't until the third swerve a few steps on that I saw the pattern in her gait. Perhaps caused by a hip injury?

Just then I realized that a necklace of lights had been forming across the throat of the brick buildings along the canal. At night, Amsterdam opens its veins and pours forth the neon milk of cities. We are obsessed with lights. Not random lights, but carefully arranged ones. Perhaps it is our way of hurling the constellations back at the sky.

We crave pattern. We find it all around us, in sand dunes and pinecones; we imagine it when we look at clouds and starry nights; we create and leave it everywhere like footprints or scat. Our buildings, our symphonies, our fabrics, our societies—all declare patterns. Even our actions. Habits, rules, rituals, daily routines, taboos, codes of honor, sports, traditions—we have many names for patterns of conduct. They reassure us that life is stable, orderly, and predictable.

So do similes or metaphors, because seemingly unrelated things may be caught in their pincers, and then the subtle patterns that unite them shine clear. This is how the mind sometimes comforts itself, and often how the mind crosses from one unknown continent of perception or meaning to another, by using the land bridge of metaphor. In conversation, we meander like a river. Rocking with grief, a mourning woman keens like a wind-bent willow. The river sings. Unanswered letters dune on a cluttered desk. Families branch. Music curves, spirals, and flows. The spidery mind spins a fragile, sticky web between like things, gluing them together for future use. Patterns can charm us, but they also coax and solicit us. We're obsessed with solving puzzles; we will stand for hours before a work of abstract art, waiting for it to reveal itself.

Why do the world's patterns require our attention? Perhaps because we are symmetrical folk on a planet full of similar beings. Symmetry often reveals that something is alive. For example, the five deer standing at the bottom of the yard right now all blend perfectly into the winter woods. Their mottling of white, brown, and black echoes the subtle colors of the landscape. No doubt the deer were there for some time before I detected them. What gave them away was the regular pattern of legs, ears, and eyes. Then all at once the word *deer* flashed through my mind, and I retraced them with my eyes, this time picking out some flanks and noses, too. *Deer!* my mind confirmed, checking the pattern.

Once is an instance. Twice may be an accident. But three times or more makes a pattern. We crave something familiar in a chaotic world. Thought has its precincts, where the cops of law and order patrol, looking for anything out of place. Without a pattern, we feel helpless, and life may seem as scary as an open-backed cellar staircase that has no railings to guide us. We rely on patterns, and we also cherish and admire them. Few things are as beautiful to look at as a ripple, a spiral, or a rosette. They are visually succulent. The mind savors them. It is a kind of comfort food.

In the courtyard of my house, two doves are strutting like petitioners. Bobbing and posing, tossing in the occasional operatic warble, they are caught up in a drama whose goal is to establish territory, make alliances, and keep the peace. Each knows the dance steps the other will perform. It is the habit of the dove to bob and strut. Societies like to invent new rituals, to cushion nature's laws under some of their own. So they agree upon rules for everything, even for flirting, courtship, marriage, and the other so-called customs of love. But, when all is said and done, they reflect one of our oldest and deepest needs: to fill the world with pathways and our lives with design.

THE COURTSHIP

A man and a woman are seated at a small, candlelit table in a restaurant. He has invited her out to dinner, and as they eat and talk their eyes meet often. They hold each other's gaze a little longer than normal, an extra second or two. She smiles, tilts her head up, and looks shyly at him, then drops her gaze and glances away for a moment. She looks back, laughs, tosses her hair. As they talk, he rests his arm near hers on the table. His blue eyes shine with animation, excitement, and a tinge of nervousness. The pupils, normally narrow as pencil leads, now are swelling open wide like the shutter of a camera, allowing more and more of her in. The couple talk about everything, about nothing. They try to present themselves as positively as possible to each other, and yet also to reveal their real selves, hurts, and dreams. Gradually, subtly, because they are in step emotionally, they begin to move to the same rhythm, to mirror each other's gestures. When he leans forward, she leans forward. When she takes a drink, he drinks, too. They are like unconscious ballroom dancers. As she flirts with him, her pupils swell like his. It signals emotional or sexual interest, but she can't help herself. Nor does she wish to. They are not teenagers; they have been down this road before. Neither of them mentions how much they long for the taste of the other's mouth, the touch of the other's caress, the scent of the other's body, the heat of the other's passion.

This is called a dinner date. But what it really is is "courtship feeding." Many animals do it. Males who wish to copulate with females first offer them food or some other present. Penguins do it.

Apes do it. Scorpions do it. Fireflies do it. Humans do it. The purpose is to prove to the female that the male will be a good provider and meet her needs. We think of men as the great seducers in mating dramas, but women do much of the choosing. Women more often initiate a flirtation, women give subtle signs that it's all right for the courtship to continue, and women decide if they want to go to bed with the men. This also happens among most other animals. Males display for females, who then choose which males they desire. Among the cottontop tamarins, small forest-dwelling monkeys of South America, males do much of the child rearing. If a male wants to mate with a female, he shows up carrying a baby cottontop on his back. That turns the female on. Essentially, the male is telling the female: "See what a caring father I'd make? I'd be great with your kids."

What else do females choose in a male? High on the list is health. Females recoil from signs of disease, parasites, or infirmity. An exhausting courtship display doesn't just impress a female with a male's seriousness, it tells her if the male is hardy, if his cardiovascular system is strong, if he has the stamina to be her mate. She could also learn this through athletics, spirited play, or sending him out on quests. Or she could make him serenade her. Female gray tree frogs are attracted to operatic males that will sing sprightly numbers long into the Caribbean night. The males use vast amounts of oxygen in the process and tire themselves; but that suits the female fine. She wants a robust, vigorous crooner who will sire hearty offspring. For some species of frogs, more than exhaustion is at stake. A few years ago, bat biologist Merlin Tuttle discovered how *Trachops cirrhosus,* a Central American bat, stalked its prey by sound. Preferring the taste of the frog *Physalaemus,* the bat listens for the male frog's mating call. The louder the song, the plumper and juicier the frog. This puts the frog in an awkward position. It needs to sing for a mate to perpetuate its kind—and in the tropical night it is full of sexual longing—but singing also reveals its whereabouts to any hungry *Trachops cirrhosus* bat. Should it sing halfheartedly, the female frogs won't be impressed, even though the bat may think it's a lovesick runt. If it sings about its prowess with large, croaking, swollen pride, then a bat is bound to court the frog in ways too ghoulish to describe.

Wealth is also important. A female wants a generous male who will protect and support her offspring. When a male *Pyrochroidae* beetle desires a female, he shows her a deep cleft in his forehead as one of his display moves. She's impressed all right. It's a hell of a deep cleft. In beetle terms, he's a hunk, a handsome, well-endowed beetle. So she grabs his head, licks it, and permits him to mate. What the male carries in his cleft is a small dose of a poison she's immune to that will protect her future eggs from ants and other predators. He gives her just a taste of it during foreplay to let her know that it would be in her best interest to mate with him, because during intercourse she would receive a huge gift of the precious chemical along with his sperm. "It's as though he's showing her a fat wallet," entomologist Tom Eisner explains, "and saying, 'There's more in the bank where that came from.' "

Female bowerbirds of New Guinea choose multitalented males, those who collect the most ornaments, design the most extravagant nests, and put on the best sideshow dance. Any male who isn't a gifted interior decorator and builder is a nerd. So males construct architectural wonders (sometimes nine feet tall) out of sticks, lichens, ferns, and leaves. Then they decorate the nests with orchids, snail shells, butterfly wings, flowers, bits of charcoal, bird-of-paradise feathers, seeds, fungi, beetle carapaces, ballpoint-pen tops, toothbrushes, bracelets, shotgun cartridges, or whatever else they can find. A sense of decor drives the males wild. As the flowers wilt, they freshen them daily. There is always a carefully considered color scheme, blue being the favorite. Researchers have counted as many as 500 decorations on a single bower. Because fierce battles arise between piratical males trying to plunder a neighbor's nest for decorations, a well-stocked bower advertises a male's power. Females are attracted to males with large, artistically designed bachelor pads in good repair. For the bowerbird to build a seductive bower, Jared Diamond explains, "a male must be endowed with physical strength, dexterity and endurance, plus searching skills and memory—as if women were to choose husbands on the basis of a triathlon contest extended to include a chess game and sewing exercise." When a female is attracted to the bowerbird equivalent of a ritzy flat and a flashy red sports car, the male grovels at her feet, cackles and squeaks his appeals as he dances around her, pointing to various objets d'art with his bill. All the male wants to give her is his seed. Therefore a razzmatazz seduction is essential; courtship is his all. The male hopes to attract and mate with as many females as possible. But the female needs to get pregnant by just one extraordinary male, and then fly off to build a modest, inconspicuous nest where she'll raise her young by herself.

If our couple decides to go dancing after dinner, or to a nightclub, or a bar, they'll bathe their minds in pop songs. It won't matter if the songs are rock, country, or easy-listening—all will be about love. Popular music has an obsession with love. Occasionally, there will be a work song, or, rather, a "take this job and shove it" song. Or a poignant song about the sacrifices Mom or Dad made to raise the kids. But there are no songs about the joys of heli-arc welding or how much fun it is to go sledding. Pop songs vivisect relationships. They are the primary source of love education for adolescents. The airwaves have become our troubadours. People all over the country can turn on their car radios, television sets, or CD players, and hear the same songs at the same time. In pop songs we share our myths and ideals about love. In a tough, mercantile way, they warn us what love may cost. But they also alert us to what grandeur it may bring. They offer advice on whom to love, how to know if it's the real thing, what to do if one's betrayed, how to cope if love disintegrates. We are constantly in love, looking for love, losing love, or hurt by love; in short, we are "Bewitched, Bothered, and Bewildered." Our songs say it all.

In evolutionary terms, humans have not required music for mating, but we do find it hypnotic and seductive. A language of pure emotion, music heightens courtship, and most cultures include music in their mating rituals. For the Cheyenne Indians, courtship took time and was suffused with romance. A brave would hide in the woods waiting for his sweetheart to pass and then serenade her on a special love flute. In time, his melodies worked their way into her heart. Then he would woo her with compliments, gifts, and attentions. But she would not make love with him before they wed. A Cheyenne girl put on a chastity belt at puberty and wore it until she married. She might keep her beau waiting for five years or so, which gave him plenty of time to master the flute, a phallic symbol of the beautiful music his body had to offer.

The Cheyenne maiden wouldn't have been comfortable if her beau sang songs with sexually explicit lyrics. I can't imagine what she'd make of such pop songs as "Sexual Healing." Love songs of the twenties "sang of carefree nights and frenetic days," says Richard Rodgers, "that rushed headlong into the nightmare and fantasy of the thirties. . . . Breadlines seemed less burdensome if one could sing." During the thirties, forties, and fifties, women yearned in love songs for love to save them, to give their lives meaning and direction. Without love, a woman was worthless. Nothing a man could do to a woman was too great a price to pay for the gift of his love. Hence the popularity of such songs as "Can't Help Lovin' That Man," in which the man is shiftless and unworthy but the singer is glad to love him anyway. Men idealized women as angelic creatures with a talent for sorcery, who stole their hearts, enslaved their thoughts, and made them feel irrational. Women called the shots in most love-song relationships. The ability to drive a man crazy with love was the only real power a woman had. Enjoying sex was not something women could talk about openly. If singers like Billie Holiday sometimes cooed "The meat is sweeter closer to the bone," it was deliciously scandalous. When rock and roll hit in the fifties and sixties, love songs suddenly reflected social revolution, uninhibited sex, love as mysticism, and a rejection of middle-class taboos. Love was a religion again, one that could save the world, as the Beatles and other groups proclaimed. By the time the eighties rolled around, men in pop songs were loners who wanted sex but not commitment. "Baby, baby, don't get stuck on me," a typical song warned, because men were tough and lean and troubled and they just weren't "the marrying kind." Today, pop songs tend to be clever and cynical. Now that sex is freely available, and inhibition and denial have given way to frankness, songs have changed from coy, romantic euphemisms to yowls of blunt desire. The lyrics have gotten sexier, even raunchy at times, and simple lamentation has turned into hard truths and stark reality. But in many of today's songs singers croon again for head-over-heels love, and psychologists Schlachet and Waxenberg think perhaps this

> renewed interest in enduring love is a backlash against a culture of narcissism and consumption that emphasizes the primacy of the individual over the human need to relate in an interdependent way, which leaves its members feeling empty and alienated with nothing but the quick fix of a new sensation to provide temporary comfort.

They see hope in the popularity of albums by Linda Ronstadt, Barbra Streisand, and Carly Simon that return to ballads of the thirties and forties.

Why do so many people listen to love songs? In imaginative envy, we idealize what we don't have. The act of yearning for something transmutes it from base metal into gold. Anyway, putting a lid on sexuality inspires romance, because people are then driven to fantasize about it. Romantic love does occur in tribes where sex is freely available (particularly if one is forced to marry someone they don't prefer), but not as often and not as an institution. Denial, repression, and inhibition all feed romantic love, because people obsess about satisfying their biological drives, yet cannot avoid the confines of morality. In that climate, pop songs stoke the hottest fantasies and keep the idea of romance alive. For some people, down-and-dirty love songs are all the romance they can find, and whether it reminds them of yesteryear or defines what they're waiting for, it sounds good. It's a little like waving slabs of beef before a caged lion so he doesn't forget the scent of a fresh kill. Men who can't put their feelings in words without embarrassment and discomfort are often able to sing passionate and sentimental love songs. Singing someone else's lyrics gives them a railing to hold on to. Just as the worst stutterers can (usually) sing fluently, men who are emotional stutterers can express their feelings through song. "If music be the food of love," Shakespeare wrote, "play on."

After their dinner date, our couple feels a mixture of hope and uncertainty, the twin ingredients necessary for romance to thrive. Both of them have gone through agonizing divorces. He still has dark circles under his heart from his ex-wife's infidelities and the painful breakup. Her key problem with her ex-husband was that she was married to Hammurabi, a man who thought he was the ultimate judge and deviser of laws. Nothing begins with so much excitement and hope, or fails as often, as love. But, despite that, they are searching again for "the glory, jest, and riddle of the world," as Alexander Pope called love. They have many things in common—their age, work, taste in music, attitudes about life—but, most of all, timing. They are both ready to risk love: a critical stage. Once someone is ready, willing, and able to love, they often fall for the next appropriate person they meet. Both are tantalized by love's slow dance, which they know can begin in the damnedest places: on back roads that spin along like time itself; an interlude in a redneck's arms; in the company cafeteria; on the spine-cracking seat of an old pickup truck; while gutter-crawling through ramshackle country pubs. What starts as a simple arithmetic of limbs and desire can suddenly become a calculus of powerful feelings. Until then, not even the low soughing of the elms, blood-dark under the August moon, not even the apple tree in the yard, sweeping one heavy bough like a censer, not even pond glow frizzled bright as a marquee, can shake the heart from its waiting.

"Falling in love," we call it, as if into a pothole, and "falling out of love," as if out of an airplane. When you're in love, you're in a bowl of its thick stew. The sides of the bowl are slippery and no matter how hard you try to climb out you keep sliding back in. As this couple strolls arm in arm, other couples are falling in love in Finland, in Patagonia, in Madagascar. Conducting a worldwide study of 168 cultures, anthropologists William Jankowiak and Edward Fischer found romantic love in 87 percent of them. In most of those, the men give the women food or other small gifts as part of the courtship. Despite their different cultures, fashions, and worldviews, they would all understand the dinner date. They would all know how it feels to free-fall through the atmospheres of infatuation, with hope as the only parachute. They all long to be "a couple," that emotional jigsaw puzzle with only two pieces.

FLESH OF MY FLESH:
THE MARRIAGE

The first marriages were by capture. When a man saw a woman he desired (usually from another tribe), he took her by force. To kidnap a bride, a groom enlisted the aid of a warrior friend, his "best man." Capture marriage dominated the prehistoric world, and was even legal in England until the thirteenth century. However, marriage by purchase became the preferred tradition, and even when it wasn't an overt sale of the bride for cash, everyone understood that she was being bartered for land, holdings, political alliance, or social advancement. A girl was a useful pair of hands in the father's household, but she was invaluable to the groom's, where she could work equally hard and also bear offspring. The Anglo-Saxon word *wedd* referred to the groom's pledge to marry, but also to the purchase money or its equivalent in horses, cattle, or other property that the groom paid the bride's father. So a "wedding" was literally the purchase of a woman for breeding purposes, involving an element of risk. The word derives from a root that meant to gamble or wager. The groom's family usually told him whom to marry, and they rarely let him see his prospective bride, because if he didn't like her looks he might balk at the marriage. The father "gave the bride away" to the buyer, who, on his wedding day, lifted her veil to see her face for the first time.

We think of the honeymoon as romantic days of sensual bliss under a tropic sky, but the original honeymoon had a more somber purpose. Right after a groom captured or bought a bride, he disappeared with her for a while, so that her family and friends couldn't rescue her. By the time they found the couple, the bride would already be pregnant. Our western idea of a love marriage occurred late in human history; and many cultures throughout the world still practice marriage by capture or purchase.* But let's consider a more commonplace sight, a marriage in San Francisco, California.

Carol and Jerry are getting married. He pops the question, she accepts, then they happily tell their families and friends that they're tying the knot. Jerry gives Carol an engagement ring and she shows it to her girlfriends and wears it proudly on the third finger of her left hand. Her girlfriends give a wedding shower for her. Her parents

---

*According to *The Guinness Book of World Records,* the longest marriage on record lasted eighty-six years, between Sir Temulji Bhicaji Nariman and Lady Nariman, who wed in 1853, when they were five years old. The longest engagement was between Octavio Guillen and Adriana Martinez of Mexico, who took sixty-seven years to make sure they were right for each other. The largest wedding present was the entire city of Gezer, which the Bible explains was a gift from the pharaoh to Solomon when he married the pharaoh's daughter (I Kings, 9:16). The most expensive wedding in recent times took place in 1981, when Mohammed, son of Sheik Rashid Bin Saeed Al Maktoum, married Princess Salama in Dubai. The wedding lasted for seven days, hosted 20,000 guests, and took place in a stadium that had been built for the occasion.

offer to pay for a lavish church wedding and reception. His parents offer to pay for a lavish honeymoon. Carol begins collecting dainties for her trousseau. She asks her sisters and best girlfriends to be part of the bridal party, and she chooses a favorite niece as flower girl and a nephew as ring bearer. Jerry asks his brother to be best man and his friends to be ushers. The evening before the wedding, the best man and the ushers throw a stag party for him. On the day of the wedding, a minister performs the ceremony at a local church. As the ceremony closes, the bride and groom exchange rings and a kiss.

Then everyone goes to a reception hall for eating, drinking, and dancing. The bride and groom cut the first piece of a huge, three-tiered wedding cake. They dance the first dance. They gratefully accept presents of cash and goods. The best man leads a series of toasts. Later, the bride tosses her bouquet into a crowd of unmarried women; her garter she tosses to a crowd of unmarried men. Then she and the groom climb into a car that has mismatched shoes dangling from the rear bumper, and the words JUST MARRIED painted in whitewash on the trunk; and the guests throw rice at them as they drive off to board a flight to Hawaii.

In later years, paging through a scrapbook of photographs, they may cherish the look on his mother's face, or smile at the picture of her uncle playing the harmonica, or laugh at the way his brother mugged for the camera. They may marvel at how young and happy everyone seemed. They probably won't be thinking of the ancient array of rituals they kept alive. Let's consider, in terms of human culture, what really happened to them. The expression "to tie the knot" dates back to the Romans, when the bride wore a girdle secured by a knot, which the groom then had the fun of untying. The two threads of the couple's life were also tied together. Rituals of binding and tying have been popular throughout the world. In ancient Carthage, the couple's thumbs were laced together with a strip of leather. In India, the Hindu groom knotted a ribbon around his bride's neck, and once he'd tied it, the marriage was legal and binding. People have always been superstitious about knots, which were credited with magic powers. In Egypt, any holy mystery was a "she-knot." Jews were afraid of the magic power of knots, and thus rabbinic law forbids the tying of knots on the Sabbath. For much of history, rope was the most powerful way to connect things, and it symbolized fate, so it made sense to talk of people "tying the knot" or being "hitched." Our vocabulary hasn't caught up with our adhesives, which still seem to us a novelty. Wedding slang may one day include Velcro, superglue, or some other invention.

We have records of engagement rings being given in Anglo-Saxon days, and no doubt they have a much longer history. Circles or rings have always symbolized eternity—one sees them in the Egyptian hieroglyphics, for example. So it's not surprising that rings were given to show favor between two people, seal agreements, or symbolize something sacred. In Gen. 41: 41–42, we find: "And Pharaoh said unto Joseph, See, I have set thee over all the land of Egypt. And Pharaoh took off his ring from his hand, and put it upon Joseph's hand." Although engagement rings were always popular, it was the medieval Italians who favored a diamond ring, because of their superstition that diamonds were created from the flames of love. The word *diamond* comes from the Greek *adamas,* which means "invisible." Tempered by heat and pressure, its crystals are the hardest on earth, and the romantic Italians felt that was also true of many-faceted love. Then, too, diamonds looked like the frozen tears of past grief or future joy.

It was the soldiers of ancient Sparta who first staged stag parties. The groom feasted with his male friends on the night before the wedding, pledging his continued loyalty, friendship, or love. The friends probably provided the Spartan version of strippers, porno movies, and women leaping out of cakes. The function of this rite of passage was to say good-bye to the frivolities of bachelorhood,* while swearing continued allegiance to one's comrades. It was important for the groom to reassure his friends that they wouldn't be excluded from his life now that it included a family. Bridal showers were also meant to restate bonds and to prepare the bride with gifts and moral support for the marriage. However, the term "shower" is fairly recent. In the 1890s, a woman held a party for her newly engaged friend at which the bride-to-be stood in the middle of the room while a Japanese paper parasol filled with little gifts was turned upside down

---

*Actually, our word *bachelor* meant the Latin equivalent of *cowhand,* and it was a term that implied that one was still young and inexperienced.

over her head, producing a wonderful shower of presents. When word of this hit the fashion pages, it so charmed readers that everyone wanted to have a "shower" of their own.

The idea of the bridal group has many origins, one of which dates back to the Anglo-Saxons. A man planning to capture a woman to be his bride needed help from his bachelor pals, otherwise known as the "bridesmen" or "bride-knights." The bride-knights made sure she got to the church for the ceremony, and to the groom's house afterward. The bride had her own "bride's maids" and a married "bride's woman" to help her. The wedding usually happened after nightfall, to keep angry family members and rivals in the dark, so they were torchlight ceremonies, and the guests were heavily armed. The flower girl is a medieval addition to the ceremony; originally she carried wheat to symbolize fertility. The ring bearer also appeared in the Middle Ages—perhaps for symmetry—and was a young page.

The white wedding dress, now traditional in the western world, was first worn in 1499 by Anne of Brittany on the occasion of her marriage to Louis XII of France. Prior to this, a woman wore her best dress, often yellow or red. In biblical days, blue, not white, symbolized purity, and both bride and groom wore a blue band around the bottom of their wedding attire, which is where the idea of the bride's "something blue" comes from. In China and Japan, brides have traditionally begun their wedding day by wearing white—but only because white symbolizes mourning, and, when a bride leaves the family of her birth to join that of her husband, she undergoes a symbolic death.

The bride's veil, which hides her beauty behind a smokescreen of fabric, is a sign of modesty and submission; in some cultures the veil covers a woman from head to foot. She is her husband's ransom; he alone gets to lift her veil. Physical beauty is such a valuable commodity for women that many religions specify ways in which new brides are to make themselves *less* beautiful—by hiding their face, hair, or body, or even by cutting off their hair. Depending on the religion, this is so the bride doesn't accidentally tempt other men, or doesn't think herself pretty enough to initiate involvements with other men; or doesn't arouse her husband too much, since sex is meant strictly for procreation.

Brides have always worn or carried flowers, though not bridal bouquets. In the fourteenth century, when it was popular for the bride to toss her garter to the men (reenacting how a lady would toss her ribbon or colors to her knight), things sometimes got out of hand, with drunken guests trying to remove the garter ahead of time. Tossing her bouquet was less worrisome.

Wedding rings are very ancient indeed, and historians aren't sure when the first one was worn, but it was probably made of iron. The main thing was that the ring be of plain, strong metal, so that it didn't break, which would have seemed a disastrous omen. Naturally, there are romantic interpretations of the band—that it symbolizes harmony, unending love, and so on—but it originally served as a notice and reminder that a woman was bound to her husband (who didn't have to wear a ring). The Romans felt that a small artery—the *vena amoris,* or "vein of love"—ran from the third finger to the heart, and that wearing a ring on that finger joined the couple's hearts and destiny. Paintings from Elizabethan days show the wedding ring worn on the thumb, which presumably was the fashion of the time, although it doesn't sound very comfortable. In traditional Jewish weddings, the ring is worn on the first finger of the left hand. But why wear a symbolic token on the hand at all, why not around the neck, as some African women do, or around the ankle? Why not wear a symbolic girdle or hat? For that matter, why give a woman's "hand in marriage"? Our hands, with which we build cities, diaper babies, till fields, caress loved ones, throw spears, discover the mysterious workings of our body—our hands teach us about our limits, they connect us to the world. They are bridges between *I* and *Thou,* living and nonliving, friend and foe. Much of our slang uses the hand as a symbol for the whole person: "give me a hand," "one hand washes the other," "handout," "factory hand," "I heard it firsthand," "she'll have a hand in that decision," for example. We take a child's hand to instruct and protect it; we take a loved one's hand for comfort or romance. Our hands link us to other lives, and to discoveries; they lead us out of ourselves on the pilgrimage of experience we call life. A ring symbolizes how that outward journey has been limited. A married woman is tethered to her husband. For so light an object, a ring weighs heavily on her life. But, in love marriages, the sheer weight of the commitment is one of the keenest paradoxes, because love makes one both heavy and happy—too heavy to go anywhere one pleases anymore, but happy to be so confined.

Fertility symbols have always accompanied weddings. In some cultures, a bride wore shafts of wheat, phallic symbols, or even ears of corn, attached to her belt. The ancient Romans baked a special wheat or barley cake, which they broke over the bride's head as a symbol of her fertility. Wheat crumbs were also thrown at the bride and groom, and scrambled for by guests. These simple cakes evolved into the elaborately styled wedding cake during the reign of England's King Charles II, whose French chefs decided to take the traditional cake, turn it into an edible palace, and ice it with white sugar. It became the custom for English newlyweds to pile small cakes one upon the other as high as they could, and then try to kiss across the tower without knocking it down. If they did, it meant a lifetime of prosperity. To ensure their good fortune, a tactful baker would weld the tiers together with icing. From that heap of spiced cake and sugar-glue we get the stately, many-tiered wedding cake of today.

The best man's toast originated with the French, who placed a piece of bread in the bottom of a glass, then drank down "to the toast." Here's an especially lovely Old English toast to the bride:

> Love, be true to her; Life, be dear to her;
> Health, stay close to her; Joy, draw near to her;
> Fortune, find what you can do for her,
> Search your treasure-house through for her,
> Follow her footsteps the wide world over,
> And keep her husband always her lover!

Tying shoes to the car bumper seems an odd custom, but it reflects the symbolic power that shoes had for ancient cultures. The Assyrians and Hebrews used a sandal as a pledge of good faith when they sealed a business deal. Tossing one's shoe onto a piece of land meant that you were claiming it ("Upon Edom I cast my shoe"—Psalms 108:9). The Egyptians exchanged sandals when they exchanged property or authority, and so a father would give the groom his daughter's sandal to show that she was now in the groom's care. The world she walked would be his. This was also the custom in Anglo-Saxon marriages, and the groom tapped the bride lightly on the head with the shoe to impress upon her his authority. In later days, people began throwing shoes at the couple, and finally, in the automobile age, tying shoes to the car.

However, people have always thrown *something* at the bride and groom, usually grain or fruit. The Greek groom used to take his new bride to his hearth and shower her with dates, figs, nuts, and small coins. In Slavic countries, the bride and groom were showered with corn and hops. In India, flower petals are sprinkled over the bride and groom. From Sanskrit, Greek, and many other sources come reports of similar pelting customs. Why has the symbolic stoning, or raining down upon, or attack with fragrant missiles been such an important feature of the wedding ceremony? Does it hark back to the time when marriage was by capture, and spears or stones were being hurled at the groom? Is it a symbolic baptism in fertile, seedlike emblems? Is it a long-distance form of touching by a crowd of well-wishers who can't all embrace the couple at once? Is it meant to bribe or repel devils and ward off the evil eye? Does it remind all present that the bride is "arable land"? Is it an instinctive, now-merely-ceremonial way to drive the young out of the nest at puberty, a behavior we so often see in its life-and-death form among other animals?

Of course, if we were attending a wedding in Africa, it would look much different. The Mbuti pygmies, who roam the forests of Central Africa, begin preparing a girl for marriage and motherhood when she reaches puberty. Then, for two to three months, she lives inside a special hut with other girls her age, and receives instruction on sexuality, marriage, and women's ways. Toward the end of this period, a battalion of the girls' mothers stands outside the hut with baskets of well-chosen stones. The young men of the village come calling; of course, the mothers are well acquainted with their families and character, and have a good idea which daughter a certain boy might be hankering for. If a mother doesn't approve of the suitor, her aim is blunt and severe. If she likes him, her attack is halfhearted. In any case, if a boy passes unscathed through the barrage of mothers, he may make love to the girl of his choice, who then becomes his fiancée. He still must ask her parents formally for her hand, and present them with a killed deer, to prove that he will be a good provider. However, it's only when the girl becomes pregnant that the engagement period is officially over and the marriage begins.

Among the Bantu Kavirondo in East Africa, the bride and groom consummate the marriage in the presence of many women and girls, to prove to all that the union has been completed. Among the G'wi Bushmen of Botswana, girls and boys are betrothed when they're very young. When a girl menstruates for the first time, she's expected to fast and sit absolutely still for four days, with her legs held straight out in front of her. Then the groom joins her, and both are ritually washed and tattooed. Their hands, feet, and backs are cut with razors, their blood is mixed together and applied to their cuts, thus making them blood-wed. A paste of ashes and medicinal roots, rubbed into the cuts, guarantees that they'll heal as raised scars. The bride's father formally introduces her to the groom's people, her new clan. Relatives on both sides lend the newlyweds their most precious ornaments to wear for a few days. When the couple returns the ornaments, their normal married life begins.

Some wedding customs seem to be universal: sprinkling the couple with seed or symbols of fertility, pretending to bind the couple with ropes or ribbons (a custom to be found from China to Italy to Africa), mixing the couple's blood literally or symbolically, the taking of sacred vows. Even in the Catholic nun's "marriage" to Christ, we find a ring and the imagery of binding together and blending of flesh and blood. This roping together of lives is perfectly understandable, but mixing flesh and blood with the loved one is quite a different challenge. In a minute sense, we can become one. Every molecule of air, every atom of matter is shared throughout the planet and throughout time. In that sense, I may indeed become one with John Donne, Colette, Marie Curie, Leonardo. Matter returns to matter, as so many creation myths tell us. But the only way for two people to become one flesh (unless they're Siamese twins) is to be mother and fetus. Subconsciously, all these traditions may be echoing the only perfect love humans know, one based on absolute devotion, self-sacrifice, and protection—the love between a mother and her newborn. In anthropological terms, they are saying to each other: I want you to love me and protect me as if you were genetically connected to me—flesh of my flesh—because that will be your connection to our offspring.

Once a couple marry, they have a brand-new collection of customs, rules, and regulations to contend with. It's as if society didn't hand round enough edicts, relatives didn't issue enough demands, because married couples like to invent their own private rituals, too. Most couples I know have evolved elaborate customs about which holidays to spend with which in-laws, which nights to "have a date" in the bedroom, how to spend Sunday. For example, they may habitually spaniel* together with a half-read newspaper on sunny afternoons in winter, or have brunch at a favorite deli and then spend a few hours mousing† around the countryside.

Remembering Valentine's Day is a must. But who knows who Valentine was? One legend claims that Valentinus, a priest in fourth-century Rome, secretly married couples even though the emperor Claudius had temporarily forbidden it. Claudius was waging a war and believed that bachelor soldiers would fight harder. Another legend paints Valentinus as a Christian imprisoned for refusing to worship pagan gods. Making friends with the jailer's blind daughter, he cured her through prayer; and on the day of his execution, February 14, he sent her a farewell note signed "Your Valentine." Other legends link him to erotic festivals in ancient Rome, which happened to take place during February (named after Juno Februata, goddess of love's fever). For whatever reason, he was canonized in the Middle Ages and he's been the patron saint of lovers ever since.

Passion may crave spontaneity and disorder, but love likes its holidays to be reliable, even commemorative, and invents rituals to give the marriage a sense of history and society. In time, long after the romance may have waned, it's not just a couple's vows that unite them, but a wealth of shared habits, customs, and events. For long-time spouses, the marriage becomes their homeland, complete with

---

*spaniel *v.* (fr. *spaniel,* any of several breeds of medium-sized dogs): To find a shaft of sunlight pouring through a window on a cold winter day, curl up in the puddle of warmth it creates on the rug, and doze with doglike dereliction. "I think I'll just spaniel for an hour or so before I begin work."

†mouse *v.* (fr. *mouse,* any of numerous small rodents of the families Muridae and Cricetidae): To explore a town with the eager curiosity of a mouse nosing down alleyways and peeking into corners, always on the lookout for hidden marvels. May refer to shopping, but only if it's done with rodentlike verve, appetite, and joyous exploration, say, of quaint boutiques. "Okay, you stay here and make the world safe for democracy; I'll go mouse the shops." Other forms: *mousing, mouser, moused, mouseable.* "What I love about Santa Fe is how mouseable it is." Should not be used when referring to natural wonders. For example, it would be inappropriate to say at a cocktail party: "Have you moused the Grand Canyon yet?" But it would be in perfect form, on the same occasion, to observe: "Napoleon—now there was a man who could mouse a whole country."

its own laws, myths, and routines. Divorce seems like exile, because they are citizens of the marriage, in whose bustling city-state they dwell.

OF COCKS AND CUNTS

We have records of *cock* being used as a slang term for the penis as early as the Middle Ages. Most scholars suggest that the word must have come from the sound of a rooster crowing *cock-a-doodle-doo*: the rooster was nicknamed a cock, then a crowing penis was nicknamed a rooster. I think it more likely came from the *cock* used in plumbing during the Middle Ages—a valve or faucet. Any four-teen-year-old boy could provide a fine compendium of slang terms for the penis. One old mideastern euphemism was "knee." Indeed, the Mesopotamians used a single word, *birku,* for both knee and penis: In an important ritual, a father would set a boy on his knee and formally acknowledge him as his son. Our word *genuine* ("of the knee") arose from that symbolic act. In Latin, the word *birku* became *virtu,* and meant virility, male-spirited, or erectness.

Every time we say the word *fascinate* we are referring to penises. In Latin, a *fascinum* was the image of an erect penis that people worshiped, hung up in the kitchen or bedroom, or wore around the neck as an amulet. Penises were powerful and praiseworthy, and could even ward off the evil eye. In time, anything worth appreciation and study, anything potent and magical, anything as truly terrific as a penis, was called fascinating. This penis-worship continued for some time. In fact, hundreds of Renaissance churches claimed to have part of Christ's penis as a holy relic. His circumcised prepuce, the only mortal part of him left on earth when he ascended to heaven, was treasured as a miraculous fertility aid. Women prayed at Christ's foreskin for help in conceiving. Thirteen of those relics survive today. The best known, at the Abbey Church in Chartres, was said to be responsible for thousands of pregnancies.

The word *cunt* has an equally fascinating heritage. I'd like to think, as Chaucer did, that it derives from the word *quaint,* which meant a many-layered infolded mystery. The *O.E.D.* offers examples of usage starting as early as 1230, and including at least one street name, "Gropecuntlane," a red-light district in medieval Oxford, later changed to "Magpie Lane." However, a likelier possibility is that the word came from India. The Hindu goddess Kali, personifying the life-giving vulva energy of the world, was called *Cunti* or *Kunda.* Old Norse for the female genitals was *kunta,* perhistoric German was *kunton.* Cognates can be found throughout the Indo-European languages. If we look back even further, we find its origins in the Indo-European root *geu,* which meant "a hollow place." Unlike *cock, cunt* isn't slang, but an ancient part of our vocabulary. Many of our everyday words derive from that female source, such as cunning, kin, country, and kind.

The Elizabethans, who liked saucy puns, had many euphemisms for the female genitals, their favorites being "lap," "ring," "eye," "circle," and "nothing." Hence the ribald jokes in Shakespeare's *Hamlet,* when Hamlet and Ophelia are getting ready to watch a play:

> HAMLET: Lady, shall I lie in your lap?
> OPHELIA: No, my lord.
> HAMLET: I mean, my head upon your lap.
> OPHELIA: Aye, my lord.
> HAMLET: Do you think I meant country matters?
> OPHELIA: I think nothing, my lord.
> HAMLET: That's a fair thought to lie between maids' legs.
> OPHELIA: What is, my lord?
> HAMLET: Nothing.
> OPHELIA: You are merry, my lord.
> HAMLET: Who, I?

In time, of course, he'll suggest she go to a nunnery (slang for a brothel), but at this stage he's love's pauper, who dreams of lying in the luxury of her lap.

It's worth noting that when we talk about gender we say that a man has a penis and a woman has a vagina. This distinction, which we take for granted, hides a prejudice about the baseness of women. A man's pleasure organ is his penis, and a woman's pleasure organ is her clitoris, not her vagina. Even if we're talking about procreation, it's not accurate: a man's penis delivers sperm and can impregnate, and a woman's womb contains eggs, which can become fertile. Equating the man's penis with the woman's vagina says, in effect, that the natural order of things is for a man to have pleasure during sex, and for a woman to have a sleeve for man's pleasure.* It perpetuates the notion that women aren't supposed to enjoy sex, that they're bucking the natural and social order if they do. I don't think this will change very soon, but it reminds me how many of our mores travel almost invisibly in the plasma of language.

If *cock* and *cunt* have a quaint and long history as language, they have an equally lush background as instruments for breaking laws, disturbing the peace, and challenging moral codes.

LOVE ON THE EDGE: ADULTERY, EXTRAVAGANT GESTURES, AND CRIMES OF PASSION

For sensitive, refined, affectionate, altruistic folk, we humans can certainly be a savage and sadistic lot. Even knowing what we do about our biological heritage, and having been less than angelic myself at times, even reading the shocking accounts of butchery in Bosnia in the newspapers, I still do not understand in a personal, intimate way how one can feel gratuitous malice, sadism, or the wish to torture another human being, regardless of how much anger or hatred may be bottled up inside. Or even how both complexions of good and evil can rule us simultaneously. Intellectually, of course, I understand only too well.

---

*In classical Latin *vagina* means "sheath for a sword." Aeneas would put his sword into his *vagina*.

There have been times and places when committing adultery, for example, was the most daredevil and extravagant act anyone could risk. During the Middle Ages, husbands competed in the degree of cruelty they showed to their adulterous wives. To be less cruel than one's neighbor was to lose face. Horror stories abound. One lady was forced to embalm her dead lover's heart and then eat it. Another was presented to a group of lepers, who were invited to rape her. Another's husband had his wife's lover butchered and his bones put in a chapel, where she was sent daily to contemplate her crime and drink out of his skull. Only rarely were adulterous husbands punished. The wives risked, at the least, public humiliation (often accompanied by having their hair cut off), and at the most, gruesome torture and/or death. Their lovers risked castration or death. And yet they dallied. They gambled life and limb. They climbed onto the motorcycles of their passion, gunned the engines, and raced toward the edge of a great precipice, leaping into thin air at high speed, never knowing if they would land safely on the far rim. With so much at stake, it's amazing people risked adultery at all; but they found it irresistible as a drug, one well worth hazarding death or dismemberment.

My backyard contains some living monuments to love's extremes. Deep in the woods, a large mulberry tree rakes its branches across any passerby. Occasionally I prune it, but that simply encourages it to grow hardier and more compact, and the next season its broad shoulders reach even farther. According to legend, the berries of the mulberry once were white, but turned red after the death of the lovers Pyramus and Thisbe. Neighbors in the cramped warrens of Babylon, the two grew up together, and fell deeply in love, though their parents forbade them to marry. Night after night, they would whisper romantic confidences through a hole in the wall between their bedrooms. Finally, unable to bear even this separation any longer, Pyramus suggested a rendezvous at the tomb of Ninus, beside a mulberry tree both knew. Thisbe crept out first and headed straight for the tomb, but when she got there she startled a lioness at a fresh kill, its mouth dripping blood. As Thisbe fled, the lioness tore her cloak, but she managed to escape. Soon Pyramus arrived, saw her torn cloak and the lioness devouring a carcass, and assumed that his lover was being ripped to shreds as he watched. Agonizing over Thisbe's death, crazed with despair, he drove away the lioness, then took his sword and rammed it into his side; and blood spurted all over the white mulberries.

Eventually, Thisbe began working her way back to the tomb. From afar, she could see that the lion was gone, and she hurried to await her lover, as planned. But to her horror she found him lying dead on the ground, saw his sword and her bloodstained cloak beside him, and understood at once what must have happened. "Your love for me killed you," she cried. "All right, I too can be brave. I too will prove my love. Only death could have separated us, but now not even death will keep us apart." With that, she plunged his sword into her heart and died beside him. As the only witness to this tragic scene, the mulberry tree felt such pity for the lovers that it stained all of its berries blood red, a reminder to passersby of the lovers' fate, and of the lengths to which people will go for love.

If this story sounds like that of Romeo and Juliet or Tristan and Iseult, it's because many ancient tales of tragic love contain the same elements: young lovers, forbidden love, a rendezvous to consummate their love, the apparent death of one lover, followed by the suicide of the other, then the suicide of the first. A natural monument often marks the spot. Such stories revolve around the agony of separation, the sexual stimulant of having to surmount obstacles, and the need to prove the sincerity of one's love.

Not all gestures are so solemn or absolute. Some are culinary—and a few silly. Legend has it that tortellini were created to honor Venus's belly button: a Bolognese innkeeper spied on Venus through a keyhole, noted the anatomical details, and decided his love was best expressed through pasta. When a mistress of Louis XIV became petulant and jealous, the king decided that only a bold gesture would appease her. Insisting she lie down with her naked breasts revealed, he asked his artisans to cast a mold from one breast and produce glasses in its exact shape, so he could always sip champagne from her bosom. Today we still drink champagne from glasses fashioned after his mistress's breast.

Why does love require such extravagant gestures? Why do lovers believe that life will be unlivable without that one, particular love? According to the hard economy that guides our lives, the more one pays for something the more precious the goods seem both to oneself and to one's neighbors. So only a Taj Mahal is capacious enough, only a fifty-carat diamond brilliant enough, only suicide sacrificial enough.

"How was *Phantom of the Opera*?" I overheard someone ask a friend recently.

"To die for," her friend replied in raptures.

The mulberry in the yard thrives in damp woodland soil. In the spring, the young twigs put out bushels of dark-green, saw-toothed leaves, which feel rough on the top but softly hairy underneath. Smallish green flowers sprout in clusters, and when the coblike fruits appear, songbirds eat them. I often see them sitting on a branch devouring what looks like congealed blood. A milky sap oozes from cuts in the mulberry bark; and in the fall, the leaves glow with a soft amber light.

Scattered around the forest, sleeping narcissus bulbs commemorate the abduction of a beautiful princess. According to one version of the Greek myth, Zeus created the flower to help his brother, the lord of the Underworld, who was in love with Persephone, Demeter's daughter. One day, Persephone was gathering flowers with her friends when she spied a brilliant blossom across the meadow. Her friends hadn't noticed it, and she laughed as she ran to discover what it was. She had never seen one so radiant before, with so many flowers bursting from the stems, and a seductive fragrance both sweet and animal. Just as she reached out a hand to caress it, the earth yawned open at her feet, and "out of it coal-black horses sprang, drawing a chariot and driven by one who had a look of dark splendor, majestic and beautiful and terrible." He grabbed her and held her tight, and galloped away with her to his world of the dead, far from the sunlit joys of springtime.

Leucothoe, a squat, bushy shrub outside my window, was named after a Persian princess, whose jealous husband chased her off a cliff and into the surging ocean below. Apollo took a fancy to her and changed her into a sea goddess, and, when he tired of her frothy ways, into a sweet-smelling plant. The bright red anemones which will bloom here in the summer take their name from Adonis, who was out hunting one day when a wounded boar turned and gored him in the groin, castrating him. It was an excruciating and deadly wound. By the time his lover, Venus, found him, he was delirious and nearly dead. Weeping, clinging to him, she moaned

Kiss me yet once again, the last, long kiss,
Until I draw your soul within my lips
And drink down all your love.

But, by then, he was far from her words or tears, down in the Underworld where she couldn't reach him. As each drop of his blood fell to the ground, delicate red flowers bloomed. His severed penis was said to have run off and become his son, the erotic god Priapus.

Soon a meander of purple and plum hyacinths will sprout along a stone pathway near the garage. Hyacinths get their name from a young sweetheart of Apollo's, a boy he accidentally killed. The two were having a friendly discus-throwing match when Zephyr, the west wind, who wanted the boy for himself but had been spurned, got into a jealous rage and blew on Apollo's hand so that it slipped. The discus flew off at a freak angle and broke the boy's neck. Horrified, Apollo pressed him to his heart and wept. As the boy's blood trickled onto the grass, a single phallic flower grew from it, a beautiful purple column on whose petals two letters spell the Greek word "Alas."

Today's newspapers offer equally extreme (even mythic) sagas. A recent revenge scandal involves a highly respected chief judge of New York State, married for forty-one years with four children. Apparently, he was committing adultery with a woman who dropped him for someone else. The judge became unhinged. He began harassing the woman and her daughter with psychotic phone calls and blackmail. When he threatened to kidnap the little girl, the frightened mother notified the police, and thus began a public tale of passion, rejection, and desperation. The judge's life was in tatters. His ex-girlfriend wanted nothing to do with him, his marriage was a disaster, and the political career he worked so hard at for so many years lay in ruins. Many had been touting him for governor. Having broken the law, he won't ever be able to keep his job as judge. What interests me about this case, and those of crimes of passion in general, is how love may inspire people to act in ways that are obviously self-destructive. What the judge had to lose was vastly greater than what he stood to gain. Having lost control of his girlfriend's love, he was willing to make do with controlling her fear. That's not much of a replacement. He knew what the consequences would be. And yet he couldn't stop himself.

Spurned lovers sometimes choose imaginative forms of revenge. One woman I know, whose husband left her for a younger woman, took the breakup very hard. It was a social aggression, as well as a blow to her self-esteem. She had defined herself as her husband's wife; and after the divorce she continued to define herself through him—but now as his ex-wife. She indulged in large and small acts of revenge. For various reasons, she decided to move out of town, letting her husband and his new bride have the house as part of the divorce settlement. It was a large, modern, magnificently landscaped house with many rare plants in its gardens. The summer before she left town, she ripped up all the perennials and planted just enough annuals to enjoy that season. By the time her husband and his bride moved in, they'd find all the gardens dead.

I also know a woman, married to a writer, who left her husband somewhat melodramatically by creeping out of their bed one morning, filling her side of the bed with his books, and pulling the covers up over them. Another woman, when her boyfriend jilted her, dumped a big panful of heavily used Kitty Litter on her ex-boyfriend's porch, with a note that read: *Consider yourself lucky I don't raise elephants.* Yet another woman first learned that her boyfriend had found someone else when he called to say he was coming over to pick up his toiletries. That gave her just enough time to take his toothbrush, scrub the toilet bowl with it, then place it neatly back in his kit.

Men are vengeful, too, but they tend to be less subtle and more violent about it. The front page of my hometown newspaper ran this headline today: MAN ALLEGEDLY DECAPITATES FOUR CATS. The story explained that a twenty-nine-year-old man, "distraught" because his live-in girlfriend had left him, decapitated her mother cat and its three kittens and then turned on the natural gas in his duplex apartment and threatened to blow up the building. Ultimately, he surrendered to the police and was sent to a psychiatric hospital.

One popular novel about extreme revenge is Fay Weldon's *The Life and Loves of a She-Devil.* An ugly, heavy set, happily married suburban mother of two discovers that her accountant husband is having an affair with one of his clients, a petite, rich, delicately beautiful writer of pulp romances who lives in a fashionably renovated lighthouse. Insulted, degraded, and spurned, the wife christens herself a she-devil and plots diabolical schemes to totally humiliate and bankrupt her husband and his mistress. The schemes all work, and soon the lovers are in deep personal, financial, and professional turmoil. Then she goes one step further and, having sent her husband to prison for embezzling money she had secretly squirreled away in Switzerland, she metamorphoses into his mistress. With the help of massive plastic surgery (which includes having her legs shortened), she becomes the evil twin to her husband's mistress, who by now has been harassed into an early death. Then the she-devil gets her semide-ranged husband out of prison, purchases the lighthouse, and takes him to live with her in what had once been his illicit love nest. There she keeps him in poverty and poor health, has lovers while he watches, and generally torments him to the end of his days.

This tale, which clearly touched a chord in the hearts and spleens of many, was made into not one but two popular movies. Even crimes that break moral laws, insult the legal system, and send shivers down the erect spine of bourgeois society, seem less craven when explained by love. Like truth, love is a rock-solid defense. Subconsciously, we picture love as a powerful geyser which builds up inside a person and has to vent its fury somewhere, be it for good or evil. We also realize that lovers need to prove their love, graphically, absolutely, with gestures that sometimes get out of hand and can become a soul-consuming end in themselves. We're fascinated by passionate extremes and don't always think they're deplorable. It's exciting to watch someone explore the body in a new way, to challenge old styles and ideas, and reinvent love. Breaking taboos, or just watching others break them, can be a positive, ennobling thrill. After all, every great work of art is a crime of passion.

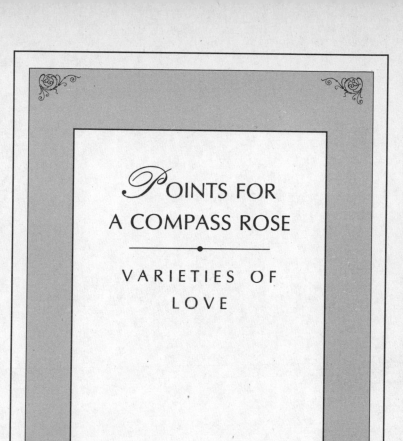

POINTS FOR A COMPASS ROSE

·

VARIETIES OF LOVE

ALTRUISM

One day a few years ago, on the isle of Jersey, a young couple took their infant son to the zoo. The boy seemed especially enchanted by the large, brawny gorillas, so his parents lifted him onto the wall of the enclosure for a better look. To their horror, the boy suddenly slipped over the side and fell down into the midst of the animals. A huge silverback—the dominant male—ran over to the baby and sat between him and the rest of the gorillas, and there he stayed, protecting the baby, until a keeper could be called.

Why did the senior gorilla protect the human child? Was it an act of altruism? Why do people sometimes risk their own lives to save the lives of strangers? Of all the varieties of love, altruism is perhaps the hardest to understand. It seems contrary to the self-interest that drives us all. Our first instinct is to stay alive, and our second to make sure our kin survive. Why help hungry and homeless strangers? Why save other species? Why sacrifice one's life for one's comrades in wartime? Altruism impresses us. We admire the trait. We teach our children that it is a good and noble feeling. But we're puzzled by it all the same. It just doesn't seem to make sense in the brutal economy of life. We keep thinking there must be some secret motive, some hidden gain. A behaviorist would argue that the gorilla didn't save the baby because it felt anything like compassion. As top male, the gorilla acted automatically. It was hard-wired to protect young primates, and when it saw one in danger—even a weird-looking, hairless one—it soberly plunked itself down as a living shield.

Some animals appear to be altruistic because we don't fully understand their motives. They're actually involved in a subtle form of commerce, an exchange of services or favors, called by scientists "reciprocal altruism." On the coast of Patagonia, some years ago, I watched mother and baby right whales pausing in a nursery bay on their way to the rich feeding grounds of Antarctica. Males knew they'd find females there, and frequently came into the bay to mate. Working together, a group of three or four males would trap and rape a female. The female would try to avoid mating by rolling onto her back with her vulva in the air, though of course this meant that her blowhole was underwater and she couldn't breathe. The males would surround her—one on either side and one underneath—so that when she rolled over to breathe one of them would have access to her vulva. It took several males to make sure that even one male could mate, because the female would bolt if she wasn't trapped. Why did the males cooperate? Probably for two reasons: first, it may be that males join forces with related males, so that the family's genes will survive, regardless of which male gets to sire the offspring. Second, because it encourages the exchange of favors—one day Fred makes sure Barney gets to mate; the next day Barney makes sure Fred does. When we buy a round-trip ticket, we have the full journey in mind, the outbound and the return. Reciprocal altruism is a round-trip ticket, the second half of which is momentarily hidden.

What of humans? We are virtuosos of favor-swapping, we love the old quid pro quo, the you-scratch-my-back-I'll-scratch-yours, the one-hand-washes-the-other. In smug moments, we label this a virtue—"cooperation"—which we praise as a holy act of goodness, trust, and decency. Psychologists don't like us to feel smug for very long about it. They usually explain it either as hedonism (we perform altruistic acts because they make us feel good, and it's the pleasure we crave) or an attempt by the ego-damaged to raise their sense of self-worth. The minute one imagines oneself in the victim's predicament, and moves to save him, it becomes an act of self-love.

That may be true. But if indeed we are cooperative by nature, it's an ancient skill, the genes for which got passed along because they gave the more cooperative among us a better chance to survive. The urge to help people in distress is partially learned—some families and cultures prize it more than others—but it's also deeply rooted in biology. As children grow, they automatically discover compassion. Around the age of two, they start to feel sympathy when they see someone in trouble, and they try to help. Add to this cooperative spirit a preference for the known over the unknown—people prefer what's familiar, are frightened of what's new—and you can see how warfare between so-called enemies might evolve as a sort of evolutionary twitch. Cross-cultural studies show that people prefer their family first; in-laws second; neighbors third; also people who remind them of family members, in-laws, or neighbors. Alien faces scare them, and they can be convinced by despots to regard them as subhuman.

What about self-sacrificing altruism? This can be seen throughout the animal kingdom, especially among insects. Insects are social, too, so it's tempting to imagine ourselves in their terms. But insects differ from us in one important way: they are closely related to each other, sharing the same gene pool, which they ruthlessly protect. It's not only in their best interest to work for the common good, they might as well give their all for it. Humans speak lovingly of extended families, but to an ant the whole society is close kin, and it will die rather than allow its genetic line to dry up. Humans, on the other hand, are related in very small, nuclear families which are in glaring competition with one another. Unlike the ants, we must abolish our self-interest to work together, and that's asking a great deal. It makes altruism all the more remarkable.

Although this book is mainly concerned with romantic love, there are other varieties—parental, altruistic, religious, patriotic, and so on—which are equally intense and powerful expressions of our hunger to love and be loved. Over the years, I've been privy to many acts of kindness, some openly heroic, others simply generous-hearted. The two dramas that follow linger in my memory as examples of deeply felt altruistic love.

FOR THE LOVE OF
CHILDREN: INTERPLAST

San Pedro Sula sits in the northwest corner of Honduras, between the glyph-covered Mayan stairway at Copán and the coral atolls of the coast. In September, beneath a giant Coca-Cola sign floating like a patron saint on a near hill, the downtown bustles with people keen to run their errands before the hot sticky hours of afternoon cascade into thick humid nights. On a tree-shaded street in the center of town stands San Pedro Sula's public hospital, a sprawling maze of one-story buildings, porticoes, and courtyards. Its corrugated roofs have grown rusty over the years, and the peeling walls are painted pink and maroon, with a ribbon of green, yellow, and red (the national colors) dancing at eye level. Outdoor benches, overflowing with patients and their families, sit on a checkerboard of yellow and green tiles. People fill the wards, crowd the walkways, and spill into the courtyards. Many of life's joys and afflictions are on parade: a woman with a machete wound just delivered by a jealous lover slowly enters the eye clinic; a badly burned man, cocooned in gauze, hobbles out of the men's ward to get some fresh air; a man in a straw hat, holding the elbow of a pregnant woman, guides her toward a sign that says FARMACIA; a man and a woman exchange rapid, staccato accusations, while their hands make small slashes in the air; a young mother sits in a corner, nursing a baby, in her eyes the narcotic of her love; twin boys, each with a cleft mouth, race toy trucks along the cement. Here and there a policeman sits on a bench, rifle at his side, guarding a prisoner in a ward. Two parents and a little boy picnic under a cashew tree, its thick branches heavy with curved green nuts. A mango tree offers shade to a Honduran nurse, a pretty curly haired woman in her twenties, who methodically peels an orange until the rind looks like a projection of the world. Though she is shaded and sitting, sweat beads on her face. In Honduras, the sun's opus grants a lavish array of fruits—mangoes, bananas, papayas, oranges, pineapples, and some of the sweetest grapefruits on earth. But, even sitting still, one is covered in a sticky, humid film. When you move, sweat saturates your clothes. Nonetheless, people often wear long sleeves and trousers; dengue fever, endemic in Honduras, is carried by mosquitoes, and there is no cure for it.

Across the courtyard, in the clinic waiting room, a hundred people sit back-to-back on long train-station benches. All are waiting to see the doctors of Interplast, an organization based in Palo Alto, California, which for the past twenty years has been sending out volunteers to provide reconstructive surgery to needy children in the third world. Donald Laub got the idea for Interplast in 1965, when, as chief of plastic and reconstructive surgery at Stanford University Medical Center, he repaired the cleft lip and palate of a fourteen-year-old boy from Central America. The experience moved him profoundly, and he volunteered more and more time for such operations, finally enlisting the help of colleagues. In 1969, he founded Interplast, to repair children riddled by birth defects, but also to train host-country doctors in the latest techniques, and help them set up burn units. Among the handful of reconstructive groups of this sort, Interplast is one of the largest and best run. It has already changed the lives of 18,000 children with a wide range of deformities. In 1990 alone, Interplast sent medical teams on twenty trips, to Honduras, Ecuador, Peru, Colombia, Nepal, Mexico, Chile, Brazil, Western Samoa, and Jamaica. Its surgeons operated on 1,313 patients, provided 15,000 free teaching hours, and donated $3,209,840 worth of surgeries. Five hundred dollars covers the cost of one child's operation, and as little as $15,000 will finance an entire trip. Most of Interplast's money comes from individual donors. Despite the generosity of corporations, which provide anesthesia, antibiotics, and other necessities, on occasion the teams have had to cut short their trips and turn children away because they ran out of an essential supply like sutures.

A typical team includes four surgeons, four anesthesiologists, six nurses, a pediatrician, and three support personnel. Although I have no medical training, I've joined the group as one of the support people, to help out wherever possible. Housed with local families, a team works with their Honduran counterparts; and high school students act as translators. David Fogarty, a plastic surgeon from Morgantown, West Virginia, usually acts as team leader. He donates a month or more every year to traveling with Interplast to locales from Cuzco to Nepal. When children need repairs that can't be done in their own country, they're sent to the United States as part of Interplast's domestic program. The Fogartys have seven children of their own—two of them adopted (a girl from Honduras, a black American boy) and he often takes in Interplast children and operates on them himself.

GUARDE SILENCIO a printed sign commands from one wall, but the room is abuzz with adults chattering to one another, parents comforting children, and children playing with small toys or occasionally crying. A large thermometer, part of an Alka-Seltzer sign, gives the temperature indoors as 90°F. A wall clock, part of a Phillips Milk of Magnesia sign, says that it is only 9:30 A.M. A thick line of people winds among the benches. Parents have brought children with lost or malformed eyes, children with cleft lips and twisted feet, children with webbed hands, children with bad burns. Mingling with them are the success stories: children returning for touch-up operations, or to have their progress checked. Some families have been waiting for twenty-four hours, others have traveled great distances, on foot and by bus, from the mountains and the coast. Babies are being fed or changed; older children play or lie sleeping. Overhead, two large fans turn slowly, stirring but not cooling the hot, soupy air. At either side of the maroon-and-cream hallway stand resin-colored doors, and above each is a hand-drawn number on a wooden plaque.

A stocky man with thick red hair and a red beard, wearing a blue-and-white batik shirt over his trousers, and leather sandals, Fogarty appears from one corridor with his arm around a shy, part-Indian girl, whom he guides through the mob. This is "Clinic Day" for the Interplast team, which flew in last night. Before the operations begin, the surgeons have to see the children, carefully examine their problems, and conduct a difficult triage. The sad truth is that someone with a defect requiring all day to do will have to be turned away, since a greater number of people could be helped in the same time. Eye surgery is also out, as well as anything else that could lead to massive complications. The hospital doesn't have the equipment, the cardiac facilities, or the supplies of blood and other necessities for a crisis, so they must choose reasonably healthy children, with defects operable under severely limited conditions. Although the team members have many reasons for making the trip, some purely altruistic, some more self-concerned, learning to *make do* with the minimum—indeed, discovering what that minimum is—is probably one of them.

They will also have a chance to take part in tough, challenging operations they may only have read about; to do medicine the way it was done in the days before high technology; to improvise with few supplies and much cunning; to solve problems that, left untreated for too long, have become nightmarish and almost unsolvable, except through high-wire acts of virtuoso surgery; to learn techniques from others faced with the same rigors. That it will stir them deeply, and may prompt them to inspect their feelings about medicine, is also part of the draw. In a sense, it is a way to renew their vows.

In Room 9, surgeons Ruth Carr and Dean Sorensen sit behind two wooden desks, waiting for their first patients. Ruth is trim and petite with shoulder-length blond hair, wearing a denim skirt and a green shirt with a small pink polo player on the chest. She practices in Santa Monica and has a twenty-month-old son. This is her second Interplast trip. On her desk, a brown plastic pot of tongue depressors stands next to a purse-size flashlight—her only examination instruments. Across the room, behind the second desk, sits Sorensen, a tall, athletic, sandy-haired man, wearing a starched white coat over tan pants and a green shirt. Ruth speaks Spanish, but we also have in the room a teenage girl from the local international high school, who acts as an interpreter. Schoolmates of hers circulate throughout the other clinic rooms, translating, carrying Coca-Colas and files, and running errands.

A young mother enters, cradling a two-month-old girl named Isabel in her arms. Dean seats them on a stool beside his desk. Dressed in a blue shift, with a simple black cross on a black thread around her neck, the mother sits with the baby pressed snug against her shoulder, and arranges the baby's bright red blouse, red socks, and diapers held by yellow-capped safety pins. Isabel's hair is a small cyclone of dark brown. The mother rocks her as she cries.

"Why is the child here today?" Dean asks through the interpreter.

The mother turns her baby's face toward us, so we can see the completely cleft mouth and exposed nasal passages. It is a savagely disfiguring birth defect, in which the mouth appears to be split in two and turned partly inside out. Otherwise, she is a stunning little girl, with loam-brown eyes and mocha skin. Because her cleft is so wide, she won't be able to touch her tongue to the roof of her mouth to speak during the crucial language-learning years. Many of the children Interplast sees today will have equally severe clefts, a birth defect that strikes one in every 600 people. Because the United States has so large a population (260 million), and birth defects are operated on right away, people with clefts aren't as visible as they are in Honduras, whose population is only 4 million, and where inbreeding and malnutrition may be contributing factors. Dean peers into Isabel's mouth, using a flashlight and a tongue depressor, questions the mother about the child's general health, then takes her photograph, and at last jots down her name on a master sheet. She is an ideal candidate for surgery.

Dean explains to the mother that the girl requires two operations, a cosmetic one to make the mouth look normal, and a practical one to fix the palate. He reassures her that the operations will be free, that she can stay with her child, that she will need only to spend a couple of days right now, but that she will have to return in six months for the second operation. They can do only one part of the procedure at a time, and it is far more urgent that the child's mouth look normal and be flexible. At the moment, Isabel is incapable of smiling, and that makes her helpless, vulnerable, and unarmed. Her life will be simpler if she can speak normally, but it would be a dreadful nightmare if she couldn't smile.

For an infant, a smile is the real human coin of the realm, as valuable to a Maori girl as it is to a boy from New Jersey. A child needs to be able to engage adults in a broad, open smile that can stop them in their tracks, elicit love, and turn antipathy to goodwill. Smiles are infectious, and rejuvenative. In 1906, French physician Israel Waynbaum offered a theory of how facial expressions affect our moods. Just shaping the mouth into a smile increases the blood flow to the brain and we feel elated, he said. More recently, at the University of Michigan in Ann Arbor, psychologist Robert B. Zajonc has been updating and extending Waynbaum's findings. It now appears that smiling also changes brain temperature and the release of neurotransmitters. Studies conducted by a psychologist at the University of California at San Francisco suggest that facial expressions conveying disgust, sadness, fear, and anger trigger nerves, which in turn signal brain areas responsible for heart rate and emotion. Although this is still a controversial issue among psychologists, the evidence strongly suggests that changing your facial expression can

change your feelings. Norman Cousins, a longtime advocate of rio-
therapy, argued the usefulness of laughter against a variety of ail-
ments, and told of his own success with watching guffaw-producing
films in his fight against cancer. Adults find smiling, happy children
more attractive, and attractive children receive more attention from
teachers and more encouragement and affection from their parents.
Smiling is an essential part of the shy pantomime we call flirting.

But a child also needs a normal mouth to perform that large
repertoire of nonverbal signs we make with our faces, revealing
moods according to a set pattern that people instinctively understand
and expect. There is a code of basic facial expressions which all
humans share—happiness, anger, fear, surprise, disgust—which are
recognizable to people from different cultures, who speak different
languages, who have never met, who seem to have nothing in common. A face is only bone, cartilage, tissue, and skin. And yet when
these components work in unison as they were meant to, they create
many thousands of subtle expressions. Children who are born blind
make the same expressions as those who are sighted. Spontaneous,
automatic, the face forms words before the mind can think them. We
often rely on facial semaphore to tell us truths too subtle or shameful
or awkward or intimate or emotionally charged or nameless to speak.
Cancel that language of the smile and glance and you doom a child
to a lifetime of emotional formality and effort, you cast it out of
normal society.

Isabel leaves, and the parade of children continues: a mother with
wide-set eyes brings in a girl who has Apert's syndrome. Seventeen
months old, the baby has twisted feet with six toes fused in pairs on
each. Her hands have fused fingers. Ruth and Dean study X rays of
the hands, and decide to separate one finger on each so that at least
she will be able to grip things. Next comes Nubia: a four-year-old
with short, curly hair and unusually long eyelashes, wearing a blue-
and-red plaid jumper with a white-collared blouse under it and frilly
anklets. She has fingers which surgeons fixed last May. Crying and
hiding her face, she allows Ruth to open her hands, where only small
white scars remain between her fingers. Ruth inspects them, and
nods; they have healed beautifully. Now Jessica arrives: a three-
month-old whose hair, just starting to grow, stands up in an unruly
quiff. She has a wide cleft palate; one half of the lip vanishes into the

nose. Then David: a five-year-old with a badly deformed ear that looks more like a small, dangling doll. After David, José: a nine-year-old with a badly burned leg on which the scars look like small mountain ranges. He had been carrying firecrackers in his pocket and they went off.

By midafternoon, all the children begin to blur into one compound child, afflicted with itself, temporarily betrayed by its body. Many would profit from going to the United States for treatment, but Interplast can afford to send only twenty children a year, since it depends entirely on private donations of money, air tickets, and supplies. On principle, it has no government funding (and therefore no political interference), and the air tickets, especially, are expensive. So, instead, an Interplast doctor will often begin reconstructive work—to remove part of a burn scar, say, or do the first part of a cleft mouth-and-palate operation—on a child whom another Interplast doctor will continue operating on six months later. This works out all right for the children, and it unites the surgeons in a powerful invisible chain. For, although the doctors who patrol the world for Interplast seldom meet face-to-face, they often meet in the body of a single child. In May, one doctor will operate on a cleft mouth; in September another will examine his predecessor's work and go on to do the palate; the following May yet another doctor will pick up the scalpel and perhaps fix a small hole in the roof of the mouth; the following September, another doctor may try to give the nose a longer and more natural philtrum. In this way, a child's life sentence is rewritten, over many months, by many hands, with sutures. In a U.S. hospital, a cadre of psychologists, surgeons, orthodontists, and pediatricians would probably confer about such children. Here, decisions must be made fast. But on tricky cases, Ruth and Dean sometimes call in Dave Thomas or Dave Fogarty or Luis Bueso (who heads the project in Honduras), or all of them at once, to examine a child stricken with some delicately bizarre abnormality, and discuss what can be done.

Cleft mouths are by far the most frequent deformity. According to the folklore of many countries, the "harelip" is a result of a pregnant mother being frightened by a rabbit. One variation on this is that a mother only has to step over a rabbit's nest to produce a deformed child, a catastrophe she can undo by ripping her petticoat in a certain way. This was so widespread a belief in Europe that an old Norwegian law actually forbade butchers from hanging up rabbits in public view. It's hard to say why rabbits were chosen as the spell-carriers. True, a rabbit's upper lip is cleft, but so is a cat's—many animals share the trait. Along with cats, rabbits were thought to be witches' alter egos, a supposedly harmless animal form they took when they wanted to get up to mischief. Throughout the ages, and in many cultures, rabbits have been associated with the moon. One African myth tells how the angry moon split the rabbit's lip. And in ancient Mexico, a pregnant woman who watched a lunar eclipse supposedly caused her child to have a cleft lip. But it was always the mother's evil, sin, or contract with the Devil for which the deformed child was a punishment. During the Middle Ages, if a child's deformity looked in any way animal-like it was concluded that the mother had had sex with the animal, and the deformed child was their offspring. Such children were killed. So, fixing a child's cleft lip also, in part, repairs the supernatural burdens of a family.

Many of the Interplast children are part European, part Maya Indian. The surgeons are making them "normal" according to contemporary European standards of beauty. But in the days of the Mayas, they would have wished to look quite different. The Mayas, who were a naturally broad-headed people, deliberately deformed the skulls of their children to accentuate that feature, making them look as different as possible from their narrow-headed neighbors. Four or five days after birth, a child would have a flat wooden board tied to the back of its head, and another board tied to its forehead. The two boards, lashed tightly together, prevented the child's head from expanding normally, and because it was soft and malleable enough to bend easily under pressure, it would grow upward. After a few days, the boards were removed, but the child's head stayed flattened for the rest of its life. The sculptures one sees on Mayan monuments show profiles with loaf-shaped heads—dramatically receding foreheads that run straight down to the nose. (The Mayans weren't alone in their passion for skull shaping. Africans, Minoans, Britons, Egyptians, and others changed the shape of their skulls.) Why did the Mayans prefer long, pointed heads? Perhaps because they lived among similarly shaped temples, arching toward the heavens in the geometry of holiness. Because the Mayans also found crossed eyes beautiful, a mother would attach balls of resin and other small objects to a child's hair, allowing them to dangle between the eyes, attracting the child's gaze and training the eyes inward. Beards were unfashionable, so Mayan mothers scalded the faces of their male children to prevent facial hair from growing. Men would burn a round patch of skin on top of their heads, to keep that spot bald, but they grew the rest of their hair quite long, braiding it, wrapping it around their heads, and allowing it to fall into a long ponytail behind. Both men and women filed their teeth to jagged points that looked like saw blades. Boys painted their faces and bodies black, but only until they were married, at which point they painted them red, "for the sake of elegance," as Sylvanus Griswold Motley reports. Adult Mayas often wore tattoos all over their bodies.

But these twentieth-century Honduran children want only to look *normal* according to our western ideal, set in part by pictures in magazines and on television, and in part by the faces of their families and neighbors. That translates into features with a simple, rounded symmetry.

By 6:00 P.M. the waiting room holds only a few adults, the clinic rooms have grown dimmer. The fans continue mixing the thick, hot air. Tongue depressors lie on the floor. A long crack in the wall of Room 9 meanders like a healing scar. The single fluorescent light casts a glare over the room, in one corner of which sit two empty Coca-Cola bottles. In this room alone, Ruth and Dean have examined eighty patients. "It's a bottomless well," Ruth says, leaning wearily against the wall.

Wrung out and sweaty, we gather up our belongings and head across the courtyard and down an alley to the parking lot, where a mustachioed driver waits to ferry us home. We are all lodging with upper-class San Pedro Sula families, at houses walled in and splendid, patroled by men with rifles, and most nights there will be dinner waiting for us and the oasis of an air-conditioned bedroom in which to sleep.

Operations begin the next morning, so I head straight for the "break room," a tiny place dominated by a large red Coca-Cola refrigerator and dozens of boxes of patients' charts. In a dim narrow corridor, I slip on a lavender scrub dress, blue-and-white shoe covers, shower cap, and mask. I walk down a long hallway. Swinging doors open onto a small room, glared over by exposed fluorescent lights, where two operating tables stand parallel, about ten feet apart. The blue tile walls give way to green paint at shoulder level, and the olive-green tiled floors look ready for a track meet. Waves of people wearing identical masks and scrubs bustle through the room.

Then the surgeons go into the hallway to wash at two white porcelain sinks, which stand beneath two large barrels of water, methodically soaping and scrubbing their hands, fingernails, and arms up to the elbows. Ten minutes later they return and enter the operating room with their hands held high, as if ready to cast a spell in unison. A nurse holds a glove open. Dave Thomas, a tall, stately surgeon in his late thirties from Salt Lake City, makes a purse of his fingers and slides the hand into the glove. Pursing the other hand, he slides it into the second glove. Then he works the latex down snug around the fingers with small tugging snaps. The three operating rooms are over eighty years old, and one of them has an opaque wall of glass bricks. A few years ago, when the electricity failed during an evening operation, Luis Bueso ran outside and pointed his car's headlights at the glass wall, and nurses held flashlights above the operating tables. Two tables will be in use simultaneously, something that is strictly forbidden in the United States because of the possibility of cross-contamination. But in Honduras, operating rooms are scarce, and there are no malpractice suits to worry about. The absence of malpractice laws also means that I can serve as a circulating nurse, bridging the sterile and nonsterile worlds of the operating room, a privilege impossible for a nonmedical person in the States. In any case, most of today's operations will be on mouths, and the mouth is full of germs to begin with. In this twin-tabled room, doctors float from one operation to the other, advising and observing, and the experience is doubled, condensed.

A small, part-Indian boy is carried in and laid on the near table. His skin looks waxy in the lamplight, and he sleeps in a blue turban like a miniature prince. A shiny aluminum clamp, holding the wrap closed, dangles over the top of his head like a jewel. An anesthesiologist tapes his eyes closed and an air tube into his mouth. Then she clamps a plastic clothespinlike device onto one of his toes, to measure pulse, blood pressure, and the amount of oxygen in the blood. Nurses arrange shiny, color-coded instruments in the correct order on a "back table," grouping them according to size and species. Dave Thomas bends his gloved fingers and holds them up as if praying. It is an old habit, not letting his hands drop lest they become contaminated. At last he settles himself on a stool at the head of the operating table, and Dean, sitting down on a stool at one side, gets ready to assist, and I join them.

"*Teinte,*" Dave Thomas says to a nurse, and she hands him a small gleaming inkwell. Drawing the blue-tipped stick from it, he dots blue along the nose and mouth, diagramming the future "Cupid's bow." With small calipers, he measures the philtrum on the right, then computes where the left side of the nose and mouth should be, and discusses with Dean how best to assemble it. Taking a needle, he burrows under the skin, injecting norepinephrine-laced lidocaine all around the areas where he'll be working. Then he puts on a headlamp attached to a wide black band around his forehead, at the front of which a small halogen lightbulb sits above his line of sight. An electrical cord running down his back connects the lamp to a battery pack worn on a white belt at his waist. He tilts the lamp's mirrorlike dish to the correct angle. Then he calls for a scalpel.

Holding the blade steady, as if it were a single-haired paintbrush, he traces his blue diagram with movements fine, light, and feathery. In fact, he doesn't seem to be making contact with the skin at all, and for a moment I wonder if perhaps he is just rehearsing his first incision. A thin line of blood wells behind his strokes, the blue ink turns to red as if by magic. With a tweezers, he lifts a flap of skin and cuts its edges loose with small gnawings of the scalpel. My eyes zoom in on the open flesh shining in the light, as I watch Dave begin to cut free one side of the nose, which is fused to the cheek. His wrists arch and pivot. His long fingers pick up an instrument, bend at several joints, assume acute angles as they work inside the mouth. At times they flex and pose like a praying mantis. He removes a large bolus of extra flesh from under the nose. Peering into the mouth, I can see where the pink, soft, emery-boardlike skin stops and the white, glossy lining of the nose begins. As he cuts, blood wells and he pinches the spot with tweezers, and Dean zaps the tweezers with a cautery gun which carries the current down to the flesh. A spark sizzles at the spot, then turns it black. Dave carves free the fused part of the nose so that he can pull it back where it belongs, more than an inch away.

A red crescent appears, then a deeper red canyon. With a tweezer, he stretches the nose, now freed from the bone, to where it should be. "Going to be tight," he says, more as a sigh than a statement. The chart says this is Rigoberto, a four-month-old boy from Santa Barbara. I remember seeing him with his father in the clinic. A Peace Corps worker, a twenty-seven-year-old woman from Michigan who found them in the mountains, told them of Luis Bueso's program, and accompanied them on their bus journey. The trip had cost his father six lempiras, a full day's wages.

Seeing blood and gore, in the absence of brutality, is not upsetting, but beautiful, fascinating, inspiring. It is when malice accompanies it that blood quickly becomes unbearable. I cannot glimpse a slasher movie without turning my head away in horror and disgust; but to watch an operation is to be enthralled by the red-and-white estuaries of the human body, and the finesse of surgeons who sail into them. There is no vicarious bridge, no sense that this could be me on the table as, hypnotic and beautiful, the body reveals its colors and textures. True, at first, there is a mild shock at seeing someone's insides exposed to the light. But that is swiftly followed by a jolt of privilege, as you peer into the many levels of what is usually a closed crypt. The body is just a collection of hide, flesh, and fluid. But when you consider that from it come all-weather thinkers like Montaigne or artists like La Tour, that on a pedestal of flesh sits a mind, discomfort evaporates. Instead, you find yourself thinking: how amazing that mere matter should lead to this. How amazing that a dialect of fluid and bone can produce acts of mercy, heroism, and love.

At last, nearly two hours later, Dave begins stitching, piercing the skin with a curved needle and pulling the catgut slowly through. Then he loops the suture around a clamp, grabs the other end of the suture, and slides the loop down the clamp, making quick, intricate knots between the instruments and his fingers. The motion is like a spider arranging its web. He draws the threads taut, and a nurse snips them. Then he pushes the needle through for another stitch. In the background, Linda Ronstadt croons a bluesy "What'll I do, when you are far away, and I'm so blue . . . what'll I do?" When she finishes, silence falls like a cleaver. Then, a few moments later, Patsy Cline begins swoonfully singing "I'm crazy . . . "

Meanwhile, on another table across the room, Isabel lies showered in light. Luis Bueso and Dave Fogarty face each other across her mouth, which they have opened up like an unfolded origami crane. Their glances meet at the crossroads of her skewed lips. A nurse seated low at the head of the table waits for their requests, her gloved hands folded. There is a certain kitchen intimacy to the group—two people sitting on worn stools at a table under a central light, with others standing close by and leaning forward; everyone's attention is focused on the same spot. A painter, a Dutch master, would make much of this scene—the luster of concentration in the eyes of the surgeons, the overhead lamp rinsing the child's face with white and casting the doctors in stark shadows. Light cascades over the hills, planes, and valleys of their faces, over Dave Fogarty's prominent brows and Luis's large glasses. Together they break open the mansion of her flesh, and roam through it with their hands. All their knowledge, training, and history run like voltage down their arms. To have hands as steady and probing as theirs is to touch life where it lives, in the cell, blood, and bone, in the pastures of yellow fat that bloom like wildflowers above the soft tissues. Their mouths are masked, and what they say is of no consequence, but their hands speak a silent, fluent Esperanto. Exchanging instruments, touching one another and the child, their hands are relentlessly eloquent, lyrical, and profound as they converse in an argot of tendon and nerve. Hours later, after orating inside the girl's body, their hands will at last have argued persuasively with her flesh; and when they leave they will stitch up the entrance with a small trail of stars.

Back at table one, a little girl lies swaddled in sheets. The child looks so peaceful, she might be sleeping normally and dreaming. But I know that isn't possible. Anesthesiologists prefer to give children drugs that will render their brains electrically silent. The brain's metabolism, its requirement for oxygen for nutrition, then drops to a very low level. This is protective in various situations, but especially when a doctor is operating in a way that could interrupt the brain's blood supply—on a blood vessel that supplies part of the brain, for example, or during a face or heart operation. Indeed, any time there's a risk to the brain, it's often desirable to have an anesthetic that will silence the brain. As a result, the children don't dream during the operations, and they remember nothing afterward; their brains are idling. But the children don't look dead. Their skin glows with a soft candle-wax sheen, and they seem suspended in time and space, like small hibernating astronauts.

Ruth pauses a moment, lifts a triangle of skin with a pair of tweezers, arranges and rearranges it, trying out various syllogisms. Her face seems to be saying: *If I move this around, and that above, and this under, and that through, then those pieces of skin will fall there.* Hours pass, but eventually the small face follows her logic into a more orderly mouth and nose. She pushes the cleft together to make a whole. All the pieces now fit like a machine-tooled jigsaw puzzle. Ruth rolls her cramped shoulders and straightens her back a moment, then leans forward again and continues stitching.

All the surgeons are raunchy and funny in the operating room, which sometimes sounds like an episode of *M*A*S*H*. Although some American surgeons prefer a quiet operating room, most don't. Flirtatious, joking, and crude banter happen there so often that it makes one wonder if there isn't a deep psychological need at work. Surgeons perform an act of controlled violence—unmalicious violence, therapeutic violence, ritualized violence—but violence just the same. We have evolved with certain instinctive responses to horror. And it *is* horror to cut open the protective armor of someone's body, and expose the thick porridges inside. Although we don't like to think of ourselves in that way, we are a heap of bright fluids in a sac; and we're taught never to break the sac open, because life can pour away so easily. Surgeons seem to defuse the horror in various ways—by blanking out any personal details about the patient, by draping the patient's body so that it's unrecognizably human, by allowing their hands to perform acts profound, solemn, and holy while their minds retreat into the opposite realm of the coarse, the casual, and the profane. "Is this a little girl or a little boy?" I sometimes ask Dave Thomas, and he always says, "I don't know." Only minutes before, he was looking at the patient's chart, which includes personal details and a photograph, as well as evaluations made during clinic. How could he "forget" only minutes later if it's a girl or a boy?

"When you're operating, are you aware of the patient as a person?" I ask Dean Sorensen, while he's stitching a cleft palate back together. He looks up at me, above the magnifying part of the loops. For a moment, his blue eyes fix me solidly. "If I did that I'd be petrified."

It is what makes it possible for Ruth Carr, before an operation on a man who has been burned on almost every part of the front of his body except the penis, to say: "He must have been wearing his flameproof jockstrap that day." It's what prompts Luis Bueso, during an operation on a well-built teenage girl, to say: "A good pair of tits have more pulling power than an oxcart." It is what allows David Fogarty, while he tries to thread a suture needle, whose eye he misses, to say with a smirk to a male Honduran doctor: "If that hole were surrounded by hair, I wouldn't have missed." The banter is the anesthetic for the surgeon.

As the morning gives way to the afternoon and early evening, Spanish, French, Portuguese, and English mix in the operating rooms, where a procession of children arrives from their villages, appear suddenly on the tables, have their faces and lives rearranged while they are unconscious, and disappear into the recovery room and then into the pediatrics ward. Not only the children dwell in this shudder out of time. All of us are temporarily yanked out of the normal course of our lives. There is a war-zone feel to the day. In their normal practices, cosmetic surgeons can afford to do subtle, elective surgeries, touch-ups, and all the niceties. Interplast teams burst into a town like a squad of commandos, to operate on gross deformities. Teams are thrown together in emotionally charged circumstances, and, as a result, people often form intense friendships and interdependencies. Then the red alert of the trip ends suddenly, like a small death, and, returning home, team members often sink into parabolas of depression.

"It's strange not knowing the before and after," Dave Thomas says, as he operates on a boy with one upper arm that is so constricted it looks like an animal someone has twisted out of balloons. Opening the constriction, he does a "Z-plasty," a favorite type of operation for lengthening, in which two pennants of skin are cut loose and rotated from the horizontal to the vertical plane. Lifting up a sail-shaped wedge of upper-arm skin, he folds it in one direction, then takes a second flap and folds it in the opposite direction. A small geyser of blood hits his smock and mask. "Bleeder," he says matter-of-factly. He clamps it, cauterizes it, and goes on to put in two stitches, which he draws together to make a harlequin pattern of the skin. A Z becomes an N. "Suddenly these children appear with their predicaments," he continues. "Then they vanish. You only see them at that one moment in time. In that moment, you may be changing the whole course of their lives. But you never see them again. The good part is that plastic surgery is unique in that, with many surgeries—a hernia, for example—you can't see the result right away. But I can see right away what I've done to reconstruct an arm or, especially, a face."

By midweek, there are signs of our presence on all the children: colored deputy sheriff badges, colored barettes and earrings, toy trucks and tops and puzzles, new dresses and T-shirts. In the children's ward, rows of full beds and cribs line the room. There is a sweet, mousey smell of pus, urine, and illness. On one wall, a framed, yellowing picture of a Gerber baby's smiling and perfect face is the center of a large, open, dewy red rose. A hand-drawn rabbit with a merry smile and long lashes watches from the wall, near Raggedy Ann and Andy clothes hooks. Although the hospital is old and worn, it is very clean, and it is staffed by a caravan of devoted nurses. They get paid little—indeed, sometimes don't get paid for weeks—yet they keep coming to work. In the same blue dress she wore to the clinic, Isabel's mother feeds her daughter with an eyedropper. Shaped normally now, her mouth wears a design of fine stitches. Cardboard splints on her arms will keep her from pestering the stitches until they dissolve. Whenever possible, the doctors use dissolvable stitches because they can't rely on the compliance of the patients, who might not have enough money to make a return trip. Mother bundles Isabel up in her arms, hugs her close. Smiling, relieved, she says good-bye and thanks everyone, emotionally, then turns around and thanks them all over again. The moment she leaves the room, nurses clean the crib and change its linens. Soon another young mother arrives with her baby, which is installed in the crib. Below the girl's frizzy, golden topknot of hair, an unsightly cyst bulges; tomorrow, the doctors will remove it.

After the last operation of the day, the team gathers in the break room to change back into street clothes and try to find places to rest on the benches and school desk-chairs. Some sit on a table, or lean against a wall. We have finished earlier than expected—it is only 6:30. Lightning flashes from the black batteries of the sky, and the rain falls thick as rubber. The rain is so dense we joke about needing a machete instead of an umbrella, and no one wants to run through the downpour to the parking lot to see if the driver is waiting with the blue van. Grabbing our rucksacks and satchels filled with scrub clothes, medicine, and personal items, we finally sprint to the van and arrive drenched, laughing. All fourteen of us pile on board. After dinner at a restaurant downtown, we head for a glitter-ball–hung discotheque full of colored lights, loud music, local beer, and never-ending songs. Today there were twelve hours of operations, and we are shot through with every caliber of exhaustion. Tomorrow there will be twelve hours more. Strobes splatter the dancers with light, cutting them into fast, dizzying snapshots. Overwrought from the day, and filled with too many warring emotions to name, people dance out their pent-up furies. Midnight arrives like an express train, and we leave. Tomorrow there will be another sea of faces to heal; over a hundred will be operated on by the week's end. Swamped by fatigue, we pile into the van. If possible, the starless night has grown even hotter. The rain has stopped, but lights continue to sizzle overhead. As part of a fiesta to celebrate a local political candidate, fireworks fill the sky like small perfect cauteries.

FOR THE LOVE OF STRANGERS: LIFE AND DEATH IN THE SOUTH SEAS

In the South Seas, the morning sun scalds the water, the air feels close and damp, and a single hot breath pours around the islands. One could die in the suffocating stammer of the winds that blow for days on end without ever cooling or refreshing. One could live in the relentless searchlight of the sun that will find you wherever you hide and hold you in its glare, the sun that also sneaks like a bright rodent into the smallest and grimmest holes, and at some point fills every shadowy corner with a moment of illumination. The sun that brands one's retinas with yellow sparks, and hurls comets of blinding glitter onto the waves. Beneath such a sun one lives in the penitentiary of one's own body. Beneath such a sun one wears an ocean of sweat wherever one wanders. But, at twilight, the heat lathers out of the sky behind a heap of red plumes, the moon rises with its seas stark and clear, and night lays a cold compress on the brow of the Pacific.

It was April, and we had set sail from Tahiti, once an almost mythic place, now tawdry and cheap in the way that tourist lay-bys come to be. We arrived at Makatéa Island, in the Tuamoto Archipelago, and dropped anchor near the port of Temao, where the rusty derricks of an abandoned phosphate mine stood offshore like a species of giant seabird. For sixty years, the thriving mine filled the pockets and bellies of the 1,200 islanders, and then at last the phosphate ran out, and the locals fled to Tahiti and other spots. What is it about such ports of call that people always find irresistible? You would think that degradation had its own small magnetisms of decay, a force strong enough to draw decent and simple people over ornery seas and impassable lands to become part of a neon swill. Anyone who has watched the carcass of an animal for any length of time, seen the insect armies arrive and begin boiling in the flesh, knows that it is the habit of the fly to leave the sound parts of an animal and rush to the festering wounds. I do not know why. When the phosphate ran out, the people of Makatéa fled to Tahiti, and took jobs in its factories, hotels, restaurants, and sin parlors. They left behind a small green gazebo of an island.

The loading platform collapsed long ago, ravaged by the salty talons of tropic storms, and undone by time, that great mindless rearranger of places and people. Occasionally, the local authorities tried to blow up the rusting structures for fear someone might get injured on them, but such efforts always failed, leaving the jagged cranes shuffled around a little, but still above water. One could see where the main conveyor belt had been, and the loading chutes, in the tangle of metal now green with algae and pitted by salt. Beyond the shore, a thick expanse of vine-clad trees led up a winding hill, where fairy terns fluttered like small, white, perfect angels; hibiscus and chenille plants spilled their intense red; and a small village lay nestled with cast-off machinery among the dense undergrowth. All this was visible in the distance, through binoculars, and the passengers clustered at the cruise ship's rails for their first glimpse of an island remote in time, distance, and culture.

Then a six-note bell sounded—what the crew call the "ding-dong"—landing instructions followed, and, as usual, everyone headed for the boat deck, where they lined up in a narrow corridor, took blue horse-collar-shaped life vests from hooks, slipped them over their heads, and secured the waist straps. Filing out to the waiting Zodiacs, they passed a large wooden board holding numbered tags on metal hooks. Next to the board, a manifest listed each passenger's name and its corresponding tag number. Whenever someone left the ship, they turned their number to the red side; returning, they turned the tag back to black. In that way, the staff knew who was on shipboard and whether or not someone was late on shore.

Though it was only 8:30 A.M., the same ferocious sun had begun to climb the sky by the time the Zodiacs set off down the main channel through the coral reef to a small protected cove. A dump truck waited at the base of the hill to take nonhikers to the village and then farther inland to a freshwater cave for a noon swim. Fifty-five people were already ashore, climbing into the truck, and walking along the trail. I had just started up the trail myself, when something made me turn to look back at the shore. There was no sound or alarm or anything out of the ordinary, just an invisible tugging at my mental sleeve. I saw a full Zodiac heading through the channel, its driver a length of orange standing at the rear beside the motor. Suddenly and inexplicably the Zodiac turned broadside to the beach, ran parallel for a few moments, then caught a wave underneath, skidded up in slow motion, and tumbled over in the surf, spilling the driver and twelve passengers into the violent water just outside the reef. My arm rose as if suddenly weightless, as if I could reach across space and grab them. Peter, one of the crew members, saw the same thing in that instant and we began running toward the water, where half a dozen men were already lunging out into a strong, heaving surf. A rescue Zodiac cut fast through the water and picked up most of the people— including two little girls and a woman in her late seventies who was badly cut around the head and neck. Meanwhile, Steve and Mike, two more crew members, hauled her husband out of the surf. He was naked from the waist down—the force of the water had sucked his clothes off—but he still wore his shirt and his blue life vest, from the straps of which hung a length of Zodiac rope. Perhaps he had tried in vain to hold on to the rope as the raft flipped over. Staggering in our arms, he was a man in his eighties, slightly potbellied with reddish hair plastered to his arms and legs; his skin was deathly white and covered with freckles. Blood trickled from a gash on his forehead. One eye was badly bruised and swelling. There was something appallingly human about his nakedness.

"I was in an amphibious unit during the war," he said in a sort of walking faint, as we held him up and guided him toward the waiting arms of others near shore. "I remembered to hold my breath and swim for the surface . . . I knew what to do."

"That's right, that's right, you did the right thing," I said, trying quickly to assess his injuries, and hoping he wouldn't ask about his wife, whom I had seen pulled, badly hurt, into the rescue Zodiac. It was good that his mind had snagged on this small precision. Fresh hands came to guide him, and we ran back toward the surf out of which Anna, the ship's photographer, was walking all by herself with a zombielike stare. It was then, already minutes after the accident, that we saw an orange shape tumbling in the surf, and we ran to it, Peter, Steve, and I. The men pulled the figure out, lifted him by the arms and legs, and I stooped, trying to give him mouth-to-mouth resuscitation as we hurried toward shore. Holding his nose closed with one hand, and his jaw down with the other, I forced my mouth onto his and blew hard into his chest, regularly, heavily, as best I could while he swung between the two men and the surf broke over us. At last we reached the overturned Zodiac in the shallows, and hoisted him on top of it. Peter straddled his waist and began CPR, and I kept forcing breath into him. It felt like screaming into a cave that had no echo. His sharp teeth sliced open my gums, and all the fluids in his stomach poured out through his mouth and nose. I washed them away quickly with the salt water, and kept breathing into him. I think it was then that Peter recognized the man as Tavita, a Philippine Zodiac driver he had worked with for years, and cried out his name with a combination of recognition and anguish. A white foam, a kind of lather, welled up from inside Tavita. Pulling back his eyelids, I saw large open pupils. There was no pulse. But I kept breathing hard into him. Peter was screaming at him not to go, calling him by name—"Tavita, my friend! Come back! come back!" Steve leapt on top of the raft to spell Peter, then me. The doctor, trembling and shaken as the rest of us, kept checking Tavita's pulse, directing our movements. What a confused, strange horror it is to kiss a man with a fully open mouth as one would a lover, hold him in your arms, assume some of the gestures of passion, even exchange fluids with him—but all in the arena of death. As his jaws grew stiffer, his teeth felt sharper, and they lacerated the insides of my lips as I tried to force air deeper and deeper into him. In the end, an hour later, when at last we gave up, and he lay dead among us, my mouth was full of blood.

From both the shore and the ship, people watched the scene unfold, their tense faces frozen in the rictus of horror. Where was the oxygen we kept crying out for the ship to send? How soon could a helicopter arrive to carry the injured to Papeete? We laid Tavita on the ground against a sea wall, a striped T-shirt over his face. Next to him the red-haired man, a minister, sat stoically with a dislocated shoulder, a broken arm, and a gashed head; his wife had been taken to the ship, where she died. A crewman had face injuries a reconstructive surgeon would need to repair. Anna lay in a fetal position on the stone landing, putting on a brave face but complaining that she couldn't move her hip. Lying crumpled on the ground, she looked frail and broken. Anna always wore a scopolomine patch behind one ear to ward off seasickness, a natural side effect of which was that it made her pupils huge. Now her pupils were small and tight; it was the first time I had ever seen them that way. Across the landing, at the loading dock, a crew member stood with her back turned to the passengers on shore and discreetly cried.

At last there was nothing more to do but things automatic and grim. A passenger and a crewman had died. Four others were injured. It was best to clear the area while the final details were attended to, so, incredibly, Peter led the ship's passengers on the scheduled tour up the hill and through the village. In the context of all that had just happened, this seemed the impossible and unnatural event, this simple walk. I went, too, because my adrenaline was pounding; there was too much pent-up action and helplessness to stand still with; and there was nothing further I could do now. Indeed, what I really needed was to run until exhausted. An important battle had just been fought and lost, and I felt it. I cannot speak for the others. I only know that on a few occasions in my life I have found death unfolding in front of me, and I have always acted before I had time to think about it. I suppose, in retrospect, on all of those occasions, I acted fast and well. But one doesn't think those things through on such a battleground. There is no pride or glory. There are no scorekeepers. One doesn't even fight believing one will win. In the end, the victor is always the same. One fights in order to keep alive a necessary attitude about life. I knew Tavita only as an acquaintance, but I liked him. I had relied on his expertise on other sailings. He had a wife and children and many friends. He was forty-three years old.

Soon helicopters arrived from Papeete to lift the injured into the sky and spirit them off to the distant Oz of a hospital in Tahiti. The passengers returned to the ship, the captain lifted anchor, and we set sail by early afternoon. In the evening, the captain and staff gathered the passengers in the lounge, and tried to sum up the day's events as best they could. Then the passengers went to dinner, talking quietly. The staff sat in the bar late into the night. How had it happened? A rogue wave? A misread signal from the local guide standing on shore? A failed motor? A lapse of attention? A cardinal rule of Zodiac driving is never to let your Zodiac run broadside to the waves. What had happened to cause Tavita, a senior driver with much experience, to make that fatal error? I did not know. No one knew. It was a freak accident. I went to my cabin and sat stupefied on the bed, rattled now that it was safe to feel at all, and trying to make peace with everything that had happened. A wiring problem made it impossible to turn the radio completely off, and so Vaughan Williams's "Greensleeves" played quietly, almost below the range of hearing. It had always been one of my favorite pieces of music; now I found it mournful and lugubrious and knew I would never be able to enjoy it again.

In the days that passed, the passengers were taken ashore to see villages or to go snorkeling in lagoons, and the ship's staff made a valiant effort to get them over the trauma and back on track with the cruise. But, behind the scenes, the ship was full of the chaos and unrest that death sets in motion. Life is process and has its own momentum, which continues for a while even after life stops. It is the way a broad jumper, straddling the air with open legs, lands hard, then continues to tumble forward even though the jump is finished. Halfway around the world, there was more than the usual red tape. There were the French Polynesian policemen to deal with. Autopsies had to be performed. Church services were held on an island in the Tuamotos. It was a beautiful, otherworldly service, with hymns sung in high, close harmony and flowers handed to the congregation.

Tavita's body was laid out in the crew's quarters so that respects could be paid. There were many Filipino men and women working on board, and, superstitious about death, they insisted on an exorcism of the ship. While the passengers were sent on glass-bottom boat rides and to a resort for drinks and swimming, the police conducted interviews and the coffins were off-loaded. Sitting under a thatched hut at the end of a dock, I looked at the ship through my binoculars, and saw long orange boxes lifted out of a side door of the ship and arranged on a small yacht.

At every landing we made during the next week, island women greeted us with thick pungent leis of plumeria and herbs. Within hours the flowers wilted, but that did not stop the locals from stringing the leis, or wearing them until they dried, or greeting strangers by garbing them, if only for a few hours, in the brief, extravagant, all-encompassing scent of their petals.

ON RELIGIOUS LOVE

San Xavier del Bac, the finest remaining example of the Spanish colonial missions that ruled frontier America, floats like a heat mirage outside Tucson, Arizona. The local Indians have many names for it, as their ancestors did: white dove of the desert, meringue wedding cake, a nun's starched hat, where the waters gather. For, in the trumpeting desert sun, or even in the wet season when the rains are thick as jelly, it looks otherworldly and miraculous. Chalk white, embellished with huge lions and scrolls, it is the tallest structure for miles. Elaborate outside, ornate within, it stands against the backdrop of cactus, dust, and one-story reservation buildings like something dropped from outer space.

Coming from a distance almost as alien as space, Father Eusebio Francisco Kino, a Jesuit from the Tyrolean Alps, arrived on the desolate spot in 1700, and decided to build his mission. The Indian name for the village was *bac*, "where water springs"; so he coupled that with the name of his patron saint, Francisco Xavier, and the result was something cross-culturally melodic: San Xavier del Bac. Although Father Kino laid the foundations for the church in 1700, it wasn't really finished until 1797. For almost two hundred years, the church has figured in the lives of the Papago Indians.

The outside is plaster, paint, and lime mortar; hand-hewn mesquite beams, and sun-parched adobe. It twists and towers in the sun. There is an inner patio and cloisters, a fountain, grape arbor, corral, and tolling bells, and the overall apparition is ghostly. Inside, it's even stranger: a bazaar of Byzantine, Moorish, and late Mexican baroque architecture, including trompe l'oeil, padlocked wooden doors that will never open, except to those who walk through walls or are on their way to Heaven. A giant red python, its scales painted a fierce red, sprawls beneath the windows. Dozens of rows of wooden benches are finished in carved half-moons, all looking front like a permanent congregation facing the altar. A crimson heart, nesting in a green-and-white garland, sits on one of the beams overhead, a crack through its center. Age has done this, not the pangs of brokenhearted-ness, but, to the believers, who can say? Rolling blue waves pour around the ceiling in a narrow frieze, over which runs a thin red vein. And the main altar! Encrusted with red and gold, baroque as watch-works, it towers high into the sanctuary. All the apostles are present, as well as God, Mary, Saint Ignatius of Loyola and Saint Xavier. The walls are six feet thick, like those of a grave, and the sanctuary's columns of square, oblong, and inverted pyramids in eye-drenching gold make your ribs quiver. Today, right in front of the altar, a black dog paces like the devil on foot, while a tape plays a resounding mass conducted by the brothers of the monastery and the local Indians.

But what is especially startling and poignant is the display of angels, whose wings have realistic feathers. They are all blond European women wearing calicos, pastels, matching petticoats, collars, and elaborate lace cuffs. In their finest lace bodices and nipped waists, they tell you what heaven meant to those poor who worshiped here when the mission was being built. Where else can you find angels in calico skirts, Magritte-like false doors, and false picture frames painted on the whitewash? Two carved angels lean like figureheads from the bow of the sanctuary, looming out into the crowds of the faithful. The lions of Spain are present, too, for obeisance of a more earthly kind. Moorish tent drapes are pulled aside with blue cordons. Are we sailing through the desert, the ocean, or the waters of mortality?

In one alcove lies the tomb of Saint Francis, and supplicants have pinned macabre replicas of hands, legs, feet, arms, kneeling figures, as well as photographs and plastic hospital bracelets and other artifacts onto his white lace blanket. They hope he will cure their physical ills, as God will cure their spiritual ones. Votive candles thicken the air with a waxy vapor, and worshipers who sit on a bench close by look entranced by devotion and the lack of oxygen.

Little has changed since the first mass celebrated with music in the Southwest was held here in 1798. Not the building that stands like a frozen white garment in the scalding heat, not the angels with their Bo-Peep dresses, not the Indians, who come to worship among the cool confusion of architectural styles or to sell their wares across the street. Visitors often linger on benches in the courtyard, listening to the monumental silence of the desert, smiling about how heaven is patrolled by corseted angels, and marveling at the collision of cultures in San Xavier del Bac's carnival in stone.

What are all these saints and angels doing here? The Christians borrowed cherished customs from the Greeks and Romans, including honoring people by turning them into gods. This was especially popular during the Middle Ages, when people wanted more than one deity to worship, and the Church obliged them by creating long lists of saints. Some were pagan gods given Christian names—Artemis was canonized as Saint Artemidos; the sun god Helios was canonized as Saint Elias; one of Aphrodite's holy whores, "Love Feast," was canonized as Saint Agape; the ewe-goddess Rachel was canonized as Saint Agnes, and so on. Others were made saints because of their martyrdom, or their miraculous acts. Even Buddha was canonized as Saint Josasphat (a mispronunciation of Bodhisat). Peopling heaven with familiar angels and saints who, like earthly folk, had specific features and areas of expertise, made a bridge between worshipers and God, a bridge they crossed more easily when propelled by love.

At its most soulful and mystical, religious love sounds much like erotic love. John Donne, a clergyman as well as a poet, wrote a sensuous poem in which he invited God to "batter" his heart, to go all the way and "ravage" him. Saint Catherine of Siena claimed that

Jesus gave her his foreskin as a wedding ring, so that she became his bride "not with a ring of silver but with a ring of his holy flesh, for when he was circumcised just such a ring was taken from his holy body." She also whipped herself three times a day—once for her own sins, once for the sins of living people, once for the sins of the dead. The saints specialized in self-denial, self-torture, and feats of masochism as a way to achieve religious ecstasy. Monks, nuns, clergymen, and saints all write about "passion," "ecstasy," and "union" in language usually applied to the heights of eroticism. Consider how Saint Augustine describes the Crucifixion:

> Like a bridegroom Christ went forth from his chamber, he went out with a presage of his nuptials. . . . He came to the marriage bed of the cross, and there, in mounting it, consummated his marriage, . . . he lovingly gave himself up to the torment in place of his bride, and he joined himself to the woman for ever.

To some, I suppose, such thoughts are blasphemy. In the West, we have separated Church and state, and Church and sex. According to the teachings of Christianity, Mary conceived the son of God without having sex at all. But, as noted, the oldest pagan religions simply worshiped the vulva or the penis. Many religions still revolve around powerful sexual myths, and require true believers to perform fertility rituals of one sort or another, sometimes in public. Circumcision, which began in the Mideast, was originally a male menstruation rite, which was performed on pubescent boys who were dressed up as girls. Strictly speaking, a boy should be willing to sacrifice even his virility to God. Cutting off the foreskin served as a symbol of that devotion.

Love itself was a religion to the Greeks, who worshiped Aphrodite as the feminine ideal, a queen of uninhibited sensuality.* She was supposedly born naked and fully formed from the frothing testicles of Uranus, which had been hurled into the sea. Botticelli paints her

---

*A chic sex club in eighteenth-century France called itself "The Aphrodite," and catered to aristocrats, clergymen, and high-ranking politicians and military officers. One noblewoman, who belonged to the club for twenty years, kept a list of her sexual liaisons there, which included "272 princes and bishops, 439 monks, 93 rabbis, 929 army officers, 342 bankers, 119 musicians, 117 valets, 1,614 Englishmen and other exiles in London during the revolution, 2 uncles, and 12 cousins."

standing demurely inside an oyster shell, whose halves are spread open like the bone-wings of a pelvis, and her pearly hand hides her genitals.

But Aphrodite hid nothing from the Greeks. Enjoying passion in her name was a joyous, unneurotic, holy act that simultaneously celebrated Creation and procreation. What could be more natural? The Greeks beheld the sexuality of the world, of plants and animals and gods, understood that it was a vital force animating all things, and became part of its holy empire. Sexuality was a single thread connecting the heavens and the earth, the sacred and the profane, the powerful and the weak. But they were latecomers to their senses. In China, Tao had already evolved its Yin and Yang, representing the male and female spirit striving to be in harmony. Tao associated lovemaking with the coupling of cosmic forces. The Hindu sacred text, the *Rig Veda,* presented lovemaking as a religious act, a bringing together of universal energies, and a reenactment of the way in which the world began, with the union of Shiva and Shakti. Shiva's symbol is the phallic-shaped lingam; Shakti's is the vagina-shaped yoni. In the medieval Jewish cabala, which seems to have been heavily influenced by Indian mysticism, a male god longs for his female partner, knowing that their union will make the universe balanced and harmonious. Humans having sexual intercourse is but a mirror of that divine passion, and so sex between husband and wife is seen as a holy, reverential act. Many of the pagan religions used a cross as their symbol, often combining it with a circle to represent the male and female genitals.

Throughout the Middle Ages, in Europe, around Eastertime, Christians celebrated spring with dances around a maypole, statues of a sexually aroused Priapus, or other phallic symbols which they wreathed with sacred circles of flowers. In Naples, an image of Priapus with an exaggerated erection was paraded through the streets in great solemnity and its penis was referred to as "the Holy Member" (*il santo membro*). Saint Guignole was depicted with a large erect penis, too, from which

women scraped splinters as conception charms. So much scraping went on that the saint might have had his holy member whittled away entirely. But the priests, with commendable foresight, made his phallus of a wooden rod that passed all the way through the statue to the back, where it was hidden by a screen, and could be periodically thrust forward by a tap of a mallet as it diminished in front.

Men with potency problems could pray to such virile saints as Saint Cosmo and Saint Damiano, votive statues of whom could be purchased, as well as wax replicas of penises, and "St. Cosmo's holy oil" was said to have great invigorating powers. One British historian, exploring the altars of ancient churches (built before 1330) which had been damaged by bombing raids during World War II, was surprised to discover stone phalluses under many of them. To appeal to a wider audience, Christianity adopted and redefined pagan symbols and rituals, especially those from the goddess cult. Perhaps its most dramatic shift was from a maternal to a paternal god, which meant a radical change from picturing god as an all-embracing, nurturing mother to a demanding, judging, punitive, or rewarding—at times monstrously violent—father. A warrior god, a jealous god, a god with weapons. If one does good works and follows his rules, one may win his favor. The New Testament God is still a fickle master, still tyrannical, but he offers forgiveness and love; and he requires an uncritical, adoring love in return. However, one is supposed to fear him, which isn't difficult since he's the sort who carries a grudge a very long time. People all over the earth are born in "original sin" because of a transgression Adam and Eve committed ages ago. This God is everybody's temperamental matinee idol.

Pagan sensuality blended nicely with the idea of a white-bearded, patriarchal god and his holy son, whose body is a source of devotion. As mentioned, nuns refer to themselves as "brides of Christ," they wear his wedding ring, keep their chastity for him, experience "passion" for him, eat his body and blood during communion, when they become one with him. Priests and monks sometimes describe their religious passion in homosexual terms. Their mystic goal is a transcendent love in which one fuses with the beloved God. As Meister Eckehart wrote:

> Some people imagine that they are going to see God, that they are going to see God as if he were standing yonder, and they here, but

it is not to be so. God and I: we are one. By knowing God I take him to myself. By loving God, I penetrate him.

The literal meaning of the word *ecstasy* (from the Greek *ekstasis*) is "to stand forth naked," and mystics have often prayed in the nude, vowing that one must throw off the mask of culture, the straitjacket of fashion, the carapace of reason, to truly purify oneself enough to unite with God. Tellingly, it is when we are naked and in the throes of sexual ecstasy that lovers so often call out God's name, over and over.

The need to feel transcendent touches a primal nerve. Even though I am agnostic, and belong to no organized religion, I am a deeply religious person. An earth-ecstatic. I believe in the sanctity of life, and in the perfectibility of people. I find wilderness a holy place, and all life sacred. Often I have stood before the plunging altar of a great canyon, breathed in the incense of an ocean storm, stood beneath a tabernacle of trees in the forest, or praised the starry night in the desert, in what can only be called religious ecstasy. Our need for whole-ness, for holiness, seems as much a part of our heritage as is our need for protein. If we look at the vocabulary of the Indo-Europeans, hoping to get a sense of the texture of their lives, we discover that they invented a word for holy. It meant the healthy interconnectedness of all living things, a sense of connection to the whole, a state in which one sees and appreciates even what is hidden. They had a verb for "to retreat in awe," and another for "speaking with the deity." Their poet, who undoubtedly retreated in awe, spoke with the deity, and celebrated life's holiness, was called *wek-wom-teks,* "the weaver of words."

We ask the same questions as the first humans who feared the night, were happy to be alive, and felt awe. Who are we? Where do we come from? How should we behave? Whom should we trust? Why is life so hard? How can beings with such a powerful life force face death? Our ever-analyzing brains, questing to make sense of life, cannot do so, finally, and so make sense of it anyway through magic, miracles, and faith. At least that stops the nagging itch to know absolutely. For some. For others, the nagging never stops.

Religious love also returns us to childhood, when we love-worshiped our parents, on whom we were absolutely dependent. And what miracles they performed! Mothers could heal a wound with a kiss, make fruit hang suspended in the Jell-O, tie shoes with magic knots; fathers appeared with food and toys, and could master wild animals or monster machines.

Tonight, a crust of starlight crackles over the winter sky. To the Egyptians the dome of night was Nut, the great mother from whose breasts poured the Milky Way. In the tomb paintings, she's shown curving overhead, her arms and legs spread wide, as she touches earth's farthest corners with her fingertips and toes. Her lover, Geb, lies on the flat ground beneath her, his erect penis reaching toward her luminous body. Pharaohs often claimed to be her son or lover, and to live their lives, as Pepi II put it, "between the thighs of Nut." Orion the hunter has just risen. His sword points to Sirius; in neolithic days they foretold the coming of a messiah. Long before the Bible, Egyptians worshiped their god of gods, Osiris, a human who died and was resurrected and who offered followers salvation and eternal life. His coming had been announced by three wise men—the belt stars of Orion: Alnilam, Alnitak, and Mintaka—which pointed to his birthplace. Many of Christianity's rituals and symbols (crucifixes, rosaries, communion, holy water, and so on) were borrowed from the Osiris cult. Tonight Ursa Major, the She-Bear, is guarding the pole of the world. I tell the month and season by watching her movements. For days now, the tail has been pointing to the east at nightfall, so I know it will soon be spring. When the tail points south, summer is near. It points west to signal autumn, and north to announce winter.

Somewhere in that mysterious swirl of stars we locate "Paradise." A Persian word (*pairidaeza*) for the garden where the Tree of Life grows, a Hebrew word (*pardes*) for the garden of love where a man's virgin bride waits to be deflowered. In both gardens, the air is drenched with perfume, luscious foods are scattered everywhere, music serenades one, and a beautiful woman offers the endless comfort of her love. The lost paradise, for which we long, the world of plenty where all our needs are met, the true "land of milk and honey"—we knew it only in infancy, when we were loved and protected, and suckled in perfect bliss at our mother's breast. That rich desire touches the heart of all love, religious or erotic, a yearning for reconnection, with mother earth, mother church, mother love.

Religious love calms our terrible loneliness, and our need for family, for being special in someone's eyes, protected, noble, forgiven. The word *religion* means to bind or connect, and a sense of reunion is built into it. We enter the exalted, welcoming home of the temple or church, where all are accepted regardless of real or imaginary crimes, where instant kin is waiting, and relatives are painted on the walls or the windows—sometimes even wearing calicos and pastel ribbons. There we learn about the history we share, and look forward to a future free from heartache or hunger. We kneel before our doting father, ask his blessing, and sing him sweet songs. We praise him, we adore him, we fear him, we promise to be obedient, we wear his favorite clothes, and recite his favorite sayings. His house is a fortress, an ornate palace in which even the poorest of us can dwell. The chanting and calm, incense-thick air puts us into a hypnotic state, so that we are open and vulnerable.* It's as if everyone placed an ad in the personals column of the soul and received an answer from their ideal match. He has a thousand faces. Those in contact with God say he's ideally responsive, attuned to their private needs and woes, completely on their wavelength, able to pick out their hesitant prayer from the lamentations of millions. And nothing could be more reassuring, no embrace more comforting, no loving union closer.

ON TRANSFERENCE LOVE

This morning I went to the local deli for breakfast, and to spend time with Carol, a pretty, chestnut-haired, single woman in her forties. A zoologist, she had been away on an expedition, and we hadn't seen each other for many months. So we set out on a girlfriend expedition of our own, catching up on all the travels in each other's lives. In time, the conversation turned to her latest thought: going into therapy to construe some of the patterns in her life, and to find detours around the rocky relationships with men she always seems to plow into. She asked my advice about whether she should choose a

---

*Chemical analysis of incense reveals that it contains mind-altering steroids.

male or female therapist, and, since she is the daughter of an alcoholic father who made her early life a misery, I suggested a male. She was fearful about having an intimate relationship with someone under such artificial circumstances. That got me thinking about the goals of psychotherapy.

Uppermost in a therapist's mind are such matters as not making the client worse; putting out any roaring fires; investigating difficult conflicts; helping the client become more stable, self-reliant, and self-accepting. But one aspect of a therapist's job is to develop a safe, stable, accepting relationship with a client, showing her by example what a healthy attachment would be like, in the hope that she will then be able to recognize its features and look for the same sort of relationship outside therapy.

"You believe their duty is to offer love to each client?" Carol asked.

"If they are any good, they are serial lovers."

"I'll be meeting this guy, intimately, twice a week," she said. "What if I fall in love with him? That's the standard joke, that you have to fall in love with your analyst, right?"

"Actually the standard joke is: How many psychologists does it take to change a light bulb?"

"I give up," she said, slicing into a Mexican omelet.

"Only one. But the light bulb has to *want* to change." We laughed, as a waitress appeared with cups of hazelnut coffee.

"Falling for your therapist isn't required," I continued, "and many people don't feel anything of the kind. But the circumstance—meeting secretly in a quiet room with a man who is completely open to you at your most vulnerable, and with whom you share your fantasies, hurts, and dreams—that's very seductive, and it encourages love, it allows love to flourish."

"Suppose I fall head over heels in love with him, body and soul, hot and heavy?"

"That would be both agonizing and very helpful. True, you would find yourself in a diabolically painful, unrequited relationship with a man you feel physically rejected by, and yet have to meet regularly. You'd be sitting across from him, face-to-face, knowing that he knows how desperately you love him, and also knowing that he doesn't want you—it can't get much more humiliating than that. But you'd also have the unique luxury of being able to analyze your pain with him, pick out which elements hurt and why, which are based on reality, which are exaggerations and distortions, which reflect scars you are carrying from childhood or past relationships with other men."

"But there I would be, dying to have a real relationship with him, to do things together, to make love . . . "

"Let's suppose you get your wish. He gets sexually involved with you, and for a while that seems fabulous. He's most likely married, and the odds are that he's not going to leave his wife. I say this because statistically that's the picture—roughly 7 percent of male therapists have affairs with their clients, but only .01 percent of that figure go on to marry them. Soon enough all sorts of man/woman problems would arise. There you would be, having another bad relationship with a man. His job is not to add to your list of unsatisfactory relationships; it's to help you learn from them and avoid them. To that extent, he would have betrayed your trust. And, of course, it would make continuing therapy impossible. How would you feel if you were paying a man you were having sex with? Wouldn't that make you feel exploited? You would almost certainly end up in therapy with someone else just to deal with your bad relationship with your first therapist."

"All right, let's suppose I don't fall in love with him. A long time ago, I was in therapy briefly with a woman, and I couldn't bear the broken relationship at the end. Here you have this intense intimacy with someone you care for and trust, and then suddenly the reverse is true and you never see them again. I felt so disposed of; it was crushing."

"From the therapist's point of view, I guess that's the safest course to follow. Sometimes in novels or movies, strangers meet on a train and don't even tell each other their full names. But they have the freedom to be unparalleled lovers, acting out any fantasy, feeling unjudged and totally uninhibited. They can reveal anything, be anything. Psychotherapy is like that. Most therapists feel that they cannot become friends with their clients—even after therapy ends— because it would prevent that intense, liberating anonymity if the client should ever need to return for help. So their policy is: once an intimate always a stranger. Freud himself didn't practice this principle; over the years, he became dear friends with a few of his patients whom he particularly liked. They often socialized, and neither he nor they reported any problems resulting from the fullness of their friendship. Indeed, I know a psychiatrist in Manhattan, a wonderful woman in her seventies, who has outside friendships with some of her patients; and they rave about her as a person and as an effective therapist. But that requires remarkable people who can compartmentalize exceptionally well, and most therapists can't manage that, or don't want to as a general principle. In any case, you are having the most intimate relationship of your life with him, but he is having intimate relationships with many people. His day is filled with tumultuous human dramas and towering moments of empathy. Dealing with them often requires pinpoint concentration. After hours, he undoubtedly wants to clear his mind of all that, and for his own mental health he needs to. Probably the last thing he wants is to fill his leisure time with the same psychic carnage, or even with people who remind him of it. I very much doubt that many therapists have relationships with their friends—or for that matter with their families—which are as intense as the ones they have with their clients."

"And yet you still believe it's worth doing, despite everything, despite the ordeal."

"Because of the ordeal. Because learning how to love in a way that's not self-destructive is essential for survival. At this point, your world seems littered with hidden snares and bombs, some of which life dropped when you weren't looking, and some of which you have set for yourself. Defusing them is an ordeal. How could it be otherwise? But the world will be a safer place for you if you *can* defuse them."

I knew I was sending her to her salvation, but perhaps also to considerable torment. In the ancient hieroglyphic poems, love is a secret. It is so obsessive, so all-consuming, so much like insanity, that one is ashamed to admit how much life one has surrendered. Caught in the undertow of a powerful transference, Carol might not be able to reveal to her therapist how much of her mental and emotional life he consumes. Because she has a sensitive and tender heart, she will love him honestly, beautifully, with all the ampleness of her spirit, but because he will not return that love, or even comfortably acknowledge its seriousness and proportions, it will seem shameful. She may feel self-hatred, since it seems to be her fault alone for loving him so one-sidedly. She will not understand that the love has formed—to use Stendhal's image—as naturally as a crystal of salt does on a branch in a sealed salt mine. She could not have stopped it; it did not arise because of some defect in her. It is an entity that sometimes grows in the caverns of psychotherapy, particularly if the therapist encourages it to flourish. But it will burn in her open wounds, it will torture her.

Carol may walk willingly into the primeval forest of deep transference, but will she be able to get out safely? Although neither is simple or without peril, it's marginally easier to leap onto a dragon's back than to climb off it. Dragons come naturally to mind because transference love is, in many ways, medieval in structure. It's a love heightened by obstacles, taboos, and impossibilities, as was courtly love. That makes it all the more delectable. The therapist is like a knight who must prove his devotion by *not* lying down with his lady. Or rather, in effect, by lying down with her but not touching her. That was, after all, the final and truest test of a knight's love, if he could steal into his lady's chamber and climb into bed beside her, while her naked body appealed to all his normal male appetites, without laying a hand on her. In therapy, the patient lies down— literally or figuratively—and is more naked than naked, more exposed than mere nudity could ever reveal. The therapist proves his devotion by not responding sexually. His quest is to restore what has been lost or stolen from the castle of her self-regard. It is a difficult task, which they both construe as a journey fraught with obstacles and danger and strife. There are dragons to slay. There are whirlwinds to tame. There are enemies without. There are monsters within.

ON THE LOVE OF PETS

One Saturday morning in midsummer, at the Farmer's Market down by the lake, a young woman was walking her pet ferret on a leash. Many people stopped to inquire about the animal. They stroked its wiry fur, commented on its pungent odor, studied its small black eyes which flashed like hot licorice. In time, she strolled on and a man arrived walking his two Irish wolfhounds. Well-mannered and tightly leashed, each dog stood almost four feet high. Roughly the size of small Shetland ponies, they ate ten pounds of food each day, and no doubt their defecations filled the fields behind their home. Both owners shone with pride about their animals. What special favor does a pet convey? Is it the controlled lawlessness implied by walking unmolested beside a wild animal? In admiration and relief, are we reminded of what we share, and don't share, with other creatures?

We live in a panic about our origins, we fear our animal nature as if it didn't belong to us, as if it were a predator that could steal our humanity when we turn off the lights. We prey on ourselves. Civilization has made us schizophrenic and we live double lives— animal and not-animal—each one frightened of dying at the hands of the other. Our desperation to distinguish ourselves from the rest of the animal kingdom is so violent that many people reading this sentence will wince even at hearing themselves described as animals. The thought is unbearable. It suggests that human life is irrational, savage, unplanned. We struggle to prove to ourselves that we are not "mere" animals, that no hyena lurks in the bathroom mirror, that we will not revert to the animal inside. We picture such a fate as a carnal circus of predators and prey where one is never strong enough to best the bigger, stronger beast around the corner. "Raise up your young to be fiends and teach them to be sly, teach them to be brutal," might be an adage for a mother in such a world. As I imagined that scenario, in the back of my mind I saw vague, human-dingolike creatures; but what interests me more is that they moved in darkness. The night world, where our senses falter and our reason is of little help, scares us all. Other creatures master that world—bats, cats, snakes, rats, insects, lions. To make hell seem all the more loathsome, theologians depicted it as a dark world lit only by the flickering confusion of flames. Actually, an overly bright world of compulsive order, repetitive forms, and suffocating cleanliness would be equally hellish.

We see it grazing in a field: some lost version of what we were or who we are—animal. We do not know our future. Animals such as albatrosses and porpoises have always seemed to us messengers and portents, full of oracular magic, able to offer us a companionship we crave, but somehow cannot give to one another, an antidote to our terrible loneliness in our alabaster cities, a connectedness with our primitive past. We look at them and know they dwell in a realm somewhere between us and our beginnings. We have littered our myths and homes with images of animals, which accompany us throughout our lives; they are the first crib toys we give to our children; women sometimes marry them in fairy tales; we use them as zodiacal signs to count the hours in our days. We understand how animals fit into the scheme of nature. As for ourselves, we aren't so sure who we are, or where we've come from, and even less what we wish to become.

When we hold the gaze of a wild animal, it assumes that we mean to bedevil it in some way, either to devour or to mate with it. Small wonder it charges or turns tail and dashes away. The best way to sneak close to grazing deer is not to make eye contact with them, but to pretend to graze idly in the soft morning light, while casually drifting closer. Hold a pet's gaze too long, and it assumes you expect something from it. It becomes unsettled, it shifts its eyes askance, then it bolts. We are used to having cats and dogs as companion animals, warm-blooded creatures that enjoy affection and some eye contact. They help bridge that no-man's-land between us and Nature, between apehood and civilization. We are still apes, of course. It is still a wilderness. We attempt to cross it with camera lens or idea, but the deeper we penetrate the frontier the vaster it seems. We long to merge with nature, and yet we also struggle to keep it at arm's length.

The imminent encroachment of nature alarms us, the weeds on the lawn, the sowbugs creeping in, the bacteria everywhere. We try to obliterate all of it, and keep the house "sanitary," neat and clean. We scrub away our own sweat and the sweat of our houses. Then we just as obsessively fill the house with potted plants and clean our floors with pine-scented liquids. Could anything be more contradictory? We build walls to keep out the elements; then we equip our homes with furnaces, lamps, and air conditioners, so that we live in a perpetual breeze or bake. To be safe from wild animals, we build fences and set traps. Even a groundhog or raccoon alarms us. A harmless garter snake loose in the house causes havoc. An invasion of ants or daddy-long-legs leads to chemical warfare. But something deep inside us remembers being accompanied by animals. We have worn the same costumes, we have heard the same outcries, we have known the same square dance in our cells. Their journey is our journey. We adopt pets and, if a cat sitting on a couch doesn't look or smell exactly like a lion resting at a watering hole, well, perhaps it's close enough. Just as we do with the elements, or with smells, we make animals tidy by putting them on leashes or in zoos. We project our values onto them, giving them dishes to eat from, sweaters and rhinestone-studded collars to wear, and we prefer it when they're well behaved.

An animal on a leash is not tamed by the owner. The owner is extending himself through the leash to that part of his personality which is pure dog, that part of him which just wants to eat, sleep, bark, hump chairs, wet the floor in joy, and drink out of a toilet bowl. We still need a pack to travel with, and sometimes we create our own group. In a world of increased helplessness and intersecting hierarchies as arbitrary as they are impenetrable, at least we can be the alpha male or female in our own house, the top dog in the eyes of our pets. Their relative stupidity makes us feel exceptionally smart. They do not seem to judge us, as children don't when they're small, and yet they need and look up to us. Acting submissive, they treat us as the ultimate top dogs. We are their kidnappers, we keep them locked away from their kind. It's no surprise that, like prisoners of war, they turn to us for food, comfort, acceptance, and affection.

A recent Gallup Poll found that 58 percent of American households have pets. Forty percent of the people have dogs; 26 percent have cats. But 90 percent of the people said that they regarded their pet as a "part of the family," bringing a sense of fullness and completion to their lives. Owning a pet is an important factor in the health and longevity of elderly people. Merely stroking a domestic animal lowers one's blood pressure. So does watching it sit. Seeing nature being calm calms us. Most pet fondling takes place almost unconsciously, the way one's hands absentmindedly stroke each other, or the way spouses press together as they sleep. Soothing, quieting, having a pet lie beside one tranquilizes the nerves. "Companion animals," as they're rather sweetly called, also provide an unflagging friendship and give owners a sense of playfulness and purpose. The minute a pet enters a household, it joins the family dynamics, and that can be either good or bad, depending on the people involved. For example, pets sometimes become the outpatients of a troubled family. When I was growing up, I had a friend, Barbara, whose parents bought a cocker spaniel. They named it Babe, and it became the "good little girl" in their household, as they so often told it, sometimes saying such things as: "Here comes your mother, Babe," or, "Babe, go to your sister." Barbara's parents quarreled a lot, and they often spoke to each other through the dog. Her father might say something like: "Babe, tell your mother I'm not going to the store, and that's final!" And her mother might answer: "Babe, tell him I'm going whether he likes it or not!" Babe became deeply attached to Barbara's mother, whom she followed like an acolyte from room to room, next to whom she slept in bed every night, and whose absence made her too depressed even to eat. Once, when Barbara's parents were on vacation in Europe, her mother called the dog-sitter to make sure Babe was eating all right. If she hadn't been, the vacation would have been cut short. When it came to looking after Babe, nothing was too much trouble, not even baking her meatloaflike meals. Barbara, on the other hand, was entering puberty and she and her mother always seemed to be fighting about her friends, her taste in clothes, her music, her politics, and a hundred other things. Her father worked all day and came home tired and bad-tempered; except for yelling, he rarely spoke to her at all.

Barbara's mother developed a powerful love for the dog, which loved her back devotedly, wet the floor in excited rapture whenever she returned home, never yelled at her or disagreed with her or confronted her with thorny child-rearing problems, didn't make complex demands, and wasn't expected to fulfill her potential. It was easy to shower affection on the dog, which she kissed and cuddled and groomed, and which indeed had become the good little girl in the family. Barbara, Babe's "sister," was relegated to the status of bad little girl. The pet enabled Barbara's parents, who didn't feel comfortable expressing love with each other or with their children, to bestow it on some living thing. This made Barbara feel resentful, as she watched her parents express love for the dog with a generosity they could not seem to muster for her. The dog joined the family, but Barbara felt excluded from it.

Pets become family members so easily because they remind us of children, which stimulates our instinct for nurturing them. As ethologist Konrad Lorenz surmised in his classic study of human behavior, what we call "cute" in animals are features they share with human infants: a large head in proportion to the body, with a high, bulging forehead; big eyes; round cheeks; short limbs and rather clumsy movements; behaviors like submissiveness and playfulness, which we associate with childhood. When we look at such beings, tenderness flows and we yearn to protect them. They seem instrinsically lovable. It doesn't matter that we are programmed to find them so; we can't help ourselves. This is not only true of animals; those characteristics appeal to us in adults, too. Unlike most other species, humans are neotenous, that is, they keep many of their juvenile features into adulthood. The people we call "pretty" retain more of those features than other people do. Dolls, cartoon characters, and stuffed animals are designed with these same features, but slightly exaggerated, to make them seem even cuter. Give a child a teddy bear with big amber eyes, small nose (unlike the pointy snout of a real bear), a gently bulging face, and stubby limbs, and the child instinctively adopts it, wants to cuddle and protect it. Why? you ask the child, who answers: "Because he's so cute." The stuffed animal touches an evolutionary tripwire inside the child, and a small explosion of nurturing ensues. Many of our favorite companion dogs have been bred to emphasize these appealing features. Just as birds have been known to feed anything that looks like a hungry fledgling (including an open-mouthed carp at the surface of a pond), humans will nurture many things, some animate, some inanimate.

We are driven to anthropomorphize animals, and often do, in cartoons, myths, and theme parks. Anthropologist Colin Turnbull discovered to his surprise and dismay that many people feel disappointed when they visit Africa, where the wilderness sprawls and the wild animals keep a distance, because it's not as intimate an experience of "nature" as people seem to have at Disneyland, among cute animals that talk and come right up and embrace visitors. Juvenile behavior—the wobbly walk of penguins, a newborn calf struggling to its feet, shyness, the submissiveness young animals show their parents, or any version of play—has the same effect, inspiring us to parent and protect. People love their pets as children, that is, as specially exempt children. They will never grow to human size, or join in a game of canasta, or pass their college boards, or play saxophone, or refrain from rude noises when company's around. They are not expected to develop, achieve greatness, or fulfill a private fantasy to be a doctor, baseball player, or rock star. They do not disappoint us, scandalize us, or cheat our expectations. We allow them the freedom to be exactly what they are, without worrying about what they must become. We let them live on their own schedule, at their own pace, as we rarely do with real children. And, because we expect nothing more, we love them, for pets perpetually please us.

POSTSCRIPT: THE MUSEUM

The first time I entered New York City's American Museum of Natural History, I knew nothing of its layout or holdings. Pure serendipity led me to the lower level on Central Park West. There I drifted into a small, quiet gallery, and stood in front of a display of miscroscopic invertebrates, creatures that inhabit the minute wetlands of our lives. Whisker-perfect glass models of rotifers and protozoans shone from their display case. These models, vastly enlarged for the exhibit, are actually single-celled organisms that live in lakes, ponds, puddles, on damp soil, in mosses, between sand grains on beaches, and even in small depressions in rocks. Protozoans also live in or on most animals as parasites or symbionts. Some are colonial; some are phosphorescent; one was shaped like the lunar landing module, another like the gem-encrusted tiara of Queen Elizabeth, yet another like a Christmas-tree ornament. Others resembled snowflakes, Amazon fig trees with their root systems exposed, jellyfish trailing gothic church spires.

Relishing their intricacy and variety, I felt so startled by joy that my eyes teared. It was a religious experience of power and clarity, limning the wonder and sacredness of life, life at any level, even the most remote. I have often been touched by the cathedral-like architecture of the microscopic, which I love to study in photographs taken through scanning electron microscopes. One year, I spent off-duty hours hooking rya rugs after the patterns of amino-acid leucine (seen by polarized light), an infant's brain cells, a single neuron, and other objects revealed by such photographic delving.

If I could have formulated the emotion I felt in words at the invertebrate exhibit, it would have been something like this: even the world around us, though invisible to the naked eye, is packed with marvels. Creatures unimaginably complex, breathtakingly frail and yet sturdy, durable, filled with the self-perpetuating energy we call life. Creatures that are omnipresent, wherever water rests. As tiny and frail as these life forms are, they survive hurricanes, earthquakes, the casual chaos of human feet. I felt what Walt Whitman may have when he wrote of the starry night, "the bright suns I see and the dark suns I cannot see are in their place." His intuition bespeaks both the faith in the unknown and the extrapolation of belief that love and religion require. The part stands for the whole, the single instance for the general truth, as it does in natural history museums, which say, in effect, *Here is a wildebeest on the African savanna, but there are many more of them, it's part of a species. This is what they need. This is what they fear. This is how they behave. Trust in it.* I wasn't thinking those things then, or worrying about what protozoan can do to one's digestive system, just feeling saturated by wonder. Only praise leapt to mind, praise that knows no half-truth and pardons all.

What is a natural history museum? It's a silent oasis in the noisy confusion of the world, isolating phenomena so that they can be seen undistractedly. What is being collected are not the artifacts themselves but the undivided attention of the visitors. *That* is the museum. It lies in the mind of the viewers. Its real holdings are the perpetuation of wonder amid a maelstrom of social and personal distractions. "Collection" is a good word for what happens—not to them, but to you. One becomes collected for a spell, gathering up one's curiosity the way rainwater collects on the ziggurat roofs of Caribbean homes. Every museum is really a museum of one's high regard. That's why we visit them so often, even though we know the holdings by heart. It functions as a sort of pilgrimage and vigil. We go there to express our love, our humility, our worship. Museums are where we store some of our favorite attitudes about life.

The ceilings in the American Museum of Natural History look drafty and high, the galleries lead through many mazes and levels. For instance, to get from the invertebrates to the Hall of Minerals and Gems you must first pass through the North American Forests, the Mollusks, and the Meteorites—with perhaps a side trip to the carvings of the Northwest Coast Indians, or to see the ninety-four-foot-long blue whale in the Hall of Ocean Life. I've always felt this meandering layout appropriate, since curiosity needs to rise and fall through many elevations and troughs. It's like prowling around a huge attic, in which the trunks and scrapbooks have been opened. No sooner are you fascinated by the ancestors of the horse than you become equally enchanted by totem poles. In the Hall of Minerals and Gems, I usually pause at the colossal slabs of jade and amethyst; the apricot topaz the size of an ox head; the cluster of black azurite crystals (some of them five inches long) which is considered to be the finest mineral specimen in existence; the Fabergé menagerie of exquisitely carved gems, including an agate pig with ruby eyes and carnelian teats. I marvel at all the shapes and color of sparkle that people have given each other as tokens of love. Then I make a beeline for the opals, whose buxom kaleidoscopes captivate me. They are only a form of wet sand, I remind myself, with light skidding among the particles of silica and the spaces between them. And yet they flash lightning bolts of color. I know how they do it, but am still perpetually bowled over by them. Next to the opals are open clamshells glazed with nacre. In each one, pearls have formed by coating stray grit with a smooth, gemlike luster. How odd that women wear them to look elegant and proper, that divers risk bursting their lungs to gather them like rigid posies from the ocean depths. Like clams, whales produce ambergris to coat jagged annoyances that they have ingested (squid beaks and such). Both pearls and ambergris result in great beauty, and I love looking at them because they offer a Zen-like lesson about how to deal with irritations.

In the new Hall of Human Biology and Evolution, one diorama in particular haunts me, and I know I will often be returning to it: a full-size, startlingly lifelike "Lucy" and her mate as she must have looked walking upright across Ethiopia three million years ago. Based on scientific fact and educated guesswork, these models are deeply evocative. Our earliest prehuman relatives (*Australopithecus afarensis*), they had lower IQs than we have, but were very human in stance, movements, and basic emotions. Standing about three-and-a-half-feet tall, weighing sixty pounds or so, Lucy apparently suffered from arthritis and died in her twenties. Her slender fingers and toes curved more than ours, and she had more body hair than modern women do, but she traveled by foot through the forests and plains. Her friends and relatives would be with her, and a special male friend with whom she dines and loves; she holds their child in her arms. She needs the male for food, protection, and something unsayable— perhaps the feeling of peace and wholeness she knows when they lie together in the tall grass. She would be jealous of other females, possessive about her male, and yet find other males appealing. Occasionally, she might be tempted to sneak off with one for a dangerous liaison. In a few years, she and her male might break up and start second families. But that emotional cataclysm would be the farthest thing from her mind as she travels with her lover.

A volcanic eruption, shown in the background, is coating the landscape with white ash; and as they walk through the savanna, they leave a trail of footprints. Lucy's head is turned left, her mouth open. She seems startled by us. She does not know what she will become. Looking forward as he walks, her mate has his arm around her shoulder in a familiar gesture of tenderness. She doesn't know about dinner dates, Valentine's Day, custody battles. What was their courtship like? What worries them? Do they imagine a future? What delights their senses? How do they comfort their young? I long to meet them face-to-face, to reach through time and touch them. It is like recognizing one's kin across the street in a bustling city.

Since then, a long caravan of humans has evolved from love to love. Men have always been described by basic words, pure as minerals. (*Man* is a Germanic word that simply means "man.") But words for women suggest more about love. In ancient days, the word for woman—*hlaefdige*—meant "kneader of bread," and also mistress of the household, bread maker: lady. In Latin, she was the shaper of loaves, identified with the word *fingere,* from which we get *feign, fiction, figment*. Both women and fiction stroll down the same etymological road, back to *dhoigho-,* a wall that was made of clay or mud bricks; it is also one derivation of the word "paradise." A woman kneads the bread of the family, shaping it, warming it, combining the ingredients of different personalities. From her doughy body, she bears them; with her stubborn hands she forms them; in the oven of her love, she binds them together. Her task is nothing less than the creation of paradise.

Lucy does not know this, as she drinks in the hot sun of the plains. The dry grass smells musty, and a breeze cuts through it like an invisible scythe. Birds call from a distant stand of trees, and cicadas scrape song from their legs. Flies pester the baby clinging to her breast, and she brushes them away from its face with her hand. The baby smiles and she smiles back. Her mate stretches out his arms to carry the baby for a spell, and it scrambles onto his shoulder and wraps an arm around his neck. Clouds mix overhead, changing shape and color. One of them reminds him of Lucy's face, and he laughs. She looks quizzically at him, and he playfully touches her cheek. It is a serene moment for both of them, just to be alive and together. Is what they feel love? Some version of it. Our treasury of emotions, even the most delicate, evolved from their wealth of experiences. We are their heirs. Only two of them walk across this museum exhibit, but that's enough to give a sense of love's lineage.

If a museum's purpose is to be an accumulation, then it can only fail. But if its purpose is to give a sense of family and neighborhood, then it will succeed by being incomplete. There will be sections straight as a narrative, all sorts of portraits, histories, and souvenirs, and many curios. Studied separately, they will fascinate; and, taken together, they will give a small sense of the vast mosaic. In the jargon of space-faring people (as we now are), natural history museums offer us a contingency sample of life on earth.

In that sense, the heart is just such a museum, filled with the exhibits of a lifetime's loves. We remember them frozen in time, illuminated by distance, rinsed in the most unnatural light at times, the better to reveal their finer points. Can they breathe and embrace us? No. But neither can they threaten and wound us, if they're restrained by glass. They are commemorative. The heart issues them like emotional stamps. They are emblematic. Ransack the museum of your heart for love-sappiness, and you'll find it for sure, just the right example. My mother once told me how, when she was a teenager, she was so in love with a certain boy that she secretly picked up the Popsicle sticks he tossed away and kept them under her pillow, kissing them at night. To this day, she remembers that as a perfect specimen of girlish infatuation. That same boy, now in his late seventies, bumped into her brother recently and asked tenderly about her. He hasn't forgotten her, either. The heart is a living museum. In each of its galleries, no matter how narrow or dimly lit, preserved forever like wondrous diatoms, are our moments of loving and being loved.

SELECTED BIBLIOGRAPHY

Abdel-Kader Hatem, M. *Life in Ancient Egypt*. Los Angeles: Gateway Publishers, 1976.

Ackerman, Diane. *A Natural History of the Senses*. New York: Random House, 1990.

Adams, J. N. *The Latin Sexual Vocabulary*. Baltimore: Johns Hopkins University Press, 1982.

Al-Masudi. *Les Prairies d'Or,* trans. C. Barbier de Meynard and C. Pavet de Courteille. Paris: Edition, 1861.

Anderson, Bonnie S., and Judith P. Zinsser. *A History of Their Own*. New York: Harper & Row, 1988. 2 vols.

Angier, Natalie. "Hard-to-Please Females May Be Neglected Evolutionary Force." *The New York Times,* May 8, 1990, C 1.

———. "Mating for Life? It's Not for the Birds and the Bees." *The New York Times,* August 21, 1990.

Aries, Philippe, and Georges Duby. *A History of Private Life*. Cambridge: Harvard University Press, 1987–90. 4 vols.

Aschan, Ulf. *The Man Whom Women Loved: The Life of Bror Blixen*. New York: St. Martin's Press, 1987.

Auden, W. H. *Epistle to a Godson*. New York: Random House, 1972.

Baldick, Robert. *Dinner at Magney's*. London: Harmondsworth, 1973.

Barnes, Julian. *A History of the World in 10½ Chapters*. New York: Knopf, 1989.

Barry, Joseph. *French Lovers*. New York: Arbor House, 1987.

Batten, Mary. *Sexual Strategies*. New York: Putnam, 1992.

Bédier, Joseph. *The Romance of Tristan and Iseult,* trans. Hilaire Belloc. New York: Pantheon, 1945.

Bergmann, Martin S. *The Anatomy of Loving*. New York: Columbia University Press, 1987.

Beye, Charles. *Ancient Greek Literature & Society*. New York: Anchor, 1975.

Bligh, E. W. *Sir Kenelm Digby and His Venetia*. London: Sampson Low, Marston & Co., 1932.

Bowlby, John. *The Making and Breaking of Affectional Bonds*. London: Routledge, 1989.

———. *Attachment and Loss*. Vol. I, *Attachment,* New York: Basic Books, 1982.

———. *Attachment and Loss*. Vol. II, *Separation: Anxiety and Anger,* New York: Basic Books, 1973.

———. *A Secure Base*. New York: Basic Books, 1988.

"Brain Receptors Shapes Voles' Family Values." *Science News,* July 4, 1992.

Brazelton, T. Berry. *Touchpoints*. Redding, MA: Addison-Wesley, 1992.

Brecher, Edward M. *The Sex Researchers*. San Francisco: Specific Press, 1979.

Brody, Jane E. "Designing Birds Impress Their Mates with Fancy Decor." *The New York Times,* March 5, 1991, C 1.

Budge, Sir E. A. Wallis. *Amulets and Talismans*. New York: University Books, 1968.

———, trans. *Book of the Dead*. New York: Bell Publishing, 1960.

Burbank, Katherine Victoria. "Passion as Politics: Romantic Love in an Aboriginal Community." Paper presented at the American Anthropological Association Meetings, Session: The Anthropology of Romantic Passion, San Francisco, December 1992.

Carcopino, Jérome. *Daily Life in Ancient Rome*. New Haven: Yale University Press, 1940.

Castleman, Michael. "Setting the Mood for Love." *New Woman,* February 1991, Vol. 21, Issue 2, pp. 97–98.

Connell, Charles. *Aphrodisiacs in Your Garden*. New York: Taplinger, 1965.

Cross, Milton. *Encyclopedia of Great Composers and Their Music*. Vol. 1, New York: Doubleday, 1962.

Darwin, Charles. *The Expression of the Emotions in Man and Animals*. London: Murray, 1872; Chicago: University of Chicago Press, 1965.

———. *The Descent of Man and Selection in Relation to Sex*. New York: Collier, 1963.

de Gourmont, Rémy. *The Natural Philosophy of Love,* trans. Ezra Pound. New York: Collier, 1972.

Delluc, Brigitte and Gilles, and Ray Delvert. *Discovering Lascaux,* trans. Angela Moyon. Paris: Editions Sud-Ouest, 1990.

de Roche, Max. *The Foods of Love*. Boston: Little, Brown, 1991.

de Rougemont, Denis. *Love in the Western World,* trans. Montgomery Belgion. New York: Schocken Books, 1983.

de Waal, Frans. *Peacemaking Among Primates*. Cambridge: Harvard University Press, 1989.

Diamond, Jared. *The Third Chimpanzee*. London: Radius, 1991.

Duby, Georges, and Robert Mandrou. *A History of French Civilisation*. London: Harmondsworth, 1965.

Ellis, Havelock. *Studies in the Psychology of Sex*. Vol. I. New York: Random House, 1936.

Everson, William K. *Love in the Film*. Secaucus, N.J.: Citadel Press, 1979.

"Explanation for Premature and Delayed Labor." *Science News,* June 13, 1992.

Fisher, Helen. *Anatomy of Love.* New York: W. W. Norton, 1992.

Foucault, Michel. *The History of Sexuality,* trans. R. Hurley. 3 vols. New York: Pantheon, 1990.

Freud, Sigmund. *Sexuality and the Psychology of Love,* trans. Philip Rieff. New York: Collier, 1963.

———. *On War, Sex, and Neurosis.* New York: Arts & Sciences Press, 1947.

———. *Totem and Taboo,* trans. A. A. Brill. New York: Vintage, n.d.

Friday, Nancy. *My Secret Garden: Women's Sexual Fantasies.* New York: Pocket Books, 1973.

Frith, Dawn and Clifford. "Say It with Bowers." *Wildlife Conservation,* January/February 1991.

Fromm, Erich. *The Art of Loving.* New York: Harper & Row, 1956.

Fullard, W., and A. M. Reiling. "An investigation of Lorenz's 'babyness.' " *Child Development,* 47, 1976, pp. 1191–93.

Gay, P. *The Bourgeois Experience: Victoria to Freud.* London: Oxford University Press, 1983.

———. *Freud: A Life for Our Time.* New York: Anchor, 1988.

Gaylin, Willard, and Ethel Person, eds. *Passionate Attachments: Thinking About Love.* New York: Free Press, 1988.

Gill, Michael. *Image of the Body.* New York: Doubleday, 1989.

Glassner, Barry. *Bodies.* New York: Putnam, 1988.

Gottman, John M. "Predicting the Longitudinal Course of Marriages." *Journal of Marital and Family Therapy,* Vol. 17, No. 1, 1991.

Grimal, Peter. *Love in Ancient Rome,* trans. Arthur Train, Jr. Norman, Okla.: University of Oklahoma Press, 1986.

Hamilton, Edith. *Mythology.* Boston: Little, Brown, 1942.

Hansen, Ron. *Mariette in Ecstasy.* New York: HarperCollins, 1991.

Harlow, Harry. "The nature of love." *American Psychologist,* 13, 1958.

———. "Lust, Latency and Love: Simian Secrets of Successful Love." *The Journal of Sex Research,* 11, 1975.

———, Harry, and Margaret Harlow. "Social Deprivation in Monkeys." *Scientific American,* 206, 1962.

———. *Learning to Love.* New York: Ballantine, 1973.

Hart, Clive. *Images of Flight.* Berkeley: University of California Press, 1988.

Hayman, Ronald. *Proust: A Biography.* New York: HarperCollins, 1990.

Hazan, Cindy, and Phillip R. Shaver. "Attachment as an Organizational Framework for Research on Close Relationships." *Psychological Inquiry,* October 1993.

Higham, T. F., and C. M. Brown, eds. *The Oxford Book of Greek Verse.* London: Oxford University Press, 1938.

"Historic Priapism Pegged to Frog Legs." *Science News,* Vol. 139, January 5, 1991.

Hoage, R. J., ed. *Perceptions of Animals in American Culture.* Washington: Smithsonian Institution Press, 1989.

Hofer, Myron A. "Early Social Relationships: A Psychobiologist's View." *Child Development,* 58, 1987.

Hughes-Hallett, Lucy. *Cleopatra: History, Dreams and Distortions.* New York: HarperCollins, 1990.

Hunter, Dard. *Papermaking: The History and Technique of an Ancient Craft.* New York: Dover Publications, 1974.

Ibn-Hazm. *The Ring of the Dove: A Treatise on the Art and Practice of Arab Love,* trans. A. J. Arberry. London: Luzac, 1953.

Jankowiak, William R. *Sex, Death, and Hierarchy in a Chinese City: An Anthropological Account.* New York: Columbia University Press, 1993.

———, and Edward F. Fischer. "A Cross-Cultural Perspective on Romantic Love." *Ethnology,* April 1992, vol. 31, No. 2.

Jung, Carl G. *Man and His Symbols.* New York: Dell, 1964.

Just, Roger. *Women in Athenian Law & Life.* London: Routledge, 1988.

Kaplan, Louise. *Female Perversions.* New York: Doubleday, 1991.

Karen, Robert. "Becoming Attached." *The Atlantic Monthly,* February 1990.

Kern, Stephen. *The Culture of Love: Victorians to Moderns.* Cambridge: Harvard University Press, 1992.

King, Margaret L. *Women of the Renaissance.* Chicago: University of Chicago Press, 1991.

Konner, Melvin. *The Tangled Web: Biological Constraints on the Human Spirit.* New York: Holt Rhinehart and Winston, 1982.

Lasky, Judith F., and Helen W. Silverman, eds. *Love: Psychoanalytic Perspectives.* New York: New York University Press, 1988.

Lawrence, D. H. *St. Mawr* and *The Man Who Died.* New York: Vintage, 1953.

Le Chapelain, André (Andreas Capellanus). *Art of Courtly Love.* New York: Columbia University Press, 1941.

Lewis, C. S. *The Allegory of Love.* London: Oxford University Press, 1938.

Liebowitz, Michael. *The Chemistry of Love.* Boston: Little, Brown, 1983.

Lorenz, Konrad. *Studies in Animal and Human Behavior.* Cambridge: Harvard University Press, 1971.

———. *King Solomon's Ring.* New York: Simon & Schuster, 1952.

———. *The Foundations of Ethology.* New York: Simon & Schuster, 1981.

———. *On Aggression.* New York: Oxford University Press, 1973.

"The Love Hormone." *Mademoiselle,* Vol. 96, No. 11, November 1990.

Lovell, Mary S. *Straight on Till Morning: The Biography of Beryl Markham.* New York: St. Martin's Press, 1987.

Lucretius. *De Rerum Natura (The Way Things Are),* trans. R. Humphries. Bloomington, Ind.: Indiana University Press, 1968.

McCullers, Carson. *The Heart Is a Lonely Hunter.* New York: Bantam, 1953.

MacLean, Paul. *A Triune Concept of the Brain and Behavior.* Toronto: University of Toronto Press, 1973.

McGuire, W., ed. *The Freud/Jung Letters.* Bollingen Series 94, Princeton, N.J.: Princeton University Press, 1974.

Manniche, Lise. *Sexual Life in Ancient Egypt.* New York: KPI Ltd., 1987.

Margulis, Lynn, and Dorian Sagan. *Mystery Dance.* New York: Summit Books, 1991.

Markham, Beryl. *The Splendid Outcast: Beryl Markham's African Stories.* San Francisco: North Point Press, 1987.

———. *West with the Night.* San Francisco: North Point Press, 1983.

Masters, John. *Casanova.* New York: Bernard Geis Associates, 1969.

Meader, William G. *Courtship in Shakespeare.* New York: Octagon Books, 1971.

Mednick, Sarnoff, and Karen Finello. "Biological Factors and Crime: Implications for Forensic Psychiatry." *International Journal of Law and Psychiatry,* 6, 1983.

Menninger, Karl. *Love Against Hate.* New York: Harcourt Brace and World, 1942.

Money, John. *Love & Love Sickness: The Science of Sex, Gender Difference, and Pair Bonding.* Baltimore: Johns Hopkins University Press, 1980.

Montagu, Ashley. "A Scientist Looks at Love." *Phi Beta Kappan,* 51, 1970.

Morris, Desmond. *Intimate Behavior.* New York: Bantam, 1973.

Murstein, Bernard I. *Love, Sex and Marriage.* New York: Springer, 1974.

Nelli, Réne. *L'Erotique des troubadours.* 2 vols. Paris: Edition, 1974.

Nin, Anaïs. *The Diary of Anaïs Nin.* Vol. 1. New York: Swallow Press, 1966; New Haven, Conn.: Yale University Press, 1988.

Nunberg, H., and E. Federn. *Minutes of the Vienna Psychoanalytic Society.* 4 vols., 1906–1918. New York: International Universities Press, 1962–1975.

Ortega y Gasset, José. *On Love,* trans. T. Tallbot. New York: Meridian Books, 1957.

Ovid (Pioblus Ovidius Naso). *Metamorphoses,* trans. R. Humphries. Bloomington, Ind.: Indiana University Press, 1955.

———. *The Erotic Poems,* trans. Peter Green. New York: Penguin, 1982.

Ozment, Steven. "The Family in Reformation Germany: The Bearing and Rearing of Children." *Journal of Family History,* 8:159–76.

Plato. *The Symposium,* in *The Republic and Other Works,* trans. B. Jowett. Garden City, N.Y.: Dolphin, 1960.

Plotnicov, Leonard. "Love, Lust, and Found in Nigeria." Paper presented at the American Anthropological Association Meetings, Session: The Anthropology of Romantic Passion, San Francisco, December 1992.

Plutarch. *Makers of Rome,* trans. Ian Scott-Kilvert. London: Harmondsworth, 1965.

Pope, Kenneth S., and Jacqueline C. Bouhoutsos. *Sexual Intimacy Between Therapists and Patients.* New York: Praeger, 1986.

Pound, Ezra, and Noel Stock, trans. *Love Poems of Ancient Egypt*. New York: New Directions, 1962.

Proust, Marcel. *The Sweet Cheat Gone*, trans. C. K. Scott-Moncrieff. New York: Vintage, 1970.

———. *Remembrance of Things Past*, trans. C. K. Scott-Moncrieff and Terence Kilmartin. 3 vols. New York: Vintage, 1982.

Reik, Theodore. *Of Love and Lust*. New York: Pyramid, 1958.

Richardson, Donald. *Greek Mythology for Everyone*. New York: Avenel, 1989.

Ruspoli, Mario. *The Cave of Lascaux*. New York: Abrams, 1986.

Sagan, Carl, and Ann Druyan. *Shadows of Forgotten Ancestors*. New York: Random House, 1992.

St. Augustine. *Confessions*, trans. R. S. Pine-Coffin. New York: Penguin, 1961.

Sarnoff, Suzanne and Irving. *Sexual Excitement/Sexual Peace*. New York: M. Evans and Company, 1979.

Sartre, Jean-Paul. *Saint Genet*, trans. Bernard Frechtman. New York: George Braziller, 1963.

Seyffert, Oskar. *Dictionary of Classical Antiquities*. New York: Meridian, 1957.

Shakespeare, William. *Romeo and Juliet*, ed. T. J. B. Spencer. New York: Penguin, 1967.

Shipley, Joseph T. *The Origins of English Words*. Baltimore: Johns Hopkins University Press, 1984.

Simpson, W. K., ed. *Literature of Ancient Egypt*. New Haven: Yale University Press, 1973.

Singer, Irving. *The Nature of Love*. 3 vols. Chicago: University of Chicago Press, 1987.

Small, Meredith. *Female Choices*. Ithaca: Cornell University Press, 1993.

Smith, Robin. *The Encyclopedia of Sexual Trivia*. New York: St. Martin's Press, 1990.

Sobel, Dava. "Rare Views of Freud Emerge from Amateur Films." *The New York Times*, December 30, 1980, C 3.

———. "Sex, as Therapy, Said to Harm Client." *The New York Times*, August 29, 1981, C 9.

Solomon, Robert C., and Kathleen M. Higgins, eds. *The Philosophy of Erotic Love*. Lawrence, Kan.: University Press of Kansas, 1991.

Stallworthy, J., ed. *A Book of Love Poetry*. London: Oxford University Press, 1974.

Stendhal (Marie Henri Beyle). *Love*, trans. Gilbert and Suzanne Sale. New York: Penguin, 1975.

Sternberg, Robert J., and Michael L. Barnes, eds. *The Psychology of Love*. New Haven, Conn.: Yale University Press, 1988.

Stevens, Wallace. *The Palm at the End of the Mind*. New York: Vintage, 1972.

Stoller, Robert J. *Sexual Excitement: Dynamics of Erotic Life*. Washington: American Psychiatric Press, 1979.

———. *Observing the Erotic Imagination*. New Haven: Yale University Press, 1985.

———. *Pain and Passion: A Psychoanalyst Explores the World of S & M*. New York: Plenum, 1991.

———, and Gilbert Herdt. *Intimate Communications: Erotics and the Study of Culture*. New York: Columbia University Press, 1990.

Tannahill, Reay. *Sex in History*. New York: Stein and Day/Scarborough House, 1992.

Tannen, Deborah. *You Just Don't Understand*. New York: Ballantine, 1990.

Tennov, Dorothy. *Love and Limerence*. New York: Scarborough House, 1989.

Thomas, Dylan. *The Collected Poems*. New York: New Directions, 1957.

Tiger, Lionel. *The Pursuit of Pleasure*. Boston: Little Brown, 1992.

Tuchman, Barbara. *A Distant Mirror*. New York: Knopf, 1978.

Turnbull, Colin. *The Mountain People*. New York: Simon & Schuster, 1972.

———. "East Africa Safari." *Natural History*, 5:26, 1981, pp. 29–34.

Vaillant, George. *Adaptation in Life*. Boston: Little, Brown, 1977.

Veyne, Paul, ed. *A History of Private Life*. Vol. I. Cambridge: Harvard University Press, 1987.

Virgil. *The Aeneid of Virgil*, trans. C. Day Lewis. London: Oxford University Press, 1952.

Walsh, Anthony. *The Science of Love*. Buffalo: Prometheus Books, 1991.

Walters, Mark Jerome. *Courtship in the Animal Kingdom*. New York: Anchor, 1988.

Weldon, Fay. *The Life and Loves of a She-Devil*. New York: Ballantine, 1983.

West, Paul. "Marcel's Wave." *Gentlemen's Quarterly*, vol. 63, No. 8, August 1993, pp. 83–88.

Whitman, Walt. *Leaves of Grass*. New York: New American Library, 1955.

Wilson, E. O. *On Human Behavior*. New York: Bantam, 1979.

Wilson, Glenn. *Love and Instinct*. New York: Quill, 1981.

Windybank, Susan. *Wild Sex*. New York: St. Martin's Press, 1991.

Wolkstein, Diane. *The First Love Stories*. New York: HarperCollins, 1991.

INDEX